Thomas Taylor Plotinus, George Robert Stow

Select works of Plotinus

Translated from the Greek with an introduction containing the substance of

Porphyry's life of Plotinus

Thomas Taylor Plotinus, George Robert Stow

Select works of Plotinus
Translated from the Greek with an introduction containing the substance of Porphyry's life of Plotinus

ISBN/EAN: 9783337282097

Printed in Europe, USA, Canada, Australia, Japan

Cover: Foto ©ninafisch / pixelio.de

More available books at **www.hansebooks.com**

BOHN'S PHILOSOPHICAL LIBRARY.

SELECT WORKS OF PLOTINUS.

'Αρχὰ καὶ αἰτία καὶ κανὼν ἐντὶ τᾶς ἀνθρωπίνας εὐδαιμοσύνας ἁ τῶν
θείων καὶ τιμιωτάτων ἐπίγνωσις.   THEAGES PYTHAG.

"The knowledge of things divine and most honourable, is the principle, cause, and rule of human felicity."

He who has not even a knowledge of common things is a brute among men. He who has an accurate knowledge of human concerns alone, is a man among brutes. But he who knows all that can be known by intellectual energy, is a God among men.

SELECT WORKS OF PLOTINUS

TRANSLATED FROM THE GREEK WITH AN INTRODUCTION CONTAINING THE SUBSTANCE OF PORPHYRY'S LIFE OF PLOTINUS BY THOMAS TAYLOR & A NEW EDITION WITH PREFACE AND BIBLIOGRAPHY BY G. R. S. MEAD B.A. M.R.A.S. SECRETARY OF THE THEOSOPHICAL SOCIETY

LONDON GEORGE BELL & SONS YORK STREET COVENT GARDEN AND NEW YORK 1895

CHISWICK PRESS:—CHARLES WHITTINGHAM AND CO.
TOOKS COURT, CHANCERY LANE, LONDON.

CONTENTS.

		PAGE
PREFACE		vii
BIBLIOGRAPHY		xxxv
INTRODUCTION		xxxix
I.	On the Virtues (II. ii.)	3
II.	On Dialectic (I. iii.)	14
III.	On Matter (II. iv.)	22
IV.	Against the Gnostics (II. ix.)	44
V.	On the Impassivity of Incorporeal Natures (III. vi.)	80
VI.	On Eternity and Time (III. vii.)	115
VII.	On the Immortality of the Soul (IV. vii.)	142
VIII.	On the Three Hypostases that rank as the Principles of Things (V. i.)	162
IX.	On Intellect, Ideas, and [Real] Being (V. xi.)	182
X.	On the Essence of the Soul (IV. ii.)	199
XI.	A Discussion of Doubts relative to the Soul (IV. iii.)	204
XII.	On the Generation and Order of Things after the First (V. ii.)	253
XIII.	On Gnostic Hypostases, and That which is beyond Them (V. iii.)	257
XIV.	That the Nature which is beyond Being is not Intellective, etc. (V. vi.)	290
XV.	On the Good, or the One	299
ADDITIONAL NOTES		325

PREFACE.

FOREWORD.

IN presenting to the public a new edition of Thomas Taylor's "Select Works of Plotinus" it will not be out of place to show cause for what may be considered by many a somewhat temerous proceeding. What has the present English-reading public to do with Plotinus; what still further has it to do with the translations of Thomas Taylor?

In the following paragraphs I hope to show that the temper of the public mind of to-day, with regard to the problems of religion and philosophy, is very similar to that of the times of Plotinus. The public interest in the philosophy of mysticism and theosophical speculation has so largely developed during the last twenty years that a demand for books treating of Neoplatonism and kindred subjects is steadily increasing.

Now of Neoplatonism Plotinus was the coryphæus, if not the founder. What Plato was to Socrates, Plotinus was to his master, Ammonius Saccas. Neither Socrates nor Ammonius committed anything to writing; Plato and Plotinus were the great expounders of the tenets of their respective schools, and, as far as we can judge, far transcended their teachers in brilliancy of genius. Therefore, to the student of Neoplatonism, the works of Plotinus are the most indispensable document, and the basis of the whole system. Just as no Platonic philosopher transcended the genius of Plato, so no Neoplatonic philosopher surpassed the genius of Plotinus.

The "Enneads" of Plotinus are, as Harnack says, "the primary and classical document of Neoplatonism;" of that document there is no translation in the English language. There are complete translations in Latin, French, and German, but English scholarship has till now entirely neglected Plotinus, who, so far from being inferior to his great master Plato, was thought to be a reincarnation of his genius. ("*Ita ejus similis judicatus est, ut . . . in hoc ille revixisse putandus sit.*"— St. Augustine, " De Civitate Dei," viii. 12.) A glance at the Bibliography at the end of this Preface will show the reader that though French and German scholars have laboured in this field with marked industry and success, English scholarship has left the pioneer work of Thomas Taylor (in the concluding years of the past century and the opening years of the present) entirely unsupported. Taylor devoted upwards of fifty years of unremitting toil to the restoration of Greek philosophy, especially that of Plato and the Neoplatonists. In the midst of great opposition and adverse criticism he laboured on single-handed. As Th. M. Johnson, the editor of " The Platonist," and an enthusiastic admirer of Taylor, says, in the preface to his translation of three treatises of Plotinus:

" This wonderful genius and profound philosopher devoted his whole life to the elucidation and propagation of the Platonic philosophy. By his arduous labours modern times became acquainted with many of the works of Plotinus, Porphyry, Proclus, etc. Since Taylor's time something has been known of Plotinus, but he is still to many a mere name."

Taylor was a pioneer, and of pioneers we do not demand the building of government roads. It is true that the perfected scholarship of our own times demands a higher standard of translation than Taylor presents; but what was true of his critics then, is true of his critics to-day: though they may know more Greek, he knew more Plato. The present translation nevertheless is quite faithful enough for all ordinary purposes. Taylor was more than a scholar, he was a philosopher in the Platonic sense of the word; and the translations of Taylor are still in great request, and command so high a price in the second-hand market that slender purses cannot procure them. The expense and labour of preparing a complete translation of the "Enneads," however, is too great a risk without first testing the public interest by a new edition of the only partial translation of any size which we possess. A new edition of Taylor's "Select Works of Plotinus" is, therefore, presented to the public in the hope that it may pave the way to a complete translation of the works of the greatest of the Neoplatonists. That the signs of the times presage an ever-growing interest in such subjects, and that it is of great importance to learn what solution one of the most penetrating minds of antiquity had to offer of problems in religion and philosophy that are insistently pressing upon us to-day, will be seen from the following considerations.

THEN AND NOW.

The early centuries of the Christian era are perhaps the most interesting epoch that can engage the attention of the student of history. The conquests of Rome had opened up communication with the most distant parts of her vast empire, and seemed to the conquerors to have united even the ends of the earth. The thought of the Orient and Occident met, now in conflict, now in friendly embrace, and the chief arena for the enactment of this intellectual drama was at Alexandria. As Vacherot says:

"Alexandria, at the time when Ammonius Saccas began to teach, had become the sanctuary of universal wisdom. The asylum of the old tradition of the East, it was at the same time the birth-place of new doctrines. It was at Alexandria that the school of Philo represented hellenizing Judaism; it was at Alexandria that the Gnôsis synthesized all the traditions of Syria, of Chaldæa, of Persia, blended with Judaism, with Christianity, and even with Greek philosophy. The school of the Alexandrian fathers raised Christian thought to a height which it was not to surpass, and which was to strike fear into the heart of the orthodoxy of the Councils. A strong life flowed in the veins of all these schools and vitalized all their discussions. Philo, Basilides, Valentinus, Saint Clement, and Origen, opened up for the mind new vistas of thought, and unveiled for it mysteries which the genius of a Plato or an Aristotle had never fathomed " (i. 331).

Indeed, the time was one of great strain, physical, intellectual, and spiritual; it was, as Zeller says, " a time in which the nations had lost their independence, the popular religions their power, the national forms of culture their peculiar stamp, in part if not wholly; in which the supports of life on its material, as well as on its spiritual side, had been broken asunder, and the great civilizations of the world were impressed with the consciousness of their own downfall, and with the prophetic sense of the approach of a new era; a time in which the longing after a new and more satisfying form of spiritual being, a fellowship that should embrace all peoples, a form of belief that should bear men over all the misery of the present, and tranquillize the desire of the soul, was universal" (v. 391-92, quoted by Mozley).

Such was the state of affairs then, and very similar is the condition of things in our own day. It requires no great effort of the imagination for even the most superficial student of the history of these times, to see a marked similarity between the general unrest and searching after a new ideal that marked that period of brilliant intellectual development, and the uncertainty and eager curiosity of the public mind in the closing years of the nineteenth century.

The tendency is the same in kind, but not in degree. To-day life is far more intense, thought more active, experience more extended, the need of the solution of the problem more pressing. It is not Rome who has united the nations under her yoke, it is the conquests of physical science that have in truth united the ends of the earth, and built up an arterial and nervous system for our common mother which she has never previously possessed. It is not the philosophy of Greece and Rome that are meeting together; it is not even the philosophy of the then confined Occident meeting with the somewhat vague and unsystematized ideas of the then Orient; it is the meeting of the great waters, the developed thought and industrious observation of the whole Western world meeting with the old slow stream of the ancient and modern East.

The great impetus that the study of oriental languages has received during the last hundred years, the radical changes that the study of Sanskrit has wrought in the whole domain of philology, have led to the initiation of a science of comparative religion which is slowly but surely modifying all departments of thought with which it comes in contact. To-day it is not a Marcion who queries the authenticity of texts, but the "higher criticism" that has once for all struck the death-blow to mere bible fetishism. The conflict between religion and science, which for more than two hundred years has raged so fiercely, has produced a generation that longs and searches for a reconciliation. The pendulum has swung from the extreme of blind and ignorant faith, to the extreme of pseudo-scientific materialism and negation; and now swings back again towards faith once more, but faith rationalized by a scientific study of the psychological problems which, after a couple of centuries of denial, once more press upon the notice of the western nations. The pendulum swings back towards belief once more; the phenomena of spiritualism, hypnotism, and psychism generally, are compelling investigation, and that investigation forces us to recognize that these factors must be taken into serious account, if we are to trace the sweep of human evolution in all its details, and have a right understanding of the history of civilization. The religious factor, which has been either entirely neglected by scientific evolutionists, or has remained with an explanation that is at best fantastically inadequate, must be taken into primary account; and with it the psychic nature of man must be profoundly studied, if the problem of religion is to receive any really satisfactory solution.

Thus it is that there is a distinct tendency in the public thought of to-day towards a modified mysticism. It is a time also when the human heart questions as well as the head; the great social problems which cry out for solution—over-population, the sweating system, the slavery of over-competition—breed strikes, socialism, anarchy; in brief, the desire for betterment. Humanitarianism, altruism, fraternity, the idea of a universal religion, of a league of peace, such ideas appear beautiful ideals to the sorely-suffering and over-driven men and women of to-day. Yes, the times are very like, then and now; and once more the hope that mystic religion has ever held out, is offered. But mysticism is not an unmixed blessing. Psychism dogs its heels; and hence it is that the history of the past shows us that wherever mysticism has arisen, there psychism, with its dangers, errors, and insanities, has obscured it. Have we not to-day amongst us crowds of phenomenalists, searchers after strange arts, diabolists, symbolists, etc., a renaissance of all that the past tells us to avoid. All these vagaries obscure the true mystic way, and at no time previously do we find the various factors so distinctly at work as in the first centuries of the Christian era. It was against all these enormities and the wild imaginings that invariably follow, when the strong power of mystic religion is poured into human thought, that Plotinus arose, to revive the dialectic of Plato and rescue the realms of pure philosophy from the hosts of disorderly speculation, while at the same time brilliantly defending the best that mysticism offered. It will, therefore, be of great interest, for those who are inclined to believe in mystical religion in the present day, to consider the views of perhaps the most acute reasoner of the Greek philosophers, who not only combined the Aristotelean and Platonic methods, but also added a refined and pure mysticism of his own, which the times of Plato and Aristotle were unable to produce.

The reader will doubtless be anxious to learn what was the attitude of Plotinus to Christianity, and whether the Christian doctrine had any influence on the teachings of the greatest of the Neoplatonists. Much has been written on the influence of Christianity on Neoplatonism and of Neoplatonism on Christianity, especially by German scholars, but it is safer to avoid all extreme opinions and be content with the moderate view of Harnack, that " the influence of Christianity— whether Gnostic or Catholic—on Neoplatonism was at no time very considerable," and with regard to the first teachers of the school entirely unnoticeable. Nevertheless, " since Neoplatonism originated in Alexandria, where Oriental modes of worship were accessible to everyone, and since the Jewish philosophy had also taken its place in the literary circles of Alexandria, we may safely assume that even the earliest of the Neoplatonists possessed an acquaintance with Judaism and Christianity. But if we search Plotinus for evidence of any actual influence of Jewish and Christian phraseology, we search in vain; and the existence of any such influence is all the more unlikely because it is only the later Neoplatonism that offers striking and deep-rooted parallels to Philo and the Gnostics." But Porphyry (c. xvi.) distinctly states that the Gnostics against whom Plotinus wrote, were Christians.

And yet there can be no doubt, that the strong spiritual life and hope which the teaching of the Christ inspired in the hearts of his hearers, brought a reality into men's lives that would not be content with the mere envisagement of a cold ideal. Those who were fired with this hope, taught that this ideal was realizable, nay, that it had already been realized. With such a fervid spirit of hope and enthusiasm aroused, philosophy had to look to its laurels. And in the words of Mozley, based on Vacherot, "the philosophers were kindled by a sense of rivalry; they felt, present in the world and actually working, a power such as they themselves sought to exercise, moralizing and ordering the hearts of men; and this stirred them to find a parallel power on their own side, and the nearest approach to it, both in character and degree, was found in Plato. To Plato they turned themselves with the fervour of pupils towards an almost unerring master; but they selected from Plato those elements which lay on the same line as that Christian teaching whose power elicited their rivalry."

Nor were the better instructed of the Christian fathers free from a like rivalry with the philosophers; and from this rivalry arose the symbols of the Church and the subtleties of an Athanasius. Curiously enough in our own days we notice a like rivalry in Christian apologetics in contact with the great eastern religious systems; a number of the most enlightened Christian writers striving to show that Christianity, in its purest and best sense, rises superior to what is best in the Orient. The theory of direct borrowing on either side, however, has to be abandoned; indirect influence is a thing that cannot be denied, but direct plagiarism is unsupported by any evidence that has yet been discovered. As Max Müller says:

"The difficulty of admitting any borrowing on the part of one religion from another is much greater than is commonly supposed, and if it has taken place, there seems to me only one way in which it can be satisfactorily established, namely, by the actual occurrence of foreign words which retain a certain unidiomatic appearance in the language to which they have been transferred. It seems impossible that any religious community should have adopted the fundamental principles of religion from another, unless their intercourse was intimate and continuous—in fact, unless they could freely express their thoughts in a common language. . . .

"Nor should we forget that most religions have a feeling of hostility towards other religions, and that they are not likely to borrow from others which in their most important and fundamental doctrines they consider erroneous" ("Theosophy, or Psychological Religion," London, 1893, pp. 367-369).

And though Plotinus cannot be said to have borrowed directly either from Christianity or other oriental ideas, nevertheless it is beyond doubt that he was acquainted with them, and that too most intimately. By birth he was an Egyptian of Lycopolis (Sivouth); for eleven years he attended the school of Ammonius at Alexandria; his interest in the systems of the further East was so great, that he joined the expedition of Gordian in order to learn the religio-philosophy of the Persians and Indians; his pupils Amelius and Porphyry were filled with oriental teaching, and it was in answer to their questioning that Plotinus wrote the most powerful books of the " Enneads." Porphyry, moreover, wrote a long treatise of a very learned nature "Against the Christians," so that it cannot have been that the master should have been unacquainted with the views of the pupil. Numenius again was highly esteemed by Plotinus and his school, and this Pythagoreo-Platonic philosopher was saturated with oriental ideas, as Vacherot tells us (i. 318):

" Numenius, a Syrian by origin, and living in the Orient, is not less deeply versed in the religious tradition of Syria, Judæa, and Persia, than in the philosophical doctrines of Greece. He is perfectly familiar with the works of Philo, and his admiration goes so far as to ask whether it is Philo who platonizes, or Plato who philonizes; he dubs Plato the Attic Moses. If the doctrines of Philo have at all influenced the philosophy of Greece, it is owing to Numenius, the father of this Syrian School out of which Amelius and Porphyry came into Neoplatonism.

" The oriental tendency of the philosopher is shown by the following words of Eusebius: 'It must be that he who treats of the Good, and who has affirmed his doctrine with the witness of Plato, should go even further back and take hold of the doctrines of Pythagoras. It must be that he should appeal to the most renowned of the nations, and that he should present the rituals, dogmas, and institutions which—originally established by the Brâhmans, Jews, Magians, and Egyptians—are in agreement with the doctrines of Plato '" (VIII. vii., " De Bono ").

We, therefore, find in Plotinus two marked characteristics: the method of stern dialectic on the one hand, and a rational and practical mysticism on the other that reminds us very strongly of the best phase of the yoga-systems of ancient India.

As Brandis remarks: " The endeavour which, as far as we can judge, characterized Plotinus more than any other philosopher of his age was . . . to pave the way to the solution of any question by a careful discussion of the difficulties of the case." And though the method is somewhat tedious, nevertheless the philosophy of Plotinus is one of remarkable power and symmetry. In the opinion of Mozley : " There is a real soberness in the mind of its author ; the difficulties connected with the divine self-substance and universality, in relation to the individuality of man, though they cannot be said to be solved, are presented in a manner to which little objection can be taken intellectually, and against which no serious charge of irreverence can be brought." This is a great admission for a man writing in a dictionary of Christian biography, and the word " serious " might well be omitted from the last clause as totally unnecessary, if not supremely ridiculous, when applied to such a man as Plotinus.

The part of the system of our great Neoplatonist that has been and will be the least understood, is that connected with the practice of theurgy, which consummates itself in ecstasy, the Samâdhi of the yoga-art of Indian mystics. For years Plotinus kept secret the teachings of his master Ammonius Saccas, and not till his fellow-pupils Herennius and Origen (not the Church father) broke the compact, did he begin to expound the tenets publicly. It is curious to notice that, though this ecstasy was the consummation of the whole system, nowhere does Plotinus enter into any details of the methods by which this supreme state of consciousness is to be reached, and I cannot but think that he still kept silence deliberately on this all-important point.

Ammonius, the master, made such an impression on his times by his great wisdom and knowledge that he was known as the " god-taught " (θεοδίδακτος); he was more than a mere eclectic, he himself attained to spiritual insight. The pupil Plotinus also shows all the signs of a student of eastern Râja Yoga, the " kingly art " of the science of the soul. In his attitude to the astrologers, magicians, and phenomena-mongers of the time, he shows a thorough contempt for such magic arts, though, if we are to believe Porphyry, his own spiritual power was great. The gods and dæmons and powers were to be commanded and not obeyed. " Those gods of yours must come to me, not I to them " (ἐκείνους δεῖ πρὸς ἐμὲ ἔρχεσθαι, οὐκ ἐμὲ πρὸς ἐκείνους) (Porphyry, x.).

And, indeed, he ended his life in the way that Yogins in the East are said to pass out of the body. When the hour of death approaches they perform Tapas, or in other words enter into a deep state of contemplation. This was evidently the mode of leaving the world followed by our philosopher, for his last words were : " Now I seek to lead back the self within me to the All-self " (τὸ ἐν ἡμῖν θεῖον ἀνάγειν πρὸς τὸ ἐν τῷ παντὶ θεῖον) (Porphyry, ii.).

Indeed, Plotinus, "in so far as we have records of him, was in his personal character one of the purest and most pleasing of all philosophers, ancient or modern" (Mozley); it is, therefore, of great interest for us to learn his opinions on the thought of his own time, and what solution he offered of the problems which are again presented to us, but with even greater insistence, in our own days. We will, therefore, take a glance at the main features of his system.

The System of Plotinus.

The whole system of Plotinus revolves round the idea of a threefold principle, trichotomy, or trinity, and of pure intuition. In these respects, it bears a remarkable similarity to the great Vedântic system of Indian philosophy. Deity, spirit, soul, body, macrocosmic and microcosmic, and the essential identity of the divine in man with the divine in the universe—the τὸ ἐν ἡμῖν θεῖον with the τὸ ἐν τῷ παντὶ θεῖον, or of the Jîvâtman with the Paramâtman—are the main subjects of his system.

Thus from the point of view of the great universe, we have the One Reality, or the Real, the One, the Good (τὸ ὄν, τὸ ἕν, τὸ ἀγαθόν); this is the All-self of the Upanishads, Brahman or Paramâtman.

Plotinus bestows much labour on the problem of the Absolute, and reaches the only conclusion possible, viz., that it is inexpressible; or, in the words of the Upanishads, "the mind falls back from it, unable to reach it." It must, nevertheless, produce everything out of itself, without suffering any diminution or becoming weaker (VI. viii. 19); essences must flow from it, and yet it experiences no change; it is immanent in all existences (IV. iii. 17; VI. xi. 1)—" the self hidden in the heart of all," say the Upanishads; it is the Absolute as result, for as absolutely perfect it must be the goal, not the operating cause of all being (VI. ix. 8, 9), as says Brandis; and Harnack dubs the system of Plotinus "dynamic Pantheism," whatever that may mean. But we are in the region of paradox and inexpressibility, and so had better hasten on to the first stage of emanation.

First, then, there arises (how, Plotinus does not say, for that question no man can solve; the primal ways of the One are known to the Omniscient alone) the Universal Mind, or ideal universe ($\nu o\tilde{\nu}\varsigma$ or $\kappa \acute{o}\sigma\mu o\varsigma$ $\nu o\eta \tau \acute{o}\varsigma$); the Îshvara or Lord of the Vedântins. It is by the thought ($\lambda \acute{o}\gamma o\varsigma$) of the Universal Mind that the World-Soul ($\psi \upsilon \chi \grave{\eta}$ $\tau o\tilde{\upsilon}$ $\pi a\nu \tau \acute{o}\varsigma$ or $\tau \tilde{\omega}\nu$ $\H{o}\lambda \omega \nu$) is brought into being. As Tennemann says (§ 207):

"Inasmuch as Intelligence ($\nu o\tilde{\nu}\varsigma$) [Universal Mind] contemplates in Unity that which *is possible*, the latter acquires the character of something determined and limited; and so becomes the *Actual* and *Real* ($\H{o}\nu$). Consequently, Intelligence is the primal reality, the base of all the rest, and inseparably united to real Being. [This resembles the Sach-Chid-Ânandam of the Vedântins, or Being, Thought, Bliss.] The object contemplated and the thinking subject, are identical; and that which Intelligence thinks, it at the same time *creates*. By always thinking, and always in the same manner, yet continually with new difference, it produces all things [the logos idea]; it is the essence of all imperishable essences ['the base of all the worlds' of the Upanishads; 'on it all worlds rest'];

the sum total of infinite life." (See En. VI. viii. 16 : IV. iii. 17 : VI. vii. 5, 9 ; viii. 16 : V. i. 4, 7 ; iii. 5, 7 ; v. 2 ; ix. 5 : VI. vii. 12, 13. And for an exposition of the logos theory in Plotinus, see Vacherot, i. 317.)

We thence pass on to the World-Soul, the Hiranyagarbha (resplendent germ or shining sphere or envelope) of the Upanishads.

"The image and product of the motionless nous is the soul, which, according to Plotinus, is like the nous, immaterial. Its relation to the nous is the same as that of the nous to the One. It stands between the nous and the phenomenal world, is permeated and illuminated by the former, but is also in contact with the latter. The nous is indivisible [the root of monadic individuality; the Sattva of the Buddhist theory of Ekotibháva as applied to man]; the soul *may* preserve its unity and remain in the nous, but at the same time it has the power of uniting with the corporeal world, and thus being disintegrated. It therefore occupies an intermediate position. As a single soul (world-soul) it belongs in essence and destination to the intelligible world; but it also embraces innumerable individual souls, and these can either submit to be ruled by the nous, or turn aside to the sensual, and lose themselves in the finite " (Harnack).

This is precisely the same idea as that of the Hiranyagarbha, the individual souls arising by a process of differentiation (Panchikarana, or quintuplication of the primary "elements") from it. Its nature and function are thus summarized by Tennemann (§§ 208, 209) from En. V. i. 6, 7, and vi. 4 ; VI. ii. 22 ; and III. viii. :

" The Soul (*i.e.*, the *Soul of the World*) is the offspring of Intelligence (νοῦς), and the thought (λόγος) of Intelligence, being itself also productive and creative. It is therefore Intelligence, but with a more obscure vision and less perfect knowledge; inasmuch as it does not itself directly contemplate objects, but through the medium of intelligence; being endowed with an energetic force which carries its perceptions beyond itself. It is not an original but a reflected light, the principle of action and of external Nature. Its proper activity consists in contemplation (θεωρία); and in the production of objects by means of this contemplation. In this manner it produces, in its turn, different classes of souls, and among others the human; the faculties of which have a tendency to elevation or debasement. The energy of the lowest order, creative, and connected with matter, is Nature (φύσις).

"Nature is a contemplative and creative energy, which gives form to matter (λόγος ποιῶν); for form (εἶδος—μορφή) and thought (λόγος) are one and the same. All that takes place in the world around us is the work of contemplation."

It is here that the system of Plotinus is somewhat weak; it is true that he has a strong admiration for the beauties of Nature, but, in dealing with the problem of matter, he scarcely avoids stumbling, and though he criticises the view of certain Gnostic schools which made matter the root of all evil, he does not entirely clear himself from a similar conception. It is the object of the World-Soul so to pervade the natural world that all its parts shall be in perfect harmony, " but in the actual phenomenal world unity and harmony are replaced by strife and discord; the result is a conflict, a becoming and vanishing, and illusive existence. And the reason for this state of things is that bodies rest on a substratum of matter. Matter is the basework of each (τὸ βάθος ἑκάστου ἡ ὕλη); it is the dark principle, the indeterminate, that which has no qualities, the μὴ ὄν. Destitute of form and idea it is evil; as capable of form it is neutral."

The Vedântins, on the contrary, pair the root of matter (Asat, Prakriti, Mâyâ) with the Universal Mind, and make it of like dignity. It is by the removal of this primal veil that the great secret of the Self is revealed.

Attempts have been made to trace correspondences between the three first principles of Plotinus and the Christian Trinity; God the Father and the One Absolute, Jesus Christ and the First Intelligence or Universal Mind, and the Holy Spirit and the World-Soul (Jules Simon, i. 308).

So much for the macrocosmic side. The microcosmic is necessarily to a large extent interblended with the above, and also views man by means of a trichotomy into spirit (νοῦς), soul (ψυχή) and body (σῶμα); by which prism the rays of the primal unity are deflected. This again is precisely the same division as that of the Vedântins: viz., Kâranopâdhi, the causal vesture, or spiritual veil or impediment of the Self; Sûkshmopâdhi, the subtle vesture, or psychic veil or impediment of the Self; and Sthûlopâdhi, the gross vesture, or physical body. The remarkable agreement between the view of Plotinus as to the three spheres of existence, or states of consciousness, or hypostases of being, in man and the universe, the one being but a reflection of the other, and that of Shankarâchârya, the great master of the

Advaita Vedântin school of ancient India, may be seen from the following brilliant *résumé* from the point of view of a mystic. It is based on the *Tattrabodha*, or Awakening to Reality, one of the most remarkable of Shankara's small treatises, so far unfortunately not translated into any European language, and is taken from the work of a mystic, entitled "The Dream of Ravan" (a reprint from "The Dublin University Magazine" of 1853, 1854; London, 1895, pp. 211-215).

"Man is represented as a prismatic trinity, veiling and looked through by a primordial unity of light— gross outward body [Sthûlopâdhi—σῶμα]; subtle internal body or soul [Sûkshmopâdhi—ψυχή]; a being neither body nor soul, but absolute self-forgetfulness, called *the cause-body* [Kâranopâdhi—νοῦς], because it is the original sin of ignorance of his true nature which precipitates him from the spirit into the life-condition. These three bodies, existing in the waking, dreaming, sleeping states, are all known, witnessed, and watched by the spirit which standeth behind and apart from them, in the unwinking vigilance of ecstasy, or spirit-waking."

The writer then goes on to speak of *four* spheres, but the "innermost" is in reality no sphere, but the state of simplicity or oneness (ἅπλωσις, ἕνωσις). This is the state of ecstasy of Plotinus.

"There are four spheres of existence, one enfolding the other—the inmost sphere of Turiya, in which the individualized spirit lives the ecstatic life; the sphere of transition, or Lethe, in which the spirit, plunged in the ocean of Ajñâna, or total unconsciousness, and utterly forgetting its real self, undergoes a change of gnostic tendency [polarity?]; and from not knowing at all, or absolute unconsciousness, emerges on the hither side of that Lethean boundary to a false or reversed knowledge of things (viparîta jñâna), under the influence of an illusive Prâjña, or belief in, and tendency to, knowledge outward from itself, in which delusion it thoroughly believes, and now endeavours to realize; whereas the true knowledge which it had in the state of Turîya, or the ecstatic life, was all within itself, in which it intuitively knew and experienced all things. And from the sphere of Prâjña, or out-knowing,—this struggle to reach and recover outside itself all that it once possessed within itself, and lost,—to regain for the lost intuition an objective perception through the senses and understanding,—in which the spirit became an intelligence,—it merges into the third sphere, which is the sphere of dreams, where it believes in a universe of light and shade, and where all existence is in the way of Âbhâsa, or phantasm. There it imagines itself into the Linga-deha (Psyche), or subtle, semi-material, ethereal soul. . . .

"From this subtle personification and phantasmal sphere, in due time, it progresses into the fourth or outermost sphere, where matter and sense are triumphant; where the universe is believed a solid reality; where all things exist in the mode of Âkâra, or substantial form; and where that which successively forgot itself from spirit into absolute unconsciousness, and awoke on this side of that boundary of oblivion into an intelligence struggling outward, and from this outward struggling intelligence imagined itself into a conscious, feeling, breathing nervous soul, prepared for further clothing, now out-realizes itself from soul into a body. . . .

"The first or spiritual state was ecstasy; from ecstasy it forgot itself into deep sleep; from profound sleep it awoke out of unconsciousness, but still within itself, into the internal world of dreams; from dreaming it passed finally into the thoroughly waking state, and the outer world of sense."

These ideas will help us exceedingly in studying our philosopher and in trying to understand what he meant by ecstasy, and why there are three divisions in the morals of Plotinus, and how the metempsychosis in which he believed was neither for him the caressing of a dream nor the actualizing of a metaphor. The most sympathetic notice of the latter tenet is to be found in Jules Simon's "Histoire de l'École d'Alexandrie" (i. 588 sq.), based for the most part on En. I. i. 12; II. ix. 6; IV. iii. 9; V. ii. 2; and on Ficinus' commentary, p. 508 of Creuzer's edition:

"There are two degrees of reward; pure souls, whose simplification is not yet accomplished, return to a star [the sidereal region rather] to live as they were before the fall [into the world of sense] (En. III. iv. 6); souls that are perfectly pure [or simplified] gain union [or at-one-ment] with Deity. But what of retribution? Here comes in the doctrine of metempsychosis, which Plotinus met with everywhere around him, amongst the Egyptians, the Jews, and his forerunners in Neoplatonism [Potamon and Ammonius Saccas]. Does Plato really take the doctrine of metempsychosis seriously, as the 'Republic' would have us believe? Does he not speak of it merely to banter contemporary superstition, as seems evident from the 'Timæus'? Or is it not rather one of those dreams which Plato loved to fondle, without entirely casting them aside or admitting them, and in which he allowed his imagination to stray when knowledge failed him? Whatever may have been the importance of metempsychosis for Plato, we can hardly suppose that Plotinus did not take it seriously. He rehabilitates all the ironical and strange transformations of the 'Timæus' and the myth of Er, the Armenian. Souls that have failed to raise themselves above [the ordinary level of] humanity, but who have nevertheless respected that characteristic in themselves, are reborn into a human body; those who have only lived a life of sensation, pass into animal bodies, or even, if they have been entirely without energy, if they have lived an entirely vegetative existence, are condemned to live the life of a plant. The exercise of the merely political virtues [the lowest class], which do not deserve rebirth into a human form, bestows the privilege of inhabiting the body of a sociable animal, πολιτικὸν ζῶον, for instance, that of a bee; while tyrants and men notorious for their cruelty animate wild beasts. Those who have erred through a too great love of music, become singing birds, and too speculative philosophers are transformed into eagles and other birds of soaring flight (En. III. iv. 2). [The εἰρωνεία, or ironical vein, of Plato is more than apparent in the above.] A more terrible punishment is reserved for great crimes. Hardened criminals descend to the hells, ἐν ᾅδου ἐλθόντα (En. I. viii. 13), and undergo those terrible punishments which Plato sets forth in the 'Republic' (Book X.). [This reminds us of the Pâtâlas of the Brâhmans and the Avîchi of the Buddhists.]

"Even though admitting that this doctrine of metempsychosis is taken literally by Plotinus, we should still have to ask for him as for Plato, whether the human soul really inhabits the body of an animal, and whether it is not reborn only into a human body which reflects the nature of a certain animal by the character of its passions. The commentators of the Alexandrian school sometimes interpreted Plato in this sense. Thus, according to Proclus, Plato in the 'Phædrus' condemns the wicked to live as brutes and not to become them, κατιέναι εἰς βίον θήρειον, καὶ οὐκ εἰς σῶμα θήρειον (Proclus, ' Com. Tim.,' p. 329). Chalcidius gives the same interpretation, for he distinguishes between the doctrines of Plato and those of Pythagoras and Empedocles, ' qui non naturam modò feram, sed etiam formas.' Hermes ('Comm.' of Chalcidius on 'Timæus,' ed. Fabric., p. 350) declares in unmistakable terms that a human soul can never return to the body of an animal, and that the will of the gods for ever preserves it from such a disgrace (θεοῦ γὰρ νόμος οὗτος, φυλάσσειν ἀνθρωπίνην ψυχὴν ἀπὸ τοσαύτης ὕβρεως)."

Moreover, Marinus tells us that Proclus, the last great master of Neoplatonism, was persuaded " that he possessed the soul of Nichomachus, the Pythagorean." And Proclus in his Commentaries on the " Timæus " vindicates the tenet, with his usual acuteness (v. 329), as follows:

" It is usual," says he, " to inquire how human souls can descend into brute animals. And some, indeed, think that there are certain similitudes of men to brutes, which they call savage lives: for they by no means think it possible that the rational essence can become the soul of a savage animal. On the contrary, others allow it may be sent into brutes, because all souls are of one and the same kind; so that they may become wolves and panthers, and ichneumons. But true reason, indeed, asserts that the human soul may be lodged in brutes, yet in such a manner as that it may obtain its own proper life, and that the degraded soul may, as it were, be carried above it and be bound to the baser nature by a propensity and similitude of affection. And that this is the only mode of insinuation, we have proved by a multitude of arguments in our Commentaries on the 'Phædrus.' If, however, it be requisite to take notice that this is the opinion of Plato, we add that in his 'Republic' he says, that the soul of Thersites assumed an ape, but not the body of an ape; and in the 'Phædrus,' that the soul descends into a savage life, but not into a savage body. For life is conjoined with its proper soul. And in this place he says it is changed into a brutal nature. For a brutal nature is not a brutal body, but a brutal life." (See "The Six Books of Proclus on the Theology of Plato," Taylor's translation; London, 1816; p. l., Introd.)

To return to the view of Jules Simon, the distinguished Academician concludes his dissertation with the following words:

"These contradictory interpretations have very little interest for the history of the philosophy of Plato; but we conclude from the care which the old commentators have taken to tone down the strangeness of the dogma of metempsychosis in Plato, that it was not a literal doctrine with Plotinus."

I would venture to differ somewhat from M. Jules Simon, and to suggest that the contradictory interpretations of commentators and the difficulties of modern criticism on this important tenet have arisen because sufficient distinction has not been drawn between the spiritual and psychic envelopes of man. The idea of union runs through the whole doctrine, and if the Psyche does not centre itself in the Nous, it risks to pass through the Cycle of Necessity (κύκλος ἀνάγκης). But the Psyche, or soul-vesture, is not the real man. The doctrine of metempsychosis, with its twin doctrine of reincarnation, or Punarjanman, is arousing much interest in our own times, and it may be possible ere long to reconcile much that appears contradictory in these doctrines, by a more profound study of the psychic and spiritual nature of man than has as yet been attempted in the western world. Speaking of reincarnation, Max Müller goes as far as to say, " it is well known that this dogma has been accepted by the greatest philosophers of all centuries " ("Three Lectures on the Vedânta Philosophy," London, 1894, p. 93); and quoting the well-known lines of Wordsworth on " the soul that rises with us, our life's star," he endorses them, and adds tentatively, " that our star in this life is what we made it in a former life, would probably sound strange as yet to many ears " in the West (p. 167). This brings us to the consideration whether or not Plotinus also puts forward the doctrine of Karma, which is the complementary doctrine of rebirth. That he did so is evident from the summary of Tennemann (§ 213):

"Every thing that takes place is the result of Necessity, and of a principle identified with all its consequences (in this we see the rudiments of Spinozism, and the 'Theodicée' of Leibnitz). All things are connected together by a perpetual dependency (a system of universal Determinism from which there is only one exception, and that rather apparent than real, of *Unity*). Out of this concatenation of things arise the principles of natural Magic and Divination." (See En. III. ii. 16 ; IV. iv. 4, 5, 32, 40 ; VI. vii. 8-10 ; VII. ii. 3.)

Though the doctrine is not sufficiently insisted upon in its moral bearings by Plotinus, and as applied to the theory of rebirth, nevertheless the general idea is there.

This next brings us to speak of the practical ethic of Plotinus, which was based on his trichotomy of man, and reminds us of the Gnostic division into Psychics (ψυχικοί) and Pneumatics (πνευματικοί), and the perfected Christ.

There are, says Jules Simon (i. 562), "three divisions in the ethic of Plotinus : the political virtues necessary for all men, whose sole aim is the negative avoidance of evil ; the higher or cathartic virtues (καθάρσεις), which can only be attained to by philosophers, and whose aim is the destruction of the passions and the preparation of the soul for mystic union ; and lastly, the at-one-ment of the soul with God."

Thus it will be seen that the political virtues pertained to the Soul, the cathartic to the Nous, and the consummation of virtue was the union with the One. It was by the practice of these virtues that the end of true philosophy was to be reached. As Tennemann says (§ 204) :

"Plotinus assumes as his principle that philosophy can have no place except in proportion as knowledge and the thing known—the Subjective and Objective—are identified. The employment of philosophy is to acquire a knowledge of the Unity, the essence and first principle of all things; and that not mediately by thought or meditation, but by a more exalted method, by direct intuition (παρουσία), anticipating the progress of reflection." (See En. V. iii. 8, v. 7 *sq.*; VI. ix. 3, 4.)

This is put very clumsily by Tennemann, and with a far from careful selection of terms, but the idea is clear enough for the student of mysticism, especially that of the East. Meditation is a means whereby the soul is prepared to receive " flashes " of the supreme wisdom. It is not the gaining of something new, but the regaining of what has been lost, and above all the realization of the ever-present Deity. This is precisely the same view as that enshrined in the great logion of the Upanishads, " *That* art *thou.*" The divine in man is the divine in the universe, nay, is in reality the Divinity in all its fulness. We have to realize the truth by getting rid of the ignorance which hides it from us. It is here that the doctrines of reminiscence (ἀνάμνησις) and ecstasy (ἔκστασις) come in. These are admirably set forth by Jules Simon (i. 549):

" Reminiscence is a natural consequence of the dogma of a past life. The Nous [the spirit or root of individuality] has had no beginning; the man [of the present life] has had a beginning; the present life is therefore a new situation for the spirit; it has lived elsewhere and under different conditions."

It has lived in higher realms, and therefore (p. 552) " it conceives for the world of intelligibles [τὰ νοητὰ, κόσμος νοητός, the proper habitat of the νοῦς] a power-

c

ful love which no longer allows it to turn away its thought. This love [ἔφεσις] is rather a part than a consequence of reminiscence." But ecstasy is the consummation of reminiscence (p. 553). "Ecstasy is not a faculty properly so called, it is a state of the soul, which transforms it in such a way that it then perceives what was previously hidden from it. The state will not be permanent until our union with God is irrevocable: here, in earth life, ecstasy is but a flash. It is a brief respite bestowed by the favour of Deity. [Such flashes are resting-places on our long journey, ἀνάπαυλαι ἐν χρόνοις.] Man can cease to become man and become God; but man cannot be God and man at the same time."

And that Plotinus was not a mere theorist, but did actually attain unto such a state of consciousness, is testified to by Porphyry (c. xxiii.). Plotinus also treats of this in the last book of the "Enneads" (see also En. V. v. 3), but, as he says, it can hardly be described (διὸ καὶ δύσφραστον τὸ θέαμα). Thus we reach the borderland of philosophy as we understand it. Beyond this region lie the realms of pure mysticism and the great unknown. And if any one can lead us by a safe path to those supernal realms, avoiding the many dangers of the way, and in a manner suited to western needs, Plotinus is a guide that can be highly recommended.

G. R. S. MEAD.

LONDON, 1895.

BIBLIOGRAPHY.

Complete Editions.

Perna (Petrus). Basle, 1580, in-folio. A faulty Greek text, to which the Latin translation of Ficinus (Florence, 1492) was appended. Title: "Plotini Platonici Operum Omnium Philosophicorum Libri LIV."

Creuzer (Fridericus). Oxford, 1835, 4to, 3 vols. Certainly the best text yet produced, with the translation and commentaries of Ficinus appended; and with additional notes by Wyttenbach and an apparatus criticus by Moser. It gives all the variæ lectiones from the codices, and is an admirable production. Title: "Plotini Opera Omnia."

Dübner (F.). Paris, 1855, 8vo. In M. F. Didot's "Library of Greek Authors." This is merely a reproduction of Creuzer's text. Title: "Plotini Enneades."

Kirchoff (M.). Leipzig (B. G. Teubner), 1856, 8vo. Endeavours to correct the faulty punctuation of Creuzer; abandons Porphyry's order of the Books, and adopts a chronographical order. There are neither notes nor annotations.

Müller (H. F.). Berlin, 1878 (Weidmann), 8vo. Based on Creuzer again. Title: "Plotini Enneades."

Volkmann (R.). Leipzig (Teubner), 1883, 1884, 8vo, 2 vols. Text simply, without various readings. Title: "Plotini Enneades."

Complete Translations.

Ficinus (M.). Florence, 1492, in-folio; Basle, 1580 (Perna's ed.), also 1615, in-folio; Oxford, 1835 (Creuzer's ed.). Title: "Plotini Opera."

Bouillet (M. N.). Paris, 1857, 1861, 8vo, 3 vols. An excellent and painstaking work. Title: "Les Ennéades de Plotin."

Müller (H. F.). Berlin (Weidmann), 1878; Leipzig, 1880, 8vo. Title: "Die Enneaden des Plotin."

Partial Translations.

Taylor (T.). London, 1787. Reprinted with another title-page, 1792, 12mo, pp. xx, 47. A paraphrase of En. I. vi. Title: "Concerning the Beautiful."
Taylor (T.). London, 1794, 8vo, pp. 228. Contains "On Felicity," "On the Nature and Origin of Evil," "On Providence," "On Nature, Contemplation, and the One," and "On the Descent of the Soul." Title: "Five Books of Plotinus."
Taylor (T.). London, 1817, 8vo, pp. 560. This is the work which is now reproduced. Title: "Select Works of Plotinus."
Taylor (T.). London, 1834, 8vo, pp. 129. Contains translations of En. I. ix., VI. iv., v., and extracts from En. VI. vii. Title: "On Suicide."
Johnson (T. M.). Osceola, Mo., 1880, 8vo. Contains three Books only, the work of an enthusiastic admirer of Taylor. Title: "Three Treatises of Plotinus."

The above represents the sum total of the labours of English translators of Plotinus.

Engelhardt (J. G. V.). Erlangen, 1820, 1823, 8vo. Only a partial translation, with notes and explanations. Title: "Die Enneaden des Plotinus."
Anquetil and Barthélemy Saint-Hilaire have each translated En. I. iv. 6, under the title: "Traité du Beau;" and Salvini translated two Books in "Discorsi Academici," 1733.

Essays and Articles.

Winzer (J. F.). Wittemberg, 1809, 4to. Title: "Adumbratio Decretorum Plotini de Rebus ad Doctrinam Morum Pertinentibus."
Gerlach (G. W.). Wittemberg, 1811, 4to. Title: "Disputatio de Differentia quae inter Plotini et Schellingii Doctrinas de Numine Summo intercedit."
Heigl (G. A.). Landshut, 1815, 8vo. Title: "Die Plotinische Physik."
Engelhardt (J. G. V.). Erlangen, 1820, 8vo. Title: "Dissertatio de Dionysio Areopagita Plotinizante."
Jahn. Bern, 1838. Title: "Basilius Plotinizans."
Steinhart. "De Dialectica Plotini Ratione" (1829), and "Meletemata Plotiniana" (1840).

Neander (A.). "Ueber die welthistorische Bedeutung des 9. Buchs in der 2. Enneade des Plotinos," in the "Abhandl. der Berliner Akademie" (1843).
Kircher. Halle, 1854. Title: "Die Philosophie des Plotin."
Also the two following "Theses for the Doctorate":
Matter (M. J.). Strasbourg, 1817, 4to. An excellent study by the well-known author of "Histoire Critique du Gnosticisme." Title: "Commentatio Philosophica de Principiis Rationum Philosophicarum, Pythagoræ, Platonis atque Plotini."
Daunas (A.). Paris, 1848, 8vo. Very superficial and patronizing. Title: "Études sur le Mysticisme, Plotin et sa Doctrine."
Valentiner. "Plotin u. s. Enneaden," in the "Theo. Stud. u. Kritiken" (1864).
Loesche. "Augustinus Plotinizans" (1881).
Steinhart. "Plotin," in Pauly's "Realencyklop. d. klass. Alterthums."
Brandis (C. A.). "Plotinus," in Smith's "Dictionary of Greek and Roman Biography" (1870).
Harnack (A.). "Neoplatonism," in the "Encyclopædia Britannica," 9th ed. (1884).
Mozley (J. R.). "Plotinus" and "Neoplatonism" (for admirable digest of system), in Smith and Wace's "Dictionary of Christian Biography" (1887).

See also articles in Bayle's "Dictionnaire Historique;" Fabricius' "Bibliotheca Græca" (v. 691-701); Dounan's "Biographie Universelle," and Franck's "Dictionnaire des Sciences Philosophiques." Also Ravaisson (M. Fr.), Paris, 1846, "Essai sur la Métaphysique d'Aristote" (ii. 380-467). And the histories of philosophy of M. de Gérando (III. xxi.); of Tiedemann (iii. 281 sq.); and of Tennemann (vi. 166 sq.); "Geschichte der Philosophie" (Leipzig, 1798, 1819, 8vo); or §§ 203-215 of the English and French translations, where a capable digest of the philosophy of Plotinus is to be found; Johnson (A.), Oxford, 1832; and Cousin (V.), Paris, 1839.

But by far the most important works to consult are:
Simon (Jules François). Paris, 1845, 8vo, 2 vols. Vol. i., Book ii., pp. 197-599, are entirely devoted to Plotinus. Title: "Histoire de l'École d'Alexandrie."
Vacherot (Étienne). Paris, 1846, 8vo, 2 vols. Consult the whole of the Introduction to Book II.; also vol. i., pp. 364-599, for a full and sympathetic description of Plotinus' system.

Richter (A.). Halle, 1867, 8vo. A painstaking, exhaustive, and enthusiastic work. Title: "Neuplatonische Studien: Darstellung des Lebens und der Philosophie des Plotins."

General.

Zeller, "Die Philosophie der Griechen," 3rd edition, 1881, iii. 2, pp. 418-865; Hegel, "Gesch. d. Philos.," iii. 3 sq. ; Ritter, iv. pp. 571-728 ; Ritter und Preller, "Hist. Phil. Græc. et Rom.," pp. 531 sq. ; also the histories of philosophy by Schwegler, Brandis, Brucker (ii. 228 sq.), Thilo, Strümpell, Ueberweg (gives the fullest account of the literature, according to Harnack), Erdmann, Cousin, Prantl, and Lewes.

G. R. S. M.

INTRODUCTION BY THOMAS TAYLOR.

TO
GEORGE MEREDITH, Esq.
AS A TRIBUTE OF THE WARMEST GRATITUDE,

FOR THE ASSISTANCE WHICH HE HAS GIVEN,

IN CONJUNCTION WITH HIS BROTHER,

WILLIAM MEREDITH,

TO THE PROMULGATION OF THE PHILOSOPHY OF

PLATO AND ARISTOTLE,

AND A TESTIMONY OF GREAT ESTEEM

FOR HIS CHARACTER,

THIS WORK IS DEDICATED

BY THE TRANSLATOR,

THOMAS TAYLOR.

INTRODUCTION.

THE philosophy of Plato is deeply indebted to two very extraordinary men, who rank among the chief of its leaders and hierophants, viz. Plotinus and Proclus; to the former for its restoration, and to the latter for the complete development of all its sublimities and mysteries.

It is indeed a remarkable historical fact, though but little known, that the depths of this philosophy, as I have elsewhere observed,[1] were not perfectly fathomed, except by his immediate disciples, for more than five hundred years after its first propagation.[2] For though Crantor, Atticus, Albinus, Galen and Plutarch, were men of great genius, and made no common proficiency in philosophic attainments, yet they appear not to have developed the

[1] See the General Introduction to my translation of Plato.
[2] This fact must necessarily be very little known at present, as the philosophy of Plato is no longer studied as it was in ancient times, having become for many centuries obsolete. And yet it is no uncommon thing with the literati, and particularly with the critics of the present age, to decide with as much confidence on the dogmas of this philosophy, and on the writings of its most celebrated votaries, as on the nugatory and fungous productions of the day. These men forget, when they boast of having consumed the best part of their life in the study of the Greek and Latin languages, that philology is a very different thing from philosophy, and that there is extreme danger in being *well-grounded* at great Grammar schools, of being at the same time *well-ground*. Their presumption however is by no means wonderful when we

profundity of Plato's conceptions; they withdrew not the veil which covers his secret meaning, like the curtains[1] which guarded the adytum of temples from the profane eye; and they saw not that all behind the veil is luminous, and that there divine spectacles[2] every where present themselves to the view. This task was reserved for men who were born indeed in a baser age, but who being allotted a nature similar to their master were the true interpreters of his sublime and mystic speculations. Of these Plotinus was the leader, and to him this philosophy is indebted for its genuine restoration, and for that succession of philosophic heroes, who were luminous links of the golden chain

consider that they have been disciplined by the spectre of the Dunciad,

"Whose beaver'd brow a birchen garland wears,
Dropping with infants' blood, and mothers' tears."

And whose language is,

—— "Since man from beast by words is known,
Words are man's province, words we teach alone.
When Reason doubtful, like the Samian letter,
Points him two ways, the narrower is the better.
*Plac'd at the door of learning, youth to guide,
We never suffer it to stand too wide.*
To ask, to guess, to know as they commence,
As Fancy opens the quick springs of Sense,
*We ply the memory, we load the brain,
Bind rebel Wit, and double chain on chain;
Confine the thought, to exercise the breath,
And keep them in the pale of Words till death.
Whate'er the talents, or howe'er design'd,
We hang one jingling padlock on the mind.*"
Dunciad, Book IV.

[1] 'Επὶ τῶν λεγομένων τελετῶν, τὰ μὲν ἄδυτα ἦν, ὡς δηλοῖ καὶ τοὔνομα, τὰ δὲ παραπετάσματα προβέβληνται, ἀθέατα τὰ ἐν τοῖς ἀδύτοις φυλάττοντα. Psellus in Alleg. de Sphin.

[2] See my dissertation on the "Eleusinian and Bacchic Mysteries" in Numbers XV. and XVI. of the "Pamphleteer."

of deity. The commencement indeed of this restoration of philosophy originated from Ammonius Saccas, but the completion of it was the work of Plotinus. For the former of these, who was by birth an Alexandrian, and at first nothing more than a porter, opened a philosophical school at Alexandria, but with a determination not to commit the more abstruse and theological dogmas of his philosophy to writing. Indeed, this truly great man was so fearful of profaning these sublime mysteries, by exposing them to vulgar inspection, that he revealed them to his disciples Erennius, Origen, and Plotinus, on the condition of inviolable secrecy, and under the guard of irrevocable oaths. However, fortunately for posterity, Erennius dissolved the compact, and Origen (not the Christian father of that name) imitating Erennius, disclosed a part of his master's secrets, in a curious treatise on Dæmons, which unfortunately is lost. But the publications of these two great men were but trifling efforts to restore the mystic wisdom of antiquity, since the evolution of it into light free from the enigmas in which it had been before enveloped, was reserved for the divine genius of Plotinus.

Of this very extraordinary man there is a long and interesting life extant by his disciple Porphyry, from which the following particulars are selected for the information of the English reader.

Plotinus was by birth an Egyptian, and was a native of Lycopolis, as we are informed by Eunapius; for Porphyry is wholly silent as to this particular. Indeed, this is not wonderful, if we consider what Porphyry asserts of him in the beginning of his life, viz. *that he was ashamed that his soul was in body.* Hence, says he, he would neither tell the race, nor the parents from whom he originated, nor would he patiently relate in what country he was born. This I know will be considered by a genuine modern, as either rank enthusiasm, or gross affectation; but he who has fathomed the depth of his writings will immediately subscribe to its truth. The same vehement love for intellectual pursuits, and contempt for body, made him disdain to sit for his picture; so that when Amelius, one of his disciples, begged that he would permit his likeness to be taken, his answer expressed the true greatness of his mind: "As if (says he) it was not sufficient to bear this image, with which nature has surrounded us, you think that a more lasting image of this image should be left as a work worthy to be inspected." However, the wish of Amelius was at length accomplished, by the ingenious contrivance of one Carterius a painter, who by frequenting the school of Plotinus, and viewing his countenance with fixed attention, produced at length from his memory a happy likeness of the philosopher. Though he was often afflicted with the colic, he always refused the assistance of clysters, asserting that remedies of this kind were not fit for a man advanced in years. Nor would he ever receive the assistance of theriacal antidotes, since he said his nourishment was not derived from the bodies of even tame animals. He likewise abstained from baths; but daily used frictions at home. But when a grievous pestilence raged[1] at Rome, and the servants who were accustomed to rub him, fell victims to the disease; from neglecting remedies of this kind, he gradually became a prey to the pestilence. So great was the violence of this distemper, and its effects so dreadful on Plotinus, as Eustochius informed Porphyry who was then absent, that through a very great hoarseness, all the clear and sonorous vigour of his musical voice was lost; and what was still worse, his eyes were darkened,

---

[1] This pestilence was in the time of the Emperor Gallienus, and raged so vehemently, according to Trebellius Pollio, that five thousand men perished through the same disease in one day. This happened in the year of Christ 262, and of Gallienus 9, 10; and not long after Porphyry applied himself to Plotinus.

and his hands and feet were covered with ulcers. Hence, becoming incapable of receiving the salutations of his friends, he left the city, and went to Campania, to the estate of one Zethus, an ancient departed friend. Necessaries were here administered to him from the hereditary possessions of Zethus, and were likewise brought from Minturnus, from the fields of Castricius.[1] But when this divine man drew near to his dissolution, that period which is no less the dread of the vulgar than the transport of the philosopher, and which to Plotinus must have been the moment of extatic rapture, Eustochius, who dwelt at Puteolus, was not very hasty in his approaches; doubtless not imagining that Plotinus was on the point of making his triumphant exit from a corporeal life. However, when he came into the presence of this departing hero, he was just in time to receive his dying words, and to preserve the sacred sentence to posterity. *As yet* (says he) *I have expected you, and now I endeavour that my divine part may return to that divine nature which flourishes throughout the universe.* Such were the last words of this mighty man, which like those contained in his writings, are great and uncommon, admirable and sublime. He died at the conclusion of the second year of the reign of M. Aurelius Flavius Claudius; and was at the time of his death in the sixty-sixth year of his age, according to the information given to Porphyry by Eustochius. Porphyry afterwards informs us, in perfect agreement with the genius of Plotinus, that he would never tell to any one, the month, or day in which he was born; because he by no means thought it proper that his nativity should be celebrated with sacrifices and banquets. Indeed we cannot suppose that he who had such a vehement contempt for a corporeal life, would be anxious that his entrance into mortality

---

[1] This is the Firmus Castricius to whom Porphyry inscribes his treatise "On Abstinence from Animal Food."

should be solemnized with festivity; but rather, considering himself with Empedocles, as

Heaven's exile straying from the orb of light,

he would be disposed to lament his captivity, and mourn the degradation of his nature. However, he was not averse to celebrate the nativities of Socrates and Plato; for he assisted at the sacred rites, and invited his friends to a philosophic banquet, where it was required that every guest should recite a written oration, adapted to the occasion of their amicable association.

The few particulars which this great man condescended to relate of himself in familiar discourse, are the following: when he was eight years of age, and was even under the tuition of a literary preceptor, he used to frequent his nurse, and uncover her breasts, through an avidity of sucking her milk. And this custom he continued, till being accused of troublesomeness, and covered with shame through the reproof, he abandoned this extraordinary custom. This story, however trifling it may appear, indicates in my opinion, the native innocence, and genuine simplicity of manners which so eminently marked the character of Plotinus. When he was in the twenty-eighth year of his age, being vehemently inflamed with the love of philosophy, he was recommended to the most excellent masters of Alexandria; but he left their schools with sorrow and disappointment. By a fortunate event however, he told a certain friend, who was well acquainted with the disposition of his mind, the cause of his affliction, and he brought him to the celebrated Ammonius, whose school Plotinus had probably overlooked, among the great multitude with which that illustrious city abounded. But when he entered the school of Ammonius, and heard him philosophize, he exclaimed in transport to his friend, *this is the man I have been seeking*. From that day he gave himself up to Ammonius with sedulous attention for eleven years; and made such rapid advances in his philosophy, that he determined to study also the philosophy of the Persians, and the wisdom particularly cultivated by the Indian sages. For this purposes, when the Emperor Gordian marched into Persia, in order to war upon that nation, Plotinus joined himself to the army, being at that time in the nine and thirtieth year of his age. But after Gordian was destroyed about Mesopotamia, Plotinus fled to Antioch, where he received a fortunate shelter from the dangers and devastations of war; and in the reign of the Emperor Philip came to Rome, in the fortieth year of his age.

It was a long time before Plotinus committed his thoughts to writing; and gave the world a copy of his inimitable mind. That light which was shortly to illuminate mankind, as yet shone with solitary splendour, or at best beamed only on a beloved few. It was now, however, destined to emerge from its sanctuary, and to display its radiance with unbounded diffusion. But a disciple like Porphyry, was requisite to the full perfection of its appearance. Amelius was indeed laborious, but he was at the same time verbose. He neither appears to have possessed the inquisitive spirit, nor the elegant genius of Porphyry ; and his commentaries were too voluminous to be exquisitely good. Porphyry gives a singular specimen of his endurance of labour, when he informs us that he committed to writing almost all the dogmas of Numenius, and retained a very considerable part of them in his memory. He was not, however, though an excellent philosopher, calculated to urge Plotinus to write, or to assist him in writing; but this important task was reserved for Porphyry, who, in the words of Eunapius, "like a Mercurial chain let down for the benefit of mortals, by the assistance of universal erudition, explained every thing with clearness and precision." Plotinus, indeed, began to write in the first year of the Emperor Gallienus; and he continued to note such questions as occurred to him, for the ten following years, in the last of which he became acquainted with Porphyry, who was at that time in the thirtieth year of his age. He had then composed one-and-twenty books, which were in the hands but of a few: for the edition was difficult to be procured, and was not universally known. Besides, Plotinus was neither hasty nor rash in his publications; but he gave those only to the light, which had been approved by a mature and deliberate judgment. The one-and-twenty books we have just mentioned, after various inscriptions, at length obtained the following titles.

On the Beautiful. Ennead I. lib. 6.
On the Immortality of the Soul. IV. 7.
On Fate. III. 1.
On the Essence of the Soul. IV. 1.
On Intellect, Ideas, and Being. V. 9.
On the Descent of the Soul into Bodies. IV. 8.
How things posterior to the First, proceed from the First, and on *the One*. V. 4.
Whether all Souls are one? IV. 9.
On *the Good*, or *the One*. VI. 9.
On the three Hypostases that rank as the Principles of Things. V. 1.
On the Generation and Order of Things posterior to the First. V. 2.
On the two Matters [*i.e.* the Intelligible and the Sensible]. II. 4.
Various Considerations. III. 9.
On the Circular Motion of the Heavens. II. 2.
On the Dæmon allotted to us. III. 4.
On the reasonable Exit from the present Life. I. 9.
On Quality. II. 6.
Whether there are Ideas of Particulars. V. 7.
On the Virtues. I. 2.
On Dialectic. I. 3.
How the Soul is said to be a medium between an impartible and partible Essence. IV. 2.

These one-and-twenty books were finished when Porphyry first became acquainted with Plotinus; and when this great man was fifty-nine years old. During the six years in which Porphyry was his companion as well as disciple, many questions of a very abstruse nature were discussed in their philosophical conversations, which, at the joint request of Porphyry and Amelius, Plotinus committed to writing, and produced from their investigation, two elaborate and admirable books, *On true being, demonstrating that it is every where one and the same whole.* "Ennead" vi. lib. 4, 5. And afterwards he wrote two others, one of which shows, *That the nature which is beyond being is not intellective, and what that is which is primarily, and also that which is secondarily intellective.* "Ennead" v. 6. But the other is, *On that which is in capacity, and that which is in energy.* "Ennead" ii. 5. He likewise wrote the following books:

On the Impassivity of Incorporeal Natures.[1] Ennead III. 6.
On the Soul, two Books. IV. 3, 4.
On the Soul, a third Book, or On the Manner in which we see. IV. 5.
On Contemplation. III. 8.
On Intelligible Beauty. V. 8.
That Intelligibles are not external to Intellect; and concerning Intellect and *the Good.* V. 5.
Against the Gnostics. II. 9.
On Numbers. VI. 6.
Why things seen at a distance appear to be small. II. 8.
Whether Felicity consists in an extension of Time. I. 5.
On Total Mixture. II. 7.
How the multitude of Ideas subsists, and concerning *the Good.* VI. 7.
On the Voluntary. VI. 8.

---

[1] It is strange that Fabricius should think this treatise ought to be entitled, περὶ τῆς ἀπαθείας τῶν σωμάτων, "On the Impassivity of Bodies." For the man of intellect who reads it, must immediately see that such a title would be ridiculous.

On the World. II. 1.
On Sense and Memory. IV. 6.
On the Genera of Beings, three Books. VI. 1, 2, 3.
On Eternity and Time. III. 7.

But while Porphyry resided in Sicily, and about the fifteenth year of the Emperor Gallienus, Plotinus composed the five following Books, which he sent to Porphyry for his revision.

On Felicity. Ennead I. 4.
On Providence, two Books. III. 2, 3.
On Gnostic Hypostases, and that which is beyond them. IV. 3.
On Love. III. 5.

These books were transmitted to Porphyry in the first year of the Emperor Claudius' reign. And about the beginning of the second year, and a little before his death, he sent him the following, and the last:

On what things are Evil, and whence Evils originate. Ennead I. lib. 8.
Whether the stars effect any thing. II. 3.
What Man is, and what Animal is? I. 1.
On the First Good, and other Goods. I. 7.

The whole amount therefore, of the books written by Plotinus, connecting the preceding with those just enumerated, is fifty-four, which Porphyry has divided into six enneads, assigning, agreeably to the meaning of the word, nine books to every ennead. But they bear evident marks, says Porphyry, of the different periods, at which they were composed. For the first one-and-twenty, which were written in the former part of his life, if compared with the next in order, seem to possess an inferior power, and to be deficient in strength. But those composed in the middle of his life, exhibit the vigour of power, and the acme of perfection. And such with a few exceptions are the four-and-twenty we have already enumerated. The last nine, however, which were composed in the decline of life, bear the marks of remitted energy, and drooping vigour. And this the four last exhibit more evidently than the preceding five.

Plotinus had many auditors, and likewise a multitude of zealous partizans, and philosophic familiars. Among the latter of these, Amelius the Tuscan, and Paulinus the Scythopolitan, a physician, held a distinguished rank. To which may be added Eustochius of Alexandria, a physician, who enjoyed the familiarity of Plotinus to the last, was present at his death, and giving himself entirely to the doctrines of Plotinus, assumed the habit of a genuine philosopher. Besides these Zothicus, a critic and poet, was conversant with Plotinus, who amended the works of Antimachus, and rendered the Atlantic history very poetically in verse; but after this he became blind, and died a short time prior to Plotinus. Zethus, too, was very familiar with our philosopher, who derived his origin from Arabia, and married the wife of one Theodosius, the familiar of Ammonius. This Zethus was deeply skilled in medicine, and very much beloved by Plotinus, who endeavoured to dissuade him from engaging in the administration of public affairs. Such indeed, was his familiarity with our philosopher that, as we have already observed, Plotinus spent the last hours of his life at his rural retreat. Porphyry likewise informs us, that not a few senators were the sedulous auditors of Plotinus. Philosophy indeed, as it is the most noble and liberal of all pursuits, ought never to be separated from noble birth and exalted rank. It is naturally allied to every thing great, and is calculated to confer dignity, even on greatness itself. It exalts the majesty of the monarch, stamps nobility with true grandeur, and raises the plebeian to immortality. Among this illustrious body of men, Marcellus Orontius diligently applied himself to philosophy, and made rapid advances in its attainment. This too was the case with

Sabinillus, and above all with the senator Rogatianus.[1]
So deeply enamoured was this last-mentioned nobleman
of the charms of wisdom, and the discourses of Plotinus,
and so attentive to the care of separating his soul from his
corporeal life, that he neglected his wealth and secular
affairs, dismissed his servants, and rejected the dignities
of the state. Hence, when he was chosen prætor, and the
lictors waited for his appearance, he neither came into
public, nor regarded the duties of his office, nor dwelt in
the house allotted for his reception; but he supt and slept
with certain of his friends and familiars, and gave himself
to absolute retirement in the day. By this negligence and
carelessness of life, (says Porphyry) from being so vehemently afflicted with the gout, that he was obliged to be
carried in a chair, he resumed his pristine strength and
vigour. And from being so diseased in his hands, that he
could not extend them when necessary, he so recovered
their use by philosophic endurance, that he could employ
them with greater expedition than the manual mechanic.
This great man, as we may suppose, possessed a principal
place in the esteem of Plotinus, who was not sparing in
his praise of so uncommon a character, and proposed him as
an illustrious example to the pupils of philosophy. Happy
Rogatianus! who could relinquish power for knowledge,
and prefer the perpetual inheritance of wisdom to the

[1] This Rogatianus is doubtless the person to whom Porphyry
alludes in his] treatise "On Abstinence," lib. i. p. 106, in the
following passage: "There was once an instance, where a negligence of terrene concerns, and a contemplation and intuition of
such as are divine, expelled an articular disease, which had infested
a certain person for the space of eight years. So that at the very
same time, that his soul was divested of a solicitous concern for
riches, and corporeal affairs, his body was freed from a trouble-
some disease." What Porphyry here says is perfectly conformable
to the Chaldæan oracle, "By extending a fiery (*i.e.* a divine) intellect to the work of piety, you will preserve the flowing body."

gaudy splendours of title, and the fleeting honours of command. Alexandrinus Serapion, too, was one of his associates, who was at first a rhetorician, but afterwards gave himself to philosophical discussions; though, shameful to relate, he was at the same time a slave to usury and avarice.[1] Besides all these, says Porphyry, he reckoned me, a native of Tyre, among his most friendly adherents, and whom he also appointed to correct his writings.

The following particulars relative to composition are related by Porphyry of this extraordinary man. He could by no means endure to review twice what he had written, nor even to read his composition, through the badness of his sight. But while he was writing he neither formed the letters with accuracy, nor exactly distinguished the syllables, nor bestowed any diligent attention on the orthography; but neglecting all these as trifles, he was alone attentive to the intellection of his wonderful mind; and, to the admiration of all his disciples, persevered in

[1] Aristotle, in his "Nicomachean Ethics," has shewn with his usual accuracy, that avarice is worse than profusion. First, because it is incurable. For it is the vice of old age, and increases with age. It is also manifold, and has nothing in common with liberality. In the third place, it is not useful to any one, not even to him who labours under it. Hence the proverb, that the avaricious man never benefits, but when he dies; for then he begins to be useful. And in the fourth place, men more frequently sin in this vice than in that of profusion. But prodigality is less a vice than avarice, first, because it may be easily cured and corrected, partly by increase of age, and partly by a defect of wealth. For poverty at length compels the prodigal to stop his profusion. And in the next place, prodigality is more allied to liberality than avarice; so far as, by giving, it is also useful to others; and on that account it is likewise sometimes praised. In short, if there is not any thing more excellent than goodness, and because there is not, we call God *goodness itself*, and if the very essence of goodness consists in imparting in a becoming manner, there cannot be any thing worse than avarice, since the very essence of it consists in *failing to give*.

this custom to the end of his life. To the mere critic and philologist, Plotinus will doubtless appear inexcusable for such *important* omissions; but to the sublime and contemplative genius, his negligence will be considered as the result of vehement conception, and profound ratiocination. Such, indeed, was the power of his intellect, that when he had once conceived the whole disposition of his thoughts from the beginning to the end, and had afterwards committed them to writing, his composition was so connected, that he appeared to be merely transcribing from a book. Hence he would discuss his domestic affairs without departing from the actual intention of his mind; and at one and the same time transact the necessary negociations of friendship, and preserve an uninterrupted survey of the things he had proposed to consider. In consequence of this uncommon power of intellection, when he returned to writing, after the departure of the person with whom he had been conversing, he did not review what he had written, owing, as we have observed, to the defect of his sight; and yet he so connected the preceding with the subsequent conceptions, as if his composition had never been interrupted. Hence he was at the same time present with others and with himself, so that as Porphyry observes, the self-converted energy of his intellect was never remitted, except perhaps in sleep, which the paucity of his food (for he frequently abstained even from bread) and his incessant conversion to intellect, contributed in no small degree to expel.

Several women also vehemently admired the doctrines of Plotinus; and also many noble persons of both sexes, when at the point of death, committed their children and all their property to Plotinus, as to a certain sacred and divine guardian. Hence, says Porphyry, the house of Plotinus was filled with boys and virgins (among the number of which was Potamon), whom he educated with diligence and care. Nor was he wearied in hearing the procurators of his pupils, rendering an account of their conduct, or paying an accurate attention to the expenditure of their income, affirming, that as they did not yet philosophize, they ought to possess their own property, and receive their annual rents without detriment. Yet though he was so attentive to his pupils in the necessary concerns of life, the intellectual energy of his soul while he was awake, never suffered any interruption from externals, nor any remission of vigour. He was likewise extremely mild in his manners, and was easy of access to all his friends and adherents. Hence, so great was his philosophic urbanity, that though he resided at Rome six-and-twenty years, and had been the arbitrator of many litigious causes, which he amicably dissolved, yet he had no enemy throughout that vast and illustrious city.

But though Plotinus was so greatly esteemed at Rome, and in general by all who had the happiness of his acquaintance, yet he had one vehement enemy in the person of Alexandrinus Olympius, who had been for a short time the disciple of Ammonius, and who arrogantly conceived himself to be the first of philosophers, and conducted himself contemptuously towards Plotinus. So deadly, indeed, was his hatred of our philosopher, that he attempted to invade him, by drawing down, through magical arts, the baneful influences of the stars. The attempt was however vain, and noxious to its author. For the sidereal defluxions, instead of being hurtful to Plotinus, were reflected on Olympius. Hence he exclaimed to his companions, "that the soul of Plotinus possessed such a mighty power, that it immediately repelled malignant influences directed upon his person, on the authors of the evil." But Plotinus, when Olympius first machinated his sidereal inchantments, was conscious of his design, and said to his friends: "Now the body of Olympius is contracted like a purse, and all his members are bruised together." After Olympius, therefore, had often found to his own detriment, that the baneful influences intended for Plotinus was repelled on himself, he desisted from such base and fruitless undertakings. Indeed, says Porphyry, Plotinus naturally possessed something greater than the rest of mankind, which the following extraordinary relation abundantly evinces. A certain Egyptian priest, who at that time was at Rome, and who became known to Plotinus through one of his friends (perhaps Porphyry himself), being desirous to exhibit his wisdom in that illustrious city, persuaded our philosopher to attend him, for the purpose of beholding, through his invocations, his familiar dæmon; to which request Plotinus readily consented. But the invocation was performed in the temple of Isis; this being the only pure place in Rome the Egyptian priest was able to find. However, instead of a dæmon, as was expected, a God approached, who was not, says Porphyry, in the genus of dæmons. The Egyptian astonished at the unexpected event exclaimed, "Happy Plotinus, who hast a God for a dæmon,[1] and whose familiar attendant does not rank among the inferior kind!" This extraordinary, however, and delightful vision was of short duration. For the priest affirmed, that it was not then lawful to ask any question, or any longer to enjoy the vision, because a certain friend who was present at the

[1] "The most perfect souls (says Proclus in MS. Comment. in 'Alcibiad.' I.) who are conversant with generation in an undefiled manner, as they choose a life conformable to their presiding God, so they live according to a divine dæmon, who conjoined them to their proper deity when they dwelt on high. Hence, the Egyptian priest admired Plotinus, as being governed by a divine dæmon. And prior to this he observes, that "the first and highest dæmons are divine, and who often appear as Gods, through their transcendent similitude to the divinities. For that which is first in every order preserves the form of the nature prior to itself."

spectacle, suffocated some birds which he held in his hands for the sake of safety, either impelled by envy or terrified through fear. As Plotinus therefore was allotted a dæmon belonging to the diviner orders, the divine eye of his soul was perpetually elevated to this guardian deity. On this account, he composed a book, "On the Dæmons" which are allotted to us, in which he diligently endeavours to assign the causes of the diversity subsisting among these attendants on mankind.

Plotinus likewise appears to have possessed a most extraordinary skill in physiognomy, as is evinced by the following circumstance. A lady named Chion, who together with her daughters resided in his house, and there happily passed a chaste widowhood, was fraudulently deprived of a very valuable necklace. In consequence of this, all the servants and domestics were summoned into the presence of Plotinus, who regarded their several countenances, selected one of them, and accused him of the theft. The man was immediately chastised, and for some time denied the fact, but at length confessed his guilt, and restored the necklace. In a similar manner (says Porphyry) he wonderfully predicted the destiny of the young men of his acquaintance; as of one Polemo, he foretold, that he would be very much addicted to love, and would live but for a short time, which happened according to his prediction. But the last instance of his sagacity, related by Porphyry, excels all the rest, both in the singular skill which it displays, and the happy consequences it produced. Porphyry, as we are informed by Eunapius in his life of him, on his first acquaintance with Plotinus, bade a final farewell to all his preceptors, and wholly applied himself to the friendship and confidence of this wonderful man. Here he filled his mind with science, and drew abundantly without satiety, from the perennial fountain. seated in the sanctuary of the soul of Plotinus. But afterwards, being vanquished as it were, by the magnitude of his doctrines, he conceived a hatred of body, and could no longer endure the fetters of mortality. "Hence," says Porphyry, "I formed an intention of destroying myself, which Plotinus perceived, and as I was walking home stood before me, and said that my design was not the dictate of a sound intellect, but was the effect of a certain melancholy disease. In consequence of this, he ordered me to depart from Rome, and accordingly I went to Sicily, particularly as I heard that a certain worthy and elegant man dwelt at that time about Lilybæum. And thus indeed I was liberated from this [deadly] intention, but was hindered from being present with Plotinus till his death."

But the great reputation of this divine man was not confined to the senate and people of Rome: for the emperor Gallienus and his wife Salonina honoured his person and reverenced his doctrine. Indeed, so highly was he esteemed by the emperor, that relying on his benevolence, he requested that a city in Campania, which had been formerly destroyed, might be restored, and rendered a fit habitation for philosophers; and besides this that it might be governed by the laws of Plato, and called Platonopolis. The emperor indeed assented to his wishes, and the philosopher would have easily accomplished his intentions, if some of the emperor's familiars, impelled by envy or indignation, or some other depraved cause, had not impeded its execution.

This very extraordinary man, as we are informed by Porphyry, was strenuous in discourse, and most powerful in discovering and conceiving what was appropriate; but in certain words he was incorrect. While he was speaking, however, there was an evident indication of the predominance of intellect in his conceptions. For the light of it diffused itself as far as to his countenance, which was indeed at all times lovely, but was then particularly beautiful. For then a certain attenuated and dewy moisture appeared on his face, and a pleasing mildness shone forth. Then, also, he exhibited a placid gentleness in receiving questions, and demonstrated a vigour uncommonly robust in the solution of them. When Porphyry once had interrogated him for three days, on the manner in which the soul is present with the body, he persevered in demonstrating the mode of its conjunction. And when a certain person, named Thaumasius, entered his school, for the purpose of discussing general questions in philosophy, and premised that he wished to hear Plotinus explain the books that were read in his school, but that he was prevented by the questions and answers of Porphyry, Plotinus replied: "Unless we dissolve the doubts of Porphyry, we shall not be able to explain any thing in the book which you wish us to make the subject of discussion." He wrote as he spoke, strenuously [1] and with abundance of intellect. His style also is concise, and abounds more with profundity of conception than copiousness of words. "He poured forth many things," says Porphyry, under the influence of inspiration; and was wonderfully affected with the subjects he discussed. The latent dogmas of the Stoics and Peripatetics, are mingled in his writings; and he has condensed in them the metaphysics of Aristotle. He was not ignorant of any geometrical, arithmetical, mechanical, optical, or musical theorem, though he never applied these sciences to practical purposes. The commentaries of the Platonic philosophers, Cronius, Numenius, Gaius, Atticus, &c.; as also of the Peripatetics, Aspasius, Alexander, Adrastus, &c., were read in his school; but he borrowed nothing whatever from these. For his conceptions were entirely his own, and his theory was different

[1] In the original σύντομος; but from what follows, it is evident that it should be σύντονος.

from theirs. In his investigations he exhibited the intellect of Ammonius. He was also rapidly filled with what he read; and having in a few words given the meaning of a profound theory, he arose. Having once read the treatise of Longinus "concerning principles," he said "that Longinus was indeed a philologist, but by no means a philosopher." When in the celebration of Plato's nativity, Porphyry recited a poem which he called "the Sacred Marriage,"[1] and a certain person who was present observed that Porphyry was mad, because many things were said in the poem mystically and latently, accompanied with a divine afflatus, Plotinus openly exclaimed, "You have shown yourself at the same time a poet, a philosopher, and an hierophant." On a certain time too, an orator named Diophanes read an apology for the intoxicated Alcibiades in the Banquet of Plato, endeavouring to prove that it was proper for the sake of learning virtue, that the lover should expose himself to the object of his attachment, and not even refuse venereal congress. But while he was reading this licentious defence, Plotinus often rose from his seat, as if he would suddenly leave the assembly; but he restrained himself till it was finished. However, when he

[1] According to the Orphic theology as we learn from Proclus, that divinity who is the cause of stable power and sameness, the supplier of being, and the first principle of conversion to all things, is of a male characteristic; but the divinity which emits from itself all-various progressions, separations, measures of life, and prolific powers, is feminine. And a communication of energies between the two, was denominated by this theology *a sacred marriage*. Proclus adds, "that theologists at one time perceiving this communion in co-ordinate Gods, called it the marriage of Jupiter and Juno, Heaven and Earth, Saturn and Rhea. But at another time surveying it in the conjunction of subordinate with superior Gods, they called it the marriage of Jupiter and Ceres. And at another, perceiving it in the union of superior with inferior divinities, they denominated it the marriage of Jupiter and Proserpine." Vid. Procl. in " Tim." et in " Parmenid."

left the company, he desired Porphyry to confute the oration. But when Porphyry requested the orator to lend him his discourse for this purpose, and was refused, he answered him from recollection, and delivered his answer in the presence of the same auditors as had attended Diophanes. On this occasion Plotinus was so delighted, that he often repeated in the assembly,

" Thus write and you'll illuminate mankind."[1]

Plotinus likewise applied himself to the canons concerning the stars, but not according to a very mathematical mode. That is, we may presume, he very little regarded the calculation of eclipses, or measuring the distance of the sun and moon from the earth, or determining the magnitudes and velocities of the planets. For he considered employments of this kind, as more the province of the mathematician, than of the profound and intellectual philosopher. The mathematical sciences are indeed the proper *means* of acquiring wisdom, but they ought never to be considered as its *end*. They are the bridge as it were between sense and intellect, by which we may safely pass through the night of oblivion, over the dark and stormy ocean of matter, to the lucid regions of the intelligible world. And he who is desirous of returning to his true country, will speedily pass over this bridge without making any needless delays in his passage. But he more accurately investigated the doctrine of Astrologers about the influences of the stars, and not finding their predictions to be certain, he frequently confuted them in his writings.

At that time there were many Christians and others, who forsaking the ancient philosophers became the followers of Adelphius and Aquilinus. These men

---

[1] A line somewhat altered from Homer. The original is,

Βάλλ' οὕτως αἰκέν τι φόως Δαναοῖσι γένηαι.
Iliad, 8. v. 282.

possessed many writings of Alexander Libycus, Philocomus, Demostratus, and Lydus; and openly exhibited certain revelations of Zoroaster, Zostrianus, Nicotheus, Allogenes, Mesus, and others of a like kind. They also deceived many, and were themselves deceived, asserting that Plato had by no means penetrated the depth of an intelligible essence. On this occasion, Plotinus urged many arguments in his conferences against these impostors, and composed a treatise in confutation of their tenets, which Porphyry inscribed "against the Gnostics." But Amelius wrote forty books against the treatise of Zostrianus; and Porphyry showed by a variety of arguments that the book which they attributed to Zoroaster was spurious and recent, and was fabricated by the propagators of the heresy, in order that their opinions might pass for the genuine dogmas of the ancient Zoroaster.

Porphyry farther informs us, that some Greeks falsely accused Plotinus of being a plagiary of the doctrines of Numenius; which calumny Tryphon, a Stoic and Platonist, told to Amelius. On this occasion Amelius wrote a treatise, inscribed by Porphyry, *on the difference between the dogmas of Plotinus and Numenius*, which he dedicated to Porphyry. Each of the books indeed of this truly great man bears such evident marks of original thought and singular depth, the execution in each is so similar, and the conceptions so uncommonly abstruse, that no one can understand his meaning, and believe him indebted to the labours of others. Porphyry adds, that he was likewise considered by many as a mere trifler, and treated with contempt, because, says he, they could by no means understand what he said. Besides, the manners of Plotinus contributed to produce and increase this disdain. For he was foreign from all sophistical ostentation and pride; and conducted himself, in the company of disputants, with the same freedom and ease as in his familiar discourses.

With the superficial and the vain indeed, a haughty carriage and severe aspect are considered as the badges of wisdom; but nothing in reality is more foreign from its possession. For true wisdom when it is deeply possessed, gives affability and modesty to the manners, illumines the countenance with a divine serenity, and diffuses over the whole external form an air of dignity and ease. Add to this, that Plotinus did not hastily disclose to every one the syllogistic necessities which were latent in his discourse. "The same thing," says Porphyry, "happened to me, when I first heard Plotinus. On which account I endeavoured to excite him by writing against him, and striving to show *that intellections are external to intellect.*" But after the writings of Porphyry on this subject were read to Plotinus, he said smiling: "It must be your employment, Amelius, to dissolve these doubts, occasioned by his ignorance of our opinion." After Amelius, therefore, had composed no small treatise against the objections of Porphyry, and Porphyry had again contradicted his writings, and was once more answered by Amelius; "At length," says Porphyry, "having scarcely after all these attempts fathomed the depth[1] of Plotinus, I changed my

---

[1] If therefore a man of such great sagacity and penetration as Porphyry, and who from the period in which he lived possessed advantages with respect to the attainment of philosophy which are denied to every modern, found so much difficulty in fathoming the profundity of Plotinus, there must necessarily be very few at present by whom this can be accomplished. Let no one therefore deceive himself by fancying that he can understand the writings of Plotinus by barely reading them. For as the subjects which he discusses are for the most part the objects of intellect alone, to understand them is to see them, and to see them is to come into contact with them. But this is only to be accomplished by long familiarity with, and a life conformable to the things themselves. For then, as Plato says, "a light as if leaping from a fire, will on a sudden be enkindled in the soul, and will then itself nourish itself." See Plato's 7th Epistle.

opinion, wrote a recantation of my error, which I recited in his school; considered the books of Plotinus ever after as most worthy of belief, and excited my master to the ambition of disclosing his opinions in a more particular and copious manner."

The testimony of the celebrated Longinus also concerning our philosopher, sufficiently evinces his uncommon excellence and worth; and in the present age will probably be more esteemed than the eulogium of Porphyry. In a letter, therefore, which he wrote to Porphyry desiring him to come from Sicily into Phœnicia where he resided, and to bring with him the books of Plotinus, he writes among other things as follows: "These books (meaning those written by Plotinus) are not moderately faulty, so that I have no means of using them, though I desire above measure to inspect what Plotinus has written on the soul, and on being." And again, "Do not send these books but bring them with you, and not these alone, but any others which may have escaped the notice of Amelius. *For why should I not inquire with the greatest diligence after the writings of this man, since they deserve the highest honour and veneration?* This indeed I have always signified to you, both when present and absent, and when you resided at Tyre, that I could not understand many of the hypotheses of the books of Plotinus; *but that I transcendently loved and reverenced the manner of his writing, the density of his conceptions, and the very philosophic disposition of his questions. And indeed I judge that the investigators of truth ought only to compare the books of Plotinus with the most excellent works.*"

This testimony of Longinus is the more remarkable, as, prior to this, he had for a long time despised our philosopher, through the ignorant aspersions of others. The wonderful genius of Plotinus, was indeed so concealed under the garb of modesty, that before fame had announced his worth it was only visible to a penetrating and sagacious few. But Longinus, says Porphyry, thought the works of Plotinus which he had received from Amelius incorrect, through the fault of the transcribers. For if any, the books in the possession of Amelius were correct, because they were transcribed from the manuscripts of Plotinus. Porphyry has likewise preserved the preface of a book composed by Longinus, inscribed, "*Concerning the End*," and dedicated to Plotinus and Amelius, in the course of which he says of our philosopher, "*That Plotinus, as it seems, has more certainly explained the Pythagoric and Platonic principles than his predecessors. For the writings of Numenius, Cronius, Moderatus, and Thrasyllus, are not to be compared for accuracy in any part, with the books of Plotinus on the same subjects.*"

If such then is the decision of Longinus concerning the abilities and writings of this extraordinary man; of Longinus, who is celebrated by one of our first poets, as "*inspired by all the Nine;*" and whose literary reputation is universal; what judgment must we form of the philosophic taste of the present age, when we find that the very name of Plotinus is known but to a few, and his works scarcely to any? The inference is obvious; let the reader draw it and lament. But, says Porphyry, if it be requisite to employ the testimony of the wise, who is wiser than a God? than a God who truly said of himself:

"The sands' amount, the measures of the sea,
Tho' vast the number, are well known to me.
I know the thoughts within the dumb conceal'd,
And words I hear by language unreveal'd." [1]

And this is no other than Apollo, who, when Amelius

---

[1] In the original:

Οἶδα δ' ἰγὼ ψάμμου τ' ἀριθμὸν, καὶ μίτρα θαλάσσης,
Καὶ κωφοῦ ξυνίημι, καὶ οὐ λαλίοντος ἀκούω.

And this is the first part of the celebrated oracle given to Crœsus, as related by Herodotus.

inquired of his oracle whither the soul of Plotinus had migrated, answered as follows:

"To strains immortal full of heav'nly fire,
My harp I tune well strung with vocal wire;
Dear to divinity a friend I praise,
Who claims those notes a God alone can raise.
For him a God in verse mellifluous sings,
And beats with golden rod the warbling strings.
Be present Muses, and with general voice
And all the powers of harmony rejoice;
Let all the measures of your art be try'd
In rapt'rous sounds, as when Achilles dy'd.
When Homer's melody the band inspir'd,
And god-like furies every bosom fir'd.
And lo! the sacred choir of Muses join,
And in one general hymn their notes combine.
I Phœbus in the midst, to whom belong
The sacred pow'rs of verse, begin the song.
Genius sublime! once bound in mortal ties,
A dæmon now and more than mortals wise.
Freed from those members that with deadly weight
And stormy whirl enchain'd thy soul of late;
O'er Life's rough ocean thou hast gain'd that shore,
Where storms molest and change impairs no more;
And struggling thro' its deeps with vig'rous mind,
Pass'd the dark stream, and left base souls behind.
Plac'd where no darkness ever can obscure,
Where nothing enters sensual and impure;
Where shines eternal God's unclouded ray,
And gilds the realms of intellectual day.
Oft merg'd in matter, by strong leaps you try'd
To bound aloft, and cast its folds aside;
To shun the bitter stream of sanguine life,
Its whirls of sorrow, and its storm of strife.
While in the middle of its boist'rous waves
Thy soul robust, the deep's deaf tumult braves;
Oft beaming from the Gods thy piercing sight
Beheld in paths oblique a sacred light:
Whence rapt from sense with energy divine,
Before thine eyes immortal splendours shine;
Whose plenteous rays in darkness most profound,

Thy steps directed and illumin'd round.
Nor was the vision like the dreams of sleep,
But seen while vigilant you brave the deep;
While from your eyes you shake the gloom of night,
The glorious prospects burst upon your sight;
Prospects beheld but rarely by the wise,
Tho' men divine and fav'rites of the skies.
But now set free from the lethargic folds,
By which th' indignant soul dark matter holds;
The natal bonds deserted, now you soar,
And rank with dæmon forms a man no more.
In that blest realm where love and friendship reign,
And pleasures ever dwell unmixt with pain;
Where streams ambrosial in immortal course
Irriguous flow, from deity their source.
No dark'ning clouds those happy skies assail,
And the calm æther knows no stormy gale.
Supremely blest thy lofty soul abides,
Where Minos and his brother judge presides;
Just Æacus and Plato the divine,
And fair Pythag'ras there exalted shine;
With other souls who form the general choir
Of love immortal, and of pure desire;
And who one common station are assign'd,
With genii of the most exalted kind.
Thrice happy thou! who, life's long labours past,
With holy dæmons dost reside at last;
From body loosen'd and from cares at rest,
Thy life most stable, and divine thy feast.
Now ev'ry Muse who for Plotinus sings,
Here cease with me to tune the vocal strings;
For thus my golden harp, with art divine,
Has told—Plotinus! endless bliss is thine."

"According to this oracle then," says Porphyry, "Plotinus was worthy and mild, gentle and endearing, and such as we truly found him to be. It also asserts that he was vigilant, that he had a pure soul, and that he was always tending to divinity, which he most ardently loved. Likewise that he endeavoured with all his might to emerge from the bitter waters of this sanguine life. Hence, when by the assistance of this divine light he had frequently raised himself by his conceptions to the first God who is beyond intellect,[1] and by employing for this purpose the paths narrated by Plato in the *Banquet*, the supreme divinity appeared to him, who has neither any form nor idea, but is established above intellect and every intelligible; to whom also I Porphyry say that I once approached, and was united, when I was sixty-eight years of age. The mark, therefore, at which all his endeavours aimed, appeared to Plotinus to be near. For the end and scope with him consisted in approximating and being united to the God who is above all things. But he four times obtained this end while I was with him, and this by an ineffable energy, and not in capacity. The oracle also adds, that while Plotinus was wandering [on the sea of life] the Gods frequently directed him into the right path, by benignantly extending to him abundant rays of divine light; so that he may be said to have composed his works from the contemplation and intuition of divinity, But from a vigilant internal and external contemplation, he is said by the oracle to have seen many beautiful spectacles, which no other philosopher has easily beheld. For merely human contemplation may indeed have various degrees of excellence, but when compared with divine knowledge, though it may be elegant and pleasing, yet cannot fathom a depth, such as is penetrated by the Gods. Hitherto the oracle has shown what were the energies of Plotinus, and what he obtained, while surrounded with body. But after his liberation from body, it declares that he arrived at the divine society, where friendship, pure desire, joy and love, suspended from deity, perpetually reign. Besides this, it also says that the sons of God, Minos, Rhadamanthus, and Æacus, are the judges of souls; and that Plo-

[1] τοῦ νοῦ is omitted in the original; but both the sense and the version of Ficinus render the insertion of it necessary.

tinus departed to these, not for the purpose of receiving their decisions of his conduct, but to enjoy their conversation, with whom also other Gods of the most excellent kind associate. It further says that Plato and Pythagoras likewise reside here, together with such other souls as stably form the choir of immortal love; and that the most blessed dæmons have here fixed their abode. And in the last place it adds, that the life of this divine society is ever flourishing, and full of joy, and perseveres in perpetuity of bliss through the beneficent communications of the Gods."

And thus much for the life of Plotinus, who was a philosopher pre-eminently distinguished for the strength and profundity of his intellect, and the purity and elevation of his life. He was a being wise without the usual mixture of human darkness, and great without the general combination of human weakness and imperfection. He seems to have left *the orb of light* solely for the benefit of mankind; that he might teach them how to repair the ruin contracted by their exile from good, and how to return to their true country, and legitimate kindred and allies. I do not mean that he descended into mortality, for the purpose of unfolding the sublimest truths to the vulgar part of mankind; for this would have been a vain and ridiculous attempt;[1] since the eyes of the multitude, as

[1] In every class of beings in the universe (as I have elsewhere observed) there is a first, a middle, and a last, in order that the progression of things may form one unbroken chain, originating from deity, and terminating in matter. In consequence of this connection, one part of the human species naturally coalesces, through transcendency, with beings of an order superior to man; another part, through diminution, unites with the brutal species; and a third part, which subsists as the connecting medium between the other two, possesses those properties which characterize human nature in a manner not exceeding but exactly commensurate to the condition of humanity. The first of these parts, from its surpass-

Plato justly observes, are not strong enough to look to truth. But he came as a guide to the few who are born with a divine destiny (θείᾳ μοίρᾳ); and are struggling to gain the lost region of light, but know not how to break the fetters by which they are detained: who are impatient to leave the obscure cavern of sense, where all is delusion and shadow, and to ascend to the realms of intellect, where all is substance and reality.

This very extraordinary man also appears to have been the first of the Platonic philosophers, who clearly and distinctly asserted the subsistence of the three hypostases that rank as principles (ἀρχικαὶ ὑποστάσεις) viz. *the good, intellect, and soul*, and who demonstrated that there can be neither more nor less than these. But these three are thus denominated, because they are not consubsistent; and they are not consubsistent, because they are essentially different from each other. For according

ing excellence, consists of a small number of mankind. That which subsists as the middle, is numerous. But that which ranks as the last in gradation, is composed of a countless multitude,

"Thick as autumnal leaves that strow the brooks
In Vallombrosa."

In consequence of this beautiful gradation, the most subordinate part of mankind are only to be benefited by good rulers, laws, and customs, through which they become peaceable members of the communities in which they live, and make a proficiency, as Maximus Tyrius well observes, not by any accession of good, but by a diminution of evil. Hence the present efforts to enlighten by education the lowest class of mankind is an attempt to break the golden chain of beings, to disorganise society, and to render the vulgar dissatisfied with the servile situations in which God and nature intended them to be placed. In short, it is an attempt calculated to render life intolerable, and knowledge contemptible, to subvert all order, introduce anarchy, render superstition triumphant, and restore, in the language of Pope, the throne of

—" Night primæval and of Chaos old."

to Plato *the good is superessential; intellect* is an *impartible, immoveable essence;* and *soul* is a *self-motive* essence, and subsists as a medium between intellect and the nature which is distributed about bodies.[1] By no means therefore is the Platonic the same with the Christian trinity, as the advocates for the latter have ignorantly and idly supposed. For *the good* or the highest God according to Plato being so perfectly exempt from all multitude, that he is even beyond essence, is not to be connumerated with any thing, or to be co-arranged with the second and third principles in the above-mentioned or any other triad. Indeed, according to the philosophy of Plato, as I have elsewhere shown, in every order of things a triad is the immediate progeny of a monad. Hence the intelligible triad proceeds immediately from the ineffable principle of things. Phanes, or intelligible intellect, who is the last of the intelligible order, is the monad, leader, and producing cause of a triad, which is denominated νοητὸς καὶ νοερὸς, i.e. *intelligible and at the same time intellectual.* In like manner the extremity of this order produces immediately from itself the intellectual triad, Saturn, Rhea, and Jupiter. Again, Jupiter, who is also the demiurgus, is the monad of the supermundane triad. Apollo, who subsists at the extremity of the supermundane order, produces a triad of *liberated Gods.* (θεοὶ ἀπόλυτοι.) And the extremity of the liberated order becomes the monad of a triad of mundane Gods.[2] This theory too, which is the progeny of the most consummate science, is in perfect conformity with

[1] See my translation of Proclus' "Elements of Theology," where all this is shown by *geometrical necessities* to be true. See also the sixth book of the "Republic of Plato," in which Socrates clearly asserts that *the good* is superessential; and the "Timæus," in which the difference between intellect and soul is most clearly indicated. See likewise the notes on the third Epistle of Plato in vol. v. of my translation of his works.

[2] See my translation of Proclus on the "Theology of Plato."

the theology of the Chaldæans. And hence it is said in one of their oracles, "*In every world a triad shines forth, of which a monad is the ruling principle.*" (παντὶ γὰρ ἐν κόσμῳ λάμπει τριάς, ἧς μονὰς ἄρχει. This likewise appears to be the peculiarity of the philosophy of Plotinus, that it considered all the above-mentioned orders, all true beings that are superior to soul, and the multiform variety of ideas, or paradigms of things, as comprehended in one supreme intellect, which it denominates the intelligible world, and as there subsisting in impartible union, without any specific distinction. Hence Plotinus was more anxiously employed in profoundly investigating the nature of this divine world, than in scientifically unfolding the order of the beings it contains. Indeed, his genius on every subject seems to have been more adapted to an intimate perception of the occult essence of a thing, than to an explanation of its gradual evolution, and a description of the mode of its participations. However, though he did not develope the more particular progressions of true beings, yet he inserted the principles of this sublime investigation in his writings; and laid the foundation of that admirable and beautiful system, which was gradually revealed by succeeding Platonists, and at last received its perfection by the acute, accurate, and elegant genius of Proclus.[1]

[1] The following beautiful extract from the treatise of Plotinus, "On intelligible beauty," is a specimen of his manner of surveying all things, as subsisting without specific distinction in one supreme intellect. The whole of the extract likewise is the result of νοερὰ ἐπιβολή, or intuition through the projecting energies of intellect. "All the Gods are venerable and beautiful, and their beauty is immense. What else however is it but intellect through which they are such? and because intellect energizes in them in so great a degree as to render them visible [by its light]? For it is not because their bodies are beautiful. For those Gods that have bodies, do not through this derive their subsistence as Gods; but these also

are Gods through intellect. For they are not at one time wise, and at another destitute of wisdom; but they are always wise, in an impassive, stable, and pure intellect. They likewise know all things, not human concerns [precedaneously] but their own, which are divine, and such as intellect sees. Of the Gods however, those that are in the sensible heaven, for they abound in leisure, always contemplate, as if remotely, what the intelligible heaven contains, and this with an elevated head. But those that dwell in the latter, occupy the whole of the heaven* which is there, and survey [its blessed] inhabitants. For all things there are heaven, and there the earth is heaven, as also are the sea, animals, plants, and men. And in short, every thing pertaining to that heaven is celestial. The Gods likewise that it contains do not think men undeserving of their regard, nor any thing else that is there [because every thing there is divine †]. And they occupy and pervade without ceasing the whole of that [blissful] region. For the life which is there is unattended with labour, and truth [as Plato says in the 'Phædrus'] is their generator, and nutriment, their essence and nurse. They likewise see all things, not those with which generation, but those with which essence is present. And they perceive themselves in others. For all things there are diaphanous; and nothing is dark and resisting, but every thing is apparent to every one internally and throughout. For light every where meets with light; since every thing contains all things in itself, and again sees all things in another. So that all things are every where, and all is all. Each thing likewise is every thing. And the splendour there is infinite. For every thing there is great, since even that which is small is great. The sun too which is there is all the stars: and again each star is the sun and all the stars. In each, however, a different property predominates, but at the same time all things are visible in each. Motion likewise there is pure; for the motion is not confounded by a mover different from it. Permanency also suffers no change of its nature, because

---

* The heaven which Plotinus here celebrates as the same with the intelligible world, and the supreme intellect, belongs, accurately speaking, to that divine order which is denominated by the Chaldæan theologians νοητὸς καὶ νοερὸς, *intelligible and at the same time intellectual*, and is beautifully unfolded by Proclus in his fourth book "On the Theology of Plato."

† From the version of Ficinus it appears that the words ὅτι πᾶν ἐκεῖ θεῖον are omitted in the original.

f

it is not mingled with the unstable. And the beautiful there is beautiful, because it does not subsist in beauty [as in a subject]. Each thing too is there established, not as in a foreign land, but the seat of each thing is that which each thing is; and concurs with it, while it proceeds as it were on high from whence it originated. Nor is the thing itself different from the place in which it subsists. For the subject of it is intellect, and it is itself intellect. Just as if some one should conceive that stars germinate from the light of this visible heaven which is luminous. In this sensible region therefore, one part is not produced from another, but each part is alone a part. But there each part always proceeds from the whole, and is at the same time each part and the whole. For it appears indeed as a part; but by him whose sight is acute, it will be seen as a whole; viz. by him whose sight resembles that which Lynceus is said to have possessed, and which penetrated the interior parts of the earth; the fable obscurely indicating the acuteness of the vision of supernal eyes. There is likewise no weariness of the vision which is there, nor any plenitude of perception which can bring intuition to an end. For neither was there any vacuity, which when filled might cause the visive energy to cease: nor is this one thing, but that another, so as to occasion a part of one thing not to be amicable with that of another. Whatever likewise is there, possesses an untamed and unwearied power. And that which is there insatiable is so, because its plenitude never causes it to despise that by which it is filled. For by seeing it more abundantly sees, and perceiving both itself and the objects of its perception to be infinite, it follows its own nature [in unceasing contemplation]. And life indeed is not wearisome to any one, when it is pure. Why, therefore, should that which leads the most excellent life be weary? But the life there is wisdom; a wisdom not obtained by a reasoning process, because the whole of it always was, and is not in any respect deficient, so as to be in want of investigation. But it is the first wisdom, and is not derived from another."

SELECT WORKS OF PLOTINUS.

SELECT WORKS OF PLOTINUS.

I.

ON THE VIRTUES.[1]

II. ii.

I. SINCE evils are here, and revolve from necessity about this [terrestrial] place, but the soul wishes to fly from evils, it is requisite to fly from hence. What therefore is the flight? To become similar, says Plato, to God. But this will be effected, if we become just and holy, in conjunction with [intellectual] prudence, and in short if we are [truly] virtuous. If therefore we are assimilated through virtue, is it to one who possesses virtue? But to whom are we assimilated? To divinity. Are we then assimilated to that nature which appears to possess the virtues in a more eminent degree, and also to the soul of the world, and to the intellect which is the leader in it, in which there is an admirable wisdom? For it is reasonable to suppose that while we are here, we are assimilated to this intellect. Or is it not in the first place dubious, whether all the virtues are present with this intellect, such as temperance and fortitude, since there is nothing which can be dreadful to it? For nothing externally happens to it, nor does any

[1] See the additional notes at the end of this Volume, for a copious account of the *political*, *cathartic* and *theoretic* virtues, the subject of the present treatise of Plotinus.

thing pleasing approach to it, which when not present it may become desirous of possessing, or apprehending. But if it also has an appetite directed to the intelligibles, after which our souls aspire, it is evident that ornament and the virtues are from thence derived to us. Has therefore this intellect these virtues? Or may we not say, it is not reasonable to suppose, that it possesses what are called the political virtues, viz. prudence indeed, about the part that deliberates and consults; fortitude about the irascible part; temperance, in the agreement and concord of the part that desires, with the reasoning power; and justice, in each of these parts performing its proper office, with respect to governing and being governed. Shall we say therefore, that we are not assimilated to divinity according to the political virtues, but according to greater virtues which employ the same appellation? But if according to others, are we not at all assimilated according to the political virtues? Or is it not absurd that we should not in any respect be assimilated according to these? For rumour also says, that these are divine. We must say, therefore, that we are after a manner assimilated by them; but that the assimilation is according to the greater virtues. In either way, however, it happens that divinity has virtues, though not such as the political.

If, therefore, some one should grant, that though it is not possible to be assimilated according to such virtues as these, since we subsist differently with reference to other virtues, yet nothing hinders but that we by our virtues may be assimilated to that which does not possess virtue. But after what manner? Thus, if any thing is heated by the presence of heat, it is necessary that also should be hot from whence the heat is derived. And if any thing is hot by the presence of fire, it is necessary that fire itself also should be hot by the presence of heat.[1] To the first of

[1] For πυρὸς θερμοῦ here, I read θερμότητος.

these assertions, however, it may be said, that there is heat in fire, but a connascent heat, so that it will follow from analogy, that virtue is indeed adventitious to the soul, but connascent with that nature from whence it is derived by imitation. And with respect to the argument from fire, it may be said that divinity possesses virtue, but that virtue in him is in reality greater than virtue [because it subsists causally]. But if that virtue indeed, of which the soul participates, was the same with that from which it is derived, it would be necessary to speak in this manner. Now, however, the one is different from the other. For neither is the sensible the same with the intelligible house [or with that which is the object of intellectual conception] though it is similar to it. And the sensible house participates of order and ornament; though there is neither order, nor ornament, nor symmetry, in the productive principle of it in the mind. Thus, therefore, we participate from thence [*i.e.* from divinity] of ornament, order and consent, and these things pertain to virtue, but there consent, ornament and order, are not wanted, and therefore divinity has no need of virtue. We are, however, nevertheless assimilated to what he possesses, through the presence of virtue. And thus much for the purpose of showing, that it is not necessary virtue should be there, though we are assimilated to divinity by virtue. But it is also necessary to introduce persuasion to what has been said, and not to be satisfied with compulsion alone.

II. In the first place, therefore, the virtues must be assumed, according to which we say that we are assimilated [to divinity,] in order that we may discover the same thing. For that which is virtue with us, being an imitation, is there an archetype as it were, and not virtue. By which we signify that there is a twofold similitude, one of which requires a sameness in the things that are similar, these being such as are equally assimilated from the same thing; but the other being that in which one thing is assimilated to another, but the latter ranks as first, and is not converted to the other, nor is said to be similar to it. Here, therefore, the similitude must be assumed after another manner; since we do not require the same, but rather another form, the assimilation being effected after a different manner. What, therefore, is virtue, both that which is universal, and that which is particular? The discussion, however, will be more manifest by directing our attention to each of the virtues; for thus that which is common, according to which all of them are virtues, will be easily apparent. The political virtues, therefore, of which we have spoken above, truly adorn and render us better, bounding and moderating the desires, and in short the passions, and taking away false opinions from a more excellent nature, by limiting and placing the soul beyond the immoderate and indefinite, and by themselves receiving measure and bound. Perhaps, too, these measures are in soul as in matter, are assimilated to the measure which is in divinity, and possess a vestige of *the best* which is there. For that which is in every respect deprived of measure, being matter, is entirely dissimilar [to divinity]. But so far as it receives form, so far it is assimilated to him who is without form. But things which are nearer to divinity, participate of him in a greater degree. Soul, however, is nearer to, and more allied to him than body, and therefore participates of him more abundantly, so that appearing as a God, it deceives us, and causes us to doubt whether the whole of it is not divine. After this manner, therefore, these are assimilated.

III. Since, however, Plato indicates that this similitude to God pertains to a greater virtue [than that which is political], let us speak concerning it; in which discussion also, the essence of political virtue will become more manifest, and likewise the virtue which is essentially more excellent, which will in short be found to be different from that which is political. Plato, therefore, when he says that a similitude to God is a flight from terrestrial concerns, and when besides this he does not admit that the virtues belonging to a polity are *simply* virtues, but adds to them the epithet political, and elsewhere calls all the virtues purifications, evidently admits that the virtues are twofold, and that a similitude to divinity is not effected according to political virtue. How, therefore, do we call these purifications? And how being purified, are we especially assimilated to divinity? Shall we say, that since the soul is in an evil condition when mingled with the body, becoming similarly passive and concurring in opinion with it in all things, it will be good and possess virtue, if it neither consents with the body, but energizes alone, (and this is to perceive intellectually and to be wise,) nor is similarly passive with it, (and this is to be temperate,) nor dreads a separation from the body, (and this is to possess fortitude,) but reason and intellect are the leaders (and this will be justice). If any one, however, calls this disposition of the soul, according to which it perceives intellectually, and is thus impassive, a resemblance of God, he will not err. For divinity is pure, and the energy is of such a kind, that the being which imitates it will possess wisdom. What then? Is not divinity also disposed after this manner? Or may we not say that he is not, but that the disposition pertains to the soul; and that soul perceives intellectually, in a way different from divinity? It may also be said, that of the things which subsist with him, some subsist differently from what they do with us, and others are not at all with him. Again, therefore, is intellectual perception with him and us homonymous? By no means; but the one is primary, and that which is derived from him secondary. For as the discourse which is in voice is an imitation of that which is in the soul, so likewise, that which is in the soul, is an imitation of that which is in something else [*i.e.* in intellect]. As, therefore, external discourse is divided and distributed, when compared to that which is in the soul, thus also that which is in the soul, and which is the interpreter of intellectual discourse, is divided when compared with it. Virtue, however, pertains to the soul; but not to intellect, nor to that which is beyond intellect.

IV. It must, however, be enquired whether purification is the same with a virtue of this kind? Or does purification indeed precede, but virtue follow? And whether does virtue consist in purifying, or in the being perfectly purified? For virtue, while in the act of purifying, is more imperfect than that which consists in complete purification, which is now as it were the end. But to be perfectly purified, is an ablation of every thing foreign. Good, however, is something else besides this. Or may we not say, that if the soul was good prior to her impurity, purification is sufficient? Purification, indeed, is sufficient; but that which remains will be good, and not purification. And what that is which remains, is to be investigated. For perhaps the nature which is left was not good; since otherwise, it would not have been situated in evil. Shall we say, therefore, that it has the form of good? Or that it is not sufficiently able to abide [perpetually] in good? For it is naturally adapted to verge both to good and evil. Its good, therefore, consists in associating with its kindred nature; but its evil in associating with the contraries to this. It is necessary, therefore, that it should associate with this nature, being purified. And this will take place, through being converted to it. Will it therefore be converted after purification? Or may we not say, that after purification it is converted? This, therefore, is the virtue of the soul, or rather that which happens to it from conversion. What then is this? The vision and impression of that which is seen, inserted and energizing in the soul, in the same manner as sight about a visible object. She did not, therefore, possess these, nor recollect them. Or perhaps she possessed them, yet not energizing, but deposited in an unilluminated state. In order, however, that they may be illuminated, and that the soul may know them to be inherent in herself, it is necessary that she should apply herself to that which illuminates. But she will not possess these, but the impressions of them. It is necessary, therefore, to adapt the impression to the true objects from which the impressions are derived. Perhaps, likewise, she may thus be said to possess them, because intellect is not foreign, and especially is not so, when it looks to the illuminating cause. But if it does not, it is foreign even when this cause is present. For sciences also are foreign, if we do not at all energize according to them.

V. We must, however, show how far purification proceeds. For thus it will be evident to whom the similitude is made, and with what God the soul becomes the same. But this is especially to enquire how far it is possible to be purified from anger and desire, and all the other perturbations, such as pain, and things of a kindred nature, and to separate the soul from the body. And perhaps, indeed, to separate the soul from the body, is for the soul to collect itself as it were, from different places, so as to become entirely impassive, and to make the necessary sensations of pleasures to be only remedies and liberations from pain,[1] in order that the soul may not be disturbed [in its energies]. It likewise consists in taking away pain, and if this is not possible, in bearing it mildly, and diminishing its power, in consequence of [the rational part] not being co-passive with it. And besides this also, in taking away anger to the

[1] Aristotle in his Nicomachean Ethics, says, that corporeal pleasures are remedies against pain, and satisfy the indigence of nature, but perfect no energy of the rational part of the soul.

utmost of our ability, and if possible, entirely; but if not, the rational part must not at the same time be angry, but the anger must be the passion of another part, and unaccompanied with deliberation. And this sudden impulse must be small and imbecile. Fear, however, must be entirely removed; for the purified soul will fear nothing. Here, also, the energy must be unattended with deliberation, except it be requisite to admonish. With respect to desire, it is evident that there must not be a desire of any thing base. And as to the desire of meats and drinks for the sake of a remission of pain, the soul herself will be without it. This likewise will be the case with the venereal appetite. But if the soul is desirous of connection, it will be I think in the natural way, and this not unattended with deliberation. If, however, it should be an unadvised impulse, it will only be so far as it is accompanied with a precipitate[1] imagination. But, in short, the [rational] soul herself will be purified from all these. She will also wish to render the irrational part pure, so that it may not be agitated. And if it is, that the agitation may not be vehement, but small, and immediately dissolved by proximity to the rational part. Just as if some one being near to a wise man, should partake of his wisdom by this proximity, or should become similar to him, or through reverence should not dare to do any thing which the good man is unwilling to do. Hence, there will be no contest. For reason being present will be sufficient, which the inferior part will reverence, so as even to be itself indignant, if it is at all moved, in consequence of not being quiet when its master is present; and it will on this account blame its own imbecility.

[1] In the original προτυπους; but it should doubtless be as in the above translation, προπετοῦς. For this is the word used by Marinus, in his Life of Proclus, when speaking of the cathartic virtues of that philosopher, and alluding to this passage in Plotinus.

VI. In conduct of this kind, therefore, there is no sin, but a correction of the man. Nevertheless the endeavour is not to be without sin, but to be a God. Hence, if any thing among the above mentioned particulars should be done without deliberation, such a one will be both a God and a dæmon, being a twofold character; or rather, having another with him, possessing another virtue. But if nothing is done unadvisedly, he will be a God alone. He will however be a God in the number of those that follow the first; for he it is who came from thence. And if he becomes by himself such as he came, he is still there. But coming hither, he will associate with intellect; and will assimilate this to himself,[1] according to the power of it. Hence, if possible, he will not be agitated, nor do any thing which may be displeasing to the master [intellect]. What, therefore, is each of the virtues to such a man as this? Wisdom, indeed, will consist in the contemplation of what intellect contains. But he will possess intellect by contact. Each of the virtues, however, is twofold; for each is both in intellect and in soul. And in intellect, indeed, each is not [properly] virtue, but virtue is in soul. What, then, is it in intellect? The energy of intellect, and that which is. But here that which is in another, is virtue derived from thence. For justice itself, and each of the virtues, are not in intellect such as they are here, but they are as it were paradigms. But that which proceeds from each of these into the soul, is virtue. For virtue pertains to a certain thing. But each thing itself pertains to itself, and not to any thing else. With respect to justice, however, if it is the performance of appropriate duty, does it always consist in a multitude of parts? Or does not one kind consist in multitude, when there are many parts of it, but the other is entirely the performance of appropriate duty, though it

---

[1] For αὐτό here, it is necessary to read αὐτῷ, conformably to the version of Ficinus.

should be one thing. True justice itself, therefore, is the energy of one thing towards itself, in which there is not another and another. Hence justice in the soul is to energize in a greater degree intellectually. But temperance is an inward conversion to intellect. And fortitude is apathy, according to a similitude of that to which the soul looks, and which is naturally impassive. But soul is impassive from virtue, in order that she may not sympathize with her subordinate associate.

VII. These virtues, therefore, follow each other in the soul, in the same manner as those paradigms in intellect which are prior to virtue. For there intelligence is wisdom and science; a conversion to itself is temperance; its proper work is the performance of its appropriate duty, and justice; and that which is as it were fortitude is immateriality, and an abiding with purity in itself. In soul, therefore, perception directed to intellect is wisdom and prudence, which are the virtues of the soul. For soul does not possess these in the same manner as intellect. Other things also follow after, similarly in soul. They are likewise consequent to purification, since all the virtues are purifications, and necessarily consist in the soul being purified; for otherwise, no one of them would be perfect. And he indeed, who possesses the greater virtues, has necessarily the less in capacity; but he who possesses the less, has not necessarily the greater. This, therefore, is the life which is the principal and leading aim of a worthy man. But whether he possesses in energy, or in some other way, the less or the greater virtues, must be considered by a survey of each of them; as for instance, of prudence. For if it uses the other virtues, how can it any longer remain what it is? And if also it should not energize? Likewise, it must be considered whether naturally the virtues proceed to a different extent; and *this* temperance measures, but *that* entirely takes away what is superfluous. And in a similar manner in the other virtues, prudence being wholly excited. Or perhaps the worthy man will see to what extent they proceed. And perhaps sometimes according to circumstances he will energize according to some of them. But arriving at the greater virtues, he will perform other measures according to them. Thus, for instance, in the exercise of temperance, he will not measure it by political temperance, but in short he will separate himself as much as possible [from the body], and will live, not merely the life of a good man, which political virtue thinks fit to enjoin, but leaving this, he will choose another life, namely, that of the Gods. For the similitude is to these, and not to good men. The similitude, indeed, to good men, is an assimilation of one image to another, each being derived from the same thing; but a similitude to God, is an assimilation as to a paradigm.

II.
ON DIALECTIC.[1]

I. iii.

I. WHAT art, or method, or study, will lead us to that end to which we ought to proceed ? That we ought, indeed, to arrive at *the good itself*, and the first principle of things, is granted, and is demonstrated through many arguments. The arguments also through which this is demonstrated, are a certain elevation to this end. But what kind of a

[1] The dialectic of Plato, which is here discussed, is not the same with that dialectic which is the subject of opinion, and is accurately investigated in the Topics of Aristotle. For the former is irreprehensible and most expeditious ; since it is connate with things themselves, and employs a multitude of powers in order to the attainment of truth. It likewise imitates intellect, from which it receives its principles, and ascends through well-ordered gradations to real being itself. It also terminates the wandering of the soul about sensibles ; and explores every thing by methods which cannot be confuted, till it arrives at the ineffable principle of things. The business, likewise, of this first of sciences, is to employ definitions, divisions, analyzations, and demonstrations, as primary sciences in the investigation of causes ; imitating the progression of beings from the first principle of things, and their continual conversion to it as the ultimate object of desire.

" But there are three energies," (says Proclus in MS. Comment. in Parmenid.) " of this most scientific method ; the first of which is adapted to youth, and is useful for the purpose of exciting their

person is it necessary the man should be who is elevated thither? Is it not, as Plato says, one who has seen all, or most things? And who in his first generation has descended into the seed of a man who will be a philosopher, or a musician, or a lover? The philosopher, therefore, the musician, and the lover, are naturally adapted to be elevated. What, therefore, is the mode? Is there one and

intellect, which is, as it were, in a dormant state. For it is a true exercise of the eye of the soul in the speculation of things, leading forth through opposite positions, the essential impression of ideas which it contains, and considering not only the divine path, as it were, which conducts to truth, but exploring whether the deviations from it contain any thing worthy of belief; and lastly, stimulating the all-various conceptions of the soul. But the second energy takes place when intellect rests from its former investigations, as becoming most familiar with the speculations of beings, and beholds truth itself firmly established on a pure and holy foundation. This energy, according to Socrates, by a progression through ideas, evolves the whole of an intelligible nature, till it arrives at that which is first; and this by analyzing, defining, demonstrating, and dividing, proceeding upwards and downwards, till having entirely investigated the nature of intelligibles, it raises itself to a nature superior to beings. But the soul being perfectly established in this nature, as in her paternal port, no longer tends to a more excellent object of desire, as she has now arrived at the end of her search. And you may say that what is delivered in the Phædrus and Sophista, is the employment of this energy, giving a twofold division to some, and a fourfold to other operations of the dialectic art. Hence it is assigned to such as philosophize purely, and no longer require preparatory exercise, but nourish the intellect of their soul in pure intellection. But the third energy, which is declarative according to truth, purifies from twofold ignorance,* when its reasons are employed upon men, full of opinion; and this is spoken of in the Sophista."

See this subject more amply discussed in the additional notes at the end of this volume.

---

* *i.e.* When a man is ignorant that he is ignorant; and this is the disease of the multitude.

the same mode for all these? Or is there a different mode for each? There is, indeed, a twofold progression to all of them; one to those who are ascending; but the other to those who have arrived at the supernal realms. For the former proceeds from things beneath; but the latter ranks among those who are now in the intelligible region, and who in that place have as it were fixed their footstep. There, also, it is necessary for them to proceed, till they have arrived at the extremity of the place. The end of the progression, however, is then obtained, when some one arrives at the summit of the intelligible world. But let this at present remain [without any further discussion]. And let us first endeavour to speak concerning this elevation.

In the first place, therefore, let these men be distinguished by us, and let us begin from the musician, and show who he naturally is. We must admit, then, that he is easily excited[1] and astonished at the beautiful; yet is not disposed to be moved from himself, but is prepared from casual occurrences as from certain types or impressions, to be excited by sounds, and to the beautiful in these, just as the timid are by noises. He likewise always flies from dissonance; and pursues in songs and rythms, that which is one, congruous, and elegant. After these sensible sounds, rythms, and figures therefore, he is thus to be elevated, viz., by separating the matter, in which analogies and ratios are inherent, and contemplating the beauty which they contain. He must also be taught that the things about which he was astonished were, intelligible harmony, and the beauty which is in it, and in short, the beautiful itself, and not a certain beauty only. The reasonings, likewise, of philosophy must be inserted in him, through which he will be led to a belief of truths of

---

[1] For ἀκίνητον here, it is necessary to read εὐκίνητον.

which he is ignorant, though he [occultly] possesses them. What these reasonings however, are, will be hereafter unfolded.

II. But the lover, into which the musician may be changed, and being changed will either remain [in that character] or will pass beyond it, has in a certain respect a recollection of beauty. Being however separated from it, he is incapable of learning what it is. But as he is struck by the beautiful objects which present themselves to the sight, he is seized with astonishment about them. He therefore must be taught not to be abjectly astonished about one beautiful body, but he must be led by the exercise of the reasoning power to all beautiful bodies, and he who does this must exhibit to him that which is one and the same in all of them, and inform him that it is different from and is derived elsewhere, than from bodies, and is rather inherent in other things, such as beautiful pursuits, and beautiful laws. For the lover will now become accustomed to incorporeal natures. He likewise must be led to the beauty which is in the arts, in sciences, and the virtues, and afterwards to that which is one and the same in all these; and he must be taught after what manner beauty is inherent in each of them. But after the virtues, he must now ascend to intellect, and being itself, and there commence the progression on high.

III. The philosopher, however, is naturally prompt, and as it were, winged, and does not require a separation [from sensible objects] like the other characters; since he is excited to the supernal region, but is dubious, and therefore is only in want of one that may point out the way. The path, therefore, must be shown to him, and he must be liberated, since he is naturally willing, and was formerly freed [from the fetters of a corporeal nature]. Hence, he must be instructed in the mathematical disciplines, in order that he may be accustomed to the perception of and belief in an incorporeal essence. For he will easily admit its subsistence, as he is desirous of learning. As he is naturally, therefore, endued with virtue, he must be led to the perfection of the virtues; and after the mathematics, he must be taught dialectic reasonings, and in short, must be rendered skilful in dialectic.

IV. What, then, is the dialectic which ought to be delivered in addition to the former particulars? It is, indeed, a habit enabling its possessor to reason about every thing, to know what each thing is, and in what it differs from other things, what the common something is which it participates, where each of these subsists, if a thing is, what it is, what the number is of beings, and again of non-beings [which are not nothing] but different from beings. This, also, discusses *the good*, and that which is not good; such things as are under *the good*, and such as are under the contrary to it; and what that is which is eternal, and that which is not a thing of this kind. All these likewise it discusses scientifically, and not from opinion. Resting, also, from the wandering about a sensible nature, it establishes itself in the intelligible world, and there has its employment, dismissing falsehood, and nourishing the soul in what is called the plain of truth, employing for this purpose the division of Plato, and also for the separation of forms. It likewise employs this division for the purpose of defining what a thing is, and in order to obtain a knowledge of the first genera of things, intellectually connecting that which results from these, till it has proceeded through the whole of an intelligible nature; and again, by an analytic process it arrives at that to which it had proceeded from the first. Then, however, it becomes quiescent, because so far as it arrives thither it is at rest, and being no longer busily employed, but becoming one, it surveys what is called logic, which is occupied about propositions and syllogisms,—just as if giving to another art, the knowledge of writing; some of which it considers as necessary, and prior to art. But it forms a judgment of these, as well as of other things, and thinks that some of them are useful, but others superfluous, and pertaining to the method by which these are discussed.

V. Whence, however, does this science derive its principles? May we not say that intellect imparts clear principles to the soul that is able to receive them? Afterwards, the soul compounds the things consequent to these principles, and connects and divides them, till it arrives at a perfect intellect. For, as Plato says, this science is the purest part of intellect and [intellectual] prudence. It is necessary, therefore, since it is the most honourable habit of those things that are in us, that it should be conversant with being, and the most honourable nature; and that prudence, indeed, should be conversant with being, but intellect with that which is beyond being. What, then, is philosophy? That which is most honourable. Is philosophy, therefore, the same as dialectic? Or is not dialectic the most honourable part of philosophy? For it must not be fancied that it is the instrument of the philosopher; since it does not consist of mere theorems and rules, but is conversant with things, and has beings as it were for its subject matter. Nevertheless, it proceeds in a path to beings, possessing things themselves together with theorems. It knows, however, that which is false and sophistical accidentally, something else being the cause of these; and it forms a judgment of them as of that which is foreign, knowing the false by the truths it contains in itself, when it is adduced by any one, because it is contrary to the rule of truth. Propositions, therefore, are not the object of its knowledge; for these are letters. But, knowing truth, it knows that which is called a proposition. And universally, it knows the motions of the soul, what the soul admits, and what it rejects, and whether it rejects that which it admits, or something else. Likewise, whether different or the same things are adduced; applying itself to them in a way resembling sense.[1] But it assigns to another power an accurate discussion of these particulars.

VI. This, therefore, is an honourable part; since philosophy has also other parts. For it speculates about nature, receiving assistance from dialectic, in the same manner as the other arts use arithmetic. Philosophy, however, proximately derives assistance from dialectic. And, in a similar manner, it speculates about manners, surveying them through dialectic, but adding habits, and the exercises from which habits proceed. The rational virtues also have habits, and what are now as peculiarities, which they derive from thence. And the other virtues, indeed, have their reasonings in peculiar passions and actions; but prudence is a certain ratiocination, and is conversant with that which is more universal. For it considers whether it is proper now to abstain or hereafter, or in short, whether another thing is better. Dialectic, however, and wisdom, introduce all things to the use of prudence, universally and immaterially. But whether is it possible to know[2] inferior concerns without dialectic and wisdom? Or may they be known in a different and defective way? It is possible, however, for a man to be thus wise and skilled in dialectic without a knowledge of these. Or this will not be the case, but they will coalesce, either previously, or together. And perhaps some one may have certain physical virtues, from which, when wisdom is possessed, the perfect virtues will be obtained. Wisdom, therefore, is posterior to the

---

[1] *i.e.* By intuition, so as to come into immediate contact with the objects of its knowledge. It does this, however, so far as its energy is purely intellectual.

[2] For εἶναι here, it is necessary to read εἰδέναι.

physical virtues, but afterwards it perfects the manners; or rather, the physical virtues existing, both are co-increased, and mutually perfected. Or, one of them being previously assumed, the one will perfect the other. For, in short, physical virtue has an imperfect eye, and imperfect manners; and the principles of both are, for the most part, derived from those things which we possess.

III.
ON MATTER.
II. iv.

1. ALL those who have spoken concerning what is called matter, and who have arrived at a conception of its nature, unanimously assert, that it is a certain subject and receptacle of forms. They dissent, however, from each other, in investigating what this subject nature is; and after what manner, and of what things, it is a recipient. And those, indeed, who alone admit bodies to be beings, and who contend that essence is in these, say, that there is one matter, which is spread under the elements, and that it is essence; but that all other things are, as it were, the passions of matter, and are matter subsisting in a certain way, and thus also are the elements. They, likewise, dare to extend matter as far as to the Gods. And, lastly, they make even the highest[1] God to be this matter, subsisting in a certain way. They, likewise, give a body to matter, calling it, *body void of quality*; and attribute to it magnitude. But others say, that matter is incorporeal; and some of these do not admit that there is only this one matter, but assert that this is the subject of bodies, and that there is another

---

[1] From the version of Ficinus, it appears, that instead of αὐτὸν αὐτῶν τὸν θεὸν, we should read, ἀκρότατον αὐτῶν τὸν θεὸν. For his version is, "summum ipsorum deum."

matter prior to this in intelligibles, which is spread under the forms that are there, and under incorporeal essences.

II. Hence we must enquire concerning this intelligible matter, whether it is, what it is, and after what manner it subsists. If, therefore, it is necessary that matter should be something indefinite and formless, but in intelligibles as being the most excellent[1] natures, there is nothing indefinite and without form, matter will not be there. If, also, every thing in the intelligible world is simple, it will not be in want of matter, in order that from it and something else, that which is a composite may be produced. To generated natures, indeed, and to such as make some things from others, matter is necessary, in which also the matter of sensibles is conceived to subsist; but it is not necessary to things which are not generated. Whence, also, does matter proceed, and how does it subsist among intelligibles? For if it was generated, it was generated by something; but if it is eternal, there are many principles; and first natures will have a casual subsistence. If, likewise, form should accede, the composite will be a body, so that body will be there.

III. In the first place, therefore, it must be said, that the indefinite is not every where to be despised, nor that which in the conception of it is formless, if it applies itself to things prior to itself, and to the most excellent natures. For thus soul is naturally adapted to apply itself to intellect and reason, being formed by these, and brought to possess a more excellent nature. In intelligibles, however, that which is a composite subsists after a different manner, and not like bodies; since reasons, also, [or productive principles] are composites, and produce a composite in energy, through nature which has an energy directed to form. But if energy is directed to something different

---

[1] For ἀορίστοις here, it is necessary to read ἀρίστοις.

from itself, it is derived from something else, and this in a greater degree. The matter, however, of generated natures, always possesses another and another form; but the matter of eternal natures always possesses the same form. Perhaps, also, the matter which is in sensibles subsists in a way contrary to that which is in intelligibles. For the former is alternately all things, and is always some different thing. Hence, nothing in it ever remains, one thing continually expelling another; and on this account, nothing is ever the same. But in the latter, matter is all things at once, and hence there is not any thing into which it can be changed. Matter, therefore, in intelligibles, is never formless, since neither is the matter in sensibles ever without form; but each of these subsists after a different manner. Whether matter, however, is eternal or generated, will be manifest when we have shown what it is.

IV. At present, however, it is supposed by us that there are forms or ideas, for this we have demonstrated elsewhere; and this being admitted we shall proceed in our discussion. If, therefore, there are many forms, it is necessary, indeed, that there should be something common in them; and also that there should be something peculiar by which one is distinguished from another. This something peculiar, therefore, and separating difference, are the appropriate form. But if there is form, there is also that which is formed, about which difference subsists. Hence, there is matter [in intelligibles], which receives the form, and is always the subject of it. Farther still, if the intelligible world is there, but this our world is the imitation of that, and this is a composite, and consists of matter [and form], it is necessary that there also there should be matter. Or how can you denominate it a world [or that which is adorned], unless you look to form? And how can you look to form, unless you assume that in which form subsists? For the intelligible world, indeed, is perfectly every where impartible; but in a certain respect is also partible. And if the parts of it are divulsed from each other, the section and divulsion are the passions of matter; for it is matter which is divided. But if the many which are there, are one [1] impartible being, the many subsisting in one,—if this be the case, they are in one matter, of which they are the forms. For this various one, is to be considered as having a multiform nature. It must, therefore, be considered as formless prior to its variety. Hence, if by intellect you take away its variety, its forms, its productive principles, and intellections, that which is prior to these is formless and indefinite, and this is no one of the things which subsist together with and in it.

V. If, however, it should be said, that because it always possesses these things, and both [the subject and the forms] are one, this subject is not matter, neither will the subject of bodies here be matter. For the matter of sensibles is never without form, but there is always the whole body. At the same time, however, this is a composite; and intellect discovers its twofold nature. For it divides till it arrives at that which is simple, and which is no longer capable of being analyzed. But so far as it is able, it proceeds into the profundity of body. The profundity, however, of each body is matter. Hence all matter is dark, because reason is light, and intellect is reason. Hence, too, intellect beholding the nature of each [*i.e.* of intelligible and sensible matter], conceives that which is beneath, as under light, to be dark; just as the eye which is luciform, extending itself to the light, and to colours which are illuminations, says, that what is under colours, is dark and material, and concealed by the colours. Nevertheless, that which is dark in intelligibles is different from that which is dark in sensibles; and the matter of the one differs as much from the matter

[1] Instead of εἰ δὲ πολλὰ ὄν, ἀμέριστόν ἐστι, in this place, it is necessary to read, εἰ δὲ πολλὰ ἓν ὂν ἀμέριστόν ἐστι.

of the other, as the supervening form of the one from that of the other. For divine matter receiving that which defines and bounds it, possesses a definite and intellectual life. But sensible matter becomes, indeed, a certain definite thing, yet neither vital nor intellectual, but an unadorned privation of life. The *morphe*,[1] also, is an image, so that the subject likewise is an image. In intelligibles, however, the *morphe* is truly form, so that the subject also is real. Hence, those who say that matter is essence, if they assert this of intelligible matter, speak rightly. For the subject there is essence, or rather, is the object of intellectual perception, together with that which it contains, and is wholly illuminated essence. To investigate, however, whether intelligible matter is eternal, is similar to the inquiry whether ideas are eternal. For they are generated, indeed, so far as they have a principle of their subsistence; but they are not generated [according to the usual acceptation of the term] because they have not a temporal beginning, but always proceed from something else, not like the natures which are always rising into existence, or becoming to be, as is the case with the world, but they *always are*, in the same manner as the world which is there [has an eternal subsistence]. For the difference which is there always produces matter; since this which is the first motion is the principle of matter. Hence, it is called difference, because motion and difference were unfolded into light together with it. But the motion and difference which proceed from the first cause of all, are indefinite, and are in want of this cause in order that they may become terminated. They are, however, terminated, when they are converted to it. But prior to this, matter and difference are indefinite, and are not yet good, but are without the light of *the good*. For if light is from *the good*, that which

[1] *Morphe* pertains to the colour, figure, and magnitude of superficies.

receives the light, prior to its reception of it, does not always possess it, but possesses it, being different from it. since the light is from something else. And thus much concerning intelligible matter, which we have discussed perhaps more than is fit.

VI. Of the receptacle of bodies, however, we must speak as follows: That it is necessary then, there should be a certain subject to bodies, which is different from them, the mutation of the elements into each other manifests. For there is not a perfect corruption of that which is changed; since if there was, there would be a certain essence which would be dissolved into nonentity. Nor again, does that which is generated proceed into being from that which in every respect is not; but there is a mutation from one form into another. That, however, remains, which receives the form of the thing generated, and casts aside another form. This, therefore, in short, corruption manifests; for corruption is of that which is a composite. But if this be the case, each sensible thing consists of matter and form. This, too, induction testifies, demonstrating that the thing which is corrupted is a composite. Analysis, likewise, evinces the same thing; as if, for instance, a pot should be resolved into gold;[1] but gold into water; and the water being corrupted, will require an analogous process. It is necessary, also, that the elements should either be form, or the first matter, or that which consists of matter and form. But it is impossible, indeed, that they should be form. For how, without matter, could they have bulk

[1] What Plotinus here says of the analysis into gold, is perfectly conformable to the assertion of Albertus Magnus, as cited by Becher in his "Physica Subterranea," p. 319, 4to. For his words are, "Non dari rem elementatam, in cujus ultima substantiatione non reperiatur aurum." That all metals, likewise, may be analyzed into water, is the doctrine both of Plato and Aristotle. See my translation of the Timæus of the former, and Meteors of the latter.

and magnitude? Nor are they the first matter; for they are corrupted. Hence, they consist of matter and form. And form, indeed, subsists according to quality and morphe; but matter according to the subject, which is indefinite, because it is not form.

VII. Empedocles, however, who substitutes the elements for matter, has the corruption of them testifying against him. But Anaxagoras, who makes the mixture of things to be matter, and who says, that it has not an aptitude to [become] all things, but has all things in energy, subverts the intellect which he introduces; not assigning to it the production of morphe and form, nor asserting that it is prior to matter, but that it subsists in conjunction with it. It is, however, impossible that intellect and matter should be consubsistent. For if the mixture participates of being, it follows that being is prior to it. But if being also is a mixture, a certain third thing is wanting to these. If, therefore, it is necessary that the demiurgus should have a prior subsistence, why is it necessary that forms should be in matter according to parvitude; and that afterwards intellect by a vainly laborious process should separate them from each other? For it is possible to impress quality in matter, since it is without quality, and to extend morphe through the whole of it. And, besides, is it not impossible that all things should be in every thing? But he who asserts that the infinite is matter, should explain what this infinite is. And if it is infinite in such a way as that which cannot be passed over, it must be observed, that there is not any such things among beings, neither if it is the infinite itself, nor if it is inherent in another nature, as an accident to a certain body. It is not, indeed, the infinite itself, because the part of it is necessarily infinite. Nor is it the infinite as an accident, because that to which it is an accident would not be of itself infinite, nor simple, and therefore evidently would not be matter.

But neither have atoms the order of matter, which indeed have no subsistence whatever.[1] For every body is entirely divisible. This opinion is also confuted from the continuity and moisture of bodies; and also from the impossibility of things subsisting without intellect and soul, which could not be formed from atoms. Again, it is not possible to fabricate any other nature, besides atoms from atoms; since no artificer is able to produce any thing from matter which is not continuous. Ten thousand other objections might and have been urged against this hypothesis, and therefore it is superfluous to dwell longer on these particulars.

VIII. What, then, is this nature, which is said to be one, continued, and void of quality? And, indeed, that it is not a body if void of quality, is evident;[2] for if it were,

---

[1] *i.e.* As things perfectly indivisible.

[2] Though from the arguments adduced here by Plotinus, it appears to be impossible that the first matter should be body void of quality, yet I think there will not be any absurdity in admitting with Simplicius, that body is twofold, one kind as subsisting according to form and productive power, and defined by certain intervals; but another as characterized by intensions and remissions, and an indefiniteness of an incorporeal, impartible, and intelligible nature: this not being formally defined by three intervals, but entirely remitted and dissipated, and on all sides flowing from being into non-being. " Such an interval as this, we must perhaps," (says Simplicius) " admit matter to be, and not corporeal form, which now measures and bounds the infinite and indefinite nature of such an interval as this, and which stops it in its flight from being. Matter, however, is that by which material things differ from such as are immaterial. But they differ by bulk, interval, division, and things of this kind, and not by things which are defined according to measure, but by things void of measure and indefinite, and which are capable of being bounded by formal measures. The Pythagoreans appear to have been the first of the Greeks that had this suspicion concerning matter but after them Plato, as Moderatus also informs us. For he, conformably to the Pythagoreans, evinced that the first one is above

it would have quality. But we say that it is the matter of all sensibles, and that it is not the matter of some, but the form of others; as clay is matter to the potter, but is not simply matter. We do not, therefore, speak of it in this way, but with reference to all things; and this being the case, we must not attribute to the nature of it any thing which is perceived among sensibles. Hence, besides not granting to it other qualities, such as colour, heat and cold, we must ascribe to it neither levity or gravity, neither density or rarity, or figure; and therefore, neither must we ascribe to it magnitude. For magnitude itself is one thing, and to be great another. And figure itself is one

being, and all essence; but he says, that forms are the second one, which is true being and the intelligible; and that the third one, which is psychical, or belonging to soul, participates of *the one*, and of forms. He adds, that the last nature from this, and which is the nature of sensibles, does not participate them, but is adorned according to a representation of them, matter which is in them being the shadow of the non-being, which is primarily in quantity, or rather depending on and proceeding from it. According to this reasoning, therefore, matter is nothing else than the mutation of sensibles, with respect to intelligibles, deviating from thence, and carried downwards to non-being.

Those things, indeed, which are the properties of sensibles are irrational, corporeal, distributed into parts, and passing into bulk and divulsion, through an ultimate progression into generation, viz. into matter; for matter is always truly the last sediment. Hence, also, the Egyptians call the dregs of the first life, which they symbolically denominate water, matter, being as it were a certain mire. And matter is, as it were, the receptacle of generated and sensible natures, not subsisting as any definite form, but as the state or condition of subsistence; just as the impartible, the immaterial, true being, and things of this kind, are the constitution of an intelligible nature; all forms, indeed, subsisting both here and there, but here materially, and there immaterially; viz. there impartibly and truly, but here partibly and shadowy. Hence, every form is here distributed according to material interval." See more on this subject in the notes to Book I. of my translation of Aristotle's Physics.

thing, and that which is figured another. It is necessary, however, that it should not be a composite, but simple, and one certain thing in its own nature. For thus it will be destitute of all things. And he who imparts morphe to it, will impart morphe as something different from matter. He will also prefer, as it were, magnitude and all things from the things which exist; for otherwise, he would be subservient to the magnitude of matter, and his production would not possess the quantity which he wished it should, but that which matter is capable of receiving. To assert, however, that the will of the artificer concurs with the magnitude of matter, is fictitious. But if the maker is prior to matter, in this case matter will entirely be such as the maker wishes it to be, and will with facility be brought to all things, and therefore to magnitude. If, however, it has magnitude, it is also necessary that it should have figure, so that it will be still more difficult to be fashioned by the artificer. Form, therefore, enters matter, bringing all things with it. But every form possesses magnitude, and the quantity which it contains is accompanied with reason [*i.e.* with a productive principle] and subsists under this. Hence, in every genus of things, quantity is defined together with form. For there is one magnitude of a man, and another of a bird. And it would be absurd to suppose, that the introduction of quantity to the matter of a certain bird, is any thing else than adding to it its proper quality. Nor must it be said that quality is a productive principle, but that quantity is not form, since it is both measure and number.

IX. How then can any thing which ranks among beings be apprehended, which has no magnitude? Perhaps every thing which is not the same with a certain quantity. For being and a certain quantity are not the same; since there are many other things besides a definite quantity. And, in short, it must be admitted that every incorporeal nature is without quantity. Matter, also, is incorporeal; since quantity itself is not a quantum [or a certain quantity], but that is a quantum which participates of quantity. Hence, from this it is evident, that quantity is form. As, therefore, a certain white thing is produced by the presence of whiteness; but that which produces a white colour in an animal, and other various colours, is not a various colour, but a various productive principle; thus also, that which produces a definite quantity, is not a definite quantity, but a quantum itself, or quantity itself, or a productive principle. Does quantity, therefore, acceding, evolve matter into magnitude? By no means. For it was not contracted into a small space; but it imparts magnitude which prior to this was not, in the same manner as it imparts quality which had not a prior existence.

X. What, therefore, is that which is void of magnitude in matter? What, also, do you conceive that to be which is in a certain way void of quality? And what is the intellection and the perception of it by the reasoning power? Shall we say it is indefiniteness? For if the similar is perceived by the similar, the indefinite also will be apprehended by the indefinite. Reason, therefore, will become bounded about the indefinite; but the intuition of it will be indefinite. If, however, every thing is known by reason and intelligence, but here, reason indeed says what it is requisite to say about it, and wishing to become intelligence, is not intelligence, but, as it were, a privation of intellect,—if this be the case, the phantasm of matter will rather be spurious, and not genuine, being composed of an imagination which is not true, and another kind of reason. And perhaps, Plato, looking to this, says, [in the Timæus] that matter is apprehended by a spurious reasoning. What, therefore, is the indefiniteness of the soul? Is it an all-perfect ignorance, such as the absence [of knowledge]? Or does the indefinite consist in a certain negation[1] in conjunction with a certain affirmation; and is it like darkness to the eye, obscurity being the matter of every invisible colour? Thus, therefore, the soul also, taking away whatever in sensibles resembles light, and not being able to bound what remains, is similar to the eye placed in darkness, and then becomes in a certain respect the same with that which, as it were, it sees. Does it therefore see? Perhaps it sees matter as something deformed, and as void of colour, and void of light; and besides this, as not having magnitude, since if it had, it would be invested with form. When, therefore, the soul understands nothing, is she not affected in the same manner as when she sees matter? By no means. For when she understands nothing, she says nothing, or rather, she suffers nothing. But when she beholds matter, she suffers such a passion as when she receives the resemblance of that which is formless; since also when she understands things that have figure and magnitude, she understands them as composites. For she understands them as things diversified, and in short as possessing qualities. Hence, she understands the whole, and at the same time both, and her intellection or sensation of the inherent properties is clear and manifest. But her perception of a formless subject is obscure; for it is not form. When, therefore, in the whole and composite, she receives the subject together with its inherent properties, and analyzes and separates them, then she understands obscurely that which reason leaves, darkly that which is dark, and sees intellectually, not understanding. And since matter itself does not remain formless, but in [sensible] things is invested with form, the soul also imme-

---

[1] In the original ἡ ἐν καταφάσει τινί, but it appears from the version of Ficinus, that we should read, ἡ ἐν ἀποφάσει τινὶ σὺν καταφάσει τινί. This emendation the sense also requires, and is adopted in the above translation.

diately impresses it with the form of things, being pained with the indefinite, as if afraid of being placed out of the order of beings, and not enduring to stop any longer at nonentity.

XI. But why is it requisite there should be something else besides magnitude and all qualities, to the composition of bodies? Or is it not necessary there should be that which is the recipient of all things? It will not therefore be bulk. For if it were bulk, it would also be magnitude. But if it is without magnitude, it will not have a place where it may receive [all other things]. For being void of magnitude, what advantage would it derive from place, if it neither contributes to form and quality, nor to interval and magnitude? the two latter of which appear to be derived to bodies from matter, wherever it may be. In short, as actions and productions, times and motions, though they have no substratum of matter in them, yet rank among beings; thus, also, neither is it necessary that the first bodies should have a matter [which is without magnitude], but that each of them should be wholly that which it is, being more various by the mixture with things that have their composition from many forms. So that this matter which is without magnitude, is a vain name. In the first place, therefore, it is not necessary that whatever receives any thing should have bulk, if magnitude is not now present with it; since soul, likewise, which receives all things, has all things at once. But if it happened to have magnitude, it would possess every thing that it contains, in magnitude. Matter, however, on this account, receives the things which it receives, in interval, because it is the recipient of interval; just as animals and plants, while they are extended with magnitude, receive at the same time the production of quality; and quantity being contracted, quality also is contracted. If, however, because a certain magnitude pre-exists in things of this kind, as a subject to the formator, some one should also require this in matter, he will not conceive rightly. For in the formation of these, not matter simply considered, is employed, but matter of a certain kind. But it is necessary that matter simply considered, should possess magnitude from something else. Hence, it is not necessary that the recipient of form should be bulk, but that at the same time it becomes bulk, it should receive another quality; and that it should have indeed the phantasm of bulk, because, as being the first matter, it is an aptitude to the reception of it. It is, however, a void bulk; and hence some assert that matter and a vacuum are the same. For the soul having nothing which it can bound, when it associates with matter, diffuses itself into the indefinite, neither circumscribing it, nor being able to arrive at any fixed point [of survey;] since otherwise it would define it. Hence, neither is it to be separately called great, nor again small; but it must be denominated both small and great. And thus it is bulk, and thus is without magnitude, because it is the matter of bulk. Being also contracted from the great to the small, and extended from the small to the great, it runs as it were through bulk. The indefiniteness of it, likewise, is a bulk of this kind, being the receptacle of magnitude in itself; but in imagination in the way before explained. For with respect to such other things without magnitude as are forms, each of them is definite; so that they bring with them no conception whatever of bulk. But matter being indefinite, and never at rest[1] with itself, and being borne along to every form, in every direction, and easily led every where, becomes multitudinous by its generation and transition to all things. And after this manner it possesses the nature of bulk.

[1] Instead of μή πω πᾶσα παρ' αὐτῆς, it is necessary to read μή ποτε παῦσασα παρ' αὐτῆς, agreeably to the version of Ficinus.

XII. Magnitude, therefore, contributes something to bodies; for the forms of bodies, are in dimensions. These forms, however, are not generated about magnitude, but about that which is amplified. For if they were generated about magnitude, and not about matter, they would be similarly void of magnitude and without subsistence, or would be productive principles alone. But forms are conversant with soul, and therefore are not bodies. Hence, it is necessary that here, many things should subsist about one thing; but this is distended with magnitude. And this [which is thus amplified,] is different from magnitude; since now also such things as are mingled, in consequence of having matter, pass into a sameness of condition, and do not require any thing else about which they may subsist, because each of the things that are mingled brings with it its own matter. At the same time, however, a certain recipient is necessary, viz. either a vessel, or place. But place is posterior to matter, and to bodies; so that bodies prior to this will be indigent of matter. Nor does it follow that because productive energies and actions are immaterial, on this account bodies also are without matter. For the latter are composites, but this is not the case with actions. Matter also imparts a subject to agents when they act, abiding in them, but not giving itself to act; for this is not investigated by material agents. Nor is one action changed into another, in order that matter may be in them; but the agent passes from one action to another, so that he has the relation of matter to the actions themselves. Matter, therefore, is necessary both to quality and magnitude, so that it is also necessary to bodies. Nor is it a vain name, but it is a certain subject, though it is invisible, and without magnitude. For if this is not granted, neither must we say that there are qualities; and for the same reason we must deny the existence of magnitude. For each of these, if assumed by itself alone, must be said to be nothing. But if these have a subsistence, though each of them obscurely exists, much more will matter have an existence, though it does not clearly subsist, and is apprehended, though not by the senses. For it is not perceived by the eyes, since it is without colour. Nor by the hearing; for it has no sound. Nor by the smell, or the taste; for it has neither moisture, nor vapour. Is it, therefore, perceived by the touch? Or is not this impossible, because neither is it a body? For the touch pertains to body, because it pertains either to the dense, or the rare, the soft, or the hard, the moist, or the dry. None of these, however, subsist about matter; so that it is perceptible by reasoning, but not by sense; and by a reasoning not derived from, but void of intellect, on which account, as we have before observed, this reasoning is spurious. But neither is corporeity about matter. For if corporeity is a productive principle, it is different from matter. But if it is a thing now made, and as it were mingled, it will evidently be body, and not matter only.

XIII. If, however, the subject of things is a certain quality, being something common in each of the elements, in the first place indeed, it must be shown what it is. And, in the next place, how quality can be a subject must be explained. How, likewise, can a thing which has quality be surveyed in that which is without magnitude, and without matter? Likewise, if the quality is defined, how can it be matter? But if it is something indefinite, it is not quality, but a subject, and matter which we are now investigating. What hinders, therefore, but that it may indeed be void of quality in consequence of not in its own nature participating any one of other things, and yet through not participating of any thing, it may be endued with quality, entirely possessing a certain peculiarity, and differing from other things, being as it were a certain privation of them? For he who suffers a privation of any thing, as for instance, a blind man, is [it may be said] a participant of quality. If, therefore, there is a privation of these things about matter, how is it possible it should not be endued with quality? But if, in short, there is privation about it, it is in a still greater degree a participant of quality, if privation is a certain something that has quality. He, however, who thus objects, what else does he do than make all things to be qualities, and the participants of quality? So that quantity, and also essence, will be quality. And if each of these is such like, quality will be present with it. It is, however, ridiculous to make that which is different from the participant of quality, and which is not such like, to be endued with quality. But if it should be said, this is because a thing that is different is a participant of quality, we reply, if indeed it is difference itself, it will not subsist as a thing that is such like, since neither is quality the participant of quality. If, however, it is different alone, it is not alone different through itself, but through difference, and is the same through sameness. Neither, therefore, is privation quality, nor the participant of quality, but is destitute of quality, or of something else, just as silence is the absence of sound or of some other thing. For privation is a negation. But a thing endued with quality consists in affirmation. The peculiarity, likewise, of matter is not morphe; for not to possess quality is not to possess a certain form. It is absurd, therefore, to call that thing quality, which is not a participant of quality, and is just as if it should be said that a thing without magnitude, in consequence of being without, possesses magnitude. The peculiarity, therefore, of matter, is not any thing else than that which matter is: nor is its peculiarity adjacent to it, but rather subsists in a habitude to other things, because matter is different from them. And other things, indeed, are not only others, but each of them is a certain thing as having form. Matter, however, may be aptly said to be alone that which is *another*. Perhaps, also, it may be appropriately denominated other things, lest by calling it in the singular number another, you should limit [its boundless nature;] but by denominating it *others*, you will indicate the indefiniteness of its subsistence.

XIV. That, however, is to be investigated, whether matter is privation, or privation subsists about matter. He, therefore, who says that both are one in subject, but two in definition, ought in justice to teach us what definition of each should be given. And to the definition of matter, indeed, he should adapt nothing of privation; and to the definition of privation, nothing of matter. For either the one is not in the definition of the other, or each is in the definition of each, or one of them only is in the definition of the other, whichever it may be. If, therefore, each is defined separately, and neither of them requires the other, both will be two things, and matter will be different from privation, though privation may happen to it. In the definition of the one, however, it is necessary that the other should not be seen, not even in capacity. But if they are as a flat nose, and flatness of the nose, thus also each of them is twofold and two. And if they are as fire and heat, heat being in fire, but fire not being assumed in heat, and matter is so privation as fire is hot,—in this case, privation will be, as it were, the form of matter, but the subject will be another thing, which it is necessary should be matter. Neither, likewise, in this way will they be one. Are they, therefore, thus one in subject, but two in definition, privation not signifying that a certain thing is present, but that it is not present, and privation being as it were a negation of beings, as if some one should say non-being? For negation does not add any thing, but says a thing is not, and thus privation will be as non-being. If, therefore, it is non-being, because it is not being but something else, will there be two definitions ; the one indeed regarding the subject, but the other privation, manifesting a habitude to other things? Or shall we say, that the definition of matter respects other things, and that this is also the case with the definition of a subject; but that the definition of privation, if it manifests the indefiniteness of it, will perhaps touch upon its nature, excepting that each is one in the subject, but two in definition? But if privation in consequence of being indefinite, infinite, and without quality, is the same with matter, how will there be any longer two definitions?

XV. Again, it must be investigated, whether if the infinite and indefinite are in another nature accidentally, how this is an accident, and whether privation happens to it. If, indeed, such things as numbers and reasons [or productive principles] are remote from infinity; for they are boundaries and orders, and arrangement is derived to other things from these; but these arrange not that which is arranged, nor the orders of things, that which arranges being different from that which is arranged; and end, bound, and reason, arrange;—if this be the case, it is necessary that what is arranged and bounded, should be infinite. Matter, however, is arranged, and also such things as are not matter, by participating or possessing the nature of matter. Hence it is necessary, that matter should be infinite. yet not infinite in such a way as if the infinite was accidental to matter. For in the first place, that which happens to any thing ought to be formative; but the infinite is not formative. In the next place, to what existing thing will the infinite be an accident? Will it be to bound, and that which is bounded? Matter, however, is neither any thing bounded, nor bound. The infinite, also, acceding to that which is bounded, loses its own nature. Hence, the infinite is not an accident to matter. Matter, therefore, is the infinite;. *since in intelligibles also, matter is the infinite which is there.*[1] And there, indeed, it is generated from the infinity or power of *the one*, or from *the ever*, infinity not being in *the one*, but proceeding from it. How, therefore, is the infinite there, and also here? Or is not the infinite twofold? And in what do they differ? They differ in the same manner as archetype and image. Is the latter, therefore, in a less degree infinite? Perhaps it is more infinite. For so far as the image flies from the reality of existence, so far it is in a greater degree infinite. For infinity is in a greater degree in that which is less bounded. For that which is less in good is more in evil. Hence the infinite which is in intelligibles, in consequence of having more of being, is but as an image [with respect to the infinity of matter]. But the infinite which is here, as having less of being, so far as it flies from existence and truth,

[1] "Power," says Proclus, (in Theol. Plat. lib. iii. cap. 9.) "is every where the cause of prolific progressions, and of all multitude; occult power, indeed, being the cause of occult multitude; but the power which exists in energy, and which unfolds itself into light, being the cause of all-perfect multitude. Through this cause, therefore, I think that every being, and every essence, has connascent powers. For it participates of infinity, and derives its hyparxis indeed from bound, but its power from infinity. And being is nothing else than a monad of many powers, and a multiplied hyparxis, and on this account being is one many.—It appears to me also, that Plotinus and his followers, frequently indicating these things, produce being from form and intelligible matter, arranging form as analogous to *the one*, and to hyparxis, but power as analogous to matter. And if, indeed, they say this, they speak rightly. But if they ascribe a certain formless and indefinite nature to an intelligible essence, they appear to me to wander from the conceptions of Plato on this subject. For the infinite is not the matter of bound, but the power of it, nor is bound the form of the infinite, but the hyparxis of it." See my translation of this work of Proclus, vol. i. p. 173.

is drawn down to the nature of an image, is a more true infinite. Is, therefore, the infinite the same thing as to be infinite? Perhaps where there are that which has a productive and forming power, and matter, each of these is different; but where there is matter alone, they must either be said to be the same, or in short, and which also is better, to be infinite is not here. For it would be reason in order that it might be infinite [*i.e.* would have a productive and forming power,] which is not in the infinite. Hence matter must be said to be of itself infinite, through having an arrangement opposite to reason. For as reason not being any thing else is reason, thus also it must be said, that matter being opposed to reason according to infinity, is infinite in such a way as not to be any thing else.

XVI. Is, therefore, matter the same with difference, or is it not the same? Perhaps it is not the same with difference simply considered,[1] but with a part of difference which is opposed to beings properly so called, and which are productive principles. Hence, also, non-being is thus a certain being, and the same with privation, if privation is an opposition to the things which subsist in reason. Will, therefore, privation be corrupted by the accession of that of which it is the privation? By no means. For the receptacle of habit, is not habit, but privation. The receptacle, likewise, of bound, is not that which is terminated, nor bound, but the infinite, and this so far as it is infinite. How is it possible, therefore, that bound approaching should not destroy the nature of the infinite, especially since this infinite has not an accidental subsistence? Or may we not say that if this infinite was infinite in quantity, it would perish? Now, however, this is not the case, but on the contrary its being is preserved by bound.

[1] It appears from the version of Ficinus, that the words ἢ οὐ ταὐτὸν ἑτερότητι ἁπλῶς, are wanting in this place in the original.

For bound brings that which the infinite is naturally adapted to be, into energy and perfection; just as that which is not yet sown [is brought to perfection] when it is sown, and as the female [when impregnated] by the male. For then the female nature is not destroyed, but possesses the female characteristic in a greater degree; since then it becomes more eminently that which it is. Is, therefore, matter evil when it partakes of good? Or shall we say it is evil on this account because it was in want of good? For it did not possess it. For that which is in want of any thing, and obtains what it wants, will perhaps become a medium between good and evil, if it is equally disposed towards both. But that which possesses nothing, as being in poverty, or rather being poverty itself, is necessarily evil. For this is not the want of wealth or of strength, but it is the want of wisdom, and the want of virtue, of beauty, strength, morphe, form, and quality. How, therefore, is it possible it should not be deformed? How is it possible it should not be perfectly base? How is it possible it should not be perfectly evil? The matter, however, which is in intelligibles is [real] being. For that which is prior to it is beyond being. But here [in the sensible region,] that which is prior to matter is being. Hence the matter which is here is not being, since it is different from it when compared with the beauty of being.

IV.
AGAINST THE GNOSTICS.[1]
II. ix.

I. SINCE it has appeared to us that the nature of *the good* is simple and the first; for every thing which is not the first is not simple; and since it has nothing in itself, but is one alone, and the nature of what is called *the one*, is the same with *the good;* for it is not first something else, and

---

[1] "At the time in which Plotinus lived," (says Porphyry in his life of our philosopher,) "there were many Christians and others, who departing from the ancient philosophy, became heretics [with respect to it]; viz. the followers of Adelphius and Acylinus, who being in possession of many of the writings of Alexander, Philocomus, Demostratus, and Lydus, and exhibiting the revelations of Zoroaster, Zostrianus, Nicotheus, Allogenes, Meses, and certain others, deceived many, and were themselves deceived. For they asserted, that Plato had not penetrated the depth of an intelligible essence. Hence Plotinus in his conferences adduced many arguments against them, and also wrote a book which we have inscribed 'Against the Gnostics,' leaving the rest to our judgment."

After this testimony of Porphyry, it is singular, as Fabricius observes, that Plotinus should not even once use the word *Gnostics*, in any part of his treatise against them. But as he was a man sparing of words beyond all other writers, he was perhaps satisfied with the inscription which he knew would be given to the book by Porphyry, and being wholly attentive to the conceptions of his own wonderful mind, did not busy himself with a repetition of names. Wherever this word, therefore, occurs in the following translation, it is inserted by me for the sake of perspicuity.

afterwards one,—nor is *the good* something else, and afterwards *the good*; this being the case, when we say *the one*, and when we say *the good*, it is necessary to think that we speak of one and the same nature; not predicating any thing of it, but manifesting it to ourselves as much as possible. It is also called *the first*, because it is most simple; and sufficient to itself, because it does not consist of many things. For if it did, it would be suspended from the things of which it consists. It likewise is not in any thing else, because every thing which is in another, is also derived from another. If, therefore, it is neither from, nor in another, and has not any composition in its nature, it is necessary that there should not be any thing superior to it. Hence, it is not requisite to proceed to other principles, but having admitted this, and next to this intellect which is primarily intellect, we ought afterwards to place soul, as the next in rank. For this is the order according to nature, neither to admit more, nor fewer than these in the intelligible. For those who admit fewer than these, must either say that soul and intellect are the same, or that intellect and that which is first are the same. It has, however, been frequently demonstrated by us, that these are different from each other.

It remains, therefore, that we should consider at present, if there are more than these three, what the natures are which exist besides these. For since the principle of all things subsists in the way we have shown, it is not possible for any one to find a more simple and elevated principle. For they [the Gnostics] will not say[1] that there is one principle in capacity, but another in energy; since it is ridiculous in things which are in energy, and immaterial, to make many natures by dividing into capacity and energy. But neither in the natures posterior to these, is it to be

---

[1] Instead of οὑ γὰρ δεῖ here, it is necessary to read οὑ γὰρ δή.

supposed that there is a certain intellect established in quiet, but that another is as it were moved. For what is the quiet of intellect, what the motion and language of it? And what will be the leisure of one intellect, and the work of the other? For intellect always possesses an invariable sameness of subsistence, being constituted in a stable energy. But motion directed to, and subsisting about it, is now the employment of soul. Reason also proceeding from intellect into soul, causes soul to be intellectual, and does not produce a certain other nature between intellect and soul. Moreover, neither, is it necessary to make many intellects on this account, that one of them perceives intellectually, but another sees that it sees intellectually. For if in these, to perceive intellectually is one thing, but another to perceive that it sees intellectually, yet there must be one intuitive perception in these which is not insensible of its own energies. For it would be ridiculous to form any other conception than this of true intellect. But the intellect will be entirely the same, which perceives intellectually, and which sees that it sees intellectually. For if this were not the case, the one would be alone intelligent but the other would perceive that it was intelligent, and the former would be different from the latter. If, however, they say that these two [only] differ from each other in conceptions, in the first place indeed, they will be deprived of many hypostases; and in the next place it is necessary to consider, whether any conception of ours can admit the subsistence of an intellect which is alone intelligent, and which does not perceive that it sees intellectually. For when a thing of this kind happens to us who are always attentive to impulses and cogitations, if we are moderately worthy, it becomes the cause to us of folly.

When, therefore, that which is truly intellect intellectually perceives itself in its intellections, and the intelligible of it is not externally posited, but intellect itself is also the intelligible, it necessarily follows that in intellectual perception it possesses itself, and sees itself. But seeing itself, it perceives itself not to be void of intelligence, but intelligent. So that in primarily energizing intellectually, it will also have a perception that it sees intellectually, both being as one; nor can there be any conception of duplicity there. If, likewise, always perceiving intellectually it is that which it is, what place can there be for the conception which separates intellectual perception from the perceiving that it sees intellectually? If, however, some one should introduce a third conception to the second, which asserts that it perceives that it sees intellectually, and should say that it understands (*i.e.*, sees intellectually), that what understands understands, the absurdity is still more apparent. And why may not assertions of this kind be made to infinity? The reason, likewise, proceeding from intellect which may be adduced, and from which afterwards another reason is generated in the soul, so as to become a medium between intellect and soul, deprives the soul of intellectual perception, if it does not derive this reason from intellect, but from some other intermediate nature. Hence it would possess an image of reason, but not reason itself. And in short, it would not have a knowledge of intellect, nor would it be intelligent.

II. Hence it must not be admitted that there are more principles than these [in the intelligible world], nor must these superfluous conceptions be adopted, which have no place there; but it must be said that there is one intellect always subsisting with invariable sameness, and in every respect without fluctuation, which imitates as much as possible its father; and with respect to our soul, that one part of it always abides on high,[1] that another part of

[1] This is one of the peculiar dogmas of Plotinus, which is however opposed, and I think very justly by Proclus, in the last

it is conversant with sensibles, and that another has a subsistence in the middle of these. For as there is one nature in many powers, at one time the whole soul tends upward in conjunction with the most excellent part, of itself, and of the universe,[1] but at another time, the worst part being drawn down, draws together with itself·the middle part. For it is not lawful that the whole of it should be drawn downward. This passion also happens to the soul, because it did not abide in that which is most beautiful, where the soul which does not rank as a part [continually] abiding, and of which we are not a part, imparts to the whole body of the universe, as much as it is able to receive from it. At the same time also, this soul remains free from all solicitude, not governing the world by the discursive energy of reason, nor correcting any thing [in itself;] but by the vision of that which is prior to itself, adorning the universe with an admirable power. For the more it looks to itself, the more beautiful and powerful it becomes, and possessing these excellencies from the intelligible world, it imparts them to that which is posterior to itself, and as it is always illuminated, it always illuminates.

III. Being therefore always illuminated, and continually possessing light, it imparts it to the natures that are in a consequent order. And these are always contained and irrigated by this light, and enjoy life through it, as far as they are able. Just as if a fire being placed in a certain

Proposition of his Elements of Theology. "For if," (as he there says) "something pertaining to the soul remains on high in the intelligible world, it will always perceive intellectually, without transition, or transitively. But if without transition, it will be intellect, and not a part of the soul. And if with transition, then from that which always, and from that which sometimes energizes intellectually, one essence will be formed. This, however, is impossible.

[1] From the version of Ficinus, it appears that instead of τοῦ ὄντος in this place, we should read τοῦ παντός.

middle, whatever is capable of receiving heat, should be heated by it as much as possible; though the fire is limited by measure. But when the powers not being measured, are never-failing, how is it possible that they should have an existence, and yet nothing should participate of them? It is, however, necessary that every thing should impart itself to something else; or *the good* will not be good, nor intellect be intellect, nor soul be soul; unless after that which lives primarily, there is also that which has a secondary life, as long as that exists which is primarily vital. Hence it is necessary that all things should be perpetually consequent to each other, and should be generated by other things, because they depend on others for their subsistence. Things therefore that are said to be generated, were not generated at a certain time, but were and will be rising into existence; nor will they be corrupted, those things excepted which they contain, into which they may be resolved. But that which has nothing into which it can be resolved, will not be corrupted. If, however, some one should say that things which are in generation may be resolved into matter, we reply, and why may not matter also be dissolved? But if it is said that matter may be dissolved, we ask what necessity there was that it should be generated? If they say it was necessary, and therefore it was generated, we reply, and it is also now necessary. But if it should be left alone, divine natures would not be every where, but would be circumscribed in a certain place, as if surrounded with a wall. If, however, this is impossible, matter is perpetually[1] illuminated [by divinity].

IV. But if they say that soul suffering as it were a defluxion of its wings, made the world, we reply, that this does not befall the soul of the universe. If also they say this soul is deceived and in error, they should assign the

---

[1] It appears that ἀεί is wanting here in the original.

cause of its deception and error. When likewise was it deceived? For if from eternity, it will for the same [1] reason remain in error. But if it began at a certain time to be deceived, why was it not deceived prior to that time? We, however, do not say that the tendency of the soul downward produced the world, but rather the non-tendency of it. But if it tends downward, it is evident that this must arise from its forgetfulness of what the intelligible world contains. And if it is forgetful of these, how did it fabricate the world? For whence can it make, except from the things which it saw there? But if it fabricates recollecting the things that are there, it has not, in short, any tendency downward. For it does not possess nor see them obscurely, if it is without this tendency. And why, if it has any recollection of them, should it not wish to return thither? For what can it suppose will happen to itself from fabricating the world? For it is ridiculous to assert that it made the world, in order that it might be honoured, and is an opinion derived from the makers of statues. If, likewise, soul fabricated by a reasoning process, and did not naturally possess a producing power, how did it make this world? When also will it destroy the world? For if it repented having made it, why does it defer its destruction? But if it does not yet repent, neither will it ever, as being now accustomed to it, and becoming through time more friendly towards it. If, also, it defers the destruction of the world on account of partial souls, waiting for their union with it, these souls ought not to have descended again into generation, having experienced in a former descent, the evils which are here; so that prior to the present time they would have ceased to descend. Nor must we grant them that this world was produced in an evil condition, because there are many molestations in it. For this

---

[1] Instead of κατὰ τὸν αὐτῶν λόγον, it is necessary to read κατὰ τὸν αὐτὸν λόγον.

arises from forming too exalted an opinion of this sensible world, and conceiving it to be the same with that which is intelligible, and not the image of it. For what more beautiful image of it could have been generated? What other fire could be a better image of the fire which is there, than the fire which is here? Or what other earth than this, of the earth which is there? What sphere, also, could be more accurate and venerable, or more orderly in its motion [than that of this sensible universe], after the comprehension which is there of the intelligible world in itself? And what other sun after the intelligible sun, can be prior to this which is the object of sight?

V. It is however truly absurd, that they having a body like other men, together with desires, pains, and anger, should not despise the power of these, but assert that *they* are able to come into contact with the intelligible, and yet that there is not in *the sun* a more impassive power, though it exists in a superior order, and has not as our bodies have, a predominant tendency to a change of quality, and that it has not likewise a wisdom more excellent than we have whose origin is recent, and who are prevented by so many impediments from arriving at truth. *Nor again, is it fit to assert that the soul of the vilest men is immortal and divine, but that all heaven and the stars that are there, do not participate of immortality, though they consist of things far more beautiful and pure [than any thing terrestrial], and though it is evident that whatever is there is orderly and elegant;* especially since they blame the disorder which is about the earth, as if an immortal soul would choose this inferior abode, and willingly though more excellent be subservient to a mortal soul. The introduction also of this other soul by them is absurd, which according to them derives its composition from the elements. For how can a composition from the elements possess any life? For the mixture of these produces either the hot or the cold, or that which is mingled from both, or the dry, or the moist, or a compound from these. How, likewise, is soul the connecting bond of the four elements, since it consists from and is posterior to them? But when they also add animadversion and will, and ten thousand other things to this soul, it may be asked why they ascribe these to it. *Farther still, they do not honour this sensible fabrication of things, nor this visible earth, but they say that there is a new[1] earth produced for them, into which they are to ascend from hence;* and that this new earth is the productive principle of the world; though why is it necessary that they should dwell in the paradigm of a world which they hate? Whence likewise does this paradigm subsist? For this, according to them, derived its subsistence from the maker of the world, verging to terrestrial natures. If, therefore, by the maker of the universe great attention is paid to the production of another world, after the intelligible world which he possesses, why is this attention requisite? And if he was thus attentive prior to the world, was it in order that souls might be saved? How is it, therefore, that they are not saved? So that the world was made in vain. But if he was thus attentive posterior to the world, receiving his knowledge by a spoliation of form from matter, in this case, the skill which souls derive from experience, is sufficient to their salvation. But if they think that the form of the world should be assumed in souls, from whence is this novel doctrine derived?

VI. And why is it requisite to speak of the other hypostases which they introduce, such as transmigrations, repercussions, and repentances?[2] For if they say that

---

[1] It appears from the version of Ficinus, that for τὸν here, we should read τέαν.

[2] Forms or ideas, according to the ancient wisdom of the Greeks, leap into matter, which is adapted by the exemplar of the universe to receive the images of them, and like a mirror gives back the

these are the passions of soul when it repents, and repercussions, when it contemplates as it were the images of beings, and not beings themselves,—these are vain assertions, adduced for the purpose of establishing a peculiar sect. For as they do not adhere to the ancient wisdom of the Greeks, they fabricate such fictions as these. For the Greeks knew and asserted without any arrogance and pride, that there are methods of ascent from the cavern [of sense] and gradual progressions to a more and more true survey [of an intelligible essence.] And, in short, some things are assumed by the Gnostics from Plato, but others are innovations of their own, in order that they may establish a peculiar philosophy, and are deviations from the truth. For the punishments and rivers in Hades, and transmigrations into other bodies, are derived from Plato. The admission, likewise, of multitude in intelligibles, viz. of being and intellect ; and another demiurgus, and soul, is assumed from what is said in the "Timæus." For Plato there says, " Intellect, therefore, perceiving ideas in which is animal itself, understood by the discursive energy of reason, that the universe should contain as many as are there." But they not understanding Plato, introduce an intellect at rest, containing all things in itself; a second intellect besides this, contemplating what the first contains; and a third intellect energizing dianoetically. Frequently, likewise, the fabricating soul is assumed by them for the reasoning intellect. And they fancy that this soul is the Demiurgus, according to Plato; not know-

influx of the ideas which it receives. Souls, therefore, falling from the intelligible world become deceived, by mistaking the resemblances of forms for forms themselves, till by repentance they return to their true country, from which they have been as it were banished, through their abode on the earth. The Gnostics perverting this doctrine, gave the names of essences to such like passions of the soul.

ing who the Demiurgus is. And, in short, they falsely ascribe to Plato the mode of fabrication which they introduce, and many other things, and pervert the opinions of the man; as if they alone understood an intelligible nature, but he, and other blessed men were ignorant of it. Denominating, likewise, the intelligible multitude, they fancy that they have accurately discovered its nature; though at the same time, by the multitude which they introduce, they draw down the intelligible nature into a similitude with that which is sensible and subordinate. For it is necessary to consider intelligible multitude as subsisting according to the least possible number, and ascribing all things to that which is posterior to the first, not to investigate any other intelligibles; *that* being all things, and the first intellect and essence, and such other beautiful essences as exist after the first nature. But we should admit that the form of soul ranks in the third place.

Moreover, we should investigate the differences of souls, in passions, or in nature, so as not in any respect to reprehend divine men, but should benevolently receive their assertions, as being sanctioned by antiquity, adopting what has been well said by them, respecting the immortality of the soul, the intelligible world, and the first God; as also, that it is necessary the soul should fly from an association with the body, and that a separation from the body is a flight from generation to real essence. For if they were clearly to assert these things, which are admitted by Plato, they would do well. *No one, however, will envy their wishing to dissent from these dogmas; nor their endeavours to establish their own opinions among their auditors, by defaming and insolently attacking the doctrines of the Greeks.* But they ought to demonstrate that their own peculiar opinions, which are different from those of the Greeks, are right; and should benevolently and philosophically adduce the opinions of the ancients. Justly, also, looking to truth when they oppose the ancients, they ought not to aim at renown by censuring those who from a remote period have been celebrated by no contemptible men, nor assert that they are better than them. For what the ancients have said concerning intelligibles, is much better, and more replete with learning than what they say; *and is easily known to be so by those who are not deceived by the fraud which at present invades mankind.* Indeed, the additions which the Gnostics have made to what they received from the ancients, will be found to be by no means appropriate; and hence in their oppositions to them, they introduce manifold generations and corruptions. They likewise find fault with this universe, reprobate the communion of the soul with body, and blame the governor of the world. They also confound the demiurgus with soul, and ascribe the same passions to the soul of the world as to partial souls.

That this world, therefore, never began, nor will ever cease to be, but will continue in existence, as long as intelligibles have a subsistence, has been elsewhere shown by us. And that the communion of our soul with the body, is not better for the soul, has been asserted prior to them. But that the soul of the universe should receive any thing from ours, is just as if some one adducing the tribe of potters or braziers, in a well-governed city, should blame the whole city [on their account]. It is necessary, however, to be persuaded that the soul of the universe governs in a way very different from ours; and not bound to body as our souls are. For besides ten thousand other differences which we have elsewhere enumerated, this also ought to be considered, that we are bound by the body, the bond being now in reality produced. For the nature of body being bound in the whole soul, binds together with itself whatever it may comprehend; but the soul of the universe is not bound by the things which it binds. For it has dominion over them. Hence it is not passively affected by them. We, however, are not the lords of these. But so much of the soul of the world as is raised to the divine nature which is above it, so much of it remains entire and simple, and without impediment; and so much of it as imparts life to the body with which it is connected, receives nothing from it. For, in short, that which is in something different from itself, necessarily receives the passive properties of that in which it is. But this no longer imparts any thing of itself to that which possesses its own proper life. Just as if one thing should be centrically inserted in another, and which is co-passive with that in which it is inserted; but the latter being decayed, should permit the former to have its own life; since, neither when the fire which is in you is extinct, is the wholeness of fire extinguished. Nor if the whole of fire should perish, this would not affect the soul of the universe, but the composition of the mundane body. And if in each of the remaining elements there should be a certain world, this would not affect the soul of the universe, since the composition of the world is different from that of each of the animals which it contains. For the soul of the world stands as it were over its body, and orders it to abide; but here the elements secretly as it were withdrawing themselves, are bound in their proper order by a secondary bond. In the former case, however, they have no place into which they can fly. Hence, it is neither necessary to contain them internally, nor by external compression to impel them inwardly; but each remains where nature from the first intended it should remain. And if any one of them is naturally moved, those things to which motion is not natural are affected by it. The bodies, however, which are naturally moved, are moved in a beautiful manner, as being parts of the whole; but certain things are corrupted, in consequence of not being able to sustain the order of the whole. Just as if in a great dance, which is conducted in a becoming manner, a tortoise being caught in the middle of the progression, should be trod upon, not being able to escape the order of the dance; though if the tortoise had arranged itself with the dance, it would not have suffered from those that composed it.

To inquire, however, why the world was made, is the same thing as to ask why soul is; and why the demiurgus made it? For this indeed, in the first place, is the inquiry of those who suppose there is a beginning of perpetuity. In the next place, they fancy that the demiurgus became the cause of the fabrication of the world, through being changed from one thing to another. Hence, they are to be taught, if they are equitably disposed, what the nature of these things is, that they may cease to revile what is honourable, which they will easily do, if they become properly cautious respecting such like particulars. For no one can rightly blame the administration of the universe, since in the first place it demonstrates the magnitude of an intelligible nature. For if it proceeds into life in such a way, as not to have an indistinct and confused life, such as the smallest natures in it possess, which are perpetually generated night and day through the abundant life it contains; but is continued, clear and abundant, and is every where a life exhibiting an inestimable wisdom, how is it possible not to assert that it is a perspicuous and beautiful statue of the intelligible Gods? But if though it imitates the intelligible paradigm it is not the same with it, this is conformable to nature; since if it were the same with, it would no longer imitate it. The assertion, however, is false, that it imitates this paradigm in a dissimilar manner. For nothing is omitted, which a beautiful and natural image can possibly possess; since it was indeed necessary that this imitation should exist, but yet that it should not be an imitation resulting from the discursive energy of reason, and an artificial care. For it was not possible that the intelligible should be the last of things; since it was necessary that the energy of it should be twofold, one indeed abiding in itself, but the other proceeding into something else. Hence it was necessary that there should be something posterior to it. For that alone which is the most powerless of all things, has nothing of itself which proceeds downwards. But an admirable power flourishes in intelligibles, so that this power perpetually[1] fabricates.

If, however, there is another [sensible] world better than this, what is it? But if it is necessary that this world should exist, and there is no other, it is this world which preserves the imitation of the intelligible universe. For the whole earth indeed, is full of various animals, and of immortal beings; and all things are replete with these, as far as to the heavens. And with respect to the stars, both those which are in the inferior spheres, and those which are in the highest orb, what reason can be assigned why they are not Gods, since they are moved in order, and revolve with such beautiful bodies? Why should they not possess virtue, or what can hinder them from obtaining it? For those things have no place there, which are the causes of evils here; nor is that evil of body there, which here is disturbed and disturbs. What, likewise, prevents celestial natures from possessing intellectual energy, since they are always at leisure, and from receiving in their intellect divinity, and the other intelligible Gods. But to assert that our wisdom is more excellent than theirs, will be said by no one who is not insane; since if souls have descended hither, through being compelled by the soul of the world, how since they suffer compulsion are they better than that soul? For in souls, that which has dominion is more

---

[1] It appears from the version of Ficinus, that ἀεὶ is here wanting in the original. And indeed, the sense requires it should be inserted.

excellent. And if souls descended hither voluntarily, why do you blame this sensible region, into which you willingly came? Especially since you may be liberated from it, if it is not agreeable to you to stay. If, however, this universe is a place of such a kind, that it is possible to obtain wisdom in it, and while dwelling here to live according to a similitude of intelligibles, does not this testify that sensible are suspended from intelligible forms?

IX. If, however, some one should blame wealth and poverty, and the inequality in the dispensation of every thing of this kind, in the first place, such a one is ignorant that the worthy man does not seek for equality in such like particulars; nor is of opinion that those who possess many things, have more [of good;] nor that rulers are better than private individuals, but suffers others to make such things as these the objects of their pursuit. He also knows that the present life is twofold, the one being that of worthy men, but the other that of the multitude. And that the life of worthy men tends to the summit, and that which is on high; but that the life which is merely human is again twofold, the one kind being mindful of virtue, and participating of a certain good, but the other pertaining to the vile rabble and to artificers, who administer to the necessities of more worthy men. But if one man slays another, or is vanquished by pleasure, through imbecility of mind, what is there wonderful in this, since the guilt is not in intellect, but in souls that are of a puerile nature? And if this should happen to be an exercise of the victors and the vanquished, how is it possible that this also should not subsist rightly? But if you should be injured, what dreadful thing is there in this to an immortal nature? And if you kill another [instead of being killed yourself,] you have what you wish. If, however, you still blame the administration of things, there is no necessity for you to continue any longer in life. But it is acknowledged that there are judicial decisions here, and punishments. How, therefore, is it right to blame a city for distributing to every one according to his desert, since virtue is honoured in it, and vice has its appropriate disgrace? There are, likewise, in the world, not only statues of the Gods, but the Gods themselves, beholding from on high, who easily, as it is said, escape the accusations of men, since they conduct all things in order from the beginning to the end, and distribute an appropriate allotment to every one, conformable to the mutations of lives, and to actions in a pre-existent state; of which he who is ignorant, is of all men the most rash and rustic in divine concerns. It is requisite, however, that you should endeavour to become a most excellent character, and not think that you alone are able to become so; for thus you will not yet be most excellent. But you ought to be persuaded that there are other transcendently good men, and also good dæmons; and much more Gods, who dwell in this world, and look to that which is intelligible; and especially that there is that most blessed soul the leader and ruler of this universe. *From hence also, it is proper that you should celebrate the intelligible Gods; and besides all these, the great king which is there, and should demonstrate that the magnitude of his nature especially consists in the multitude of Gods. For it is the province of those who know the power of God, not to contract this power into one, but to show that the amplitude of divinity is as great as he himself has demonstrated it to be; since remaining that which he is, he has produced many Gods, all of whom are suspended from, and subsist through and by him. This world, likewise, is through him, and wholly looks to his divinity, as does also each of the Gods, who prophetically announce to men what they there behold, and by oracles unfold their will.*

If, however, the Gods that proceed from, are not the same with the first God, this very thing also is according to nature. But if you wish to despise superior beings, and arrogantly extol yourself as not inferior to them, in the first place [it should be remembered,] that by how much more excellent any one is, by so much the more is he benevolently disposed towards all other beings, and towards mankind. And in the next place, it is proper to have a moderate conception of our own dignity, and unaccompanied with any rusticity: exalting ourselves only so far as our nature is able to ascend; conceiving that there is also a place with divinity for others, as well as for ourselves, and not, as if flying in a dream, arrange ourselves alone immediately after the highest God; and thus deprive ourselves of that power by which it is possible for the soul of man to become a God. But this is possible so far as intellect is the leader of the soul. To attempt, however, to pass beyond intellect, is to fall from intellect. *But stupid men are persuaded when they suddenly hear such sounds as these: " You are better, not only than all other men, but also than the Gods." For there is much arrogance among men [of the present time]. And he who prior to this was humble and modest, and a man of no consequence, becomes exalted beyond measure when he is told, " You are the son of God, but other men whom you formerly admired, are not the sons of God; as neither are those beings which men honour conformably to the rites of their ancestors. It may be shown, however, without any labour, that you are more excellent than the heavens themselves."* [1] Others, also,

---

[1] Of this most stupid and arrogant opinion was the slashing Dr. Bentley, as Pope calls him, as is evident from the following extract:

"Nor do we count it any absurdity, that such a vast and immense universe should be made for the sole use of such mean and unworthy creatures as the children of men. For if we consider the dignity of an intelligent being, and put that in the scales against brute inanimate matter, we may affirm, without over-valuing human nature, that the soul of one virtuous and reli-

vociferate the same things. Just as if some one in the company of many persons who knew not how to numerate, should hear it said that he was a thousand cubits in height. If, therefore, he should think himself so tall as this, but should hear that other men were five cubits in height, he would only have a confused imagination that a thousand was a great number.

Farther still, they acknowledge that the providence of God is attentive to human concerns. Why, therefore, does he neglect the whole world, of which we are a part? If it is because he is not at leisure to look to it, neither therefore is it lawful for him to survey that which is inferior and us. Why also, while he surveys us, does he not behold that which is external; and thus look to the world in which we are contained? But if he does not look to that which is external, in order that he may not see the world, neither will he behold us. Divinity, however, knows the order of the world, and the manner in which men who are contained in it subsist. Those, also, who are dear to divinity, bear mildly whatever happens to them from the world, if any thing necessarily befalls them from the motion of all things. For it is not proper to look to what is pleasing to an individual, but we should direct our attention to the universe, and honour every one according to his desert; hastening to that goal to which all things that are able hasten, and by the attainment of which they become blessed; some things as far as they have ability obtaining an allotment adapted to their nature. Nor should any man ascribe this ability to himself alone. For it does not follow that a man possesses what he pretends to possess; since many assert they possess that of which they know they are destitute, and also fancy they have a

gious man, is of greater worth and excellency than the sun and his planets, and all the stars in the world." See Bentley's 8th Sermon at Boyle's Lectures.

thing when they have it not, and that they alone are the possessors of that which they alone do not possess.

X. He, therefore, who investigates many other particulars, or rather every particular respecting their opinions, will be able to show copiously what the nature of them is. We, indeed, are ashamed of certain of our friends,[1] who before they were intimate with us were conversant with these opinions, and who still, I know not how, persevere in them, and endeavour to render them credible. We, however, speak to those with whom we are acquainted, and not to the many who are auditors of these men. For we shall effect nothing by endeavouring to persuade them not to be disturbed by the arguments of the Gnostics, which are not accompanied with demonstrations; (for how is it possible they should?) but are the assertions of arrogant men. For there is another mode of properly confuting those who dare to reprehend the doctrines of ancient and divine men, and a mode which adheres to the truth. We shall, therefore, dismiss the enquiry how they are to be persuaded. For those who accurately understand what has now been said, will know what the nature is of every other particular. We shall dismiss, however, the consideration of that assertion which surpasses every thing in absurdity, if it is requisite to call it an absurdity, viz. that soul and a certain wisdom verged downward, whether soul was the first that began to verge, or wisdom was the cause of this tendency to an inferior condition, or both had the same intention. They add, that other souls and the members of wisdom descended at the same time, and entered bodies, such for instance as those of men. They say, however, that the soul for the sake of which other souls descended, did not descend, as if it did not verge downward, but that it only illuminated the dark-

[1] Plotinus, I suppose, alludes here to Origen the Christian father, among others, who had formerly been one of his disciples.

ness; and that afterwards an image was from thence produced in matter. Again, also, after this fashioning an image of an image, they assert that it pervades through matter or materiality, or whatever else they may please to call it; for they call this by one name, and that by another, devising many appellations for the purpose of rendering what they say obscure. And thus they generate what is denominated by them the demiurgus. Making the world, likewise, to revolt from the mother, they say that it proceeds from the demiurgus as far as to the last of images.[1]

XI. In the first place, therefore, if this soul did not descend, but illuminated the darkness, how can it be rightly said to have verged downward? For it is not proper to say that it now verged, because something flowed from it such as light; unless one thing belonging to it was situated in the region beneath, but another proceeded locally to this region, and becoming near to it, illuminated it. But if this soul illuminated, abiding in itself, and not at all operating for this purpose, why did this soul alone illuminate, and not those natures also which are more powerful than it in the order of beings? If, however, they say that this soul, in consequence of forming a rational conception of the world, illuminated it from the discursive energy of reason, why did it not at one and the same time illuminate and make the world, but instead of this waited for the generation of images? In the next place, this rational conception of the world, which is called by them a foreign land, and which was produced as they say by greater causes, did not occasion the makers of it to

[1] After this in the original, the words ἵνα σφόδρα λοιδορήσηται ὁ τοῦτο γράψας follow, i.e. "in order that he who writes this may be more vehemently reprehended." But as I do not see what connection they have with the words immediately preceding them, I have not inserted them in the translation.

verge downward. Besides, how did it happen that matter being illuminated, made psychical images, but not the nature of bodies? For the image of soul, would not be at all in want of darkness or matter; but that which was generated would when generated follow its maker, and be suspended from him. Again, whether is this illumination from a reasoning process, essence, or as they say, a conception? For if it is essence, what is the difference between it, and that from which it proceeds? But if it is another species of soul, and this rational, perhaps it is vegetable and generative. If, however, this be the case, how will it any longer be true that it made the world in order that it might be honoured for so doing; and how did it make it through arrogance and audacity, and in short, through imagination? And still more absurd is it, that it should have made the world through a reasoning process. Why, also, was it requisite, that the fabricator of the world should have made it from matter and an image? But if this illumination is a conception, in the first place it must be shown whence the name derives its origin; and in the next place how it produces, unless it imparts to the conception a fabricative power. But how can there be production with a fiction? They will say, that this thing is first, and another is posterior to it. This, however, is asserted without any authority. Why, also, was fire the first thing produced [and afterwards other things]?

XII. After what manner, likewise, did this image when just produced attempt to fabricate? Was it through a recollection of what it previously knew? But in short it had not then an existence, neither itself, nor the mother which they assign to it, in order that it might know this. In the next place, is it not wonderful, since they came into this world, not as images of souls, but as true souls, that scarcely one or two of them being raised from the world, and recovering their recollection, have been able to remember something of what they formerly saw; and yet this image, as soon as it was generated, formed a conception, though as they say, obscurely, of supernal natures? Or that this should have been the case with the mother of it, who is a material image; and that it should not only have formed a conception of these natures, and of both this and the intelligible world, but should also have learned what the things are from which the sensible universe was generated? Whence did it conceive that fire should first be produced, and think that this was necessary? For why did it not conceive this of something else? But if it was able to produce fire from the conception of it, why did it not produce the world from a conception of the world? For it is in a similar manner requisite, that the production of the world should be simultaneous with the conception of it. For both fire and the world were comprehended in the conception of them; since this image fabricated entirely in a more physical way, and not like the arts. For the arts are posterior both to nature and the world. And even now, in the individuals which are generated by natures, fire is not first produced, afterwards each particular, and in the next place the mixture of these, but the enclosure and circumscription of the whole animal, impressed in the menstrual effluxions. Why, therefore, might not matter be there circumscribed in the impression of the world, in which impression, earth and fire and the rest of things were comprehended? But perhaps they would thus have made the world, in consequence of employing a more true soul. The artificer of the world, however, knew not how to make it in this manner, though he foresaw the definite magnitude of the heavens, the obliquity of the zodiac, the motion of the bodies under it, and [the central position of] the earth; and all this in such a way as to possess the causes through which they thus subsist; though such foreknowledge could not belong to an image, but entirely proceeded from a power derived from the best of things, and which they also though unwillingly acknowledge. For the illumination diffused through the darkness, compels them to assent to the true causes of the world. For why was it requisite to illuminate, if it was not entirely necessary? For this necessity was either according to nature, or preternatural. And if, indeed, it was according to nature, this illumination always existed; but if it was preternatural, then among supernal beings that which is irregular had a subsistence, and evils existed prior to this world. Hence, this world is not the cause of evil, but supernal beings are the causes of evils to the world. And evil to the soul is not from the universe, but the evils that are here are derived from soul. And thus by a reasoning process we are led to refer the world to the first of things. But if matter also is the cause of evil, whence does it appear that it is so? For soul verging downward, saw, as they say, the darkness, and illuminated it. Whence, therefore, did the darkness originate? For if they say that soul verging downward produced it, then it will follow that the darkness did not exist prior to this downward tendency of the soul. Nor will the darkness itself be the cause of this tendency, but the nature of soul. This, however, is the same thing as to attribute the cause to precedaneous necessities. So that the cause is from the first of beings.

XIII. He therefore who blames the nature of the world, does not know what he does, nor whither this audacity of his tends. This, however, arises from the Gnostics not knowing the successive order of things, viz. of first, second, and third natures, this order always extending itself as far as to the last of things, and from not considering that subordinate beings ought not to revile such as are first, but should mildly yield to the nature of all things; and that they should betake themselves to the first of beings, abandoning the tragic fears, which they fancy are produced from the spheres of the world, all which are the causes of bland effects. For what do they contain of a terrible nature, with which those that are unskilled in arguments, and such as are strangers to erudite and elegant knowledge, are terrified? For though the bodies of these spheres are of a fiery[1] characteristic, yet it is not proper to be afraid of them, since they subsist with commensuration both to the universe and to the earth. But they ought to look to[2] the souls of these spheres, by whom they imagine themselves to be considered as beings of a very honourable nature, though their bodies transcendently surpass ours both in magnitude and beauty, and contribute to and co-operate with natural effects. For otherwise subordinate beings would not be generated, as long as the first of things subsist. These spheres also give completion to the universe, of which they are likewise mighty parts. If men, however, possess something honourable beyond other animals, much more do the starry spheres, which do not exist in the universe for tyrannical purposes, but impart to it ornament and order. But with respect to those things which are said to be effected by them, these are to be considered as signs of future events; and that things which are generated are produced accompanied with different fortunes. For it is not possible that the same things should happen to each individual, since they are much distant from each other, in the times of their generation, the places in which they reside, and in the dispositions of the soul. Nor again, is it fit to require that all things

The fire of which the heavenly bodies consists is unburning and innoxious, perpetually shining, as Proclus says in the "Timæus," with vivific heat, illuminative power, purity, and transparent light.

[2] For εἰ δὲ τὰς ψυχὰς here, it is necessary to read εἰς δὲ τὰς ψυχὰς.

should be [perfectly] good, nor, because this is impossible, rashly to blame [the order of the universe].[1] Nor is it proper to think that these inferior differ in no respect from superior natures, or to conceive that to be evil which is more defective with respect to the possession of wisdom, and is less good, and thus always considering a thing to be evil in proportion as it is more inconsiderable. Just as if some one should say that nature is evil, because it is not sense. And that which is sensitive is evil, because it is not reason. For those who thus think must be compelled to assert that evil also subsists in the intelligible world. For there, likewise, soul is inferior to intellect, and intellect to something else [or *the good*].

XIV. After another manner, also, they especially make supernal natures not to be incorruptible. For when they write incantations, and utter them as to the stars, not only to [the bodies[2] and] souls of these, but also to things superior to soul, what do they effect? They answer, charms, allurements, and persuasions, so that the stars hear the words addressed to them, and are drawn down; if any one of us knows how in a more artificial manner to utter these incantations, sounds, aspirations of the voice, and hissings, and such other particulars as in their writings are said to possess a magical power. If, however, they are not willing to assert this, but that sounds possess certain incorporeal powers, it will follow that while they wish to render their assertions more venerable, they ignorantly subvert their renown. They likewise pretend that they can expel disease. And if, indeed, they say that they

---

[1] The words τὴν τάξιν τοῦ παντός are omitted in the original; but both the sense, and the version of Ficinus, require they should be inserted.

[2] Instead of οὐ μόνον πρὸς τὴν ψυχὴν in the original, from the version of Ficinus, it is necessary to read, οὐ μόνον πρὸς τὰ σώματα ἀλλὰ καὶ τὴν ψυχήν.

effect this by temperance and an orderly mode of life, they speak rightly, and conformably to philosophers. But now when they assert that diseases are dæmons, and that they are able to expel these by words, and proclaim that they possess this ability, they may appear to the multitude to be more venerable, who admire the powers of magicians; but they will not persuade intelligent men that diseases have not their causes either from labours, or satiety, or indigence, or putrefaction, and in short from mutations which either have an external or internal origin. This, however, is manifest from the cure of diseases. For disease is deduced downward, so as to pass away externally, either through a flux of the belly, or the operation of medicine. Disease, also, is cured by letting of blood, and fasting. Perhaps, however, [they will say] that the dæmon is then hungry, and the medicine causes him to waste away; but that sometimes health is suddenly obtained, through the dæmon departing, or remaining within the body. But if this is effected while the dæmon still remains within, why, while he is within, is the person no longer diseased? And if he departs, what is the cause of his departure? For what did he suffer? Is it because he was nourished by the disease? The disease, therefore, was something different from the dæmon. In the next place, if the dæmon enters without any cause, why is not the body always diseased? But if he enters when the cause of the disease is present, why is the dæmon necessary in order to the body becoming diseased? For the cause is sufficient to produce the fever. At the same time, however, it is ridiculous, that as soon as the cause of the disease exists, the dæmon should immediately be present, as if subsisting in conjunction with the cause. The manner, however, in which these things are asserted by the Gnostics, and on what account is evident; since for the sake of this, no less than of other things, we have mentioned these dæmons. Other particulars, however, we shall leave to the consideration of the reader. *And this must every where be considered, that he who pursues our form of philosophy, will, besides all other goods, genuinely exhibit simple and venerable manners, in conjunction with the possession of wisdom, and will not endeavour to become insolent and proud; but will possess confidence accompanied with reason, much security and caution, and great circumspection.*[1]

XV. What these assertions, however, effect in the souls of those that hear them, *persuading them to despise the world, and the things that are in it*, ought not by any means to be concealed from us. For there are two sects of philosophers with respect to the attainment of the end of life, one of which places the pleasure of the body as the end; but the other chooses the beautiful and virtue, the desire of which is derived and suspended from God. The manner, however, in which this is accomplished, must be elsewhere discussed. And Epicurus, indeed, taking away providence, exhorts us to pursue pleasure and delight, as the only things which then remain. But the doctrine of the Gnostics, as still more juvenile than this, blames the domination of providence, and providence itself, despises all human laws, and virtue which has existed in every age, and considers temperance as ridiculous, in order that nothing beautiful and good may be seen to subsist among men. Together with temperance also it subverts justice which is connascent with it in manners, and which derives its perfection from reason and exercise; and in short, it subverts every thing by which a man may become a worthy character. Hence, nothing else is left for them to pursue but pleasure, and their own concerns and utility, and not that which is common to other men : unless some one among

[1] There are four lines more in this section in the original; but the meaning of them is so very obscure, that I have not attempted to translate them.

them happens to be superior to these assertions. For none of the above-mentioned particulars are considered as beautiful by them, but something else whatever it may be which they pursue; though they ought to endeavour to correct those with whom they are well acquainted, applying themselves from a divine nature to human concerns. For it is the province of this nature which despises the pleasure of the body, to know what is beautiful and good. But those who are destitute of virtue, are not at all excited to supernal natures. This is testified by their never saying any thing about virtue, and by their entirely omitting the discussion of things pertaining to it. *Nor do they say what virtue is, or how many virtues there are, or direct their attention to the numerous and beautiful assertions which may be surveyed in the writings of the ancients, or to the means of acquiring and possessing virtue, and of cultivating and purifying the soul. For it is to no purpose to say, look to God, unless you also teach how we are to look to him. For what hinders, some one may say, but that a man may look to God who does not abstain from any one pleasure, and who suffers his anger to be without any restraint; such a one recollecting indeed the name of God, but being held in bondage by all the passions, and not at all endeavouring to expel them? Virtue, therefore, indeed proceeding to the end* [i.e. *to its perfection,*] *and being ingenerated in the soul in conjunction with wisdom, will present God to the view. But to speak of God without true virtue, is to utter nothing but a name.*

XVI. *Again, to despise the world, and the Gods, and other beautiful natures that are contained in it, is not to become a good man. For, every bad man will in the first place despise the Gods; and no one is completely bad till he does despise them. Hence, if he is not bad in every thing else, from this very thing he will become so. For the honour which the Gnostics say is paid by them to the intelligible Gods, is utterly incongruous. For he who loves any thing, is delighted with every thing which is allied to the object of his love. For you also love the children of the father whom you love. But every soul is the daughter of the father of the universe. And the souls in the mundane spheres, are intellectual, and good, and are united to intelligible essences much more than ours.* For how could this world be separated from the intelligible world; or the Gods in it, from the intelligible Gods? But these things have been discussed by us before. Now, however, we must say, that those who despise things allied to the intelligible Gods, have no knowledge of those Gods, except what is merely verbal. For how can it be pious to assert as they do, that providence does not extend to terrene affairs, and to every thing whatever it may be? How also is this consonant to their own doctrine? For they say that divinity providentially attends to them alone. Whether, therefore, did he pay attention to them while they were with supernal natures, or does he also attend to them during their existence here? For if the former, how came they to descend? But if the latter, how is it that they are still upon the earth? How, likewise, does it happen that divinity is not present in the earth? For whence does he know that they are here, and that being here and revolting from him, they have become evil? But if he has a knowledge of souls that have not become evil, he will also know those that have, in order that he may be able to distinguish the former from the latter. He will, therefore, be present to all things, and will be in this world, whatever the mode may be of his subsistence in it. So that the world will participate of him. But if he is absent from the world, he will also be absent from you; and you will not have any thing to say either about him, or the natures posterior to him. But whether a certain providence proceeds from divinity to you, or whatever you may think fit to assert respecting it, the world certainly derives its subsistence from thence, and is not, nor ever will be, deserted by him. For the providence of divinity is in a much greater degree extended to wholes than to parts; and the former of these participate of him more abundantly than the latter. And much more does he providentially attend to the soul of the world. This is evident from the existence of the world, and from the wisdom of the mode in which it exists. *For who among those that are stupidly proud, is so orderly and wise as the universe?* Indeed, to compare the one with the other is ridiculous, and is attended with great absurdity. Hence, when the comparison is made for any other purpose than that of argument, it is attended with impiety. Nor is it the province of a wise man to investigate things of this kind [as if he was dubious about them], but *of one who is mentally blind, who is entirely destitute both of sense and intellect, and who being very remote from a knowledge of the intelligible world does not look to the sensible universe.* For what musician is there, who on perceiving the harmony in the intelligible world, is not moved when he hears the harmony arising from sensible sounds? Or who that is skilled in geometry and numbers, when he beholds through his eyes that which is commensurate, analogous and orderly, is not delighted with the view? For those who view through the eyes the productions of art, in pictures, do not behold them in the same way as they do the originals of which they are the resemblances. But the geometrician and arithmetician, knowing in the sensible object the imitation of that which subsists in intellection, they are as it were agitated, and brought to the recollection of reality. And from this passion also, love is excited. He however, who sees beauty resplendent in the face, tends thither. But his mind must be dull and sluggish in the extreme, and incapable of being incited to any thing else, who on seeing all the beautiful objects in the sensible world, all this symmetry and great arrangement of things, and the form apparent in the stars though so remote, is not from this view mentally agitated, and does not venerate them as admirable productions of still more admirable causes. For he who is not thus affected, will neither direct his attention to the one, nor have a knowledge of the other.

XVII. If also, they are induced to hate the nature of body, because they have heard that Plato greatly blames it as being an impediment to the soul, and says, that the whole of a corporeal nature is inferior to the soul, yet separating this by the discursive energy of reason, it is requisite to survey what remains, viz. the intelligible sphere, comprehending in itself the form of the world, souls in an orderly series without bodies, imparting magnitude according to the intelligible, and producing it into interval; so that the magnitude of that which is generated, may as much as possible be adequate to the impartibility of the paradigm. For that which is there great in power, is here great in bulk. And whether they wish to understand this sphere as circularly moved by a divine power, which contains the beginning, middle, and end of the whole sphere, or whether they consider it as stable, and not yet governing any thing else, they will thus be led to form a proper conception of the soul which governs this universe. They ought likewise to connect body with this soul in such a manner that soul may not be at all passive, but may impart something to the body, which it is able to receive, because it is not lawful there should be envy in the Gods. They should likewise ascribe such a power to the soul of the world, as is able to render the nature of body which is not of itself beautiful, a participant of beauty as far as it is capable of being adorned; which beauty also excites divine souls. Unless, indeed, the Gnostics should say that their souls are not excited by beauty, and that they do not in a different manner survey deformed and beautiful bodies. If, however, this be the case, neither are they differently affected by base and beautiful studies, nor by beautiful disciplines and the contraries to these. Hence neither do they perceive the transcendency of the contemplative energy, nor of God himself. For on account of first natures the above-mentioned particulars subsist. If, therefore, the latter are not beautiful, neither are the former. Hence, the latter are beautiful after the former. When, however, they say that they despise the beauty which is here, they would do well to despise the beauty in boys and women, so as not to be vanquished by lust. But it is requisite to know that they ought not to boast, if they despise what is base, but if they despise what they before had acknowledged to be beautiful, and by which they were in a certain respect affected. In the next place it must be observed, that there is not the same beauty in a part and the whole, in all individuals and the universe. And in the third place, that there is so great a beauty even in sensibles, and partial natures such as dæmons, as to cause us to admire the maker of these, and to believe that they are derived from him. Hence, when we are not detained by these lower beauties, but proceed from these without reviling them to supernal natures, we then proclaim that the beauty of the latter is immense. And if, indeed, we are inwardly as well as outwardly beautiful, we must say that the one accords with the other. But if we are internally bad, we ought then to acknowledge that we suffer a diminution in things of a more excellent nature. Nothing, however, that is *truly* beautiful externally, is internally deformed. For every thing which is externally beautiful, is so in consequence of the domination of inward beauty. But those who are said to be beautiful, and are at the same time internally deformed, have a false external beauty. And if some one should say that he has seen those who are outwardly truly beautiful, but are inwardly base, I am of opinion that he has not seen such persons, but has mistaken others for them; or if he has seen them, their inward deformity has been adventitious to them, they being naturally beautiful. For there are many impediments here which prevent our arriving at the end. But what is there to prevent the universe which is externally beautiful from being so internally? Moreover, those to whom nature has not given perfection from the beginning, are perhaps incapable of arriving at the end; so that it is possible for them to become depraved. The universe, however, was never once a child so as to be imperfect; nor does it acquire any thing new [1] by proceeding, and which is added to its body. For whence could it acquire this? Since it already possessed all things. Nor can any addition to the soul of it be devised. But even if some one should grant the Gnostics that there can, yet nothing evil can be added to it.

XVIII. Perhaps, however, they will say that they by their arguments cause those who believe in them, to fly far from, and hate the body, but that our doctrines detain the soul in body. But this is just as if two persons dwelling in the same house, one of them should blame the furniture and the builder of it, and yet nevertheless stay in it; but the other should not blame either of these, but assert that the builder of it had constructed it in a most artificial manner, and should wait for the time as long as he dwells in it, in which he may be liberated, and may no longer be in want of a house. The former of these, however, is thought to be the wiser of the two, and more prepared to depart, because he knows that the house is composed of inanimate stones and wood, and is very far from being a true edifice, though he is ignorant of the great difference between bearing [properly], and not bearing things of a necessary nature; since he would not be indignant if he

---

[1] τι νέον is omitted in the original.

was moderately pleased with the beauty of the stones. It is necessary, however, that those who have a body should remain in the habitations which are fabricated by a sister beneficent soul, and who possesses an abundant power of fabricating without labour. *Indeed the Gnostics think fit to call the vilest men their brethren, but refuse thus to denominate the sun, and the other stars; and with an insane mouth separate the soul of the world from an alliance with ours.* While, therefore, we are bad, it is not indeed lawful to conjoin us with supernal natures; but then only this can take place, when we become worthy, since we are not bodies, but souls resident in bodies, and capable of dwelling in them in such a manner, as to approximate very nearly to the mode in which the soul of the universe inhabits the whole body of the world. This however, consists in being free from impulsion, in not yielding to externally-acceding pleasures, or visible objects, and in not being disturbed at any severe occurrence. The soul of the world, therefore, is not impelled; for there is not any thing by which it can be. And we dwelling in this region of sense, may indeed by virtue repel the percussions of external objects, so as by magnitude and strength of decision, to diminish some of the percussions, and prevent others from taking place. But when we proximately accede to that which cannot be impelled, then we shall imitate the soul of the universe, and the soul of the stars, and becoming near through similitude, we shall hasten to be one and the same with them. Then also those things which were the objects of their vision from the first, will be ours, in consequence of being well prepared for this [felicitous event] both by nature and study. The Gnostics, however, will not, by saying that they alone are able to survey [divine natures] behold more of them on this account; nor because they assert that when they die they shall entirely lay aside the body, though this is not permitted to the souls that always adorn the heavens. For they say this through ignorance of the meaning of being out of the body, and of the manner in which the whole soul of the universe pays attention to that which is inanimate. It is possible therefore, not to be a lover of body, to become pure, to despise death, to have a knowledge of more excellent natures, and to make them the objects of pursuit; and also not to envy those who are able to pursue them, and always do so, as if they did not. Nor should we be affected in the same manner as those who fancy that the stars do not move, because sense announces to them that they stand still. For on this account also, the Gnostics fancy, that the nature of the stars does not survey the intelligibles that are as it were external to them, because they themselves do not see the soul of them externally subsisting.

V.
ON THE IMPASSIVITY OF INCORPOREAL NATURES.

III. vi.

I. IF we should say that the senses are not passions, but energies and judgments about the passions, the passions indeed subsisting about something else, as for instance about a body affected in a certain manner, but judgment about the soul; judgment not being passion, for if it were, another judgment would again be necessary, and thus we should be obliged to proceed in an infinite ascent;—if we should thus speak, it would nevertheless be here dubious, whether judgment itself has nothing in it of the subject of its decision, or whether if it has an impression of it, it is not passively affected. At the same time, however, let us speak about these impressions as they are called, and show that the mode of their subsistence is entirely different from what it is apprehended to be, and is such as that of intellections, which being energies are able to know without passivity. And in short, neither our reason, nor our will permits us to subject the soul to such conversions and changes in quality, as are the calefactions and refrigerations of bodies. With respect to what is called the passive part of the soul also, it is requisite to see and consider, whether we must admit this likewise to be immutable, or grant that passivity belongs to this alone. This however, we shall discuss hereafter. But let us now direct our attention to the doubts pertaining to the former particulars. For it is dubious how that part of the soul, whatever it may be, is immutable, which is prior to the passive part, and to sense, since depravity is ingenerated in it, and false opinions and ignorance; and besides these, familiarity and alienation, when it is pleased and pained, is angry and envious, is emulous and desirous; and in short, which is never quiescent, but is moved and changed by every incidental circumstance. If, indeed, the soul is body and has magnitude, it is not easy, or rather is wholly impossible to show that it is impassive and immutable in any one of the particulars, which are said to take place about it. But if it is an essence void of magnitude, and it is necessary that the incorruptible should be present with it, we should take care not to ascribe to it passions of this kind, lest we should also ignorantly grant that it is corruptible. Whether, likewise, the essence of it is number or reason, as we say it is, how can passion be ingenerated in number or reason? But we ought rather to think that irrational reasons, and impassive passions are produced in it. And these being transferred to it from bodies, are each of them to be oppositely assumed, and according to analogy, so that the soul [after a manner] possessing these, does not [really] possess them, and being passive to them does not suffer. And it must be considered what the mode is of such like affections.

11. In the first place however, it is requisite to speak of virtue and vice, and to show what then takes place when vice is said to be present with the soul. For we say it is necessary to take away something, as if a certain evil was in the soul, and that virtue should be inserted in it, and it should be adorned and made beautiful, instead of being, as it was before, base and deformed. If therefore we should say that virtue is harmony, but vice dissonance, shall we adduce an opinion

conformable to that of the ancients? For this assertion will in no small degree promote the object of our investigation. For if, indeed, virtue consists in the parts of the soul being naturally concordant with each other, but vice, in their not being concordant, nothing adventitious or extraneous will take place; but each part will proceed such as it is, into an appropriate order, and being such will not enter into dissonance, like dancers who in dancing do not accord with each other; either one of them singing, when the rest do not sing, or each singing by himself. For it is not only necessary that they should sing together, but that each should sing well with an appropriate music, as far as pertains to his own part of the performance; so that then also in the soul there is harmony, when each part performs that which is adapted to it. It is requisite, however, prior to the harmony, that there should be another virtue of each of the parts, and another vice of each prior to their dissonance with respect to each other. What is it therefore, from which being present, each part is evil? Is it from vice being present? And again, is each part good through the presence of virtue? Perhaps, therefore, some one may say that ignorance in the reasoning power is the vice of it, this ignorance consisting in the negation of knowledge, and not in the presence of a certain thing. But when false opinions are inherent, which especially produce vice, how is it possible in this case that something should not be ingenerated, and that this part of the soul should not thus be changed in quality? Is not also the irascible part affected in one way when it is timid, and in another when it is brave? And is not the epithymetic [1] part likewise, affected differently when it is intemperate, and when it is temperate? Or may we not say, that when

---

[1] *i.e.* The part characterized by *desire;* the whole soul receiving a triple division, into reason, anger, and desire, which last is a tendency to the possession and enjoyment of external good.

each part possessing virtue, energizes according to the essence by which it is characterized, we then say it is obedient to reason? And the reasoning part, indeed, is obedient to intellect, but the other parts to reason. Or shall we say that to be obedient to reason is as it were to see, that which is obedient not being figured, but seeing, and being in energy when it sees; just as sight both when it is in capacity, and when in energy, is the same in essence; but energy is not a change in quality, but at once applies itself to that to which it is essentially adapted, and perceives and knows without passivity. The reasoning power also thus subsists with reference to intellect, and thus sees. And the power of intellection is this, not becoming internally, the impressions as it were of a seal, but it possesses, and again does not possess that which it sees. It possesses the spectacle indeed, in consequence of knowing it; but does not possess it, because nothing is impressed in it from the object of vision, like the figure in the wax. It is, however, necessary to recollect, that *memory is not a certain repository of impressions, but a power of the soul exciting itself in such a way as to possess that which it had not.*

What then, was it not one thing before it thus recollected, and another afterwards when it now recollects? [It was] if you are willing to call it another, and not to say that it is changed in quality; unless some one should assert that a progression from power to energy is a mutation in quality. Nothing however is here added, but that is effected which there was a natural aptitude to effect. For in short, the energies of immaterial natures are not themselves in energizing changed in quality, or they would perish, but they much rather energize by remaining permanent. But to energize with passivity is the province of things which are connected in their energies with matter. If however that which is immaterial is passively affected, it will not be able any where to abide, as in the sight, vision energizing, it is the eye which suffers [and not the energy of seeing]. And opinions are as it were visions. But how is the irascible part timid? And how also does it possess fortitude? Shall we say it is timid indeed, either because it does not look to reason, or because it looks to depraved reason; or that it is so through a defect of instruments, such as the want or the weakness of corporeal arms, in consequence of which it is either prevented from energizing, or is not moved so as to be as it were incited? But it possesses fortitude, if the contrary takes place; in neither of which cases, there is not any change of quality, or passion. Again, that part of the soul which desires, when it energizes alone, produces what is called intemperance. For [sometimes] it performs all things alone, other things not being present, whose province it is in their turn to have dominion, and to point out to this part [what it ought to do]. In the mean time the power whose province it is to see, performs something else, and not all things; but is elsewhere at leisure, in consequence of seeing as much as possible other things. Perhaps, too, what is called the vice of this part, consists very much in a bad habit of the body; but the virtue of it is a contrary habit; so that no addition is in either case made to the soul.

III. But how is it that familiarities and alienations, pains, anger, and pleasures, desires and fears, are not mutations and passions inherent and exciting? It is necessary, therefore, thus to distinguish concerning these. For not to acknowledge that changes in quality are ingenerated in us, and also vehement sensations of these, is the province of one who denies things that are evident. It is requisite, therefore, admitting the subsistence of these, that we should investigate what that is which is changed. For by asserting that these things take place about the soul, we are in danger of falling into the same absurdity as if we should admit that the soul is red, or becomes pale, not considering that these passions are produced indeed on account of the soul, but subsist about another composition [than that of the soul]. And shame, indeed, in the soul, arises from an opinion of baseness; the body (that we may not err in our conceptions) being as it were contained in the soul, and not being the same with that which is inanimate. The animated body, therefore, when it is moved with facility, undergoes a change in the blood, from the shame which subsists in the soul. And with respect to what is called fear, the principle of it, indeed, is in the soul; but the paleness produced by it, arises from the blood retreating inwardly. In pleasure, also, the sensible diffusion of it subsists about the body; but that which takes place about the soul is no longer passion. The like also must be asserted with respect to pain. For the principle of desire latently subsisting in the soul, that which proceeds from thence is recognized by sense. For when we say that the soul is moved in desires, in reasonings, and in opinions, we do not say that it produces these in consequence of being agitated, but that motions are generated from it; since also, when we assert that life is motion, we do not conceive that it is a change of quality. But the natural energy of each part of the soul, is life not departing from itself. In short, it will be sufficient if we do not admit that energies, lives, and appetites, are mutations in quality; that recollections are not types impressed in the soul; and that imaginations are not configurations described as it were in wax. For every where, in all passions and motions, the soul must be acknowledged to subsist with invariable sameness in its subject and essence; and that virtue and vice are not produced in it after the same manner as black and white, or heat and cold about the body. But it must be admitted that the soul subsists with reference to both these, and in short, about all contraries, according to the above mentioned mode.

IV. Let us, however, direct our attention to what is called the passive part of the soul; though we have already after a manner spoken concerning this, when we discussed all the passions which are produced about the irascible and epithymetic part, and showed how each of them subsists. Nevertheless, it is requisite to discuss it more amply; in the first place assuming what that which is passive in the soul is said to be. It is said, therefore, to be that about which the passions appear to subsist. But these are things to which pleasure and pain are consequent. Of the passions, however, some originate from opinions, as when some one being of opinion that he shall die, is terrified, or fancying that he shall obtain some good is delighted; the opinion indeed, being in one thing, but the exciting passion in another. But other passions are such as, existing involuntarily, produce opinion in that which is naturally adapted to opine. And we have already observed that opinion permits the nature which opines to remain immovable. Unexpected fear, however, when it accedes, will be found to originate from opinion, affording as it were a certain perception to the part of the soul which is said to be afraid. For what does this being afraid effect? Perturbation it is said, and astonishment from the expectation of evil. It is evident, however, that the phantasy is in the soul, both the first [1] which we call opinion, and the second which is derived from the first, and is no longer opinion [truly so called,] but is conversant with that which is beneath, being as it were obscure opinion, and an unadvised and rash

---

[1] The phantasy or imagination is the highest of the gnostic irrational powers of the soul. But this in its summit is united to *opinion*, or that gnostic rational power which knows *that* a thing is, but does not know *why* it is; and in its other extremity it is conjoined with sense. So far, therefore, as it is united to opinion, it may be said to be the same with it. See my Introduction to, and translation of, Aristotle's treatise "On the Soul."

imagination, such as the energy which is said to be inherent in nature, according to which it produces every thing without phantasy. But a sensible perturbation from these is produced about the body; viz. a trembling and concussion, paleness, and an inability of speaking. For these effects are not in the psychical part; since if they were, we should not say that they are corporeal. For if they pertained to the soul, that power of it whose province it is to transmit these, would no longer perform its office, in consequence of being detained by passions, and departing from itself. This passive part, therefore, of the soul, is not indeed body, but a certain form. Nevertheless, it is in matter, as are also the epithymetic, the nutritive, augmentative, and generative powers, the three latter of which are the root and principle of the epithymetic and passive form. It is requisite, however, that no perturbation, or in short passion should be present with any form; but it is necessary that form should remain permanent, and that the matter of it should be conversant with passion, when passion is produced through the presence of the exciting power of form. For the vegetable power does not itself vegetate when it causes other things to vegetate; nor is increased when it increases other things; nor in short when it moves, is moved according to the motion with which it moves, but is either not moved at all, or has another mode of motion or energy. Hence it is necessary that the nature itself of form should be energy; and should produce by being present, just as if harmony should of itself move the chords [of a musical instrument]. The passive part of the soul, therefore, will be indeed the cause of passion, whether the motion is produced by it from the sensitive phantasy, or also without the phantasy. This, likewise, must be considered, whether opinion originating supernally, that which is passive in the soul subsists alone in the form of the harmony; but the motive causes are analogous to the musician; and the things which are struck through passion have the relation of chords. For in a musical instrument also, harmony does not suffer, but the chord. And the chord is not moved, though the musician wishes that it should be, unless harmony commands it to be moved.

V. Why, then, is it requisite to endeavour to render the soul impassive by means of philosophy, if from the first it is without passivity? Shall we say, it is because a phantasm as it were proceeding into it from what is called the passive part, the consequent passion produces a perturbation [in this part] and the image of expected evil is conjoined with the perturbation? Reason, therefore, thinks it fit that a passion of this kind should be extirpated, and that it should not be suffered to be ingenerated, because where it is, the soul is not yet in a good condition. But where it is not ingenerated, there the soul is impassive, the vision which is the cause of the passion about the soul, having no longer an inherent subsistence. Just as if some one wishing to expel the visions of sleep, should recal the dreaming soul to wakefulness; or as if he should say that external spectacles produce the passions, and should assert that these passions belong to the soul. But what will the purification of the soul be, if it is in no respect defiled? Or in what will the separation of it from the body consist? May we not say that the purification of it will be, to leave it by itself alone, and not suffer it to associate with other things [that are hostile to its nature], nor permit it to look to any thing external; nor again, to have foreign opinions, whatever the mode is, as we have said, of opinions or passions; nor to behold images, nor fabricate passions from them? If, however, it is converted to supernal from inferior objects, is not this a purification and separation of the soul, which in this case is no longer in body, so as to be something belonging to it, but resembles a light not merged in turbid mire, though at the same time that which is merged in it is impassive? But the purification, indeed, of the passive part of the soul, is an excitation from the vision of absurd images. And the separation of it will consist in not verging downward, and in the imagination not being conversant with inferior natures. It will also consist in taking away those things by the ablation of which this part likewise will be separated, when it is not permitted to lie in a spirit turbid from gluttony, lest it should be suffocated in flesh, but when that in which it dwells is attenuated, so that it may be quietly carried in it.

VI. That the intelligible essence, indeed, the whole of which is aranged according to form, is necesarily impassive, has been already shown. Since, however, matter also is something incorporeal, though after another manner [than the intelligible,] concerning this likewise it must be considered after what manner it subsists; whether it is passive, as it is said to be, and in all things mutable, or whether it is necessary to opine that this also is impassive, and if it is so, the mode of its impassivity must be unfolded. In the first place, therefore, this must be assumed by those who speak concerning the nature of it, and who endeavour to show what it is, that the nature, essence, and existence of being, is not such as the multitude conceive it to be. For being which may be so denominated in reality, is *truly* being; but this is that which is entirely being; and this again is that which in no respect is deficient in existence. But since it is perfectly being, it is not in want of any thing in order that it may be preserved and be, but to other things which appear to be, it is the cause of their apparent existence. If, therefore, these things are rightly asserted, it is necessary that it should subsist in life, and in a perfect life; for if it were deficient in this, it would not be essence in a more eminent degree. This, however, is intellect and perfect wisdom. Hence it is bounded and definite, and nothing is there in capacity which does not also possess a mighty power; since otherwise it would be deficient. Hence, too, it is eternal, invariably the same, and unreceptive of any thing. For if it should receive any thing, it would receive something besides itself; and this would be non-being. It is necessary, however, that it should be perfectly being. Hence it is requisite it should accede to existence, possessing all things in itself, and being at once all things, and one all, if by these peculiarities we define being. But it is necessary that we should thus define it, or intellect and life would not proceed from being, but these would be adventitious to it, though they will not emanate from non-being, and being will be deprived of life and intellect. That which is truly non-being, therefore, will have these in such a way as it is requisite for them to subsist in less excellent natures, and in things posterior to being. For that which is prior to being, imparts these indeed to it, but is not itself indigent of these. Hence, if being is a thing of this kind, it is necessary that it should neither be a certain body, nor that which is the subject of bodies, but that existence to these should consist in non-being.

It may, however, be said, how is it possible the nature of bodies and matter should not have a [real] being, in which these mountains and rocks exist, the whole solid earth, and all resisting substances? Indeed, things which are struck, confess that their essence subsists by compulsion. If, therefore, some one should say, how is it possible that things which neither press, nor are impelled, nor resist, and which in short are not visible, viz. soul and intellect should be beings, and truly beings,—we reply, that among bodies, earth is most stable, but that which is more movable, is also less ponderous, and of this that which is on high is most movable. And hence, fire flies [as it were] from the nature of body. I am of opinion, however, that things which are more sufficient to themselves, disturb others in a less degree, and occasion them less pain. But things which are more ponderous and terrene, because they are in a defective and fallen condition, and are unable to elevate themselves, strike against others, falling on them through imbecility, and oppressing them by their descending and sluggish weight. For dead bodies cause greater molestation [1] when they fall, and strike and injure more vehemently. But animated bodies, as they participate of [real] being, are the more innoxious the more they participate of it. Hence motion, which is a certain life as it were in bodies, and an imitation of life, is in a greater degree present with those things that have less of body, as if a defect of being rendered that with which it is present, more corporeal. From what are called passions, likewise, it may be seen, that what is in a greater body is more passive, earth than other things, and other things according to the same ratio. For other things when divided, return again into one, when nothing prevents them. But when a terrene body is divided, the parts always continue separate from each other, as being naturally averse to reunion, and by a small impulse are disposed to remain as they are impelled, and be corrupted. Hence, that which becomes body in a most eminent degree, as having especially arrived at nonentity, is incapable of recalling itself into one. Ponderous, therefore, and vehement concussions, by which some things act upon others, are attended with ruin. But one debile thing falling on another, possesses with respect to it the same efficacy and power, as [2] nonentity falling on nonentity. And this we think a sufficient refutation of their opinion who place beings among bodies, and who are induced to do so by the

---

[1] For ἀειδέστερα it is necessary to read ἀηδέστερα.
[2] ὡς is omitted in the original.

testimony of impulsions and concussions; and from the phantasms produced through sense derive their belief of the truth. Such as these are affected in a manner similar to those who are dreaming, and who imagine that what they perceive is true, though it is nothing more than a dream. For sense is alone the employment of the dormant soul; since as much of the soul as is merged in body, so much of it sleeps. But true vigilance is a true elevation from, and not in conjunction with body. For indeed a resurrection with body, is a transmigration from sleep to sleep, [and from dream to dream] like a man passing [in the dark] from bed to bed. But that elevation is entirely true, which wholly rises [from the shadowy essence] of bodies. For these possessing a nature contrary to soul, have also that which is contrary to essence. And this also is testified by their generation, their flowing and corruption; all which are foreign to the nature of real being.

VII. Let us, however, again return in the first place, to the subject matter, and afterwards to the things which are said to be in matter, from which it will be known that matter itself has no [real] existence, and that it is impassive. It is therefore incorporeal, since body is posterior to it, and is a composite, and matter in conjunction with another thing [*i.e.* with form,] produces body. For thus it is allotted the same appellation according to the incorporeal, because both being and matter are different from bodies. Since, however, matter is neither soul nor intellect, nor life, nor form, nor reason, nor bound; for it is infinite; nor power; for what can it effect; but falls off from all these, neither can it rightly receive the appellation of being. But it may deservedly be called non-being. Yet it is not non-being in the same manner as motion is, or permanency; but it is truly non-being, the image and phantasm of bulk, and the desire of subsistence. And it stands, indeed, but not in that which is permanent, is of itself invisible, and flies from him who wishes to behold it. When, likewise, some one does not see it, then it is present; but is not perceived by him who strives intently to behold it. Add too, that contraries are always apparent in it; the small and the great, the less and the more, the deficient and the exceeding, being an image neither able to remain, nor yet to fly away. For it has not even power to effect this, as receiving no strength from intellect, but subsisting in the defect of all being. Hence it deceives us in whatever it announces of itself; so that if it should appear to be great, it is small; if more, it is less; and the being which we meet with in the imagination of it, is non-being, and as it were a flying mockery. Hence, also, the things which appear to be ingenerated in it, are mockeries, and images in an image, just as in a mirror, where a thing which is situated in one place appears to be in another. It likewise seems to be full and to be all things, and yet has nothing. But the things which enter into and depart from matter, are imitations and images of [real] beings, flowing about a formless resemblance; and on account of its formless nature are seen within it. They also appear, indeed, to effect something in it, but effect nothing; for they are vain and debile, and have no resisting power. And since matter, likewise, is void of resistance, they pervade without dividing it, like images in water, or as if some one should send as it were forms into what is called a vacuum. For again, if the things which are beheld in matter were such as those from which they proceeded into it, perhaps a certain power of these might be ascribed to material forms, and matter might be supposed to suffer by them. But now, since the things which are represented are of one kind, and those that are beheld in matter of another, from these also we may learn that the passion of matter is false; that which is seen in it being false, and in no respect possessing any similitude to its maker. Hence, being imbecile and false, and falling into a false receptacle, as in a dream, or in water, or a mirror, it necessarily permits matter to be impassive, though in the things which have been just mentioned,[1] there is a similitude between the representations in them, and the originals of which they are the resemblances.

VIII. In short, that which suffers ought to be a thing of this kind, so that it may be as it were in the contrary powers and qualities of the things which accede and produce passion. For to the inherent heat the change in quality is from that which refrigerates; and to the inherent humidity the change is from that which causes dryness. And we say that the subject is changed in quality, when from being cold it becomes hot, or moist from being dry. But what is called the corruption of fire, testifies the truth of this, the mutation being made into another element. For we say that the fire and not the matter is corrupted; so that passions are about that, about which corruption also subsists. For the reception of passion is the path to corruption; and to be corrupted pertains to that to which likewise it belongs to suffer. It is not however possible, that matter should be corrupted. For into what, and how can it be corrupted? But is not matter [it may be said] co-passive, since qualities in their mixture with each other suffer, and matter receives in itself myriads of heats and colds, and in short infinite qualities, and is distinguished by these, and has them as it were connascent and mingled with each other? For each of these is not separate from the rest, and matter is left in the middle of them. Unless perhaps some one should place it external to them. But everything which is in a subject, is in such a manner

---

[1] viz. In water, a mirror, and a dream.

present with the subject, as to impart something to it from itself.

IX. It must therefore be assumed, that one thing is present with another, and that one thing is in another, not according to one mode only. But sometimes together with being present, it causes that with which it is present to be better or worse, accompanied with permutation; as is seen to be the case in the bodies of animals; and at another time, it makes it to be as it were better or worse, without that being passive with which it is present, as is said to be the case in the soul. Sometimes, also, this takes place in such a way as when a figure is imprinted in wax, where there is neither any passion, so as to cause the wax to be something else when the figure is present with it, nor any defect in the wax, when the figure is destroyed. Light, also, does not produce a change in quality of the figure about that which is illuminated. Nor does a stone, when it becomes cold, possess any thing besides frigidity, from that through which it is cold, while it remains a stone. And what does a line [viz. the extension of length] suffer from colour? Nor, in my opinion, does a superficies suffer any thing from it, but perhaps the subject body. Though what can this suffer from colour? For it is not proper to say that a thing suffers when something is [merely] present with it; nor when it is invested with form. If, however, some one should say that mirrors, and in short diaphanous substances, suffer nothing from the images that are seen within them, he will not adduce an unappropriate paradigm. For the forms which are in matter are images, and matter is still more impassive than mirrors. Hence heat and cold are ingenerated in it, but do not heat [or refrigerate] it. For to be heated and refrigerated, pertains to quality leading the subject from one quality to another.

It is requisite, however, to consider, whether frigidity is

not the absence and privation [of heat]: but qualities entering together into matter, many of them act on each other, or rather are contrarily affected. For what can fragrance effect in sweetness; or colour in figure? Or what can that which belongs to one genus effect in another? Whence especially credibility may be obtained, that a thing may be in that which is different from it, without injuring by its presence that with which it is present. As, therefore, that which is injured is not injured by any thing of a casual nature, so neither does that which is changed and which suffers, suffer by any thing indiscriminately. But contraries only suffer from contraries, other things being unchanged by others; so that those things in which there is no contrariety, do not suffer by any thing of a contrary nature. Hence, it is necessary if any thing suffers, that it should not be matter, but something which is a composite of matter and form, or in short, that it should be at one and the same time many things. But that which is alone, and separate from other things, and which is entirely simple, will be impassive to all things, and will be inclosed in the middle of all things, acting on each other; just as when in the same house certain persons strike each other, neither does the house suffer any thing from the blows, nor the air which is in it. But the forms which are in matter, perform such things as they are naturally adapted to perform. Matter itself, however, is much more impassive than such qualities in it, which by not being contraries are impassive with reference to each other.

X. In the next place, if matter suffers, it is necessary that it should possess something from the passion, and that this should either be the passion itself, or that it should be disposed differently from what it was before the passion was produced in it. Hence, another quality acceding after the former, the recipient will no longer be matter, but matter with a certain quality. If, however, quality[1] itself should fail, leaving something of itself of an effective nature, the subject will in a still greater degree become something else ; and proceeding after this manner, the subject will be something besides [mere] matter, and will be manifold and multiform. Hence, it will no longer be the universal recipient, since it will be an impediment to the multitude of things which accede to it, and matter will no longer remain, and therefore will not be incorruptible. So that if it is necessary that matter should be as it was from the first, it ought thus to be always the same, since to assert that it has been changed is not to preserve it the same. Farther still, if in short every thing which is changed in quality ought, remaining in the same form, to be changed according to accidents, and not essentially;—if, therefore, it is requisite that what is changed in quality should remain, and that part of it which suffers is not that which remains, one of two things is necessary, either that matter when changed in quality should depart from itself, or that not departing from itself it should not be changed in quality. If, however, some one should say, that it is changed in quality, yet not so far as it is matter; in the first place, indeed, he cannot assign what that is according to which it is so changed; and in the next place, he must confess that thus also matter itself is not changed in quality. For as in other things which are forms, it is not possible that they can be essentially changed in quality, since their essence consists in this [i.e. in being forms], thus also, since the being of matter is to exist as matter, it cannot be changed in quality so far as it is matter, but it must necessarily remain what it is. And as there form itself is unchanged in quality, so likewise here it is necessary that matter itself should be immutable.

[1] Quality is that which imparts what is apparent in matter, and which is the object of sense.

XI. Whence, also, I think that the divine Plato [in the Timæus], having formed the same conception rightly says, that the things which enter into and depart from matter, are imitations of beings; the words *entering into and departing,* not being used by him in vain. For he wished to direct our attention to the mode in which matter participates of forms. It also appears that the doubt how this participation is effected, is not what many prior to us conceived it to be, viz. how forms proceed into matter, but rather how they subsist in it. For it seems to be truly wonderful, how these forms being present with matter, it nevertheless remains impassive; especially since the forms which enter it suffer from each other. According to Plato, however, the entering forms expel those which entered prior to them, and passion is in the composite from matter and form; yet not in every composite, but in that which is in want of the acceding or departing form; and which indeed in its composition is defective by the absence of a certain form, but is perfect by the presence of it. But matter does not possess any thing more whatever as an accession to its composition, by the entrance of any thing into it. For it does not then become that which it is through the form that enters, nor is it less by the departure of this form. For it remains that which it was at first. To the natures, indeed, which require ornament and order, it is useful to be adorned; and to these ornament may accede without transmutation, as is the case with things which we surround with decoration. If, however, any thing is so adorned as to have the ornament connascent, it will be requisite that what was before void of beauty, should be changed in quality, become different from what it was, and from being deformed be beautiful. If, therefore, matter being deformed is rendered beautiful, it is no longer that base thing which it was before; so that in being thus adorned, it loses its subsistence as matter, and especially if its deformity is not accidental. But if it is so deformed as to be deformity itself, it will not participate of ornament. And if it is so evil, as to be evil itself, it will not participate of good. Hence it does not participate in such a way as some fancy it does, viz. by being passive, but after another manner, which is that of appearing to participate. Perhaps, too, according to this mode the doubt may be solved, how, since matter is evil, it can aspire after good, because it does not through the participation cease to be what it was. For if what is called the participation of matter subsists after this manner so that it remains as we say the same, unchanged in quality, and is always that which it is, it will no longer be wonderful, how being evil it participates of good. For it does not depart from itself. But because it is indeed necessary it should participate, it participates after a certain manner as long as it exists. In consequence, however, of remaining that which it is, and the mode of participation preserving it [in its own proper nature] it is not injured in its essence by that which thus imparts something to it. And it appears not to be less evil on this account, viz. because it always remains that which it is. For if it truly participated of, and was truly changed in quality by *the good*, it would not be naturally evil. So that if some one should say that matter is evil, he will assert what is true, if he says it is impassive to *the good*, which is the same thing as to say, that it is entirely impassive.

XII. But Plato having formed this conception of matter, and not admitting that participation in it, is as if form was generated in a subject, and imparted to it morphe, so as to become one composite, the things which it participates being co-transmuted, and as it were co-mingled, and co-passive,—Plato, therefore, not being willing to adopt such a mode of participation as this, but desiring to show

how matter remaining impassive possesses forms, investigated a paradigm of impassive participation, without which it is not easy to show what those things especially are, which when present preserve the subject one and the same. He likewise excites many doubts, while hastening to obtain the object of his enquiry, and besides this, wishing to represent to us the vacuity of subsistence in sensibles, and that the region of the resemblance of reality is very ample. Supposing, therefore, that matter by figures produces passions in animated bodies, while at the same time it has itself none of these passions, he indicates by this the stability of matter; enabling us to collect by a syllogistic process that matter neither suffers, nor is changed in quality by these figures. For in these bodies indeed [which are the objects of sense], and which receive one figure after another, perhaps some one may say a change in quality is effected, asserting that the mutation of figure is an homonymous alliation.[1] Since matter, however, has neither any figure, nor any magnitude, how can it be said that the presence of figure, in whatever way this may take place, is alliation, though it should homonymously be said to be so? If, therefore, some one adopting this conception of Plato as legitimate, should assert that the subject nature [*i.e.* matter] does not possess any thing in such a way as it is thought to possess it, he will not speak absurdly. In what manner, however, does matter possess forms, if you are not willing to admit that it possesses them as figures? But the hypothesis of Plato indicates as much as possible the impassivity of matter, and the apparent presence of images in it, which are not [in reality] present.

Perhaps, however, we ought first to speak further about the impassivity of matter. Plato, therefore, teaches us that we ought to be led by usual appellations to the con-

[1] *i.e.* A change in quality.

sideration of its passivity, as when he says it becomes dry, or ignited, or moist, &c. and receives the forms of air and water. For the assertion that it receives these forms, mitigates the force of the other assertion, that matter is ignited and becomes moist. He likewise manifests when he says that matter receives forms, that it is not itself invested with morphe, but that the morphæ are in the same state as when they entered into matter; and that the term ignited is not properly applied to matter, but rather fire in generation, or becoming to be. For it is not the same thing for fire to be in generation, and for a thing to be ignited. For to be ignited is indeed effected in another thing, in which there is also passivity. But how can that which is a part of fire, be itself ignited? For this would be just the same as if some one should say, that the statue proceeded through the brass, or fire through matter, and besides this ignited it. Farther still, if that which accedes is reason or a productive principle, how will it ignite? Shall we say on account of figure? But that which ignited already consists both of matter and figure. How, therefore, can it consist of both, unless it becomes one from both? Or shall we say that though it becomes one, yet not from two things having passions in each other, but acting upon other things? Does this, therefore, arise from the agency of both, or from one of them causing the other not to fly away? When, however, a certain body is divided, how is it possible that matter also should not be divided? And matter when it is divided being passive, how is it possible it should not suffer by this very passion? Or what hinders us from asserting for the same reason that matter is corrupted? Since when body is corrupted, it must be shown why matter likewise is not corrupted. In answer to this, however, it may be said, that what suffers and is divided is a magnitude of a definite quantity, but in that which is not magnitude, the passions of magnitude are not ingenerated. And, in short, the passions of body are not inherent in that which is not body; so that those who make matter to be passive, must also admit it to be body.

XIII. It is likewise requisite that they should attend to the manner in which they say matter flies from form. For how can it fly from stones and rocks by which it is comprehended? For they will not say that it sometimes flies from form, and sometimes does not. For if it flies by its own will, why does it not always fly from it? But if it abides from necessity, there is not any time in which it is not invested with a certain form. The cause, however, must be investigated why each matter has not always the same form, and this must be in a still greater degree investigated in the forms which enter into matter. How, therefore, is matter said to fly from form? Is it by its own nature, and always? But what else will this be, than that never departing from itself, it so possesses form as if it never possessed it, or if this is not admitted, they will not be able to assign any probable reason in defence of what they assert. Plato also calls matter the receptacle and nurse of all generation. And the receptacle and nurse indeed, are different from generation; but that which is changed in quality is in generation. Since, likewise, the receptacle and nurse are prior to generation, they will also be prior to alliation. Add too, that they will preserve matter in an impassive state; as also will the assertion that each thing has an *apparent* subsistence in that in which it is ingenerated, and that it departs from thence as from a receptacle and seat. The impassivity of matter, likewise, is preserved by the assertion that it is the place of forms; for this does not ascribe any passion to it, but investigates another mode of subsistence. What, therefore, is this mode? Since, indeed, a nature of this kind ought not to be any one of, but to fly from every essence of beings, and to be entirely different from them; for they are reasons or productive principles, and have a real existence;—this being the case, it is necessary that matter in consequence of this difference should preserve the safety which it is allotted, and should not only be unreceptive of beings, but also if there is a certain imitation of them, that it should even be destitute of familiarity with this resemblance. For thus it will be entirely different from beings, since otherwise, being conversant with a certain form, and becoming something else in conjunction with it, it would cease to be different from beings, and to be the receptacle of all things; for it would not be the recipient of any thing. It is necessary, however, that matter should remain the same, while forms enter into it, and that it should be impassive during their egress from it, in order that they may always enter into and depart from it. But that which enters, enters as an image, and not being itself real, enters into that which is void of truth and reality. Does it, therefore, truly enter? But how is it possible it should be truly received by that to which it is not in any respect lawful to participate of truth, in consequence of its being false? Hence, it falsely proceeds into that which is false, and becomes similar to an object in a mirror, as long as the object is beheld within it. For with respect to matter, if you take away [real] beings, none of those things which are now seen in the sensible region, would for the smallest space of time be apparent. The mirror, therefore, of which we have just spoken, is perceived by us; for it is itself a certain form. Matter, however, not being itself any form, is not itself seen; for otherwise, it would be requisite that it should be seen by itself prior to the forms that it apparently contains. But it suffers something of the same kind as the air when illuminated, which is then also invisible, because it could not be seen without being illuminated. Hence the objects which are seen in mirrors, are believed not to have an existence, or to have it in a less degree, because that which contains them is visible, and itself remains while the objects depart. But matter is not itself perceived, neither when it has, nor when it is without forms. If, however, it was possible for the objects from which mirrors are filled to remain without being seen, yet no one would doubt the reality of the objects which are seen in them. Hence, if there is something in mirrors, sensibles also will be in matter. But if there is nothing [in reality] in mirrors, but objects have only an apparent subsistence in them, in matter also it must be said, forms have a resemblance of subsistence. The cause of this appearance, likewise, must be ascribed to the hypostasis of beings, of which beings themselves always truly participate, but non-beings not truly; since it is not proper that they should subsist in such a manner as they would, if they had an existence, and being had not.

XIV. What then, matter not existing, would nothing have a subsistence? Nothing except beings;[1] just as neither would an image have any existence, unless there was a mirror, or something of this kind. For that which is naturally adapted to subsist in another thing, cannot exist when that thing is not. For this is the nature of an image to be in something different from itself. For if any thing departs from the producing causes of its existence, it may indeed subsist without being in another thing. But since [true] beings remain, if there is a representation of them in something else, it is necessary there should be another thing imparting a seat to that which does not truly accede.[2] And this by its presence and audacity, and

---

[1] The words οὐδὲν παρὰ τὰ ὄντα are omitted in the original; but from the version of Ficinus evidently ought to be inserted.

[2] Instead of παρέχει τῷ οὐκ ἐλθόντι in this place, it is necessary to read παρέχων τῷ ὄντως οὐκ ἐλθόντι.

as it may be said, mendicity and poverty, is as it were compelled to receive. It is however deceived, by not receiving [truly], in order that its poverty may also remain, and that it may always be a mendicant. For according to the fable, after it once had a subsistence, it began to beg; the fable indicating by this the nature of it, which consists in being destitute of good. It does not, however, beg to receive those things which the giver has to bestow, but is satisfied with whatever it may receive; so that this also indicates that what is apparent in it is different [from reality]. Its name, likewise, [which is Penia or Poverty] signifies that it is not filled. And the assertion that it was connected with Plenty,[1] does not signify that this connection was with [real] being, nor with satiety, but with a certain artificial thing, *i.e.* with the wisdom of a phantasm. For since it was not possible for that to be entirely without the participation of being, which is in any respect external to it; for it is the nature of being to produce beings; but that which is entirely non-being is unmingled with being;—this being the case, an admirable thing is effected, which participates, and yet in a certain respect does not participate of being, and which also in a certain respect possesses something from proximity to being; though by its own nature it is incapable of being as it were conglutinated with it. Hence it becomes defluous, as gliding away from a foreign nature which it has received, like echo from smooth and equable places, because it does not abide there, though it appears to be there, and to proceed from thence. If, however, matter so participated and received, as some one may think it does, that which proceeds into would be absorbed by it. But now it appears, that it is not absorbed, since matter

---

[1] For πόρρῳ here, it is necessary to read πόρῳ. See the speech of Diotima in the "Banquet of Plato."

remains the same, having received nothing, but impeding progression like some repercussive seat. It is also the receptacle of forms acceding to, and mingled in it; just as those who are desirous of enkindling a light from the sun, place some smooth substance opposite to it, which they also fill with water, in order that the flame being impeded by that which is inward, and of a contrary nature, may not pass through, but may stop externally. Matter, therefore, thus becomes the cause of generation, and the forms which consist in it, are constituted after this manner.

XV. In things, therefore, which collect fire from the sun about themselves, as they receive flame from a sensible fire, they become themselves objects of sense. Hence also they are apparent, because the objects are external, successive and proximate, touch each other, and have two extremities. But the productive principle in matter, has the external after a different manner. For difference of nature is sufficient, not being indigent of a twofold boundary; but being much more alienated than every boundary by a diversity[1] of essence which is destitute of all alliance, it possesses a power repugnant to mixture. And this is the cause of its remaining in itself, because neither that which enters into it enjoys it, nor does it enjoy that which enters; just as opinions and imaginations in the soul are not mingled with each other, but each again departs, as being alone that which it is, neither attracting, nor leaving any thing, because it was not mingled, and having the external, not because it is superjacent, and is visibly different from that in which it is, but because reason distinguishes the one from the other. Here, therefore, imagination is as it were an image, (the soul not being an image naturally,) though it appears to be the leader

---

[1] For ἑρώτητι here, it is necessary to read ἑτερότητι.

of many things, and to lead them where it pleases. The soul, nevertheless, uses the imagination as matter, or as that which is analogous to matter. The imagination, however, does not conceal the soul, since the soul by its energies frequently expels the phantasy; nor would it ever be able to conceal it, though it should be wholly diffused through it, though this by the imagination appears to be sometimes effected. For the soul contains in herself energies and reasons contrary to those of the phantasy by which the acceding [phantasms] are repelled. Matter, however, is much more imbecile than the soul, and contains nothing of beings whether true or false, which is properly its own. Neither has it any thing through which it may become apparent, being a solitude of all things. It is, however, the cause to other things of their apparent subsistence; but is not able to say even this of itself, I am here [though I am by no means visible]. And if at any time a certain profound reason discovers where it is concealed among beings, it exclaims that it is something deserted by all beings, and by things which appear to be posterior to beings, that it is likewise attracted to all things, and as it seems follows, and again does not follow them.

XVI. Moreover, a certain reason acceding and extending matter as far as it proceeds into it, causes it to be great, investing it from itself with greatness, which is not in matter. But matter does not through this become quantity; for if it did, that which is great in it would be magnitude. If, therefore, some one takes away this form, the subject no longer is, nor will appear to be great. But if that which is generated was great, man and horse, and together with horse the magnitude of horse which accedes, would depart on the departure of horse. If, however, it should be said, that horse is generated in a certain great bulk and of a certain extent, and that the magnitude remains, we reply that it is not the magnitude of the horse, but the magnitude of the bulk which there remains. Nevertheless, if this bulk is fire or earth, on the departure of fire or earth, the magnitude of fire or of earth will also depart. Matter, therefore, will neither enjoy figure, nor magnitude; for otherwise it would not be something else from fire, but remaining fire, it would not become fire. Hence, matter having now become as we see, as great in extent as the universe, if the heavens should cease to exist and all they contain, together with these, all magnitude would likewise depart from matter, and at the same time all other qualities, and matter would be left that which it was before, preserving no one of the things which had a prior subsistence about it. In the natures, however, which suffer by the presence of certain things, something is still left in the recipients, when those things depart; but this is no longer the case with natures that do not suffer. Thus the air which is surrounded with light, retains nothing of the light when it departs. But if some one should wonder how it is possible, that a thing should become great which does not possess magnitude; it may also be doubted how that can become hot which has not heat. For it is not the same thing in matter, to be matter and to be magnitude; since magnitude is immaterial, in the same manner as figure is immaterial. And if we preserve matter, we must assert that it is all things by participation. But magnitude is one of all things. In bodies, therefore, which are composites, there is magnitude together with other things, yet it is not indefinite; since in the definition of body magnitude also is included. But in matter, even indefinite magnitude is not included; for it is not body.

XVII. Neither, again, will matter be magnitude itself. For magnitude is form, but not the recipient of form; and magnitude subsists by itself. If matter, likewise, cannot adapt to itself the imitations of beings,[1] on this account also it is not magnitude. Since, however, that which is placed in intellect or in soul, wishes to be great, it imparts to those things which by proceeding as it were, endeavour to imitate it, by the desire of, or motion towards it, the ability of impressing the same passion in another thing. That which is great, therefore, running in the progression of the phantasy so as to cause the smallness of matter to run in conjunction with it, occasions matter also to appear great, though it is not filled by the co-extension. For this greatness of matter is falsely great, since by not having the power to be great, and being extended towards magnitude, it becomes amplified by the extension. For since all beings produce in other things, or in another thing the representation of themselves as in mirrors, each of the agents is in a similar manner[2] great; and the universe also is great in this way. The magnitude, therefore, of each productive principle, as of that of a horse or any thing else concurs with the particular thing to which the productive principle pertains. And every appearance, indeed, of things as in a mirror is great in consequence of being illuminated by greatness itself. Each portion of them, likewise, becomes something great, and all things at once present themselves to the view from every form of which magnitude is one. From each form, also, there is, as it were, an extension to every thing and to all things, and this is to be compelled in form. Power, too, produces as much in bulk as bulk is capable of receiving; so that what is [in reality] nothing, appears to be all things. Hence colour which proceeds from what is not colour, and the quality in sensibles which is derived from what is not quality, have an equivocal appellation from their producing

---

[1] For αὐτῶν here, it is necessary to read ὄντων.
[2] Instead of ὡς αὐτὸ here, it is necessary to read ὡσαύτως.

causes. Magnitude, also, proceeds from that which is not magnitude, or from that which is homonymously magnitude; these[1] being surveyed as having a subsistence between matter itself, and form itself. And they become apparent, indeed, because they are derived from form themselves. They have, however, a false subsistence, because that in which they are apparent is not [truly]. But each of them becomes extended into magnitude, being attracted by the power of the things which are seen in matter, and which make for themselves a place. There is, however, an attraction to all things, yet not by violence, because the universe is matter. But each thing attracts according to the power which it possesses; and derives from the representation of magnitude itself, the ability of making matter so great as it appears to be. Hence the magnitude which is here is the phantasm of it which is apparent. Matter, however, being compelled to concur with this attraction, at once imparts itself wholly and every where; for it is the matter of the universe, and not some particular matter. But that which is not of itself some particular thing, may on account of something else become contrary to what it was, and having become contrary, no longer is [what is was]; since if it were, it would cease to be changed.

XVIII. If some one, therefore, possessing an intellectual conception of magnitude, should have this conception attended with a power not only of subsisting in itself, but also of proceeding as it were externally, and the power should receive a nature not existing in the intellectual perceiver, nor having a certain form, nor a certain vestige of magnitude or of any other form, what would he produce through this power? Not a horse, or an ox. For other powers would produce these. Or shall we say, that since

---

[1] viz. Colour, quality, and magnitude.

this power proceeds from a great father, nothing else [besides matter] is able to receive this magnitude, and that its possession of it will only be imaginary, and not real. Hence, to that which does not so obtain magnitude, as to be in its own nature the great itself, it remains for it to be apparently only as much as possible great. But this is not to be deficient, and not to proceed to many things in many places; but to possess in itself kindred parts, and not to leave any thing destitute of itself. For it is not possible that in a small bulk, there should still be an equal image of magnitude, since it is an image of greatness; but so far as it aspires through its hope, it accedes as far as it is possible for it to accede, and running in conjunction with that which is not able to leave it, it causes that to be great which is not great, yet not so as to appear to be the magnitude which is seen in bulk. At the same time, however, matter preserves its own nature, using this magnitude as a ¦vestment, through which it ran together with it, when magnitude running became its leader. But if at any time it should divest itself of magnitude, it would again remain the same as it was before in itself; or would be as great as form when present caused it to be. And soul, indeed, possessing the forms of beings, since she is also herself a form, contains all things at once. Since, likewise, each form is at once wholly contained in her, hence perceiving the forms of sensibles as it were converted and acceding to her, she cannot endure to receive them with multitude, but sees them divested of bulk. For she cannot become any thing else than what she is.

Matter, however, having nothing repercussive; for it has no energy; but being a shadow, stays to suffer whatever the producing cause may effect in it. That also which proceeds from the reason that is in soul, has now a vestige of the thing which is about to be effected; just as in the iconic nature of the phantasy, reason which is moved, or the motion from reason, is a division into parts; since if it was one and the same, it would not be moved, but be permanent. Matter, however, is not able to introduce at once all things into itself, for if it were able, it would be some one of all things. But since it is necessary that it should receive all things, yet not impartibly, it is requisite that existing as the place of all things, it should proceed to all things, meet with them, and be sufficient for every interval, because it is not itself comprehended by interval, but is exposed to the reception of it. How does it happen, therefore, that one thing entering into matter, does not impede other things? It is because all things cannot enter together at the same time; for if they could, there would not be anything which is first. But if there is, it is the form of the universe; so that all things are indeed simultaneous, but each has a partial existence. For the matter of the animal nature is distributed in conjunction with the division of the animal into parts. For if this were not the case, nothing would have been produced besides reason.

XIX. The things, therefore, which enter into matter as a mother, neither injure it, nor benefit it. For the impulses of these do not pertain to matter, but to each other, because the powers of these also pertain to contraries, but not to subjects, unless the subjects are considered in conjunction with the impulses. For heat destroys cold, and the black the white; or if they are mingled together, another quality is produced from the mixture. Hence, things which are mingled suffer; but with them, to suffer, is not to be that which they were before. In animated natures, also, the passions indeed, are about the bodies, the change in quality taking place according to the inherent qualities and powers. But when their state of existence is dissolved, or congregated, or transposed preternaturally, then, the passions indeed are in the bodies, but knowledge is in the souls that perceive the more vehement passions. If, however, they do not perceive them, they have no knowledge of them, but matter still remains. For matter suffers nothing, when cold departs, and heat accedes; since neither of these is either friendly or foreign to it. Hence, the appellations of a receptacle and nurse are more appropriate to it [than any other names]. But why is it called a mother? For it does not generate. Those, however, appear to have denominated it a mother, who think that a mother has the relation of matter towards her offspring, as alone receiving, but imparting nothing to the things begotten; since whatever of body there is in the offspring, is derived from the nutriment. But if the mother imparts any thing to her progeny, it is not so far as she has the relation of matter, but because she is also form. For form alone is prolific, but the other nature is barren. *Whence, also, I think the ancient wise men obscurely signifying this in their mysteries, represent the ancient Hermes always possessing the organ of generation erect, thus manifesting that it is intelligible reason which generates in the sensible universe. But they indicated the unprolific nature of matter which always remains the same, by the barren substances which were placed about it.* For they introduce the mother of all things, which they thus proclaim, receiving the principle according to the subject, and they give her this appellation in order to render their meaning manifest, wishing to indicate to those who are desirous of more accurately comprehending the nature of matter, and who do not investigate it superficially, that it is not entirely similar to a mother. By this, indeed, they demonstrate remotely, but at the same time as much as they are able, that matter is unprolific, and not perfectly feminine; but that it is of a female nature so far as it receives, but not so far as pertains to a generative power. For that which has proceeded into matter, is neither feminine, nor able to generate, but is separated from all generative power, which is alone inherent in that which continues to be of a masculine nature.

VI.
ON ETERNITY AND TIME.
III. vii.

I. WITH respect to eternity and time, we say that each of these is different from the other, and that one of them indeed is conversant with a perpetual nature, but the other about that which is generated. We also think that we have a certain clear perception of these in our souls spontaneously, and, as it were, from the more collected projections of intellectual conception; always and every where calling these by the same appellations. When, however, we endeavour to accede to the inspection of these, and to approach as it were nearer to them, again we are involved in doubt, admitting some of the decisions of the ancients about these, and rejecting others, and perhaps receiving differently the same decisions. Resting also in these, and thinking it sufficient if when interrogated we are able to relate the opinion of the ancients concerning time and eternity, we are liberated from any farther investigation about them. It is necessary, therefore, to think that some of the ancient and blessed philosophers have discovered the truth; but it is fit to consider who those are that have obtained it, and after what manner we also may acquire the same knowledge on these subjects. In the first place, however, it is requisite to investigate what those conceive eternity to be, who admit that it is different from time.

For that which is established as the paradigm being known, that also which is the image of it, and which they say is time, will perhaps become manifest. But if some one, prior to the survey of eternity, should imagine what time is, it will happen to him, procceding from hence thither by reminiscence, that he will behold the nature to which time is assimilated, if the latter has a similitude to the former.

What, therefore, is it requisite we should assert eternity to be? Shall we say it is the intelligible essence itself, just as if some one should say that time is the whole heaven and the world? For some are said to have had this opinion concerning time. For since we imagine and conceive eternity to be something more venerable, and an intelligible nature is also most venerable, we are unable to say which is the most venerable of the two; and since also, that which is beyond these is not to be predicated in the same way, some one may be induced to consider eternity and an intelligible essence as the same. For again, both the intelligible world and eternity comprehend in themselves the same things. When, however, we say that the one is in the other, we place intelligibles in eternity; and when we predicate the eternal of intelligibles, as when Plato in the "Timæus" says, "if the nature of the paradigm is eternal," we then assert that the eternal is different from the intelligible. Nevertheless, we say that it either exists about, or in, or is present with an intelligible essence. That each of them, however, is venerable, does not manifest a sameness of nature; for perhaps the venerableness of the one is derived from the other. With respect to comprehension also, that of the intelligible is as of parts, but eternity comprehends the whole at once not as a part, but because all such things as are eternal subsist according to it. Shall we, therefore, say that eternity exists according to the permanency which is in intelligibles;

just as here, time is said to exist according to motion? It may, however, be very properly investigated, whether eternity is the same with permanency, or whether it is not simply the same, but is the same with the permanency which is about essence. For if it is the same with permanency [simply considered] in the first place, we cannot say that permanency is eternal, as neither do we say that eternity is eternal. For the eternal is that which participates of eternity. And in the next place, how is motion eternal? For thus it will be stable. Farther still, how does the conception of permanency contain in itself *the ever*? I do not mean *the ever* which is in time, but such as we intellectually perceive when we speak of the eternal. But if it contains *the ever* in the stability of essence, again, we shall separate the other genera of being from eternity. Besides, it is not only necessary to conceive eternity as subsisting in permanency, but also as subsisting in one. And in the next place, we must admit that eternity is without interval, in order that it may not be the same with time. Permanency, however, so far as it is permanency, neither contains in itself the conception of unity, nor of that which is without interval. But we predicate of eternity that it abides in one. Hence, it will participate of permanency, but will not be permanency itself.

II. What, therefore, will that be according to which we say, the whole world which is there is eternal and perpetual? And what is perpetuity? Whether it is the same with eternity, or eternity subsists according to perpetuity. Shall we say, therefore, that it is necessary to conceive of eternity as one certain thing, but a certain intelligence or nature collected together from many things, whether it be something consequent to the natures in the intelligible world, or existing together with, or perceived in them, but which is able to effect and is many things. Indeed, he who surveys an abundant power collected into one, according to this particular thing which is as it were a subject, he denominates it essence; afterwards, so far as he beholds life in it, he denominates it motion; and in the next place, he calls it permanency, so far as it entirely possesses an invariable sameness of subsistence. And he denominates it different and the same, so far as all these are at once one. Thus, therefore, composing these, so as to be at once one life alone, contracting in them difference, and beholding an unceasing sameness of energy, and which never passes from one intelligence or life to another, but always possesses the invariable, and is without interval;—beholding all these, he will behold eternity. For he will perceive life abiding in sameness, and always possessing everything present, and not at one time this, and afterwards another thing, but containing all things at once, and not now some things, and again others. For it is an impartible end; just as in a point where all things subsist at once, and have not yet proceeded into a [linear] flux. It likewise abides in the same, *i.e.* in itself, and does not suffer any change. But it is always in the present, because nothing of it is past, nor again will be in future, but this very thing which it is, it always is. Hence, eternity is not a subject, but that which as it were shines forth from a subject, according to sameness itself, which it announces not concerning the future, but that which is now present, indicating that it subsists in this manner, and in no other. For what can afterwards happen to this, which it now is not? Nor again, will it be in futurity what it is not at present. For there is not any thing from which it can arrive at the present time. For it is not another thing, but this. Nor will it be this in future, which it does not now possess from necessity; nor does it possess about itself that which was. For what is there which was present with it and is past? Nor does that which will be, belong to it. For what is there which will happen to it? It remains, therefore, that in *to be*, it is that which it is. Hence, that which neither was, nor will be, but alone is, stably possessing its being, in consequence of not changing into will be, nor having been changed from the past, is eternity. The life, therefore, which is about being, and which in existence or *to be*, is at once total and full, and every where without interval, is the eternity which we investigate.

III. Nor must we think that this [eternity] happens externally to that nature [viz. to being itself], but that it is in it, and from it, and subsists together with it. For it is seen to be profoundly inherent in it. For perceiving all such other things as we say are there, to be inherent, we assert that all of them are from, and subsist together with essence. For it is necessary that things which have a primary subsistence, should exist together with first essences, and should be contained in them; since the beautiful also is in and from them, and truth also is inherent in them. And in a certain degree, indeed, the whole itself is as it were in a part, and the things which are there are as parts in a whole, as if in reality this were an *all* not collected from parts, but itself generating parts, in order that through this it may be truly all. The truth also which is there, is not a concord with something else that is intelligible, but of each thing itself of which it is the truth. It is necessary, therefore, that the whole of this which is true, if it is truly all, should not only be every thing so far as it is all things, but likewise that the all should subsist in such a way, as not to be in any thing deficient. But if this be the case, nothing *will* accede to it. For if something *will be* added to it, it was prior to the accession of this deficient. Hence, prior to this it was not every thing. But what can happen to it preternaturally? For it suffers nothing. If, therefore, nothing can accede to it, it neither is about to be, nor will be, nor was. If, indeed, you take away from generated natures, the *it will be*, since they subsist in perpetual acquisition, non-existence is immediately present with them. But to things which are not such as these, if you add the *it will be*, a departure from the seat of existence is the consequence of such an addition. For it is evident that existence is not connascent with them, if they are in any respect indebted to futurity for their subsistence. For in generated natures, indeed, essence is seen to be an extension from the beginning of generation, to the extremity of the time in which they no longer exist. This it is, therefore, for them to be; and if any one should deprive them of this extension of being, their life would be diminished. So that it is necessary that the existence of the universe also, should be an extension of this kind. Hence, it hastens to be in futurity, and is not willing to stop, since it attracts existence to itself, in performing another and another thing, and is moved in a circle through a certain desire of essence. So that we have found what existence is in such natures as these, and also what the cause is of a motion which thus hastens to be perpetually in the future periods of time. In first and blessed natures, however, there is not any desire of the future; for they are now the whole, and whatever of life they ought to possess, they wholly possess, so that they do not seek after any thing, because there is not any thing which can be added to them in futurity. Hence, neither does that happen to them in which there is the future. The all-perfect and total essence therefore of being, is not only total in its parts, but is not in any thing deficient, and is that to which nothing pertaining to non-being can happen; for it is not only necessary that all beings should be present with *the all*, and *the whole*, but likewise that nothing should be added to it of that which sometimes is not. Hence this disposition and nature of the all-perfect essence of being, will be eternity. For eternity is denominated from that which always is.

IV. He, however, will know that eternity[1] thus subsists, who by the projecting[2] energies of intellect is able to speak concerning it: or rather, he who sees it to be a thing of such a kind, that nothing in short has ever been generated about it; for otherwise it would not be perpetual being, or would not always be a certain total being. Is it therefore now perpetual? It is not, unless a nature of such a kind is inherent in it, as to procure credibility concerning it, that it thus subsists, and no longer in any other way. So that if again you survey it by the projecting energies of intellect, you will find that it is such a thing as this. What then, if some one should never depart from the contemplation of it, but should incessantly persevere in admiring its nature, and should be able to do this through the possession of an unwearied nature, such a one perhaps running to eternity, would there stop, and never decline from it, in order that he might become similar to it, and eternal, surveying eternity and the eternal by that which is eternal in himself. If, therefore, that which thus subsists is eternal, and always being, which does not decline in any respect to another nature, but the life which it possesses is now all, neither having received, nor receiving, nor being about to receive any thing in future;—that which thus subsists, will indeed be perpetual. And perpetuity is such a collocation as this of a subject, subsisting from it, and being inherent in it. But eternity is the subject in conjunction with a collocation of this kind presenting itself to the view. Hence eternity is venerable, and as our intellectual conception of it says, is the same with deity. But it says that it is the same with that God [whom we

[1] Instead of τωι here, it appears to me to be necessary to read τω αἰῶνι.
[2] The visive energies of intellect are thus denominated, because such an energy is an immediate darting forth as it were to the object of its intuition.

call by the appellation of being and life.] And eternity may be properly denominated a God unfolding himself into light, and shining forth, such as he essentially is, viz. as immutable and the same, and thus firmly established in life. It ought not, however, to be considered as wonderful, if we say that it consists of many things. For every thing in the intelligible world is many, on account of the infinite power which it possesses; since the infinite receives its appellation from a never-failing essence. And this properly, because nothing pertaining to it is consumed. Hence, if some one should thus denominate eternity, calling it life which is now infinite, because it is all, and nothing of which is consumed, because nothing pertaining to it is either past or future, since otherwise it would not be all things at once;—if some one should thus denominate it, he will be near to the true definition [1] of it. For what is afterwards added, viz. that it is all things at once, and that nothing of it is consumed, will be an exposition of the assertion, that it is now infinite life.

V. Because, however, such a nature as this, thus all-beautiful and perpetual, subsists about *the one*, proceeding from and with it, and in no respect departing from it, but always abides about and in *the one*, and lives according to it, hence I think it is beautifully and with a profundity of decision, said by Plato, that "eternity abides in one," [2] that he might not only lead it to *the one* which is in itself, but that he might also in a similar manner lead the life of being about *the one*. This, therefore, is that which we in-

[1] This definition of eternity is justly admired by Proclus in his 3rd book "On the Theology of Plato," of which see my translation. Boetius, likewise, as I have elsewhere observed, has adopted this definition in lib. 5, "De Consol. Philosoph."

[2] Plato, however, does not by *the one* in this place, mean the ineffable principle of things, but the one of being, or the summit of the intelligible order, as is shown by Proclus in the above mentioned work.

vestigate, and that which thus abides is eternity. For this very thing, and which thus abides, which is the energy of a life abiding from itself, subsisting with and in *the one*, and which neither in existing nor living is false and fictitious, will certainly be eternity. For to be truly, is never not to be, nor to be otherwise. But the former of these is to be invariably the same; and the latter is to be without diversity. Hence it has not in any respect, another and another. You must not, therefore, conceive it to have interval, nor evolve, nor extend it. Neither, therefore, must you admit that there is any thing of prior and posterior in it. Hence, if there is neither prior nor posterior about it, but the *is*, is the truest of all the things about it, and is itself, and this in such a way as to be essence and life;—if this be the case, again that which we call eternity will present itself to our view. But when we say that it is always, and that it is not at one time being, and at another time non-being, it is requisite to think that we thus speak for the sake of perspicuity; since the term always, is perhaps not properly employed, but is assumed for the purpose of manifesting its incorruptible [1] nature. And farther still, it signifies that it never fails. Perhaps, however, it would be better to call it only being. But though being is a name sufficient to essence, yet since some are of opinion that generation also is essence, it is requisite for the sake of discipline to add the term *always*. For one thing is not being, but another perpetual being; as neither is a philosopher one thing, but a true philosopher another. Because, however, some persons are only philo-

---

[1] After τοῦ ἀφθάρτου in the Greek, the words πλανῷ ἂν τὴν ψυχὴν, εἰς ἔκβασιν τοῦ πλείονος follow, which are to me unintelligible. Something, I conceive, is omitted; but I am not able to conjecture what the omission is. The version of these words by Ficinus is certainly nonsense; for it is, "animum potest reddere vagabundum per quendam in plura exitum et proventum."

sophers in appearance, the addition of a true philosopher became necessary. Thus, likewise, *the always* was added to being, and being to *the always*. So that it was called *aion;* on which account *the always* was assumed, in order that the conjunction of *being* with *the always*, might indicate that which is truly being. *The always*, likewise, must be contracted into a power devoid of interval, and which besides what it now possesses, is not in want of any thing. But it possesses every thing. Hence it is every thing and being, and is not indigent of any thing. Nor is a nature of this kind, full indeed in one respect, but deficient in another. For that which exists in time, though it may seem to be as perfect as is sufficient to body, yet it is perfect through soul, and is in want of something future, because it is deficient in time of which it is indigent; so that it exists together with time, if it is present with it, and being imperfect, runs in conjunction with it. On this account, therefore, it is equivocally said to be a perfect being. That, however, which is a thing of such a kind, as neither to be in want of futurity, nor to be measured by some other time, nor to be in futurity infinite, and this infinitely, but now possesses that which it ought to be;—this is that after which our intellectual conception aspires; the being of which is not derived from a certain quantity of extension, but is prior to all quantity. For it is fit, since it is not of a definite quantity, that it should not at all come into contact with quantity, lest the life of it being divided, should lose its pure impartibility; but that it should be both in life and essence impartible. When, however, it is said in the "Timæus" that the demiurgus *was* good, this must be referred to the conception of the universe, signifying that what is beyond the universe, does not originate from a certain time; so that neither is the world allotted a certain temporal beginning, since the cause of its existence is the source of priority. At the same time, however, Plato thus speaking for the sake of perspicuity, blames afterwards this expression *was good*, as not altogether rightly employed in things which are allotted what is called and is intellectually conceived to be, an eternal subsistence.

VI. Do we, therefore, bear witness to the things of which we now speak, as to things foreign from our nature? But how is this possible? For how can intellectual perception be effected, except by contact? And how can we come into contact with things that are foreign to us? It is necessary, therefore, that we also should participate of eternity. Since, however, we exist in time, how is this possible? But we shall know what it is to be in time, and what it is to be in eternity, when we have discovered what time is. We must, therefore, descend from eternity to time, and the investigation of time. For there, indeed, the progression was to that which is above, but we must now speak descending, yet not profoundly, but our descent must be such as that of time. If, indeed, nothing had been said concerning time by ancient and blessed men, it would be necessary that connecting from the beginning what follows with eternity, we should endeavour to speak what appears to us to be the truth on this subject, and to adapt our opinion to the conception of it which we possess. Now, however, it is necessary first to assume those assertions which especially deserve attention, and to consider if what we say is concordant with some one of them. But perhaps the assertions concerning time, ought in the first place to receive a threefold division. For time may be said to be either motion, or that which is moved, or something pertaining to motion. For to say that it is either permanency, or that which is stable, or something pertaining to permanency, will be perfectly remote from the conception of time, since it is in no respect the same [and therefore, can never accord with that which is stable]. Of those, however, who say that time is motion, some indeed assert that it is every motion; but others, that it is the motion of the universe. But those who say it is that which is moved, assert it to be the sphere of the universe. And of those who say it is something pertaining to motion, or the interval of motion; some assert that it is the measure of motion, but others that it is an attendant on it, and either on every motion, or on that which is arranged.[1]

VII. It is not, indeed, possible, that time should be motion, neither if all motions are assumed, and one as it were is produced from all of them, nor if that motion is assumed which is orderly. For each of these motions is in time. If, however, some one should say that motion is not in time, much less will motion be time; since that in which motion is, is one thing, and motion itself another[2] thing. Since, however, there are beside these other assertions, it may be sufficient to observe, that motion may indeed cease and be interrupted, but time cannot. But if some one should say that the motion of the universe is not interrupted, yet this motion, if it is admitted that the circulation [of the world] is in a certain time, will itself be carried round to the same point from whence it began; and not to

[1] Archytas the Pythagorean defined time to be the universal interval of the nature of the universe, in consequence of surveying the continuity in the productive principles of that nature, and their departure into divison. Others still more ancient defined time to be, as the name manifests, *a certain dance of intellect;* but others defined it to be the periods of soul; others, the natural receptacle of these periods; and others, orderly circulations; all which (says Iamblichus, from whom this information is derived) the Pythagoric sect comprehends. Both Archytas also and Aristotle appear to have admitted time to be *a continued and indivisible flux of nows.* See a treasure of the conceptions of the ancients on this subject, in the Additional Notes to my translation of Aristotle's "Physics."

[2] For ἀλλ' οὐ here, it is necessary to read ἄλλου.

that point in which the half of it only is accomplished. And this motion, indeed, will be the half, but the other will be double, each being the motion of the universe, both that which proceeds from the same to the same, and that which arrives only at the half. The assertion, also, that the motion of the outermost sphere is most vehement and rapid, bears witness to what we say; so that the motion of it is one thing, and time another. For that motion is the most rapid of all, which in the least time passes through the greatest interval. But other motions are slower, which are performed in a longer time, and pass through a part only of the same space. If, therefore, time is not the motion of the outermost sphere, much less will it be that sphere itself, which in consequence of being moved is conceived to be time. Is, therefore, time something belonging to motion? If indeed it is interval, in the first place, there is not the same interval of every motion, nor of uniform motion. For the motion which is in place is swifter and slower, and both the intervals may be measured by another third interval, which may with greater rectitude be dominated time. But of which of these motions will time be the interval? Or rather, will it be the interval of any one of them, since they are infinite? And if time is the interval of orderly motion, it is not the interval of every motion, nor of every motion of this kind. For these are many. So that there will also be at once many times. But if time is the interval of the universe, if indeed it is the interval in motion itself, what else will it be than motion, viz. so much; and this quantity of motion will either be measured by place, because the place which it passes through is so much in quantity, and the interval will be this. This, however, is not time, but place. Or motion by its continuity, and from not immediately ceasing, but being always assumed, possesses interval. But this will be the multitude of motion. And if some one looking to motion should assert that it is much, just as if it should be said that heat is much, neither will time here also present itself to our view, nor become obvious; but motion again and again will occur, like water repeatedly flowing, and also the interval which is beheld in it. The again and again also will be number, as the duad or the triad; but the interval will belong to bulk. Thus, therefore, the multitude of motion will be as the decad, or as the interval which is beheld as it were in the bulk of motion, which is not attended with a conception of time. But this quantity of motion will be generated in time; for otherwise, time will not be every where, but will be in motion as in a subject. It will, likewise, again happen that time will be said to be motion. For the interval is not external to motion, but is motion not at once collected together. But if it is not at once collected, if an at-once-collected subsistence is in time, in what respect does that which is not at-once-collected differ from that which is? Shall we say that they differ in time; so that the separating motion, and the interval of it, are not time itself, but subsist in time? If, however, some one should say, that the interval of motion is time, by the interval not meaning the peculiarity of motion, but that with which motion has an extension, as if running together with it, yet what this is, is not unfolded. For it is evident that time is that in which the motion was generated. This, therefore, is that which was investigated from the first, viz. what that existing thing is which is time; since this is just as if some one being asked what time is, should say that the interval of motion is in time. What, therefore, is this interval, which he calls time, who supposes it to be external to the proper interval of motion? For again, he who places temporal interval in motion itself, will be dubious where he should place the interval of rest. For as much as a certain thing is moved, so much also will something else have been quiescent. And you may say that the time of each is the same, though its relation to the one, is different from its relation to the other. What therefore is this interval, and what nature does it possess? For it is not possible that it should be local since this has an external subsistence.

VIII. In the next place, it must be considered how time is the number or measure of motion; for it is better to assert this of it, on account of its continuity. In the first place, therefore, here also it may be doubted, whether it is similarly the number or measure of every motion, in the same manner as it was dubious respecting the interval of motion. For how can any one numerate inordinate and anomalous motion, or what number or measure will there be of it, or according to what will the measure subsist? But if he numerates and measures with the same thing, both irregular and regular motion, whether swift or slow, the number and the measure will be a thing of such a kind, as if it were the decad, measuring both horses and oxen, or as if the same thing were the measure both of moist and dry substances. If, therefore, time is a measure of this kind, it has indeed been shown what the things are of which time is the measure, viz. that it is the measure of motions, but it has not yet been shown what time is. If, however, in the same manner as the decad when assumed without horses, may be understood as number, and a measure is a measure possessing a certain proper nature, though it should not yet measure any thing, thus also it is necessary time should subsist, being a measure;—if therefore time is such a thing in itself as number, in what will it differ from this number which subsists according to the decad, or from any other monadic number? But if it is a continued measure, being a certain quantity, it will be such a measure as a certain cubital magnitude. It will, therefore, be magnitude, such as a line accompanied with motion. But

K

how, since it also runs, can it measure that with which it runs in conjunction? For why should one measure rather than the other? And it is better and more probable to admit this not in every motion, but in that with which it concurs. This, however, ought to be continuous, so far as the concurrent motion is successive. But that which measures ought not to be considered as subsisting externally, nor as separate, but as at once measured motion. And what will that be which measures? Will the motion indeed be measured, but the magnitude be that which measures? And which of these will time be? Will it be the measured motion, or the magnitude which measures? For time will either be the motion which is measured by magnitude, or magnitude which measures, or that which uses magnitude, as a cubit for the purpose of measuring the quantity of the motion. In all these, however, it is more probable as we have said to suppose that the motion is equable. For without equability, and besides this, without one motion of the universe, the doubt will be greater than that which results from admitting that time is in some way or other the measure of motion. But if time is measured motion, and is measured by quantity, then just as if it were necessary that motion should be measured, it would not be requisite that it should be measured by itself, but by something else, thus also it is necessary, if motion has another measure besides itself, and on this account we are in want of a continuous measure, for the purpose of measuring it, that magnitude itself should have a measure, in order that the motion may be as much in quantity as its measure. And thus time will be the number of the magnitude attending the motion, and not the magnitude which runs in conjunction with the motion.

It is necessary, however, to doubt what this number is, whether it is monadic, and how it measures? For though some one should discover how it measures, yet he would not find time measuring, but a certain quantity of time. This, however, is not the same with time [simply considered]. For it is one thing to speak of time, and another, of so much time. For prior to the so much, it is necessary to say what that is which is so much. Is time, therefore, the number which measures motion externally? Such as the decad in horses, and not that which is assumed together with horses. What this number, therefore, is, has not been shown, which prior to measuring, is what it is, in the same manner as the decad. Shall we say it is that number which measures by running according to the prior and posterior of motion?[1] But it is not yet manifest what this number is which measures according to prior and posterior. That, however, which measures according to prior and posterior, whether by a point, or by any thing else, entirely measures according to time. This number,[2] therefore, which measures motion by prior and posterior, will be successive to, and in contact with time, in order that it may measure it. For prior and posterior, must either be assumed locally, as the beginning [and end] of a stadium, or temporally. For in short, with respect to prior and posterior, the former indeed is time ending in *the now;* but the latter is time beginning from *the now*. Time, therefore, is different from the number which measures motion according to prior and posterior, not only motion of any kind, but also that

---

[1] Time is defined by Aristotle, to be *the number of motion according to prior and posterior*, which accords with Plato's definition of it in the "Timæus," viz. *that it is an eternal image flowing according to number.* For this shows that time subsists according to number which has the relation of an image, and exists according to the order of motion, *i.e.* according to prior and posterior. In short, time is properly the measure of motion according to the flux of being, which is the peculiarity of *generation*, or *becoming to be.*

[2] For χρόνος here, it is necessary to read ἀριθμός.

which is orderly. In the next place, why when number is adjoined, whether according to the measured, or the measuring, (for the same number may be both that which measures, and is measured)—why therefore when number is added, will there be time; but motion existing, and prior and posterior entirely subsisting about it, there will not be time? Just as if some one should say that magnitude is not as great as it is, unless some one apprehends what the quantity of it is. Since time, however, is, and is said to be infinite, how will there be number about it, unless a part of it being selected is measured, in which case it will happen that it exists prior to its being measured. But why will not time be prior to the existence of soul that measures it? Unless it should be said that the generation of it is effected by soul; since it is by no means necessary that time should exist because it is measured by soul. For it would exist as much as it is in quantity, though no one should measure it. And if some one should say that it is soul which uses magnitude for the purpose of measuring time, what will this have to do with the conception of time?

IX. But to say that time is an appendix of motion, is not to teach what time is, nor ought this to be said before it is shown what the appendix is. For perhaps it may be time. With respect to this appendix, however, it must be considered, whether it has a posterior, or simultaneous, or prior subsistence; if there is an appendix of this kind. For in whatever manner it may be spoken of, it is spoken of in time. Hence, if this is time, it will follow that time is the appendix of motion in time. Since, however, we do not investigate what time is not, but what it is, and much has been said on this subject by many prior to us, according to each position, he who discusses these would rather compose a history [than discover the nature of time]. To which may be added, that we have occasionally said something concerning these different positions. Some things also may be opposed from what has been already said, to him who asserts that time is the measure of the universe, and likewise such other things as have just now been asserted respecting the measure of motion. For separate from inequality, all the other particulars may be adduced, which are adapted to their positions. It follows, therefore, that we should now show what it is necessary to think time is.

X. Again, therefore, it is requisite that we should betake ourselves to that condition of being which we have said is in eternity; a condition which is immutable, and at once total, a life now infinite and perfectly inflexible, and abiding in one, and directed to *the one*. But time was not yet, or at least was not in those natures; but was about to be generated [1] by the reason and nature of that which is posterior. Intelligibles, therefore, quietly energizing in themselves, he who desires to know how time first fell, will not perhaps call upon the Muses who did not then exist, to tell him. Perhaps, however, he will, since the Muses also then had a being.[2] Perhaps, too, he will find time itself generated, so far as it is generated and unfolded into light. But he will speak about it as follows:

Before this priority originated, and was indigent of the posterior, the former was quiescent together with the latter in being, time not yet existing; but itself also quietly abiding [*i.e.* subsisting casually] in real being. A certain

---

[1] Time, as well as the world, is said to have been generated, not because it once was not, for it always existed, but because it depends for its subsistence on causes naturally prior to itself.

[2] The Muses, considered according to their subsistence in Apollo, belong to the intellectual order, and are therefore superior to time. But if time is supposed to have had a beginning, then the Muses, according to their mundane subsistence, had no existence prior to the generation of time. To say, therefore, that the Muses did not once exist, is equivalent to the assertion that the intellectual is prior to the mundane order of them, according to nature, order, dignity, and causality.

nature, however, much conversant with action, wishing to govern, and possess authority from itself, and chusing to explore more of the present, was itself indeed moved, and together with it likewise time, always tending to hereafter and the posterior, and not to the same, but to another, and again another existence. But we from this motion producing a certain length of progression, conceive time to be the image of eternity. For since there was a certain unquiet power of the soul, wishing always to transfer what it there saw to something else, it was not willing that an at-once-collected all should be present with it. But as reason [*i.e.* a productive principle] evolving itself from a quiet seed, produces as it fancies an abundant progression, abolishing the abundant by division, and instead of the one subsisting in itself, consuming the one which is not in itself, and thus proceeds into a more imbecile length; in a similar manner, this nature of soul, producing the sensible through the imitation of the intelligible world, and being moved not with the motion which is there, but with a motion resembling it, and wishing to be its image, in the first place indeed, renders itself temporal, producing this instead of eternity. In the next place, it causes that which is generated to be subservient to time, making the whole of it to be in time, and comprehending all the progressions of it in time. For the world is moved in the nature of soul; since there is not any other place of this universe than soul, and in the time of soul it is moved. For soul exhibiting its energy successively, generates together with its energy that which is successive, and proceeds in conjunction with another reasoning process after that energy, which was not before; since, neither was the discursive energy of reason effective, nor the present life of soul similar to that which preceded it. Hence, at the same time, there is another life, and this other life will have another time. Distance of life, therefore [or the interval between one life and another], will be attended with time. The perpetual extension of life also to the anterior part, will have perpetual time: and the past life will be accompanied with past time. If, therefore, some one should say that time is the energy [1] of soul, proceeding in a transitive motion from one life to another, will he not appear to say something to the purpose? [2] For if eternity is life consisting in permanency, and in an invariable sameness of subsistence, and which is now infinite, but it is necessary that time should be the image of eternity, just as this universe is the image of the intelligible world;—if this be the case, instead of the life which is there, it is necessary there should be another life of the discursive power of the mundane soul, homonymous as it were to the life of eternity; and instead of intellectual motion, that there should be the motion of a certain part of the soul. It is also necessary, that instead of an invariable sameness and permanency of subsistence, there should be that which does not abide in the same, but always has another and another energy. Likewise, that instead of an essence which is without interval and one, there should be an image of *the one*, and which possesses unity in continuity of succession. That instead of that which is now infinite, and a whole, there should be that which proceeds ad

---

[1] The word ἐνέργεια is omitted in the original.

[2] Time, however, according to Proclus, is a medium between that which is *alone* the cause of motion, as soul, and that which is *alone* immoveable, as intellect. Hence time is truly, so far as it is considered in itself, immoveable, but so far as it is in its participants, it is moveable, and subsists together with them, unfolding itself into them. He adds, *hence it is a certain proceeding intellect*, established indeed in eternity, but proceeding and abundantly flowing into the things which are guarded by it. This definition of time by Proclus, appears to me to be uncommonly beautiful and accurate. See the whole of the passage from which it is taken, in the Additional Notes to my translation of the "Timæus" of Plato.

infinitum, according to what is perpetually successive. And that instead of an at-once-collected whole, there should be that which is a whole according to parts, and is always about to be a whole. For thus it will imitate that which is now wholly what it is, and which is at-once-collected, and infinite, if it wishes its being to consist in perpetual acquisition; since it will thus also imitate the being of eternity. It is necessary, however, not to assume time externally to soul, as neither is eternity in the intelligible world external to being. Nor again, must it be considered as any thing consecutive, or posterior to soul, as neither is eternity to being. But it must be beheld within, and subsisting together with soul, in the same manner as eternity with being.

XI. Here, however, it is necessary to understand, that this is the nature of time, viz. that it is the length of such a life as we have before mentioned, proceeding in equable and similar mutations, which themselves proceed in a silent course; this length also possessing a continuity of energy. If, therefore, we again in words make this power to revert, and the life of it to cease which it now possesses, and which is unceasing, and will never end, because it is the energy of a certain ever-existing soul, not directed to itself, nor in itself, but employed in producing and generating;—if, therefore, we suppose this power no longer energizing, but ceasing from this energy, and also this part of the soul converted to real being and eternity, and abiding in quiet, what will there any further be besides eternity? What will any longer be another and another, where all things abide in one? And what will be prior or posterior, or more extended? Where, likewise, will the soul any further betake itself to any other thing than that in which it is? Or rather, neither will it betake itself to this. For in this case, it must have first departed from it, in order that it may accede to it; since neither is it the sphere itself [of the universe] which had not an existence prior to time. For this sphere exists, and is moved in time. And though time should stop, this sphere still continuing to energize, we should nevertheless measure the duration of its permanency, as long as the permanency of eternity is external to it. If, therefore, this sphere becoming quiescent and united, time is taken away, it is evident that the commencement of its motion, round the earth, and this its life, generate time. Hence, also, it is said [in the "Timæus" of Plato], that time was generated together with the universe, because soul produced it in conjunction with the universe. For in an energy of this kind, this world was generated. And this energy indeed is time, but the universe is in time. If, however, some one should say, that the circulations of the stars are also denominated by Plato times, he should recollect that he says these were generated for the purpose of rendering time manifest and distinct, and that the measure of it might be conspicuous to us. For since it was not possible for time itself to be bounded by soul, nor for each part of it to be measured by us, since it is invisible and incomprehensible, and especially since this is impossible to those who do not know how to numerate,—hence the Demiurgus made day and night, through which mankind were enabled to apprehend two things by their difference; from which, as Plato says, they arrived at the conception of number. Afterwards receiving the interval produced by the motion of the sun from the east to the east again, they apprehended what was the quantity of time, the form of the motion being equable; adhering to which, we use a thing of this kind as a measure of time. For time itself is not a measure. For how could it measure; and what would it say if it measured? Will it say this thing is as much in quantity as I am? Who therefore is it that says I? Is it that according to which the measure subsists? Has it not therefore an existence in order that it may measure, but is not a measure? Hence the measured motion of the universe will be according to time. And time will not be the measure of motion, according to that which it is, but according to accident, so that being something else prior to this, it renders the quantity of the motion manifest. One motion also being assumed in so much time, and being frequently enumerated, leads to a conception of the quantity of time that is past. So that if some one should say that motion and circulation, after a certain manner, measure time as much as possible, as manifesting in their quantity the quantity of time, which cannot in any other way be assumed or understood, he indeed will not adduce an absurd manifestation of time. *Hence, that which is measured by circulation, viz. which is manifested, and not generated by it, will be time.* And thus the measure of motion is that which is measured by a definite motion, and is measured by it, as being different from it. For if that which measures was one thing, and that which is measured another, but is measured accidentally; in this case, it would be just as if some one should say that what is measured by a cubit is magnitude, but should not say what that is which defines the magnitude. It would also be just as if some one not being able to render motion itself manifest on account of its indefinite nature, should say that motion is that which is measured by place. For assuming the place which motion passes through, he will say that the quantity of the motion is equal to the quantity of the place.

XII. Circulation, therefore, renders time in which it is performed manifest. It is necessary, however, that time should no longer alone be that in which something is performed, but that prior to this it should be what it is, namely, that in which other things are moved and at rest, in an equable and orderly manner; and that from a certain thing of an orderly nature, it should become apparent, and shine forth to our conceptions, yet not be generated by this thing, whether it is at rest, or in motion. It becomes, however, more apparent when this thing is in motion. For motion contributes more to the knowledge, and transition to the nature of time than rest. And the quantity of the motion of a thing is more known than the quantity of its rest. Hence [some philosophers] have been induced to say that time is the measure of motion, instead of saying that it is measured by motion. In the next place, it is requisite to add what that is which is measured by motion, and not to adduce that which accidentally takes place about it, and this alternately. Perhaps, however, they do not intend to say that this takes place alternately, and we do not understand their meaning; but they clearly asserting that time is a measure according to that which is measured, we do not apprehend their conceptions on this subject. The cause, however, why we do not, is because they have not clearly shown in their writings what time is, whether it is a measure, or that which is measured, as if they were writing to those who were acquainted with their opinions, and to their auditors. Plato, indeed, does not say that the essence of time is either a measure, or that which is measured by something, but asserts in order to render it manifest, that the circulation [of the universe] is allotted something which is the smallest [*i.e.* the centre,] for the purpose of unfolding the smallest part of time; so that from hence both the quality and quantity of time may be known. Wishing, however, to manifest the essence of time, he says that it was generated together with the universe, and that it is a moveable image of its paradigm eternity; because neither does time remain, life not remaining, in conjunction with which it runs and is convolved. But he says, it was generated together with the universe, because such a life as this produced the universe, and one life fabricated both the world and time. If, therefore, this life could be converted into one, time which exists in this life would immediately cease, and also the universe, in consequence of no longer possessing this life.

If, however, some one assuming the prior and posterior of the life which is here, should assert this to be time, because this is something, but that the more true motion which has prior and posterior is not any thing, his assertion would be most absurd. For he would ascribe to inanimate motion the prior and posterior, and also time together with it, but he would not grant this to the motion through the imitation of which the inferior motion exists; though from this superior motion prior and posterior primarily subsist, since it is a self-operative motion. As, likewise, it generates its several energies, thus too it produces that which is successive, and together with the generation a transition of energies. Why, therefore, do we refer this motion of the universe to the comprehension of the more true motion, and assert that it is in time, but do not refer to this the motion of soul which subsists in itself, and proceeds in a perpetual course? Shall we say it is because that which is prior to it is eternity, which neither runs in conjunction, nor is co-extended with this motion? This first motion, therefore, is referred to time which also it generates, and which together with its own energy it possesses. How, therefore, is time every where? Because this life and motion are not absent from any part of the world, as neither does the life which is in us desert any part of us. If, however, some one should say that time consists in a non-hypostasis, or non-hyparxis, for we are deceived about its essence, in the same manner as when we say of God that he *was* or *will be*; for thus he *will be* and *was* in the same manner as that in which it is said he *will be* [*i.e.* in the same manner as time]; to assertions of this kind there belongs another mode of discussion. With respect to all that has been said, however, it is necessary to observe, that when any one assumes the quantity of space passed over by a man that is moved, he also assumes the quantity of the motion, and when he assumes the quantity of the motion, such for instance as is produced in walking, he directs his attention to the boundary[1] of motion existing in the man prior to this motion, in order that he may judge whether he has walked to the full extent of this boundary. And the body, indeed, which has been moved in so much time, he refers to so much motion; for this is the cause of its being moved; and to the time of this motion. But he refers this motion of the body to the motion of the soul which produced an equality of interval. To what, therefore, will he refer the motion of the soul? For that whatever it may be to which he may wish to refer it, will be now without interval. Hence, this subsists primarily, and is that in which the rest are contained; but it is itself no longer contained in any thing else. For there is not any thing by which it can be contained. This, therefore, is primarily; and the like takes place in the soul of the universe. Is then time in us also? May we not say that it is in every such soul, that it subsists uniformly in every similar soul, and that all of them are [in a certain respect] one? Hence, time will not be divulsed, since neither is eternity, which according to another characteristic is in all uniform natures.

[1] The word used by Plotinus here is κίνημα, which signifies in the Physics of Aristotle, *the boundary of motion*.

VII.
ON THE IMMORTALITY OF THE SOUL.
IV. vii.

I. WHETHER each [part] of us is immortal, or the whole perishes, or one part of us is dissipated and corrupted, but another part perpetually remains, which part is the man himself, may be learnt by considering conformably to nature as follows: Man, indeed, is not something simple, but there is in him a soul, and he has also a body, whether it is annexed to us as an instrument, or after some other manner. However this may be, it must be admitted, that the nature and essence of each of these must be thus divided. Since the body, therefore, is itself a composite, reason shows that it cannot remain [perpetually the same]; and sense likewise sees that it is dissolved and wastes away, and receives all-various destructions; since each of the things inherent in it tends to its own [*i.e.* to the whole form from which it was derived], and one thing belonging to it corrupts another, and changes and perishes into something else. This, too, is especially the case when the soul, which causes the parts to be in friendly union with each other, is not present with the corporeal masses. If each body, likewise, is left by itself, it will not be one, since it is capable of being dissolved into form and matter, from which it is also necessary that simple bodies should have their composition. Moreover, as being bodies they have magnitude, and consequently may be cut and broken into the smallest parts, and through this are the recipients of corruption. Hence, if body is a part of us, we are not wholly immortal. But if it is an instrument [of the soul] it is necessary that being given for a certain time, it should be naturally a thing of this kind. That, however, which is the most principal thing, and the man himself, will be that with reference to the body which form is with reference to matter, since this according to form is as body to matter; or according to that which uses, the body has the relation to it of an instrument. But in each way soul is the man himself.

II. What, therefore, is the nature of this thing [soul]? If indeed it is a body, it is in every respect capable of being analyzed. For every body is a composite. But if it is not a body, but of another nature, that also must be considered either after the same, or after another manner. In the first place, however, it must be considered into what body this body which they call soul ought to be analyzed. For since life is necessarily present with soul, it is also necessary that this body which is supposed to be soul, if it consists of two or more bodies, should have a connascent life in both, or in each of them; or that one of these should have life, but the other not, or that neither should be vital. If, therefore, life is present with one of them only, this very thing will be soul. Hence, what body will this be which has life from itself? For fire, air, water and earth, are of themselves inanimate; and with whichever of these soul is present, the life which it uses is adventitious. There are not, however, any other bodies besides these. And those to whom it appears that there are other bodies the elements of these, do not assert that they are souls, or that they have life. But if it should be said, that though no one of these bodies possesses life, yet the congress of them produces life, he who says this would speak absurdly. And if each of them has life, one will be sufficient. Or rather, it is impossible that a coacervation of bodies should produce life, and things void of intellect generate intellect. Moreover, neither will these, in whatever manner they may say they are mixed, generate either intellect or soul.[1] Hence, it is necessary there should be that which arranges, and which is the cause of the mixture; so that this will have the order of soul. For that which is compounded will not be that which arranges and produces the mixture. But neither will there be a simple body in the series of things, without the existence of soul in the universe; if reason [or a productive principle] acceding to matter, produces body. For reason cannot proceed from any thing else than from soul.

III. If some one, however, should say that an assemblage of atoms or impartibles produce soul by their union, such a one will be confuted by similitude of passion, and by apposition; since one thing will not thus be generated through the whole, nor will that which is co-passive be produced from bodies which are without passion and incapable of being united. But soul is co-passive with itself. And of impartibles neither body nor magnitude can consist. Moreover, with respect to a simple body, they will not say that it has life from itself so far as it is material. For matter is void of quality. But they will rather say that what is arranged in body according to form possesses life. Hence, if they say that this form is essence, soul will not be both, but one of these; and this will no longer be body. For this will not also consist of matter; since if it did, we must again analyze it after the same manner. But if they assert that this form is a passion of matter and not essence, they must inform us what that is from which this passion

---

[1] The words ἢ νοῦν, ἢ ψυχήν, are omitted in the original; but from the version of Ficinus it appears that they ought to be inserted.

and life are derived into matter. For matter will not give form to itself, nor insert soul in itself. Hence, it is necessary that there should be something which is the supplier of life, whether the supply is to matter, or to a certain body, this supplier being external to, and beyond every corporeal nature. Indeed, neither will there be any body, if there is no psychical power. For body [perpetually] flows, and its nature is in [continual] motion. The universe[1] also would rapidly perish if all things were bodies; though some one of them should be denominated soul. For it would suffer the same things as other bodies, since there would be one matter in all of them. Or rather, nothing would be generated, but all things would stop in matter, as there would not be any thing to invest it with form. Perhaps, too, neither would matter have any subsistence whatever. This universe also will be dissolved, if it is committed to the connexion of body, and the order of soul is given to body, as far as to names, viz. to air and a dissipable spirit, and which has not from itself any oneness. For how is it possible, since all bodies are divisible, that this universe if it is committed to any one of them, should not be borne along in a foolish and casual manner? For what order is there, or reason or intellect, in a pneumatic substance, which is in want of order from soul? But if soul, indeed, has a subsistence, all these will be subservient to it in order to the composition of the world, and the existence of every animal, a different power contributing from a different thing to [the perfection of] the whole. If soul, however, is not present to the whole of things, these will neither have a subsistence, nor any arrangement.

IV. Compelled by truth, the authors of the above mentioned hypothesis also testify, that it is necessary there should be a certain form of soul prior to and more excellent than bodies. For they introduce a spirit endued with

[1] τὸ πᾶν is omitted in the original.

intellect, and an intellectual fire, as if it was not possible there could be a better condition among beings without fire and spirit, and without a place in which it might be established, though they ought to have investigated where bodies are to be placed; for it is necessary that these should be established in the powers of soul. But if they assert that life and soul are nothing else than a spirit or wind, we must enquire what this celebrated spirit introduced by them is, and how it subsists. For they are compelled to fly to this when they admit that there is another efficacious nature besides bodies. If therefore not every spirit is soul, because there are myriads of inanimate spirits, but a spirit subsisting after a certain manner is according to them soul, we ask them whether they say that such a spirit and this habitude is something belonging to beings, or nothing. But if indeed it is nothing, it will be a name alone. And its subsistence after a certain manner will be also merely a name, and thus it will be an accident to beings. Hence, according to them nothing but matter will have an existence, and soul, deity, and every thing [except matter] will be merely names. If, however, habitude is something pertaining to beings, and different from a subject and from matter, and subsists indeed in matter, but is itself immaterial, because it is not again composed from matter;—if this be the case, it will be a certain reason [or productive principle] and will not be body, but of another nature. Farther still, from the following considerations it will be no less manifest that it is impossible for soul to be any body whatever. For it would either be hot or cold, or hard, or soft, or moist, or firm, or black, or white, and all such different qualities as are in different bodies. And if indeed it is hot alone, it will alone heat; if cold alone, it will alone refrigerate. If also it is alone light, it will by its presence cause things to be light; if heavy, it will alone render them heavy; if black, it will blacken; and if white, will cause them to be white. For it is not the province of fire to refrigerate, nor of cold to produce heat. But soul produces different effects in different animals, and contrary effects in the same animal; fixing some things, but diffusing others. And some things indeed it causes to be dense, but others rare, black, white, light and heavy; though from the nature of one body it ought to produce one quality only, and not different qualities. But now it produces many qualities.

V. With respect to motions also, why are different motions produced by the soul, and not one only, there being but one [natural] motion of every body? But if they assign deliberate choice as the cause of some motions, and reasons [or productive principles] as the causes of others, these indeed are rightly assigned. Deliberate choice, however, does not pertain to body, nor reasons, since they are different, but an elementary body is one and simple. Nor can such a body be full of productive power, except so far as this is imparted to it by that which makes it to be hot or cold. But how can it belong to body to increase at certain times, and to a certain extent, since it is naturally adapted to be increased, except so far as the power of augmenting is assumed in the bulk of matter, and is subservient to that which through it produces the increase? For if soul being body increases, it is necessary that it should also be increased, viz. by the addition of a similar body, in order that it may be of an equal bulk with that which is increased by it. And that which is added will either be soul, or an inanimate body. And if indeed it is soul, whence and how is it introduced, and how is it added? But if that which is added is inanimate, how is this animated, how does it accord with the preceding soul, and become one with it, and how does it entertain the same opinions with the former soul? Will not this added soul, as being foreign, be ignorant of what the other knows? And in the same manner as with another mass belonging to our frame, there will be an efflux from, and an influx into it, and nothing will continue the same. How, therefore, shall we remember? And how shall we recognize such things as are appropriate to us, since we shall never employ the same soul? Moreover, if soul is body, since the nature of body is divided into many parts, each of the parts will not be the same with the whole. If, therefore, soul was a magnitude of a certain quantity, if this quantity should become less, it would no longer be soul; just as the being of every quantity is changed by ablation, from what it was before. But if some one of those things which have magnitude, being diminished in bulk, should remain the same in quality, so far indeed as it is body, and so far as it is quantity, it is different from what it was; but through quality which is different from quantity it is able to preserve itself the same. What, therefore, will those say who contend that the soul is body? In the first place, indeed, with respect to each part of the soul which is in the same body, is each part soul in the same manner as the whole soul? And again, is this the case with the part of a part? For if this is admitted, magnitude will contribute nothing to the essence of the soul; though it is necessary that it should if soul is a certain quantity. The whole soul, likewise, is every where present with the body; but it is impossible for the same corporeal whole to be in many things at the same time, or for a part of it to be the same as the whole. And if they say that each of the parts is not soul, then according to them, soul will consist of things inanimate. Besides, if the magnitude of each soul is definite, it will no longer be soul, if it is either extended or diminished. When, therefore, from one copulation and one seed, twins are begotten, or as in other animals many offspring are produced, most of the seed being distributed into many places, where also each part of the seed is a whole, how is it possible this should not teach those who are willing to learn, that where the part is the same with the whole, this in the very essence of itself transcends the nature of quantity; and ought from necessity to be without quantity. For thus alone it can remain the same, quantity being withdrawn, since it has no need of either quantity or bulk, its essence being something different from either. Hence soul and reasons [or productive principles] are void of quantity.

VI. But that if soul is body, it will not be possible to perceive either sensibly or intellectually, or to know scientifically, and that there will neither be virtue, nor any thing beautiful [in human conduct,] will be manifest from the following considerations. Whatever is able to have a sensible perception of any thing, ought itself to be one, and to apprehend every thing by one and the same power. This will also be the case, if many things enter through many organs of sense, or there are many qualities about one thing, and likewise when there is a variegated appearance such as that of the face, through one thing. For one thing does not perceive the nose, and another the eyes, but the same thing perceives at once all the parts of the face. And though one thing proceeds through the eyes, but another through the ears, yet it is necessary there should be one thing at which both these arrive. Or how could the soul say that these are different, unless the perceptions of sense at once terminated in the same thing? It is necessary, therefore, that this should be as it were a centre, that the senses should on all sides be extended to this, like lines from the circumference of a circle, and that a thing of this kind which apprehends the perceptions of sense should be truly one. For if it were any thing divisible, and the informations of the senses arrived at this as at the two extremities of a line, they must either again concur in one and the same thing as a middle, or there would be another thing there and another, and each would have a sensible perception of each; just as if I should perceive one thing, but you another, even though the object of sense should be one thing, such as the face; or they must be collected into one. And this indeed appears to be the case. For visible forms are collected in the pupils of the eyes; or how through these could the greatest things be seen? Hence, in a still greater degree the forms which arrive at the ruling part of the soul, become as it were conceptions; and therefore this part also must be impartible. For if it had magnitude, it would be co-divided with the object of sensible perception. Hence, one part of it would perceive a part of the sensible object, and nothing in us would have the apprehension of the whole of a sensible thing. But the whole is one thing. For how can it be divided? For in the division, equal cannot be adapted to equal, because the ruling part is not equal to every sensible thing. Into how many parts, therefore, must the division of it be made? Must it be divided into as many parts, as the sensible perception which is introduced to it, is divided into? And will each of the parts of the soul, therefore, perceive the parts of the sensible object? Or shall we say that the parts of the soul will not have a sensation of the parts of the thing perceived? This however is impossible. But if any part whatever perceives the whole of the sensible object, since magnitude is adapted to be divided infinitely, it will happen that infinite sensible perceptions will be produced about each part; so that, for instance, there will be infinite images of the same thing in our ruling part. Moreover, if that which perceives is body, it will not be able to perceive in any other way, than as if certain images were impressed from wax in a seal; whether the sensible forms are impressed in blood, or in air. And if, indeed, they are impressed as in moist bodies, which it is reasonable to suppose they will be, if as in water, they will be confounded, and there will be no memory. But if the impressions remain, either it will not be possible for others to be impressed while they remain, so that there will be no other sensible perceptions, or if others are produced, the former will be destroyed, so that there will not be a remembrance of anything. But if it is possible to remember, and to have a sensible perception of other things after others, the former not impeding the latter, it is impossible for the soul to be body.

VII. The same thing also may be seen from pain and the sensation of pain; when a man is said to have a pain in his finger or about his finger. For then it is manifest that the sensation of pain is produced about the principal or ruling part; a portion of the spirit being pained, but the ruling part having a perception of the pain, and the whole soul in consequence of this suffering the same thing. How, therefore, does this happen? They will say by succession, the psychical spirit about the finger suffering in the first place, but imparting the passion to that which is next to it, and afterwards to something else, until the passion arrives at the ruling part. Hence, it is necessary if that which is primarily pained perceives, that there should be another sensation of that which is second, if sensation is produced according to succession. And likewise, that there should be another sensation of that which is the third in order; that there should be many and infinite sensible perceptions of one and the same pain; and that afterwards all these should be perceived by the ruling part, and besides these, that it should have a perception of its own passion. In reality, however, each of these does not perceive the pain that is in the finger; but one sensation perceives that the part of the palm of the hand which is next to the finger is pained, and another more remote sensation perceives the pain which is in a more remote part. There will also be many pains, the ruling part not perceiving the passion which is in the finger, but that which is present with itself. And this it will alone know, but will bid farewell to the others, not perceiving that the finger is pained. If, therefore, it is not possible that sensible perception of a thing of this kind should subsist according to succession, and it does not belong to body, since it is a bulk, that one part of it suffering, another part should recognize the suffering; for in every magnitude this is one thing, and that another;—if this be the case, it is necessary that the power which perceives should be a thing of such a kind, as to be every where itself the same with itself. But this pertains to any thing else rather than to body.

VIII. Moreover, that neither will it be possible to perceive intellectually if the soul is body, may be demonstrated as follows. For if to perceive sensibly is, for the soul using the body to apprehend sensibles, intellectual perception will not be an apprehension of the objects of such perception, through body. For unless this is admitted, intellectual will be the same with sensible perception. Hence, if to perceive intellectually is to apprehend without body, by a much greater priority it is necessary that the nature which thus perceives should not be body. Further still, if sense indeed is the perception of sensibles, intellection is the perception of intelligibles. If, however, they are not willing to admit this, yet there will be in us intellections of certain intelligibles, and apprehensions of things without magnitude. How, therefore, will intellect if it is magnitude, understand that which is not magnitude, and by that which is partible that which is impartible? Shall we say it will understand it by a certain impartible part of itself? But if this be the case, that which understands will not be body. For there is no need of the whole in order to come into contact with the object of its intellection; since contact according to one certain thing is sufficient. If, therefore, they admit that the first intellections, which is true, are entirely liberated from body, it is necessary that the nature which intellectually perceives the form separate from body of each thing, should know either real being, or that which is becoming to be. But if they say that intellections are of forms inherent in matter, yet they are then only apprehended when by intellect they are separated from body. For the separation [*i.e.* abstraction] of a circle and triangle, of a line and a point, is not effected in conjunction with flesh, or in short, with matter. Hence it is necessary that the soul also, in a separation of this kind, should separate itself from the body. And therefore it is necessary that it should not be itself body. I think, likewise, that the beautiful and the just are without magnitude, and consequently the intellection of these is unattended with magnitude. Hence, these approaching to us are apprehended by that which is impartible in the soul, and in the soul they reside in the impartible. How also, if the soul is body, can temperance and justice be the virtues of it, which are its saviours, so far as they are received by it?

IX. There must, therefore, be another nature which possesses existence from itself, and such is every thing which is truly being, and which is neither generated, nor destroyed. For without the subsistence of this, all things would vanish into non-entity, and this perishing, would not afterwards be generated; since this imparts safety to all other things, and also to the universe which through soul is preserved and adorned. For soul is the principle of motion, with which it supplies other things, itself moving itself, and imparting life to the animated body. But it possesses life from itself, which it will never lose, because it is derived from itself. For all things do not use an adventitious life, or there would be a progression of life to infinity. But it is necessary there should be a certain nature primarily vital, which is also necessarily indestructible and immortal, as being the principle of life to other things. Here, likewise, it is requisite that every thing divine and blessed should be established, living from itself, and existing primarily being, and primarily vital, void of essential mutation, and being neither generated nor destroyed. For whence could it be generated, or into what could it perish? If, likewise, it is necessary that the appellation of being should truly belong to this nature, it is requisite that it should not at one time exist, and at another not; just as a colour which is of itself white, is not at one time white, and at another not white. If, however, whiteness was [real] being, together with being white, it would likewise always be. But now it possesses whiteness alone. That, however, to which being is present which is from itself, and is primarily being, will always have a subsistence. Hence, this which is primarily and perpetually being, ought not to be destitute of life, like a stone, or a piece of wood, but to be vital, and enjoy a pure life, in that part of itself which is alone permanent. But that part of it which is mingled with a subordinate nature is an impediment to its possession of the best of things, yet it does not through this lose its nature, but resumes its ancient condition, when it recurs to things which are [truly] its own.

X. That soul, however, is allied to a more divine and eternal nature, is evident from its not being body as we have demonstrated, and also because it has neither figure nor colour. Moreover, this likewise may be shown from the following considerations. It is acknowledged by all of us, that every divine nature, and which is truly being, enjoys an excellent and wise life. This, therefore, being admitted, it is necessary to consider in the next place, what the nature is of our soul. We must assume the soul, however, not receiving in the body irrational desires and angers, and other passions, but as abolishing all these, and as much as possible having no communication with the body. For such a soul as this will perspicuously show that evils are an addition to the soul, and are externally derived; and that the most excellent things are inherent in it when it is purified, viz. wisdom and every other virtue, which are its proper possessions. If, therefore, the soul is such when it returns to itself, how is it possible it should not belong to that nature which we say is possessed by every thing eternal and divine? For wisdom and true virtue being divine, cannot be inherent in any vile and mortal thing; but that which is of this kind is necessarily divine, as being full of divine goods, through an alliance and similitude of essence to a divine nature. Hence, whoever of us resembles a soul of this description, will in soul itself differ but little from superior beings; in this alone being inferior to them, that he is in body. On which account, also, if every man was such, or if the multitude employed souls of this kind, no one would be so incredulous as not to believe that our soul is entirely immortal. Now, however, men perceiving that the soul of the greater part of the human race is defiled with vice, they do not reason about it, either as a divine or an immortal thing. *But it is necessary, in considering the nature of every thing, to direct our attention to the purity of it;* since whatever is added, is always an impediment to the knowledge of that to which it is added. Consider the soul, therefore, by taking away [that which is extraneous]; or rather, let him who takes this away survey himself, and he will believe himself to be immortal, when he beholds himself in the intelligible world, and situated in a pure abode. For he will perceive intellect seeing not any thing sensible, nor any of these mortal objects, but by an eternal power contemplating that which is eternal; every thing in the intelligible world, and itself also being then luminous, in consequence of being enlightened by the truth proceeding from *the good,* which illuminates all intelligibles with reality. By such a soul as this, therefore, it may be properly said,

Farewell, a God immortal now am I,[1]

having ascended to divinity, and earnestly striving to become similar to him. If, however, purification causes the soul to have a knowledge of the most excellent things, the sciences also which are inwardly latent will then shine forth, and which are truly sciences. For the soul does not by running to externals behold temperance and justice, but perceives them herself by herself, in the intellection of herself, and of that which she formerly was, and views them like statues established in herself, which through time have become covered with rust. These she then purifies, just as if gold were animated, and in consequence of being incrusted with earth, and not perceiving itself to be gold, should be ignorant of itself; but afterwards shaking off the earth which adheres to it, should be filled with admiration on beholding itself pure and alone. Then, also, it would perceive that it has no need of adventitious beauty, and would consider with itself that it is then in the best condition when it is permitted to be wholly by itself.

XI. Who, therefore, endued with intellect will doubt that a thing of this kind is not immortal, to which indestructible life is present from itself? For how is it possible it should perish, since it is not adventitious, and is not possessed in the same way as heat is present with fire? I do not mean by this, that heat is adventitious to fire, but that it is so to the subject matter of fire, though it is not to fire itself. For through this fire is dissolved. Soul, however, does not possess life in such a way, as that matter is the subject of it, but life acceding, demonstrates the presence of soul. For either life is essence, and is an essence of such a kind as to live from itself, which is soul,

[1] A celebrated line of Empedocles.

the object of our investigation, and this they acknowledge to be immortal; or they must analyze it as a composite. This, also, they must analyze, till they arrive at that which is immortal, and moved from itself, and to which it is not lawful to receive the destiny of death. Or if they say that life is a passion adventitious to matter, they are compelled to acknowledge that nature to be immortal from which this passion was imparted to matter, and which is incapable of receiving the contrary to that which it imparts. For it is one nature living in energy.

XII. Farther still, if they say that every soul is corruptible, it would be requisite that all things should have long since perished. But if they assert that one soul is corruptible, and another not, as for instance, that the soul of the universe is immortal, but ours not, it is necessary that they should assign the cause of this difference. For each is the cause of motion, and each lives from itself. Each, likewise, comes into contact with the same things by the same power, intellectually perceiving the natures in the heavens, and also those that are beyond the heavens, investigating everything which has an essential subsistence, and ascending as far as to the first principle of things. To which may be added, that it is evident the soul gave being to itself prior to the body, from its ability of apprehending what each thing is, by itself, from its own inherent spectacles, and from reminiscence. And from its employing eternal sciences, it is manifest that it is itself perpetual. Besides, since everything which can be dissolved receives composition, hence, so far as a thing is a composite, it is naturally adapted to be dissolved. But soul being one simple energy, and a nature characterized by life, cannot be corrupted as a composite. Will it, therefore, through being divided and distributed into minute parts, perish? Soul, however, is not, as we have demonstrated, a certain bulk or quantity. May it not, therefore, through being changed in quality, be corrupted? Change in quality however which corrupts takes away form, but leaves the subject matter. But this is the passion of a composite. Hence, if it is not possible for the soul to be corrupted according to any of these modes, it is necessarily incorruptible.

XIII. How, therefore, since the intelligible is separate, does the soul descend into body?[1] Because so far as in-

[1] Souls fall into bodies, (says Proclus in Tim. p. 343.) because they wish to imitate the providential energies of the Gods, and on this account proceed into generation, and leave the contemplation of true being. For as divine perfection is twofold, one kind being intellectual and the other providential, and one kind consisting in an abiding energy, but the other in motion, hence souls imitate the prolific, intellectual, and immutable energy of the Gods by contemplation, but their providential and motive characteristic, through a life conversant with generation. As the intelligence too, of the human soul is partial, so likewise is her providence; but being partial it associates with a partial body. But still further, the descent of the soul contributes to the perfection of the universe. For it is necessary that there should not only be immortal and intellectual animals, such as are the perpetual attendants of the Gods, nor yet mortal and irrational animals only, such as are the last progeny of the Demiurgus of the universe, but likewise such as subsist between these, and which are by no means [wholly] immortal, but are capable of participating reason and intellect. And in many parts of the universe, there are many animals of this kind. For man is not the only rational and mortal animal, but there are other such-like species, some of which are more dæmoniacal, and others approximate nearer to our essence. But the descents of a partial soul contribute to the perfect composition of all animals, which are at the same time mortal and rational.

Should it be again asked, Why, therefore, are partial souls descending into generation filled with such material perturbation, and such numerous evils? We reply, that this takes place through the inclination arising from their free will; through their vehement familiarity with body; through their sympathy with the image of soul, or that divisible life which is distributed about the body; through their abundant mutation from an intelligible to a sensible nature, and from a quiet energy to one entirely conver-

tellect alone is impassive in intelligibles, having an intellectual life alone, it abides there eternally. For it has not any impulse, or appetite. But that which receives appetite, and is next in order to that intellect, by the addition of appetite proceeds as it were to a greater extent, and being desirous to adorn, in imitation of the forms which it sees in intellect, it becomes as it were pregnant from them. Hence, becoming parturient, it hastens to make and fabricate, and through this festination becoming extended about a sensible nature, when it subsists in conjunction with the soul of the universe, it transcends the subject of its government, by being external to it, and thus together with the mundane soul presides over the universe with a providential care. But when it wishes to govern a part of the world, it then governs alone, and becomes [merged] in that in which it is; yet not so as to be wholly absorbed by body, but even then it possesses something external to body. Hence, neither is the intellect of this soul passive. But this soul is at one time in body, and at another ex-

sant with motion; and through a disordered condition of being, naturally arising from the composition of dissimilar natures, viz. of the immortal and mortal, of the intellectual and that which is deprived of intellect, of the indivisible and that which is endured with interval. For all these become the cause to the soul of this mighty tumult and labour in the realms of generation; since we pursue a flying mockery which is ever in motion. And the soul, indeed, by verging to a material life, kindles a light in her dark tenement the body, but she herself becomes situated in obscurity; and by giving life to the body, she destroys herself and her own intellect, in as great a degree as these are capable of receiving destruction. For thus the mortal nature participates of intellect, but the intellectual part of death, and the whole becomes a prodigy, as Plato beautifully observes in his Laws, composed of the mortal and immortal, of the intellectual and that which is deprived of intellect. For this physical law, which binds the soul to the body, is the death of the immortal life, but is the cause of vivification to the mortal body."

ternal to it. And being impelled, indeed, to descend from first natures, it proceeds as far as to such as rank in the third degree, and to those with which we are conversant, by a certain energy of intellect; intellect at the same time abiding in itself, and through soul filling every thing with all that is beautiful, being an immortal adorner through an immortal soul. For intellect itself also exists eternally, through unceasing energy.

XIV. With respect to the souls of other animals, such among these as have fallen from a better condition, and have proceeded as far as to brutal bodies, these likewise are necessarily immortal. But if there is another species of soul, it is necessary that this also should not be derived from any other source than a vital nature, since this likewise is the cause of life to animals, and besides this, of the life which is in plants. For all these proceeding from the same principle, have an appropriate life of their own. And these souls also are incorporeal, impartible, and essences. If, however, it is requisite that the soul of man being tripartite should be dissolved with the composite, we must say that pure souls which are liberated from the body, dismiss that which adhered to them in generation; but that this is accomplished by others in long periods of time. That also which is dismissed, is the worst part, nor will this be destroyed, as long as that subsists from whence it originates. For nothing which is comprehended in being perishes.

XV. And thus much has been said by us to those who require demonstration on this subject. But such things as should be adduced to those who stand in need of the evidence arising from faith mingled with sensible information, may be selected from history, which abounds with instances in confirmation of the immortality of the soul. It may also be obtained from what the Gods have delivered in Oracles, when they order the anger of souls that have been injured, to be appeased ; and likewise honours to be paid to the dead, as being still sentient, which honours all men pay to departed souls. Many souls also who once ranked among men, do not cease when liberated from bodies to benefit mankind. And these by employing divination benefit us in other respects, and demonstrate through themselves, that other souls also do not perish.

VIII.

ON THE THREE HYPOSTASES, THAT RANK AS THE PRINCIPLES OF THINGS.

V. i.

I. WHAT is the reason that souls become oblivious of divinity, being ignorant both of themselves and him, though their allotment is from thence, and they in short partake of God? The principle therefore of evil to them is audacity, generation, the first difference,[1] and the wish to exercise an unrestrained freedom of the will. When, therefore, they began to be delighted with this unbounded liberty, abundantly employing the power of being moved from themselves, they ran in a direction contrary [to their first course], and thus becoming most distant from their source, they were at length ignorant that they were thence derived. Just as children who are immediately torn from their parents, and have for a long time been nurtured at a great distance from them, become ignorant both of themselves and their parents. Hence, souls neither seeing their father, nor themselves, despise themselves through ignorance of their race, but honour other things, and admiring

[1] The five genera of being are, essence, sameness, *difference*, motion and permanency. This *difference*, therefore, which ranks as the first, and which is the source of all diversity, causes souls by predominating in them to be forgetful of deity, and themselves.

every thing rather than themselves, being vehemently astonished about, and adhering to sensible natures, they as much as possible hurl themselves [from their true parents], and thus despise the beings from which they have become elongated. Hence, the honour which they pay to sensible objects, and the contempt of themselves, happen to be the causes of their all-perfect ignorance. For at the same time they pursue and admire something else, and acknowledge themselves to be inferior to that which they admire and pursue. But the soul admitting that it is something subordinate to things which are generated and corrupted, and apprehending that it is the most ignoble and mortal of every thing which it honours, neither believes in the nature nor power of God. Hence, it is necessary that there should be a twofold discourse to those who are thus affected, in order to convert them to the contraries [to the things they admire], and to first natures, and to elevate them as far as to that which is highest, and one, and the first. What, therefore, is each of these discourses? One of them, indeed, is that which shows the cause why the soul honours these sensible objects, which we have elsewhere largely discussed; but the other teaches and reminds the soul of the greatness of its origin, and its true dignity; which discussion is prior to the former, and when manifested will render that manifest. Of this, therefore, we must now speak. For this is proximate and conducive to the object of enquiry. For that which is investigated is soul; and what it investigates should be known by it, in order that it may in the first place learn whether it has the power of investigating things of this kind; and also whether it has such an eye as is able to see them, and whether they are properly objects of its enquiry. For if they are foreign to its nature, why should it investigate them? But if they are allied to it, it is expedient and possible to discover them.

II. Every soul, therefore, ought to consider in the first place, that soul produced all animals, and inspired them with life; viz. those animals which the earth and sea nourish, those which live in the air, and the divine stars contained in the heavens. Soul also made the sun; soul made and adorned this mighty heaven. Soul, too, circumvolves it in an orderly course, being of a nature different from the things which it adorns, which it moves, and causes to live, and is necessarily more honourable than these. For these are corrupted when soul deserts them, and generated when it supplies them with life. But soul always exists, because it never deserts itself. What the mode is, however, by which life is supplied to the universe, and to each of its parts, may be considered to be as follows: Let a certain other soul whose dignity in contemplating is not small, being liberated from deception, and the allurements which fascinate other souls, be established in a quiet condition and survey a mighty soul. And let not only the surrounding body and the storms of body be at rest with respect to it, but the whole of that by which it is surrounded. Let the earth, therefore, be still; let the sea be still, the air, and the heavens themselves which are more excellent than the elements.[1] Afterwards, let this

[1] Proclus had evidently this beautiful passage in view, when, in his second book "On the Theology of Plato," he celebrates the ineffable principles of things, with the following matchless magnificence of diction.

"Let us now, if ever, remove from ourselves multiform knowledge, exterminate all the variety of life, and in perfect quiet approach near to the cause of all things. For this purpose, let not only opinion and phantasy be at rest, nor the passions alone which impede our anagogic impulse to *the first* be at peace; but let the air be still, and the universe itself be still. And let all things extend us with a tranquil power to communion with the ineffable. Let us also, standing there, having transcended the intelligible (if we contain any thing of this kind), and with nearly closed eyes adoring as it were the rising sun since it is not lawful for any

quiet soul behold that other mighty soul, externally as it were, on all sides flowing and infused into, penetrating and illuminating the quiescent mass. For just as the rays of the sun darting on a dark cloud cause it to become splendid, and golden to the view, thus also, soul entering into the body of heaven gave it life, gave it immortality, and excited it from its torpid state. But heaven being moved with a perpetual motion, through the guidance of a wise soul, became a blessed animal. It also acquired dignity through soul becoming its inhabitant, since, prior to soul, it was a dead body, viz. earth and water, or rather the darkness of matter and non-entity; and, as some one says, that which the Gods abhor. The power, however, and nature of soul will become still more apparent and manifest, if any one directs his attention to the manner in which it comprehends and leads heaven by its will. For it gives itself to the whole of this vast magnitude; and every interval, both great and small, is animated by it: one body indeed, being situated differently from another, and some bodies being opposite, but others being suspended from each other. This, however, is not the case

being whatever intently to behold him—let us survey the sun whence the light of the intelligible gods proceeds, emerging, as the poets say, from the bosom of the ocean; and again, from this divine tranquillity descending into intellect, and from intellect, employing the reasonings of the soul, let us relate to ourselves what the natures are, from which, in this progression, we shall consider the first god as exempt. And let us as it were celebrate him, not as establishing the earth and the heavens, nor as giving subsistence to souls, and the generations of all animals; for he produced these indeed, but among the last of things. But, prior to these, let us celebrate him, as unfolding into light the whole intelligible and intellectual genus of gods, together with all the supermundane and mundane divinities—as the god of all gods, the unity of all unities, and beyond the first adyta,—as more ineffable than all silence, and more unknown than all essence,—as holy among the holies, and concealed in the intelligible gods."

with soul. For it does not give life to individuals, through a division of itself into minute parts, but it vivifies all things with the whole of itself; and the whole of it is present every where, in a manner similar to its generator, both according to oneness and ubiquity. Heaven, also, though it is ample, and different parts of it have a different situation, yet is one through the power of soul. And through this the sensible world is a God. The sun, likewise, is a God, because it is animated. And this is also the case with the other stars. Whatever we too possess, we possess on account of this. For dead bodies are more worthless than dunghills. It is necessary, however, that soul, which is the cause to Gods [*i.e.* to the mundane Gods] of their being Gods, should be itself a more ancient God. Similar to this likewise is our soul. And when it is surveyed in a pure condition, without any thing extraneous adhering to it, this same thing which is soul will be found to be a venerable thing, and more honourable than every corporeal nature. For [perhaps without soul [1]] all things would be earth. And though fire should then exist, what would there be [venerable] in its burning power, or in the composites from fire and earth, even though you should add to these, water and air? But if body is an object of pursuit because it is animated, why does any one, neglecting himself, pursue another thing? Since, therefore, you admire soul in another thing, admire yourself.

III. Hence, as the soul is so honourable and divine a thing, now confiding in a cause of this kind, ascend with it to divinity. For you will not be very distant from him; nor are the intermediate natures many. In this, therefore, which is divine, receive that part which is more divine, viz. the vicinity of the soul to that which is supernal, to which

[1] It appears from the version of Ficinus, that the words ἴσως ἄνευ ψυχῆς, ought to be supplied in this place.

the soul is posterior, and from which it proceeds. For though it is so great a thing as we have demonstrated it to be, yet it is a certain image of intellect. And, just as external discourse is an image of the discursive energy within the soul, after the same manner, soul, and the whole of its energy, are the discourse of intellect, and a life which it emits in order to the hypostasis of another thing; just as in fire, the inherent heat of it is one thing, and the heat which it imparts another. It is necessary, however, to assume there, not a life flowing forth, but partly abiding in intellect, and partly giving subsistence to another life. Hence, since soul is derived from intellect, it is intellectual, and the intellect of soul is conversant with discursive energies. And again, the perfection of soul is from intellect, as from a father that nourishes it, who generated soul, as with reference to himself, not perfect. This hypostasis, therefore, is from intellect, and is also reason in energy when it perceives intellect. For when it looks to intellect, it possesses internally, and appropriately, the things which it understands, and the energies which it performs. And it is necessary to call those energies alone the energies of the soul, which are intellectual and dwell with it. But its subordinate energies have an external source, and are the passions of a soul of this kind. Intellect, therefore, causes the soul to be more divine, both because it is the father of it, and because it is present with it. For there is nothing between them, except the difference of one with reference to the other, soul being successive to, and the recipient of intellect; but intellect subsisting as form. The matter also of intellect is beautiful, since it has the form of intellect, and is simple. The great excellence, however, of intellect, is manifest from this, that though soul is such as we have described it to be, yet it is surpassed by intellect.

IV. This also will be evident to him who admires this

sensible world; who surveys its magnitude and beauty, and the order of its perpetual motion; the Gods it contains, some of whom are visible, and others invisible; and the dæmons, animals and plants, with which it is replete; and who ascends from these to its archetype, and the more true world [of which this is the image]. For there he will behold all intelligibles, which together with the intelligible world are eternal, and subsist in an appropriate intelligence and life. An undecaying intellect, likewise, and immense wisdom preside over this intelligible world; and a life which is in reality under Saturn, flourishes there; Saturn being a God, and a pure intellect. For he comprehends in himself all immortal natures, every intellect, every God, and every soul, all which subsist in him with invariable stability. For why should he seek after change, since he possesses an excellent condition of being? Or whither should he transfer himself, since he possesses all things with himself? But neither, being most perfect, will he seek to be increased. Hence, all things that are with him are perfect, in order that he may be entirely perfect, having nothing which does not partake of perfection; and possessing nothing in himself which he does not intellectually perceive. But he intellectually perceives, not investigating, but possessing.[1] Its blessedness, also, is not adventitious to it, but it possesses all things in eternity. And it is itself truly eternity, which time running round soul imitates, omitting some things, but applying itself to others. For other and again other things are about soul; since at one time the form of Socrates, and at another the form of horse present themselves to its view; and always one certain thing among the number of beings. But intellect has all things. Hence, it possesses in the same all things established in the same. It likewise alone *is*,

[1] Conformably to this, Aristotle also, in his Metaphysics, says of intellect, "that it energizes possessing," ἐνέργει δὲ ἔχων.

and *is* always, but is never *future;* for when the future arrives, it then also *is;* nor is it the *past.* For nothing there has passed away, but all things abide in the present *now;* since they are things of such a kind, as to be satisfied with themselves thus subsisting. But each of them is intellect and being. And the whole is every intellect, and every being. Intellect, therefore, derives its subsistence as intellect, from the intellection of being.[1] But being subsists as being, through becoming the object of intellectual perception to intellect, and through imparting to it, intellection and existence. There is, however, another cause of intellection, which is also the cause of existence to being. Of both therefore at once, there is another cause. For both these are con-subsistent, and never desert each other. But being two, this one thing [resulting from both] is at once intellect; and is being, intellective, and intelligible. It is intellect, indeed, so far as it is intellective; but being, so far as it is intelligible [or the object of perception to intellect]. For intellectual perception could not subsist, difference and sameness not existing. Intellect, therefore, being, difference and sameness, are the first of things. But it is likewise necessary to assume together with these, motion and permanency. And motion, indeed, is necessary if being intellectually perceives; but permanency in order that it may remain the same; and difference, in order that it may be intellective and intelligible. For if you take away difference from it, then becoming one it will be perfectly silent. It is necessary, however, that intellective natures should be different from each other; and that they should also be the same with each other, since they subsist in the same thing, and there is something common in all of them. Diversity,

---

[1] Instead of ὁ μὲν οὖν νοῦς, κατὰ τὸ νοεῖν ὑφιστάς, τὸ ὄν, it is necessary to read as in the above translation, ὁ μὲν οὖν νοῦς, κατὰ τὸ νοεῖν ὑφιστὰς τὸ ὄν.

likewise, is *otherness*. But these becoming many produce number and quantity. And the peculiarity of each of these produces quality, from all which, as principles, other things proceed.

V. This exuberant God, therefore, exists in the soul which is here, being conjoined to him by things of this kind, unless it wishes to depart from him. Approaching therefore to, and as it were becoming one with him, it enquires as follows : Who is he that, being simple and prior to a multitude of this kind, generated this God ? Who is the cause of his existence, and of his being exuberant, and by whom number was produced? For number is not the first of things ; since *the one* is prior to the duad. But the duad is the second thing, and being generated by *the one*, is defined by it. The duad, however, is of itself indefinite. But when it is defined, it is now number. And it is number as essence. Soul also is number. For neither corporeal masses nor magnitudes are the first of things. For these gross substance which sense fancies to be beings, are things of a posterior nature. Nor is the moisture which is in seeds honourable, but that contained in them, which is not visible. But this is number and reason [or a productive principle]. What are said therefore to be number and the duad in the intelligible world, are reasons and intellect. But the duad indeed is indefinite, when it is assumed as analogous to a subject. Number, however, which proceeds from it and *the one*, is each form of things ; intellect being as it were formed by the species of things which are generated it it. But it is formed in one manner from *the one*, and in another from itself, in the same manner as sight which is in energy. For intelligence is sight perceiving, both being one.

VI. How, therefore, does intelligence see; what does it see; and, in short, how does it subsist; and how is it generated from *the one*, so that it may see? For now indeed the soul perceives the necessity of the existence of these things. It desires, however, to understand this which is so much spoken of by the wise men of antiquity, viz. how from *the one* being such as we have said it is, each thing has its subsistence, whether it be multitude, or the duad, or number; and why *the one* did not abide in itself, but so great a multitude flowed from it, as is seen to have an existence, and which we think should be referred to *the one*. We must say, therefore, as follows, *invoking God himself, not with external speech, but with the soul itself, extending ourselves in prayer to him, since we shall then be able to pray to him properly, when we approach by ourselves alone to the alone.* It is necessary, therefore, that the beholder of him, being in himself as if in the interior part of a temple, and quietly abiding in an eminence beyond all things, should survey the statues as it were which are established outwardly, or rather that statue which first shines forth to the view, and after the following manner behold that which is naturally adapted to be beheld. With respect to every thing that is moved,[1] it is necessary there should be something to which it is moved. For if there is nothing of this kind, we should not admit that it is moved. But if any thing is generated posterior to that to which the moveable nature tends, it is necessary that it should always be generated in consequence of that prior cause being converted to itself. Let, however, the generation which is in time be now removed from us who are discoursing about eternal beings. And if in the course of the discussion we attribute generation to things which exist eternally, let it be considered as indicative of cause and order. Hence, that which is from thence generated, must be said to be generated, the cause not being moved. For if something was generated in consequence of that cause being moved, the thing generated

[1] Instead of πάντα τῷ κινουμίνῳ in this place, it is necessary to read ἐπὶ παντὶ τῷ κινουμένῳ.

after the motion would be the third, and not the second from the cause. It is necessary, therefore, the cause being immoveable, that if any thing secondary subsists after it, this second nature should be produced, without the cause either verging to it, or consulting,[1] or in short being moved. How, therefore, and what is it necessary to conceive about that abiding cause? We must conceive a surrounding splendour, proceeding indeed from this cause, but from it in a permanent state, like a light from the sun shining, and as it were running round it, and being generated from it, the cause itself always abiding in the same immoveable condition. All beings, likewise, as long as they remain, necessarily produce from their own essence, about themselves, and externally from the power which is present with them, a nature whose hypostasis is suspended from them, and which is as it were an image of the archetype from which it proceeded. Thus fire emits from itself indeed heat, and snow not only retains cold within itself [but imparts it to other things]. This, however, such things as are fragrant especially testify. For as long as they exist, something proceeds from them, of which whatever is near them partakes. All such things, likewise, as are now perfect generate; but that which is always perfect, always generates, and that which it produces is perpetual. It also generates something less than itself. What, therefore, is it requisite to say of that which is most perfect? Shall we say that nothing proceeds from it; or rather that the greatest things posterior to it are its progeny? But the greatest thing posterior to it, and the second, is intellect. For intellect sees it, and is in want of it alone. But this most perfect nature is not in want of intellect. It is also necessary that the thing generated from that which is better than intellect, should be intellect.

---

[1] For βουληθέντος here, it is requisite to read βουλευθέντος.

And intellect is superior to all things after the first, because other things are posterior to it. Thus, for instance, soul is the reason of intellect, and a certain energy of it, just as intellect of that first God [who is beyond intellect]. But the reason of soul is indeed obscure. For as it is the image of intellect, on this account it is necessary that it should look to intellect. After the same manner also, it is necessary that intellect should look to the highest God, in order that it may be intellect. It sees him, however, not separated from him, but because it is after him, and there is nothing between; as neither is there any thing between soul and intellect. But every thing desires its generator. This also it loves, and especially when that which is generated and the generator are alone. When, however, that which generates is the most excellent of things, the thing begotten is necessarily present with it in such a manner, as to be separated by *otherness* [1] alone.

VII. But we say that intellect is the image of this most excellent nature. For it is necessary to speak more clearly. In the first place, indeed, it is necessary that intellect should in a certain respect be generated, and preserve [in itself] much of its generator; and also that it should have such a similitude to it, as light has to the sun. Its generator, however, is not intellect. How therefore did he generate intellect [so far as it is *intellect*]? May we not say, because intellect, by conversion, looks to him? But the vision itself is intellect. For that which apprehends another thing, is either sense or intellect. And sense indeed may be compared to a line, but the other gnostic

[1] In the original ἑτερότητι, which is derived from ἕτερος *another*. And this word is *properly* used when we speak of two things only. Hence, ἑτερότης must not be considered in this place as merely signifying *difference;* for universally one thing is separated from another by difference, but as denoting the greatest proximity and alliance.

powers of the soul to a circle. A circle, however, of this kind is as it were partible. But this is not the case with intellect. Or may we not say that this also is one? But the one here is the power of all things. Hence intelligence surveys those things of which it is the power, divided as it were from the power; for otherwise it would not be intellect. For intellect now possesses from itself a co-sensation as it were of the great extent of its power; in which power, its essence, consists. Intellect, therefore, through itself defines its own being, by a power derived from him [*i.e.* from the first God,] and perceives that essence is as it were one of the parts of and from him, and that it is corroborated by him, and perfected by and from him into essence. It sees, however, itself derived from thence, as something which is as it were partible from that which is impartible; and not only itself, but life, and intellection, and all things, because the first God is nothing of all things. For on this account all things are from him, because he is not detained by a certain form. For he is one alone. And intellect, indeed, in the order of beings is all things. But he on this account is none of the things which are in intellect; and all things which have a subsistence among beings are derived from him. Hence also these are essences. For they are now definite, and each possesses as it were a form. Being, however, ought not to be surveyed in that which is as it were indefinite, but as fixed by bound and permanency. But permanency in intelligibles is circumscription and form, in which also they receive their hypostasis. This intellect, therefore, which deserves the appellation of the most pure intellect, and which is of the genus of intelligibles, originates from no other source than the first principle. And being now generated, it generates together with itself beings, all the beauty of ideas, and all the intelligible Gods. Being, likewise, full of the things which it generates, and as it were absorbing its progeny, it again contains them in itself, and does not suffer them to fall into matter, nor to be nourished by Rhea, as the mysteries and the fables about the Gods obscurely indicate. For they say that Saturn the most wise God was born prior to Jupiter, and that he again contains the things which he generates, in himself, so far as he is full, and an intellect characterized by purity. But after this they say that he generated Jupiter, who was now a boy [*i.e.*, pure and full]. For intellect, being a perfect intellect, generates soul. For being perfect it is requisite that it should generate, and since it is so great a power that it should not be unprolific. Neither here, however, is it possible that the thing generated should be more excellent than the generator; but being inferior, it is necessary that it should be an image of it. In a similar manner it is requisite that it should be indefinite, but bounded, and as it were invested with form by its generator. But the progeny of intellect is a certain reason, and an hypostasis which energizes dianoetically. This, however, is that which is moved about intellect, is the light of intellect,[1] and a vestigie suspended from it. Hence, according to one part of itself it is conjoined with it, and on this account it is replete with and enjoys it, participates of, and intellectually perceives it; but according to another part, it comes into contact with things posterior to itself, or rather, generates them, and which are necessarily inferior to soul. About these, however, we shall speak hereafter. And as far as to these is the progression of divine natures.

VIII. On this account all things are distributed by Plato in a triple order about the king of all. For he says, "that all things are about the king of all;"[2] second

---

[1] *i.e.* Is a light emanating from intellect.

[2] There is evidently a defect here in the original; for there is nothing more than φησὶ γὰρ πρῶτα. But the words of Plato in his second Epistle are περὶ τὸν πάντων βασιλέα πάντ' ἐστι, καὶ ἐκείνου

things about that which is second, and such as are third about that which ranks as the third." He also says that this king is the father[1] of cause, denominating intellect cause. For with Plato, intellect is the demiurgus. But he says that this cause produced soul in that *Crater* [mentioned by him in the Timæus]. The cause, however, being intellect, he says that the father[2] is *the good*, and that which is beyond intellect, and beyond essence. In many places, also, he calls being and intellect idea; so that from Plato we may know that intellect and idea are from *the good*, but soul from intellect. These assertions, however, are not new, nor of the present time, but were delivered by the ancients, though not explicitly, and what has now been said by us is an interpretation of them. That these opinions also are ancient, is testified and confirmed by the writings of Plato. Parmenides, therefore, prior to Plato, adopted this opinion, so far as he collects into one and the same thing being and intellect. Being, likewise, he does not place among sensibles. For he says, *that to perceive intellectually, and to be, are the same thing.* He also says, *that this is immoveable*, though he adds, *that it perceives intellectually*, removing from it all corporeal motion in order that it may abide invariably the same. And he assimilates it to the bulk of a sphere, because it contains all things involved in itself, and because its intellection is not external to but in its own essence. When, likewise, in his writings he calls it one, he alludes to the cause of it, as if this one [of intellect] was found to be many. The Parmenides, however, in Plato, speaking more accurately, divides from each other this and the first one, which is more principally one. He also calls the

ἕνεκα πάντα, καὶ ἐκεῖνο αἴτιον ἁπάντων τῶν καλῶν, δεύτερον δὲ περὶ τὰ δεύτερα, καὶ τρίτον περὶ τὰ τρίτα.

[1] παρὰ here is erroneously printed for πατέρα.
[2] There is the same error in the original here as above.

second one many, and the third, one and many. And after this manner, he likewise accords with the doctrine of the three [above mentioned] natures.

IX. But Anaxagoras, when he says that there is a pure and unmingled intellect, admits also that the first [principle of things] is simple, and that *the one* is separate. On account of antiquity, however, he omits the accurate discussion of these things. Heraclitus, also, knew an eternal and intelligible one. For he says, *that bodies are always rising into existence, or becoming to be, and flowing.* With Empedocles, strife[1] indeed divides, but friendship is *the one;* and this according to him is incorporeal. But the elements are arranged by him analogous to matter. Aristotle, however, afterwards asserts that the first principle is separate and intelligible. But when he says that it intellectually perceives itself, again he makes it not to be the first.[2] When also he introduces many other intelligibles, and as many as there are spheres in the heavens, in order that each of these may move each of the spheres, he speaks of intelligibles in a way different from Plato, and not being able to assign probable reasons, adduces necessity. It may also be opportunely observed, that it is more reasonable to refer all the spheres to one co-ordination, and to assert that they look to one thing, and the first cause of all. Moreover, it may likewise be asked, whether according to him the many intelligibles are from one first cause, or whether there are many principles in intelligibles? And if indeed they are from one first, they will be analogously arranged, like

[1] In the original, εἶκος instead of νεῖκος.
[2] Aristotle in his writings ascended no higher than the intelligible, and this with him is the first principle. And perhaps this was because he knew that the nature which is beyond the intelligible is perfectly ineffable and unknown, and therefore accurately speaking, is even beyond principle. See my translation of his Metaphysics.

the spheres in the sensible universe, one comprehending another, but one external to them ruling over all of them. So that the first will there comprehend the rest, and there will be an intelligible world. As here, likewise, the spheres are not empty, but the first is full of stars, and all the rest have stars; so there also the moving causes will contain many things in themselves, and what is there contained will have a more true subsistence. But if each is a principle, the principles will subsist fortuitously. And it may be asked, why they subsist and accord in accomplishing one work, viz. the concord of all heaven. How, likewise, are the sensible natures in the heavens equal to the intelligible and motive causes. And how are they thus many being incorporeal, since matter does not separate them from each other. Hence, those ancients who especially embraced the doctrines of Pythagoras and his followers, and of Pherecydes, were investigators of this intelligible essence. Some of them, however, committed discussions of these things to writing, but others delivered them not in writing, but unfolded them in unwritten discourses, or wholly dismissed the consideration of them.

X. It has been shown, however, as far as it is possible to demonstrate about things of this kind, that it is requisite to think that beyond being there is *the one*, such as reason wishes to unfold; that next to this, being and intellect subsist; and that, in the third place, follows the nature of soul. But, as in the nature of things there are these three hypostases, so likewise it is proper to think, that the above mentioned three subsist with us. I do not mean to assert that they are to be found in sensibles; for they have a separate subsistence; but that they are external to sensibles, and external after the same manner in man also, as the three which we have been considering are external to all heaven. This, however, is such a man as Plato calls the inward man. Our soul, therefore, is likewise something divine, and of a nature different from sensibles, such as is the whole nature of soul. But the soul is perfect which possesses intellect. With respect to intellect, however, one kind is a reasoning intellect, but another imparts the power of reasoning. He, therefore, will not err who places in the intelligible order of things this reasoning intellect of the soul, which is not in want of any corporeal organ to the subsistence of its discursive energy, but which possesses the energy of itself in purity, in order that it may reason purely, in as great perfection as possible. For we must not inquire after a place where we may establish it, but it must be arranged external to all place. For thus that which is from itself, the external, and the immaterial subsist, when they are alone, and have nothing from a corporeal nature. On this account, also, Plato in the Timæus says, "that the Demiurgus surrounded the body of the universe with soul," indicating that part of the mundane soul which abides in the intelligible. Concerning our soul, likewise, concealing his meaning, he says, in the Phædrus, that it sometimes hides its head in the heavens, and sometimes elevates it beyond them.[1] The exhortation, too, in the Phædo, to separate the soul from the body, does not relate to a local separation, which is effected by nature, but insinuates that the soul should not verge to imaginations, and to an alienation from itself, by a tendency to body. He also indicates that we should elevate the remaining [*i.e.* the irrational] form of the soul, and lead it on high together with the superior part of it; and that the part which is established in the sensible region, and is alone the fabricator and plastic maker of body, should likewise be engaged in an employment of this kind.

XI. Since, therefore, the soul reasons about things just

[1] I have followed the version of Ficinus in this place, as the original is obviously defective: for there is nothing more than, ἐπὶ δὲ ἡμῶν ἔτι κρύπτων, ἐπ' ἄκρα εἴρηκε τῇ κεφαλῇ.

and beautiful, and inquires by a reasoning process whether this thing is just, and that is beautiful, it is necessary there should be something stably just, from which the reasoning of the soul originates; or how could it reason? And if the soul at one time reasons about these things, but at another time not, it is necessary there should be an intellect in us, which does not reason about, but always possesses the just. It is likewise necessary that we should contain the principle and cause of intellect, and God; the latter of these not being divisible, but abiding, yet not in place, [but in himself,] and again being surveyed in each of the multitude of things that are able to receive him. They receive him, however, as something different from themselves; just as the centre of a circle is in itself, but each of the lines in the circle has its summit terminating in the centre, and the several lines tend with their peculiarity to this. For by a thing of this kind which is in us,[1] we also touch, associate with, and are suspended from deity. But we are established in it more or less according as we converge to it in a greater or less degree.

XII. How, therefore, does it happen, since we possess things of such great dignity, that we do not apprehend them, but for the most part are sluggish with respect to such like energies? And there are some who do not energize about them at all. Intellect, indeed, and that which, prior to intellect, is always in itself, are always employed in their own energies. Soul, likewise, is thus that which is always moved. For not every thing which is in the soul is now sensible; but it arrives to us when it proceeds as far as to sense. When, however, each thing in us energizing, does not impart itself to the sensitive power, it does not yet proceed through the whole soul. Hence we have not yet any knowledge of the energy, because we

---

[1] This is called by Proclus, *the one*, flower, and summit of the soul, and is that in which our *truest* being consists.

exist in conjunction with the sensitive power, and are not a part of the soul, but the whole soul. And farther still, each of the psychical animals in us, always energizes essentially according to its peculiarity; but we then only recognize the energy, when there is a participation and apprehension of it. It is necessary, therefore, in order that there may be an apprehension of things which are thus present, that the animadversive power should be converted to the interior of the soul, and there fix its attention. Just as if some one waiting to hear a voice which is pleasing to him, should separate himself from other voices, and excite his hearing to the perception of the more excellent sound, when it approaches. Thus, also, here it is necessary to dismiss sensible auditions, except so far as is necessary, and to preserve the animadversive power of the soul pure, and prepared to hear supernal sounds.

IX.
ON INTELLECT, IDEAS,[1] AND [REAL] BEING.

V. xi.

I. SINCE all men from their birth employ sense prior to intellect, and are necessarily first conversant with sensibles, some proceeding no farther pass through life, considering these as the first and last of things, and apprehending that whatever is painful among these is evil, and whatever is pleasant is good; thus thinking it sufficient to pursue the one and avoid the other. Those too among them, who pretend to a greater share of reason than others, esteem this to be wisdom, being affected in a manner similar to more heavy birds, who collecting many things from the earth, and being oppressed with the weight, are unable to fly on high, though they have received wings for this purpose from nature. But others are in a small degree elevated from things subordinate, the more excellent part of the soul recalling them from pleasure to a more worthy pursuit. As they are, however, unable to look on high, and as not possessing any thing else which can afford them rest, they betake themselves together with the name of virtue to

[1] For a more ample discussion of Ideas than is contained in this treatise of Plotinus, see the Introduction and Notes to my translation of the "Parmenides of Plato," and the notes to my translation of Aristotle's "Metaphysics," in which the reader will find treasures of antiquity on this subject unfolded.

actions and the election of things inferior, from which they at first endeavoured to raise themselves, though in vain. *In the third class is the race of divine men*, who through a more excellent power, and with piercing eyes, acutely perceive supernal light, to the vision of which they raise themselves above the clouds and darkness as it were of this lower world, and there abiding despise every thing in these regions of sense; being no otherwise delighted with the place which is truly and properly their own, than he who after many wanderings is at length restored to his lawful country.

II. What then is this place? And how may some one arrive at it? He, indeed, will arrive thither, who is by nature amatory, and who is truly a philosopher in disposition from the beginning. For as being amatory, he will be parturient about the beautiful, yet will not be satisfied with the beauty which is in body, but will fly from thence to the beauty of soul, to virtues and sciences, studies and laws, and will again from these ascend to the cause of the beauty contained in soul. If, also, there is a beauty prior to this, he will ascend to it, till he at length arrives at that which is first, and which is beautiful from itself. Having likewise arrived hither, he will be liberated from his parturiency, but not before. But how will he ascend, whence does he derive the power of ascending, and what is the reasoning which will conduct this love [to the desired end?] Is it the following? This beauty which is in bodies, is adventitious to bodies. For the *morphæ*, or forms themselves of bodies, are in them as in matter. The subject, therefore, is changed, and from being beautiful becomes deformed. Hence reason says that body is beautiful by participation. What is it then which causes body to be beautiful? This, indeed, is effected in one way by the presence of beauty, but in another by soul, which fashions body, and inserts in it a *morphe*, or form of such a kind.

What then? Is soul of itself beautiful or not? Certainly not; since if it were, one soul would not be wise and beautiful, but another unwise and base. Hence, the beauty which is in soul is derived from wisdom. Who is it, therefore, that imparts wisdom to the soul? Is it not necessarily intellect? But it is an intellect, which is not at one time intellect, and at another deprived of it: for it is true intellect, and which is therefore beautiful from itself. Is it then necessary to stop here as at that which is first, or is it requisite to pass beyond intellect? Intellect, indeed, as with reference to us precedes the first principle of things, announcing as it were in the vestibules of *the good*, that all things subsist in itself; as being a multitudinous impression of *the good* which entirely abides in unity.

III. This nature, however, of intellect must be considered, which reason announces to be truly being, and true essence, previously confirming, by proceeding in another way, [what we have before asserted] that it is necessary there should be a certain nature of this kind. Perhaps, therefore, it is ridiculous to investigate whether intellect ranks in the order of beings; though perhaps some persons may be dubious concerning this. And they may be in a still greater degree dubious whether there is such an intellect as we have maintained there is, and which is separate[1] [from soul]. Likewise, whether this intellect is [real] beings, and whether it contains the nature of forms, about which we now propose to speak. We see, therefore, that all the things which are said to exist are composites, and that no one of them is simple, whether they are fashioned by art, or constituted by nature. For artificial substances consist of brass, or wood, or stone, and do not yet obtain perfection from these, till they are

---

[1] For ἀχώριστός here, it is necessary to read χωριστός.

elaborated by the several arts, one of which produces a statue, another a bed, and another a house, and each effects this by the insertion of the form which it contains. Moreover, with respect to the things which are constituted by nature, such of them as are composed of many particulars, and which are said to be co-mingled, may be analyzed into the form which is inherent in all substances that are mingled together. Thus man may be analyzed into soul and body; and body into the four elements. But finding that each of these is a composite, consisting of matter and that which gives it form (for the matter of the elements is of itself formless) you will again also investigate respecting the soul, whether it now ranks among simple natures, or whether one thing in it has the relation of matter, but another, viz. the intellect which it contains, the relation of form; one indeed being analogous to the *morphe* in brass, but the other to the artist who produces that *morphe*. He, likewise, who transfers these very same things to the universe, will also here ascend to intellect, and will admit that it is truly the maker and demiurgus [of all things]. He will, likewise, say that the subject matter receiving forms, becomes either fire or water, or air, or earth; but that these forms proceed from another cause, and that this is soul. Again, also, he will assert, that soul imparts *morphe* to the four elements of the world; but that intellect becomes the supplier of productive principles to soul; just as productive principles being inserted from the arts in the souls of artists enable them to energize [according to art]. With respect to intellect, also, one which is as the form of the soul is analogous to *morphe*, but another which imparts this form, is analogous to the maker of the statue, in whom all things are inherent which he imparts. The things, however, which body receives, are now nothing more than images and imitations.

IV. Why, therefore, is it necessary to ascend to soul, and yet not admit that it is the first of things? Is it not because in the first place, indeed, intellect is different from, and more excellent than soul? But that which is more excellent is prior by nature. For soul when perfect, does not, as some fancy it does, generate intellect. For whence will that which is in capacity become in energy, unless there is a cause which leads into energy? Since if it becomes in energy casually, it is possible that it may not proceed into energy. Hence, it is necessary that first natures should be established in energy, and that they should be unindigent and perfect. But imperfect natures are posterior to them. The progeny also of imperfect, are perfected by first natures, who after the manner of fathers give perfection to what posterior natures generated imperfect from the beginning. That, likewise, which is generated, has at first the relation of matter to the maker of it, but is afterwards rendered perfect by the participation of form. But if it is necessary that soul should be connected with passion, and if it is likewise necessary that there should be something impassive, or all things would perish in time; it is necessary that there should be something prior to soul. And, if soul is in the world, but it is necessary there should be something beyond the world, on this acccount also it is necessary that there should be something prior to soul. For if that which is in the world, is in body and matter, nothing would remain the same [if that which is mundane only existed]. So that man, and all productive principles, would not be perpetual, nor always the same. Hence, that it is necessary intellect should be prior to soul, may be surveyed from these and many other arguments.

V. It is necessary, however, to consider intellect truly so called neither as intellect in capacity, nor as proceeding from the privation to the possession of intellect. For if we do not, we must again investigate another intellect prior to this. But we must assume intellect in energy, and and which is always intellect. If such an intellect, however, has not an adventitious intellection, whatever it intellectually perceives, it perceives from itself. And whatever it possesses, it possesses from itself. But if it perceives intellectually by and from itself, it is itself that which it perceives. For if the essence of it was one thing, but the objects of its perception different from it, its very essence would be destitute of intellection; and again, it would be intellect in capacity, but not in energy. Neither of these, therefore, must be separated from the other. With us, however, it is usual, from the things with which we are conversant, to separate in our conceptions intellect, and the objects of its perception. What therefore is its energy, and what does it intellectually perceive, in order that we may admit it to be those things which it perceives? Is it not evident, that being intellect, it intellectually perceives in reality, and gives subsistence to beings? Hence it is itself beings. For it either intellectually perceives them existing elsewhere, or it perceives them in itself as being itself. It is impossible, therefore, that it can perceive them existing elsewhere. For in what other place can they exist? Hence it intellectually sees itself, and perceives them in itself. For it does not perceive these, as some fancy, in sensibles. For each of the things which have a primary subsistence, is not a sensible object. For the form which is in sensibles is in matter, and is truly an image. Every form, also, which is in another thing, is derived from another thing, proceeds to it, and is the image of it. If, likewise, it is necessary that intellect should be the maker of this universe, it will not intellectually perceive things in that which does not yet exist, in order that it may produce it. Hence, it is necessary that these things should be prior to the world, not as impressions from other things, but as archetypes, and primary natures, and the essence of intellect. If, however, some should say that [seminal] productive principles are sufficient, it is evident that these must be perpetual. But if they are perpetual and impassive, it is necessary that they should subsist in intellect, and in such an intellect as is prior to habit, and nature and soul. For these are in capacity. Intellect, therefore, is truly beings, not intellectually perceiving such things as are situated out of itself. For the objects of its perception are not external to itself. But it is as it were the first legislator, or rather the law itself of existence. Hence it is rightly said, that it is the same thing to perceive intellectually and to be, and that the science of things without matter, is the same with the things themselves. I have also investigated myself as one among the number of beings. And the same thing is testified by reminiscence. For no one of [real] beings subsists out of intellect, nor is in place; but they always abide in themselves, neither receiving mutation nor corruption. Hence, also, they are truly beings; since if they were generated and corrupted, they would have an adventitious existence; and they would no longer be [real] beings, but that which is adventitious to them would be being. Sensibles, therefore, are indeed by participation that which they are said to be, the subject nature [*i.e.* matter] receiving form externally derived; as for instance, brass receiving form from the art of the statuary, and wood from the tectonic art; in consequence of art proceeding into these materials through an image. Art itself, however, abides in sameness, external to matter, and possesses in itself the true statue, and the true bed. Thus also in bodies, this universe which participates of images, evinces that real beings are different from bodies; since the former are immutable, but the latter mutable. The former, likewise, are established in themselves, and are not in want of place. For they are not magnitudes, but have an hypostasis intellectual, and sufficient to themselves. For the nature of bodies is indebted to something else for its preservation. But intellect, since it sustains through an admirable nature things which are of themselves in a perishable condition, does not seek where it may be itself established.

VI. Let, therefore, intellect be [real] beings, and possess all things in itself, not as in place but as itself, and as being one with them. But all things there subsist collectively at once, and yet nevertheless they are separated from each other; since the soul also which has many sciences in itself simultaneous, possesses them without any confusion. Each also, when it is requisite, performs what pertains to it, without the co-operation of the rest. And each conception energizes with a purity unmingled with the other inward conceptions. Thus, therefore, and in a still greater degree, intellect is at once all things; and again, not at once, because each is a peculiar power. Every intellect however, comprehends all things,[1] in the same manner as genus comprehends species, and as whole comprehends parts. The powers of seeds, likewise, bring with them an image of what we have said. For in the whole seed, all things are without separation, and the reasons [or productive principles] are as it were in one centre. That there is one productive principle likewise of the eye, and another of the hand, is known from what is sensibly generated from them. With respect, therefore, to the powers in seeds, each of them is one whole productive principle, together with the parts comprehended in it. And that which is corporeal indeed in the seeds, possesses a certain quantity of matter which is as it were moist; but the productive principle itself is according to the whole of

---

[1] πάντα is omitted in the original.

its form, and the same thing is also reason, generating a certain thing by the form of a soul, and which is the image of another more excellent soul. Some, however, denominate this principle which is inserted in the seeds, nature; which being thence excited from things prior to itself, in the same manner as light from fire, changes and gives form to matter; effecting this, not by impulsion, nor by employing levers [or any other mechanical power], but by imparting seminal productive principles.

VII. The sciences, however, of sensibles, which are in the rational soul, if it is proper to say that there are sciences of these, since the appellation adapted to them is that of opinion, in consequence of being posterior to sensible things, are the images of them. But the sciences of intelligibles, which are truly sciences, and which descend from intellect into the rational soul, understand indeed nothing sensible; but so far as they are sciences, are each of the things which are the objects of their perception; and possess internally the intelligible and intelligence. This, however, is because intellect is inward, which is primary natures themselves, is eternally present with itself, and exists in energy. It likewise does not extend itself to the objects of its perception as if it did not possess them, or as if it acquired them externally, or obtained them by a discursive process, as if they were not already present with it (for these are the passions of soul); but it stands firmly in itself, being at once all things, and does not energize intellectually in order that it may give subsistence to every thing. For it does not, when it intellectually perceives God, become God, nor when it understands motion does it become motion. Hence, if the assertion that forms are intellections signifies, that when intellect understands this particular form it then becomes that form, it is not true. For it is necessary that the object of intellection should be prior to this intellectual perception. Or how would intelligence arrive at the perception of it? For it cannot be fortuitously, nor does intelligence extend itself towards the intelligible in vain.

VIII. If, therefore, intelligence is truly one, that form which is the object of its perception and idea itself are one. What therefore is this? Intellect and an intellectual essence, each idea not being different from intellect, but each is intellect. And, in short, intellect is all forms; but each form is each intellect; just as the science which ranks as a whole is all the theorems [of the several sciences] Each theorem, however, is a part of whole science, not as separated by place; but each possesses power in the whole. This intellect, therefore, is in itself, and possesses itself in quiet, being always exuberantly full. Hence, if intellect were conceived to subsist prior to being, it would be requisite to say that intellect, by energizing and intellectually perceiving, generated and perfected beings. But since it is necessary to conceive being to be prior to intellect, it is requisite to admit that beings are established in that which is intellective, but that energy and intelligence are posterior to beings; just as the energy of fire is posterior to fire. Hence, since beings are established in intellect, they possess in themselves their own energy. Being, likewise, is energy; or rather, both are one. Hence, too, both being and intellect are one nature; and on this account also, beings, the energy of being, and an intellect of this kind, are one. Such intellections, also, are form, and the morphe and energy of being. In consequence, however, of these being divided by us, we conceive some of them to be prior to others. For the intellect which makes this division, is different from them. But impartible intellect and which does not divide, is being and all things.

IX. What then are the things in this one intellect, which we divide in our conceptions of it? For it is necessary to exhibit them quiescent, and to survey them proceeding from thence, as if from science subsisting in unity. This world, therefore, being an animal comprehending in itself all animals, and possessing its existence, and the quality of its existence from something different from itself, that also from which it is derived being referred to intellect—this being the case, it is necessary that the archetypal universe should be in intellect; and that this intellect should be the intelligible world, which Plato [in the Timæus] says exists in that which is animal itself. For as where there is reason [or a productive principle] which is a certain animal, and where also there is at the same time matter which receives the spermatic reason, it is necessary that an animal should be generated; after the same manner, an intellectual nature being present, which is all-powerful, and has nothing to impede its energy, (nothing existing between this, and that which is able to receive it) it is necessary that the recipient should be adorned, and that intellect should adorn. And that, indeed, which is adorned, possesses distributed forms, here man, and there the sun. But in the adorning cause all things are in one.

X. Such things, therefore, as are forms in the sensible world, are derived from the intelligible world; but such things as are not forms do not originate from thence. Hence, nothing preternatural is there; as neither is there in the arts any thing which is a deviation from art, or lameness in the seeds of animals. For lameness of the feet which takes place in the generation of an animal. arises from the productive seminal principle not vanquishing [the seminal matter]. But the injury which the form sustains is a casual circumstance. According qualities, therefore, and quantities, numbers and magnitudes, habitudes, actions and passions, which are according to nature, and motions and permanencies both universal and particular, are among the number of things which are in the intelligible world. Instead of time, however, eternity is there. But place is there intellectually, being the [impartible] subsistence of one thing in another. Hence, since all things there exist simultaneously, whichever of them you assume is essence, is intellectual, and participates of life. Sameness, also, and difference, motion and permanency, that which is moved, and that which is stable, essence and quality, are there, and all things there are essence. For each thing is being in energy, and not in capacity; so that quality is not separated from each essence. Are, therefore, those things alone these which the sensible world contains, or are there likewise many other things? Prior to the discussion of this, however, the things pertaining to art must be considered. For there is no paradigm of evil there. For evil here happens from indigence, privation, and defect. And evil is the passion of matter frustrated of form, and of that which is assimilated to matter.

XI. With respect, therefore, to things pertaining to the arts, and the arts themselves, the arts that are imitative, such as painting, statuary, dancing and pantomine, since they derive their subsistence from sensibles, and employ and imitate a sensible paradigm, and also transfer [to their originals] the forms, motions and symmetries which they perceive, cannot properly be referred to intelligibles, except so far as the forms in the human soul may be called intelligible. If any one, however, considers the habit in all animals arising from the symmetry of their formation, this will be a part of the power which in the intelligible world surveys and contemplates the symmetry of all things that are there. Moreover, with respect to all music which is conversant with harmony and rythm, so far as its conceptions are employed about rythm and harmony, it will subsist after the same manner as the music which is conversant with intelligible rythm. With respect to such arts as are productive of sensible things conformably to art, as the builder's and the carpenter's art,—these, so far as they employ symmetry, will derive their principles from intelligibles, and from the wisdom which is there. But as they mingle these with a sensible nature, the whole of them will not be in intelligibles, except so far as they subsist in man [*i.e.* in the human soul]. Neither will the agriculture be there which is conversant with a sensible plant; nor the medicine which surveys the health of the body, or which contributes to strength and a good corporeal habit. For there is another power, and another health there, through which all animals are sufficiently corroborated. With respect to rhetoric also, and the military art, economics, and the art pertaining to regal government, if some of these partake in actions of the beautiful, and make it the object of their contemplation,—in this case, they have a scientific allotment from the science which is there. But geometry, which is conversant with intelligibles, must be arranged in the intelligible world; as likewise must the highest wisdom which is conversant with real being. And thus much concerning the arts, and things pertaining to the arts.

XII. If, however, the idea of man is there, the ideas of the rational and the artificial are also there, and likewise the arts which are the progeny of intellect. It is also requisite to assert, that the forms of universals are there, *i.e.* not of Socrates, but of man; though it must be considered with respect to man, whether the form of a particular man is there, not because he is the same with another man, but because one man has a flat, and another an aquiline nose. These nasal differences, however, must be placed in the form of man [as certain differences of forms], just as there are differences of animals. But that one man has an aquiline nose of this, and another of that kind, originates from matter. With respect to the differences of colours, also, some of them exist in their productive principles, but others are produced by matter and difference of place.

XIII. It remains to consider whether what the sensible world alone contains is in the intelligible world, or whether as man himself is different from the sensible man, so with respect to soul, soul itself is different from the soul which is here, and intellect itself from the human intellect. In the first place, therefore, it must be said, that it is not proper to think that all things which are here, are images of archetypes; or that the human soul is the image of soul itself, but that here also one soul differs from another in dignity. Perhaps, however, soul, so far as it is here, is not soul itself. But since each [rational] soul has a real subsistence, as likewise have justice and temperance, there is also in our souls true science and not images only, nor merely the similitudes of intelligibles, as in the sensible region. For true science, justice, and temperance themselves exist here, though after another manner than in the intelligible world. For they are defined in a certain place. So that where the soul emerges from the body, there also these subsist. For the sensible world, indeed, is in one place only; but the intelligible world is every where. Such things, therefore, as a soul of this kind possesses here, these things also are there. So that if the things which are in the sensible world, are assumed to be those which are in the number of visible objects, not only the natures which are in the regions of sense are there, but also more than these. But if among the natures which are said to be in the world, soul, and what soul contains are comprehended, then all such things are here as subsist there.

XIV. Is this nature, therefore, which comprehends all things in the intelligible, to be considered as the first principle of things? But how is this possible, since that which is truly the principle is *one*, and entirely simple, but multitude subsists in *beings?* After what manner, however, this all-comprehending nature subsists besides *the one*, how multitude exists, and how all these subsist, and why and whence intellect is all these, must be shown by beginning the discussion from another principle. With respect, however, to things generated from putrefaction, and to things artificial,[1] whether there are forms of these, and also of mud and clay in the intelligible world, it must be said, that such things as intellect derives from the first principle, are all of them most excellent. But the above-mentioned particulars are not among the number of these, nor does intellect consist of the forms of such particulars. Soul, however, which is derived from intellect, receives from matter other things [besides what she receives from intellect], and such particulars as the above are in the number of these. The discussion of these, however, will be rendered clearer by recurring to the doubt, how multitude proceeds from *the one*. In the mean time it is evident that such composite natures as are casual are not derived from intellect, but from a concurrence of sensibles in themselves, and do not subsist in forms. Those things, also, which are produced from putrefaction, are the progeny of a soul which is perhaps incapable of effecting any thing else; for if this were not the case, it would produce something conformable to nature. It produces, therefore, where it is able. But with respect to the arts, such of them as are referred to things natural to man, are comprehended in [the soul of] man. The art also, which is universal, is

---

[1] Instead of χαλεπῶν here, it is evidently necessary from what afterwards follows to read τεχνικῶν or τέχνων. Ficinus, from not seeing the necessity of this emendation, has made nonsense of the passage. For he translates περὶ δὲ τῶν ἐκ σήψεως καὶ τῶν χαλεπῶν, "Ubi vero quæritur nunquid ibi sit species eorum etiam quæ ex putrefactione fiunt, *difficiliumque, et admodum molestorum.*"

prior to other arts, and soul itself is prior to universal art, or rather this must be asserted of the life which is in intellect, before it became soul, and which is necessary to the generation of soul. And this life it is requisite to denominate soul itself.

X.
ON THE ESSENCE OF SOUL.
IV. ii.

I. IN investigating the essence of soul, if we show that it is neither body, nor the harmony in incorporeal natures; and likewise if we omit what is said of its being the *entelecheia*,[1] or perfection of the body, as not true, as the words [taken literally] imply, and as not manifesting what the soul is; and if also we should say that it is of an intelligible nature, and a divine allotment, perhaps we shall assert something perspicuous concerning its essence. At the same time, however, it will be better to proceed still further than this. For this purpose, therefore, we shall make a division into a sensible and intelligible nature, and place soul in the intelligible. Hence, let it be at present admitted that it ranks among intelligibles: and let us in another way investigate that which is proximate to, or the peculiarity of, its nature. We say, therefore, that some things are primarily partible, and in their own nature dissipable; but these are such as have no part the same, either as another part, or as the whole; and in which it is

[1] The cause, according to Aristotle, by which the animal is *vitally* moved, is the rational soul, but the cause by which the animal thus moved is *defined* or *bounded*, is *entelecheia*, or form, which imparts to it perfection. See my Introduction to, and translation of, Aristotle's treatise "On the Soul."

necessary that the part should be less than all and the whole. These, however, are sensible magnitudes and masses, each of which has an appropriate place, nor is it possible among these, that the same thing should be in many places at once. But there is another essence opposed to this, which in no respect admits of a separation into parts, since it is without parts, and therefore impartible. It likewise admits of no interval, not even in conception, nor is indigent of place, nor is generated in a certain being, either according to parts, or according to wholes, because it is as it were at one and the same time carried in all beings as in a vehicle; not in order that it may be established in them, but because other things are neither able nor willing to exist without it. It likewise possesses an essence which subsists according to sameness, and is the foundation [1] of all following natures, being as it were a centre in a circle, the lines drawn from which and terminating in the circumference, nevertheless permit it to abide in itself. For they possess from the centre their generation and being, participate of the point, and have for their principle that which is impartible. They also proceed, suspending themselves from the centre. This, therefore, [of which the centre in a circle is an image] being primarily impartible in intelligibles, and the leader among beings, and again that which is in sensibles being in every respect partible,—this being the case, prior to that which is sensible, but which nevertheless is something near to and in it, there is another certain nature, which is partible indeed, yet not primarily so like bodies, but becomes partible in bodies. Hence, when bodies are divided, the form which is in them is also divided, though it still remains a whole in each of the divided parts; the same thing in this case becoming many, each of which is perfectly distant

---

[1] It appears from the version of Ficinus, that the word στήριγμα is wanting in this place in the original.

from the other, in consequence of the form becoming entirely partible. Of this kind are colours, and all qualities, and each *morphe*, which is capable of being wholly at one and the same time in many things, that are separated from each other, and which has no part suffering the same thing with another part. Hence this must be admitted to be in every respect partible.

Again, besides the nature which is perfectly indivisible, there is another essence proximately suspended from it, and which has indeed from it the impartible, but by a progression from thence, hastening to another nature, is established in the middle of both; viz. in the middle of that which is impartible and primary, and that which is divisible about bodies, and is inherent in bodies. This nature does not subsist after the same manner as colour and every quality, which are indeed every where the same in many masses of bodies, yet the quality which is in one mass, is entirely separate from the quality in another, so far as one mass is also separate from another. And though the magnitude should be one, yet that which is the same in each part, has no communion whatever so as to produce co-passivity, because this sameness is at the same time attended with [a predominant] difference. For the sameness is passion, and is not itself also essence. That, however, in this middle nature which accedes to an impartible essence, is itself essence, and is ingenerated in bodies, about which also it happens to be divided; yet it does not suffer this, till it gives itself to bodies. When, therefore, it is inherent in bodies, though it should be inherent in the greatest body, and which is every where most extended, yet though it gives itself to the whole, it does not depart from the unity of its nature. Yet it is not one in the same manner as body. For body is one by continuity, but one part of it is different from another, and is situated in a diffcrent place. Nor again is it one, in the same manner as one quality. The nature, however, which is at once partible and impartible, and which we say is soul, is not one like that which is continued, having another and another part; but it is partible indeed, because it is in all the parts of that in which it subsists; and impartible, because the whole of it is in all the parts, and likewise in each of the parts. He, therefore, who perceives this, and beholds the power of it, will know what a divine and admirable thing soul is, and that it possesses a supernatural essence; not indeed having magnitude, but being present with all magnitude, and existing in this place, and again not existing in it, and this not by a different, but the same nature. So that it is divided into parts, and again not divided; or rather, it is neither divided, nor generated divisible. For it remains with itself a whole. But it is divided about bodies, because bodies in consequence of their proper partibility, are not able to receive it impartibly. So that the distribution into parts, is the passion of bodies, and not of soul.

II. That it is necessary, however, that the nature of soul should be a thing of this kind, and that it is not possible for soul to be any thing besides this, being neither alone impartible, nor alone partible, but that it is necessarily after this manner both these, is manifest from the following considerations. For if it was like bodies having another and another part, when one part suffered, another part would not be sensible of the suffering, but that soul for instance, which is in the finger, would have a sensation of the passion, as being different, and subsisting in itself. And, in short, there would be many souls, governing each of us. One soul, likewise, would not govern this universe, but an infinite number of souls separate from each other. For with respect to what is said about continuity, unless it contributes to unity, it is introduced in vain. For that which is asserted by some who deceive themselves, is not to be admitted, viz. that the senses gradually arrive at the ruling part, by a continued succession.[1] In the first place, therefore, to say that the senses arrive at the ruling part of the soul, is said without examination. For how do they divide, and assert *this* to be one thing, but *that* another, and the ruling part something else? By how much quantity, also, do they divide each of these; or by what difference, the quality being one, and the bulk continued? Whether, likewise, is the ruling part alone sentient, or have the other parts also a sensible perception? And if this is the case with the ruling part alone, it will then perceive, when the sensible passion falls on this part established in a certain place; but if it falls on another part of the soul, which is not naturally adapted to be sentient, this part will not deliver the same passion to the ruling part, nor, in short, will there be sensation. If, also, the sensible passion falls on the ruling part, it will either fall on a part of it, and this being sentient, the remaining parts will no longer be sensitive; for it would be in vain; or there will be many and infinite sensible perceptions, and all of them will be dissimilar. Hence, one sensible perception will say, I primarily suffer, but another will say, I perceive the passion of another sense. Each sensation, likewise, except the first, will be ignorant where the passion was generated. Or each part of the soul will be deceived, fancying that the passion was there generated, where it is. If, however, not only the ruling part, but any other part has a sensible perception, why will this part be the leader, but another part not? Or why is it necessary that sensation should arrive at the ruling part? How, likewise, will the sensations arising from many senses, such as the ears and eyes, know one particular thing? But again, if the soul is entirely one, so as to be perfectly impartible, and one in itself; and

---

[1] For διαδόσει here, it is necessary to read, conformably to the version of Ficinus, διαδοχῇ.

if it entirely flies from the nature of multitude and partibility, no body which may participate of the soul, will be wholly animated; but the soul establishing itself as it were about the centre of each, will leave all the bulk of the animal without animation. Hence it is necessary that soul should be thus one and many, partible and at the same time impartible: and we ought not to disbelieve that it is impossible for one and the same thing to be in many places at once. For if we do not admit this, there will not be a nature which connects and governs all things; and which at once comprehends all things, and conducts them by wisdom. And this nature is indeed multitude, because beings are many; but it is also one, in order that the nature which comprehends may be one. By its multitudinous one, therefore, it supplies all the parts of body with life; but by its impartible one it conducts all things wisely. In those things, however, which are deprived of wisdom, that which is the leading one imitates this one of the soul. Hence, this is the meaning of what is divinely though obscurely asserted by Plato, viz. that from an essence impartible and always subsisting according to sameness, and from an essence divisible about bodies, the Demiurgus mingled a third species of essence from both.[1] Soul, therefore, is after this manner one and many; but the forms in bodies are many and one; bodies are many only; and that which is supreme is one alone.

[1] See my Introduction to, and translation of, the "Timæus" of Plato.

XI.
A DISCUSSION OF DOUBTS RELATIVE TO THE SOUL.

IV. iii.

I. Is it necessary to consider such doubts as pertain to the soul as sufficiently solved; or shall we say that the doubts themselves are accompanied with this gain, that to know the difficulty with which they are attended, will be a right discussion of the affair? For what can any one reasonably more abundantly consider and discuss than this; both on many other accounts, and also because it contributes to the knowledge of those things of which it is the principle, and of those from which it is derived? By so doing, likewise, we shall comply with the mandate of the God who calls upon us to know ourselves. And since we wish to investigate and discover other things, it is but just to enquire what this is which investigates, especially since we desire to apprehend that which is lovely in the objects of contemplation. For in every intellect there is that which is twofold;[1] so that in partial intellects it is reasonable to admit that one has [the intelligible] in a greater, but another in a less degree. It is likewise requisite to consider, how souls become the receptacles of the Gods; but this, indeed, we shall discuss when we investigate how soul subsists in

[1] viz. The intelligible and the intellectual.

body. Now, therefore, again, let us return to those who assert that our souls also are derived from the soul of the universe. For perhaps they will say it is not sufficient [in order to establish this hypothesis,] that our souls extend as far as the soul of the universe, nor that they are similarly intellectual with it; since parts are of a similar species with their wholes. They will, likewise, adduce Plato[1] as the patron of this opinion, when proving that the universe is animated, he says: "As our body is a part of the body of the universe, thus also our soul is a part of the soul of the universe." This, too, is confirmed by the assertion, that we follow the circulation of the universe. And it is clearly asserted and demonstated that our manners and fortunes are thence derived; and that as we are generated within the world, we receive our soul from the universe in which we are comprehended. Farther still, as each part of us partakes of our soul, so likewise we for the same reason, since we have the relation of parts to the whole, participate as parts of the soul of the universe. The assertion [of Plato[2]] likewise, that every soul pays a guardian attention to every thing inanimate, has the same signification, and does not leave any thing else externally of soul, after the soul of the universe. For it is this soul which pays attention to every thing inanimate.

II. In answer to these things, therefore, in the first place it must be said, that those who admit souls to be of a similar species, because it is granted that they come into contact with the same things, and ascribe to them a common genus, exclude them from ranking as parts of one soul, and will rather make one and the same soul, and each to be every soul. But making one soul, they will also suspend it from something else, which no longer being some-

[1] See his "Philebus" and "Timæus."
[2] In the "Phædrus."

thing pertaining to this thing or that, but neither belonging to the world, or to any other thing, will effect the very same thing, as is effected by [the life] of the world, and of any animated being whatever. For it rightly happens that not every soul is something belonging to another thing, since soul is an essence; but that there should be a certain soul which is wholly exempt from a subordinate nature; and that such souls as belong to something else, are from accident at certain times connected with that which is inferior to themselves. Perhaps, however, it is necessary to show more clearly how a part in such souls is to be considered. Part, therefore, belonging to bodies, whether the body is of the same or of a different species, must be dismissed; observing thus much alone, that when part is asserted of bodies consisting of similar parts, the part is according to bulk, and not according to form; such for instance as whiteness. For the whiteness which is in a part of milk, is not a part of the whiteness of all the milk; but it is the whiteness indeed of a part, and not a part of the whiteness. For whiteness is entirely without magnitude, and is void of quantity. This, therefore, thus subsists. When, however, in things which are not bodies we speak of a part, we either assume it in such a way as in numbers, as when we say that two is a part of ten; (but let this be considered as asserted in mere numbers alone) or as when we speak of the part of a circle and a line; or as a theorem is a part of science. In monads and figures, indeed, it is necessary in the same manner as in bodies, that the whole should be diminished, by a division into parts, and that the several parts should be less than the wholes [of which they are the parts]. For being quantities, and having their existence in quantity, and also not being the same quantity, they necessarily become greater and less. A part, therefore, cannot after this manner be asserted of soul. For it is not quantity in such a way as the decad is the whole, but the monad a part of the decad. Many other absurdities also will happen [from admitting that the soul is quantity]; nor are ten things one certain thing. Either, likewise, each of the monads will be soul, or soul will consist of all inanimate things. Besides, the part of the whole soul is admitted to be of the same kind with the whole; but it is not necessary in continued quantity, that the part should be such as the whole. Thus, for instance, the parts of a circle are not of the same species with the circle, nor the parts of a triangle with the triangle; at least, all the parts in these, in which a part may be assumed, are not similar [to the whole]. For all the parts of a triangle are not triangles; [and so in other figures] but there will be a difference between the form of some of the parts and that of the whole. Soul, however, is acknowledged to be of a similar form. In a line, likewise, a part of it is still a line, but here also there is a difference in magnitude. But in soul, if the difference between that soul which is partial, and that which ranks as a whole, should be considered as a difference in magnitude, soul would be a certain quantity and a body; since in this case, it would receive the difference so far as it is soul, from quantity. All souls, however, are admitted to be similar and wholes. It appears, likewise, that neither is soul divided after the same manner as magnitudes; nor do even our opponents admit that the whole of the soul can be divided into parts; since if this were the case, the whole would be destroyed. And unless the first soul was every soul, it would be a name alone; just as if it should be said, when wine is distributed into many amphoræ, that the portion of it in each amphora, is a part of the whole wine. Shall we say, therefore, that part is to be assumed in the soul, in the same manner as a theorem is a part of science? the whole science, indeed, nevertheless remaining; but the separation into parts, being as it were the utterance and energy of each. In a thing of this kind, however, each possesses the whole science in capacity, but the whole nevertheless continues to be the whole. If, therefore, a part in the whole soul and other souls is to be thus assumed, the whole soul, of which things of this kind are parts, will not be the soul of a certain thing, but will itself subsist from itself. Neither, therefore, will it be the soul of the world, but will be a certain soul, and will rank among those that are of a partial nature: hence all the parts being of a similar species, are the parts of one soul. But how is one the soul of the world, and another the soul of a part of the world?

III. Are parts, therefore, so to be assumed, as if some one should say, that the soul which is in the finger of a certain animal, is a part of the whole soul which is in the whole animal? This assertion, however, either leaves no soul independent of body, or admits every soul not to be in body, and contends that what is called the soul of the universe is external to the body of the world. But this must be considered; and now must be investigated by an image. For if the soul of the universe imparts itself to all partial animals, and thus each soul is a part [of the whole soul]; for if this soul were divided, it would not impart itself to each; in this case, in consequence of imparting itself wholly, it will be every where the same, being one and the same at once in many animals. After this manner, however, one soul will no longer rank as a whole, and another as a part, and especially in those things in which the same power is present. For where the employment of one thing is different from the employment of another, as in the eyes and ears, there it must not be said that one part of the soul is present to the sight, and another to the ears (for such a division as this belongs to other things), but the same part, though a different power energizes in each. For all the powers of the soul are in both the parts; but the apprehensions are different in consequence of the organs being different. Nevertheless, all the powers rank among forms, and are reduced to a form which is capable of being fashioned according to all things. This is evident from the necessity that all things should arrive at one thing [and concur in it]; but the nature of the instruments through which the concurrence is effected, is not able to receive all things, and the passions become different in the different instruments of sensation. The judgment, however, is from the same thing, as from a judge directing his attention to what is said and done. But it has been shown, that it is every where one thing which energizes in different actions. And if the apprehensions are as sensations, it is not possible for each of the senses to understand, but the whole soul. But if intelligence is appropriate, each intellectual perception subsists through itself. And when the soul is rational, and is rational in such a way as to be denominated wholly so, then that which is called a part is the same with the whole, and is not a part of it.

IV. What, therefore, shall we say, if it is thus one, when any one inquires, in the first place doubting, whether soul can after this manner be at once one in all things? And in the next place, when one soul is in body, but another not, [how this takes place?] For perhaps it follows that every soul is always in body, and especially the soul of the universe. For this soul does not, as ours is said to do, leave the body; though some say that even this soul abandons its body, and yet is not entirely out of the body. But if the soul of the universe is entirely out of the body, how is it that one soul leaves the body, but another does not, though both are [essentially] the same? In intellect, therefore, which is separated from itself by difference, according to parts especially distinguished from each other, but which always subsist together at once, the essence of intellect being impartible, no such doubt can arise. But

P

in the soul which is said to be divisible about bodies, how this which is one certain thing can be all souls, is attended with many doubts; unless that which is one is established in itself, without falling into body, and afterwards all souls proceed from it, both the soul of the universe, and others to a certain extent; existing as it were together with it, and being one in consequence of not belonging to any thing else [*i.e.* of not being consubsistent with something of a nature subordinate to themselves]. They must, likewise, be suspended from their boundaries, and conspire with each other in their tendencies to supernal natures, by the projecting energies of intellect; like a light which is now on the earth, and is distributed in different habitations, yet is not divided into parts separated from the whole, but is nevertheless one. Hence, the soul of the universe is always transcendent, because it does not belong to it to descend, and be converted to these inferior realms. But our souls are subordinate, because a certain part of their essence is limited to this terrene abode, and to a conversion to body which requires solicitude and care. The soul of the world, therefore, in its most inferior part, resembles a great vegetable soul, which without labour and silently governs the plant of which it is the soul [*i.e.* in the same manner as worms are generated in wounds]. But the government of the inferior part of our soul, resembles the worms that are generated in the putrified part of a plant. For thus the animated body of the universe subsists. Another soul, however, which is similar in species to the superior part of the soul of the world, resembles in its government the husbandman whose attention is directed to the worms that are generated from putrefaction in a plant, and who is solicitously employed in the cultivation of the plant. Or as if some one should say that a man who is well, and is with other men that are in health, is with those persons with whom he co-operates either in acting or contemplating; but that a diseased man, and who is employed in procuring remedies for the body, is with the body, and becomes corporeal through his attention to it.

V. How, therefore, any longer will *this* be your soul, *that* the soul of some other person, and *that* again of another? Shall we say that it is the soul of this person according to its inferior part, but not of this according to its supreme part, but of some other person? Thus, however, Socrates will indeed exist, when the soul of Socrates is in body; but he will perish when he is especially in the most excellent condition [*i.e.* when he is in the intelligible world]. But no being perishes, since the intellects which are in the intelligible do not perish, because they are not corporeally distributed into one thing, but each remains possessing in difference a sameness of subsistence, in which its very being consists. After this manner, therefore, souls also being successively suspended according to each intellect, being likewise reasons of intellects, though more evolved than an intellectual essence, and becoming as it were *much* from that which is *few*, and being in contact with it, they are now willing to be divided by each of these more impartible essences, yet are not able to proceed to the very extremity of division. For they preserve their sameness and difference, and each remains one, and at the same time all are one. We have, however, summarily shown, that all souls are from one soul, and that all of them are divisible and at the same time indivisible. The soul, also, which abides [on high], is the one reason of intellect, and from this soul partial and immaterial reasons are derived, in the same manner as there [*i.e.* in the same manner as partial intellects are derived from one intellect which ranks as a whole].

VI. Why, however, did the soul of the world being of a uniform nature make the world, but not the soul of each individual, though it likewise contains all things in itself? For we have before shown that productive power may exist at one and the same time in many things. Now, however, the reason of this must be assigned. For perhaps the manner may be known by us in which the same thing in different subjects either does or suffers a certain thing, or is with respect to it both an agent and a patient. Or rather let us consider how and why the soul of the universe made the world, but other souls govern a certain part of the world. Perhaps, however, it is not at all wonderful, that of those who possess the same science, some should rule over many, but others over few. But why, it may be said, is this the case? To this it may be answered, that the difference of souls is greater, so far as one of them does not depart from the soul of the universe, but abiding there has a body surrounding it; but other souls, body now existing, and their sister soul having dominion, are alloted an appropriate destiny, this soul preparing for them proper habitations. It may also be said, that the soul of the universe beholds that intellect which ranks as a whole, but that other souls rather behold their own intellects which are of a partial nature. Perhaps, however, these souls also are able to make the universe; but the soul of the world having made it, this is no longer possible to other souls, productive energy having commenced from the first soul. But the same doubt will arise if any other soul first began to fabricate. It is better, however, to say that the soul of the world rather than other souls fabricated the universe, because it in a greater degree adheres to intelligibles. For the power of those souls is greater that more vigorously tend to the intelligible world. For, preserving themselves in that secure region, they fabricate with facility; since it is the property of a greater power, not to suffer in the things which it produces. But power remains suspended from the supernal region. Abiding, therefore, in itself, it produces [other things] acceding. But other souls which proceed from the one soul, depart from it into the profundity [of a material nature]. Perhaps, also, that which is most abundant in them, being drawn downward, draws them likewise into an inferior condition, their own decisions conspiring with the downward impulse. What, however, is said in the "Timæus" of mixture in a second and third degree, must be considered as signifying that some souls are nearer to, but others more remote from the soul of the world; just as in our souls, all of them are not similarly disposed with reference to supernal natures, but some are united to them, others through [ardent] desire accede near, and others accomplish this in a less degree, because they do not energize with the same powers. For some, indeed, energize with a first, others with a second, and others with a third power, all souls nevertheless possessing all powers.

VII. And thus much concerning these particulars. What is said in the "Philebus," however, may lead us to suspect that other souls are parts of the soul of the universe. But the meaning of what is there asserted, is not what some one may fancy, but was useful to Plato in demonstrating that the world is animated. This, therefore, he renders credible by saying that it is absurd to assert that the universe is inanimate, and that we who have a part of the body of the universe, have a soul. For how can a part have a soul, if the universe is inanimate? The opinion of Plato, however, is especially manifest in the "Timæus;" where the Demiurgus having generated the soul of the universe, afterwards produces other souls, mingling them in the same crater in which he had mingled the soul of the world, and making them to be of a similar species with it, but assigning them a difference in a second and third degree. Nor is what he asserts in the "Phædrus" wonderful, that every soul pays a guardian attention to that which is inanimate. For what is it except soul which governs, fashions, arranges, and produces the nature of body? Nor must it be said, that one soul is naturally adapted to do this, but another not. The perfect soul, therefore, says he, revolves on high, not verging downward, but fabricates, riding in the world as it were as in a vehicle. Every other perfect soul, also governs the universe in a similar manner. But when he speaks of the soul whose wings suffer a defluxion, he evidently makes a difference between such a soul as this, and that of the universe. And when he adds, that souls follow the circulation of the universe, derive their manners from thence, and suffer from it, this does not at all indicate that our souls are parts of the soul of the world. For soul is sufficiently able to represent many things in itself, from the nature of places, and water, and air. And to this ability, the habitations of different cities, and the temperature of bodies, also contribute. And if we should grant that since we are in the universe we have something from the soul of the world, and that we suffer from the celestial circulation, yet we shall oppose to these things another soul [*i.e.*, the rational soul], and which by its resistance especially demonstrates itself to be a different soul. To the assertion, also, that we are generated within the world, we reply that the fœtus in the womb of the mother has a soul different from that of the mother, and which accedes to it externally.[1]

VIII. Such, therefore, is the solution of these particulars; the sympathy of souls being no impediment to our arguments. For since all of them originate from the same

[1] *i.e.* It has a rational soul different from that of the mother. It is better, however, to say with Proclus, that as nature does nothing in vain, the presence of the rational soul to the fœtus in the womb would be useless, as it could not then energize; but that it becomes united to the irrational soul in the very moment in which the infant leaves the womb.

source as the soul of the universe, they are co-passive. For it has been already asserted by us that there is one [first] soul, and many souls. And we have likewise shown what the difference is between part and whole ; and have in short spoken concerning the difference of souls. Now, also, we shall summarily observe, that besides bodies souls differ, especially in their manners, in the operations of the reasoning power, and from a pre-existent life. For in the "Republic" of Plato it is said, that the choice of souls is made conformably to their antecedent lives. But if any one in short assumes the nature of soul, he will assert that there are differences in the souls in which it is admitted there are second and third degrees. It has, likewise, been said by us, that all souls are all things ; and that each is characterized by that which energizes in each. This, however, is the same thing as to assert, that one soul indeed is united in energy, another in knowledge, and another in appetite. Different souls also behold different objects, and are and become the very objects which they behold. Plenitude, likewise, and perfection pertain to souls, yet all of them have not the same of either of these ; but the whole co-ordination of them is various. For every reason [or productive principle] is one, abundant, and various, in the same manner as a psychical animal, which has many forms. But if this be the case, there is co-ordination, and beings are not, in short, divulsed from each other. Nor is there any where that which is casual in beings ; not even among bodies. Hence it follows, that the number of things is definite. For again, it is necessary that beings should stop [in their progression], that intelligibles should continue the same, and that each thing should be one in number; for thus it will be *this particular thing.* For every body being naturally in a continual flux, in consequence of having an adventitious form, the perpetual existence of bodies according to form takes place through an imitation of [real] beings. The essence of the latter, however, as not subsisting from composition, consists in that which is one in number, which exists from the beginning, and neither becomes that which it was not, nor will be that which it is not; since if there were any thing in some future time which could produce them, it would not produce them from matter. But if this be the case, it is necessary to add something which is of itself essential; so that there will be a mutation about this very thing, if it now produces more or less. Why, likewise, should it produce now, and not always after the same manner? That, likewise, which is generated will not be perpetual, if it admits of the more and the less. But soul is supposed to be a thing of this kind. How, therefore, is it infinite if it is stopped [in its progression]? May we not say, that it is infinite in power, because power is infinite, since God himself is not bounded. With respect to souls, therefore, each is not that which it is, as if it were so much in quantity, through a foreign boundary; but it is as great as it wishes to be. Nor will it ever proceed out of itself, but will pervade every where, to bodies and through bodies, as it is naturally adapted to do; yet it is not divulsed from itself, when it is in a finger and a foot. Thus also in the universe, soul remains entire, into whatever it may proceed, and in another and another part of a plant. Hence, when any part of a plant is cut off, it is both in the plant as it was at first, and in the part which is separated from it. For soul is every where in the body of the universe, as in the one of it, this body being one. But when an animal becomes putrid, if many animals are generated from it, soul is then no longer the soul of the whole animal in the body; for it has not then a proper receptacle of itself; nor yet does it perish. But the putrified matter being adapted to the generation of animals, has partly the soul of these, and partly the soul of those animals, soul never being absent from any thing, though one thing is adapted to receive it, and another is not. The parts of matter, however, which thus become animated, are not the cause of there being many souls. For these [spontaneously generated] animals are suspended from one soul, so far as it remains one; in the same manner as in us, when certain parts of the body are amputated, and others grow instead of them, the soul indeed is absent from [*i.e.* is not participated by] the former, but is present with the latter, so long as it remains one. In the universe, however, it always remains one. But of the natures within the universe, some indeed have soul, but others not, the same psychical [powers] still remaining.

IX. The manner, however, in which the soul is ingenerated in the body, must be considered. For this is no less admirable, and no less deserves to be investigated. The mode, therefore, in which the soul enters into the body is twofold. For one of these modes takes place, when the soul being in one body changes it for another, and from an aerial [or fiery], becomes situated in a terrestrial body; which some do not call a transmigration, because that from which the insertion originates is immanifest. But the other mode is a transition from an incorporeal essence to any body whatever; which also will be the first communion of the soul with the body. It will be right, therefore, to consider respecting this communion, what the passion arising from this conjunction then is, when the soul being entirely pure from body, becomes surrounded with the nature of body. Let us, however, first consider how this is effected in the soul of the universe; for perhaps it is proper, or rather is necessary, to begin from hence. For it is requisite that we should explain its ingress into and animation of the body, for the sake of doctrine and perspicuity. Though there never was a time, therefore, in which this universe was not animated, and it is not possible for body to subsist if soul is absent, nor was matter ever unadorned, yet it is possible in conception and in words to separate these from each other. For by these we may analyze every composition. The truth then is as follows : If body had no existence, there would be no progressions of soul; since there is not any other place, where it is naturally adapted to be. If, however, soul intends to proceed, it will generate for itself a place, so that it will generate body. The stability of soul, however, being as it were corroborated in permanency itself, and soul also resembling the effulgence of a great light, a darkness was in the mean time generated in the very extremity of the light, which soul perceiving, gave form to it, since it was likewise the cause of its subsistence. For it was not lawful for any thing proximate to soul, to be destitute of form. Hence, by this obscure nature which was generated by soul, that which is called obscure was received. [The universe] therefore, being generated like a certain beautiful and various edifice, is not separated from its maker [soul], nor yet is mingled with it; but the whole of it is every where considered by its artificer as deserving a providential attention. It is advantageous, therefore, both to its existence and its beauty, to participate as much as possible of its maker; and to the latter this participation is not injurious. For it governs, abiding on high. And the world is animated after such a manner, that it cannot with so much propriety be said to have a soul of its own, as to have a soul presiding over it; being subdued by, and not subduing it, and being possessed, and not possessing. For it lies [1] in soul

[1] Similar to this, one of the Chaldæan Oracles, speaking of human souls, says,

Ἐν δὲ Θεῷ κεῖνται, πυρσοὺς ἕλκουσαι ἀκμαίους,
Ἐκ πατρόθεν κατιόντας, ἀφ' ὧν ψυχὴ κατιόντων
Ἐμπυρίων δρέπεται καρπῶν ψυχότροφον ἄνθος.

i.e. "But they lie in God, drawing vigorous torches [i.e. unities,

which sustains it, and no part of it is destitute of soul; being moistened with life, like a net in water. It is not, however, able to become that in which it lies; but the sea [of soul] being now extended, the net is also co-extended with it, as far as it is able. For each of the parts is incapable of existing in any other situation than where each is placed. But soul is naturally so great, because it is without quantity. Hence every body is comprehended by one and the same thing. And wherever body is extended, there also soul is. Unless, however, body existed, the attention of soul would not be at all directed to magnitude. For it is of itself that which it is. For the world is so greatly extended, through soul being present with the whole of it. And the extension of the world is bounded, so far as in its progression it has soul for its saviour. The magnitude of the shadow, likewise, is as great as the reason [or productive principle] which is suspended from soul. But the reason was of such a kind as to be able to produce as great a magnitude as the form of it wished might be produced.

X. Thus conceiving, therefore, it is requisite that again betaking ourselves to that which always subsists invariably the same, we should assume all things existing at once, such as the air, light, the sun, and the moon. And, likewise, that we should again consider light and the sun as at once all things, but having the order of things first, second, and third. Here, also, we must consider soul as being always established; and in the next place, we must assume the natures which are first, and those that are in a consequent order, as the extremity of fire in that which is posterior; from the shadow of that fire which subsists at

images of *the one*], descending from the father; and from these descending, the soul plucks of empyrean fruits, the soul-nourishing flower." See my Collection of these Oracles, in the "Old Monthly Magazine."

the extremity of things, forming a conception of the fire which ranks as the first. In the next place, we must conceive this ultimate fire to be at the same time illuminated, so as to resemble form running into that nature which is hurled towards it, which was first generated, and is entirely obscure. It is, however, adorned according to reason by the power of soul, which possesses in itself wholly a power of adorning by reasons [or productive principles]; just as the reasons in seeds fashion and give form to animals, as if they were certain little worlds. For whatever comes into contact with soul, is made to be such as the essence of soul is naturally adapted to make it. Soul, however, makes, not by an adventitious decision, nor by waiting for counsel and consideration; for thus it would make not according to nature, but according to adscititious art. For art is posterior to, and imitates soul; producing obscure and imbecile imitations, which are things of a ludicrous nature, and not of much worth, and employing many machines in the formation of images. But soul by the power of essence has dominion over bodies in such a way, that they are generated and subsist, just as she leads them, since they are unable from the first to oppose her will. For in things of a posterior nature which impede each other, matter[1] is frequently deprived of the attainment of the appropriate form which the productive principle [latent] in the seed wished it to have. There, however [*i.e.*, in the universe], the whole form being generated by soul, and the generated natures having at the same time an arrangement, that which is produced becomes beautiful without labour, and without impediment. But in the universe are fabricated, some things indeed which are statues of the Gods, others which are the habitations of men, and others which are adapted to other things. For what else ought to be gene-

[1] From the version of Ficinus, it is necessary here to supply the word ἡ ὕλη.

rated about soul, except those things which it possesses the power of producing? For the property of fire is to produce heat, and of another thing [cold] to refrigerate. But the peculiarity of soul is, partly to produce something from itself into another thing, and partly to produce something in itself. For in inanimate natures, indeed, that which is from themselves, lies in them as it were in a dormant state; but that which tends to another thing, endeavours to assimilate to itself that which is able to be passive to it. And this is common to each of them, to lead other things to a similitude to itself. That which energizes, however, in soul is something of a vigilant nature, and this is also the case with that which tends from it to another thing. Hence, it causes other things to live which do not live from themselves, and confers on them such a life as it lives itself. The life of soul, therefore, being essentialized in reason, imparts reason to body, as an image of that which it possesses itself. For that which it imparts to body is an image of life. Body, also, receives from soul corporeal *morphæ*, of which soul contains the productive principles. Soul, likewise, comprehends in itself the productive principles of Gods,[1] and of all things. Hence, the world also contains all things in itself.

XI. Those ancient wise men, likewise, who wishing that the Gods should be present with them, fabricated temples and statues, appear to me to have directed their attention to the nature of the universe, and to have intellectually perceived, that the nature of soul is every where tractable; and that it may be received the most easily of all things, if any thing is fashioned so as to be passive to it, and is able to receive a certain portion of it. But every thing is disposed to be passive which is in any way imitative, so as

[1] *i.e.* Of divine souls, each of which is a God according to participation. See the first book of my translation of Proclus "On the Theology of Plato."

to be able like a mirror to seize a certain form. For the nature of the universe has fashioned all things most artificially in imitation of those forms the participations of which it contains in itself. And since every thing is thus generated, the reason [or productive principle] in matter, which was fashioned according to a reason prior to matter, is conjoined to that God, conformably to whom it was generated, and which the soul looks to, and possesses while it fabricates. Hence it was not possible for any thing to be generated destitute of this God; *nor again, is it possible for him to descend hither;* since this God is intellect, the sun of the intellectual world. Let this, therefore, be assumed by us as the paradigm of reason. But next to this soul follows, suspended from permanently abiding intellect, and being also itself permanent. Soul, therefore, imparts the terminations of itself which are prior to this visible sun, to this sun; and causes it through itself as a medium to be conjoined to intellect, becoming as it were an interpreter of the things derived from intellect to the sun, and also of those which revert from the sun to intellect, so far as the former recurs through soul to the latter. For no one thing is very remote from another; and yet again, it is remote through difference and mixture. But every thing [in the intellectual region] is in itself, not locally, and each is united to each, and is at the same time separate from each. These, however, [*i.e.* the mundane spheres] are Gods, because they are never deserted by intellect and soul; and are suspended from the primordial soul, which is as it were departing [from mundane natures]. These, therefore, so far as they are what they are, and so far as they are said to look to intellect [are divine]; the vision of soul itself being directed no where else than to intellect.[1]

[1] The latter part of this sentence in the original is as follows: οὐδαμοῦ ψυχῆς αὐτῆς ἢ σώματος ἐκεῖ βλεπούσης; but both the sense

XII. The souls of men, however, beholding the images of themselves, like that of Bacchus in a mirror,[1] were from thence impelled to descend; yet were not cut off from their principle and from intellect. For they did not descend in conjunction with intellect, but proceeded as far as to the earth, their heads being at the same time established above the heavens. It happened, however, that their descent was more extended, because that which subsists in them as a medium, is compelled to exercise a guardian care, in consequence of the nature into which it arrives requiring solicitous attention. But the father Jupiter, commiserating laborious souls, made the bonds about which

and the version of Ficinus require that the word σώματος should be expunged.

[1] The meaning of what is here said by Plotinus, will be illustrated by the following remarkable passage from the MS. Commentary of Olympiodorus "On the Phædo." "In order," (says he) "to the soul's descent, it is necessary that she should first establish an image of herself in the body; and in the second place, that she should sympathize with the image according to a similitude of form. For every form hastens into a sameness with itself, through an innate convergency to itself. In the third place, becoming situated in a divisible nature, it is necessary that she should be lacerated and scattered together with such a nature, and that she should fall into an ultimate distribution, till through a cathartic life, she raises herself from the extreme dispersion, loosens the bond of sympathy through which she is united to the body, and energizing without the image, becomes established according to her primary life. And we may behold a resemblance of all this, in the fable respecting Bacchus the paradigm of our intellect. For it is said that Dionysius, establishing his image in a mirror, pursued it, and thus become distributed into the universe. But Apollo excited and elevated Bacchus, this God being a cathartic deity, and the true saviour of Dionysius. And on this account he is celebrated as Dionysoter. (διονυσωτήρ, for so it is requisite to read, and not διονυσοτης.)" See more on this subject in the second edition of my treatise, "On the Eleusinian and Bacchic Mysteries," in Number 16 of the "Pamphleteer," for November, 1816.

they labour mortal, causing them to have periodical cessations of their toil, and a liberation from body, that they also may become situated there where the soul of the universe always resides, without any conversion to these inferior realms. For what the world now possesses is sufficient to it, and will be perpetually through all the following revolutions and periodic restitutions of time, and this established in measures of definite lives, in which these are led to an harmonious agreement with those. At the same time, likewise, all things are arranged by one reason, with reference to the ascent and descent of souls, and every other particular. *The symphony, however, of souls with the order of the universe, which nevertheless are not suspended from the universe, but co-adapt themselves in their descent, and make one concord with the mundane circulation, is testified by this, that their fortunes, lives, and deliberate elections, are signified by the figures of the stars.* That the universe, likewise, utters as it were one voice harmonically and aptly, is asserted by the ancients more than any thing else, though obscurely. But this would not be the case, unless the universe was both active and passive through its participation of intellectual forms, in the measures of its periods, orders, and lives; souls evolving themselves according to the genera of discursive progressions, at one time in the intelligible world, at another in the heavens, and at another being converted to these inferior realms. Every intellect, however, is always in the intelligible world, and never departing from its own proper habitation, but established on high, sends through soul these objects of sensible inspection. But soul from its proximity to intellect, is in a greater degree disposed according to the form which flourishes there, and to some of the natures posterior to itself imparts a sameness of subsistence, but to others a subsistence which is different at different times, and a wandering which proceeds in an orderly course.

Souls, however, do not always equally descend, but sometimes more, and at other times less, though they may belong to the same genus. But each soul descends to that which is prepared for its reception, according to similitude of disposition. For it tends to that to which it has become similar; one soul indeed to man, but another to some other animal.

XIII. For justice, which is said to be inevitable, subsists in such a manner in a ruling nature, that every thing proceeds in that order with reference to which it was generated an image of archetypal pre-election and disposition. And that whole form of the soul, is similar to that to which it has in itself a disposition, and which then sends and introduces it where it is proper for it to be situated; not that it may then descend into body, or into this particular body; but that when the prescribed period arrives, souls may as it were spontaneously descend, and enter into that receptacle in which it is necessary for them to reside. A different soul, also, has a different time of descent; which when it arrives, souls descend, as if called by a cryer, enter into an appropriate body, and are similarly affected with those who are moved and borne along by the powers and strong attractions of magicians. They, likewise, resemble the administration which takes place in one animal, which moves each in a certain time, and generates hair, the beard, and the nature of horns, and now impels them to, and causes them to be efflorescent in things of this kind, which they did not possess before. They are also similar to the administration in the growth of trees which vegetate in orderly pre-established periods of time. Souls, however, proceed neither voluntarily, nor from compulsion. For that which is voluntary in them [when they descend] is not as if it were deliberate choice, but resembles a physical leaping, or the natural tendencies to wedlock, or the impulses to certain beautiful actions, to which we are not excited by a reasoning process. A certain particular thing, however, is always accompanied with a certain destiny. And to this thing the present time, but to another the future pertains [as to the accomplishment of the decrees of fate]. The destiny, indeed, of the intellect which is prior to the world, is to remain in the intelligible region, and from thence to impart something [to the sensible universe]. And particulars, falling under the universal law, are from thence sent hither. For in each, that which is universal is inherent. This law, also, does not receive its perfective power externally, but is imparted so as to be in the natures that use it, and to be carried about with them. When the time, likewise, arrives [which the law decreed], then that is effected which it wished to be effected, by those who possess this law. Hence, they themselves accomplish the law which surrounds them, and becomes strong through being established in them; oppressing them as it were with its weight, and producing in them a promptitude and vehement desire of arriving at that place, to which the law within them announces they should come.

XIV. These things, therefore, thus subsisting, this world having many lights, and being illustrated by souls, is adorned by other prior worlds, deriving a different gift from a different world; both from those Gods themselves, and from other intellects, through whom souls are imparted to the universe. And it is probable, that this is obscurely indicated by the fable, in which it is said that Prometheus having fashioned a woman, the other Gods also contributed to her embellishment. It is likewise said, that he mingled earth with water, and inserted the human voice; that he gave her a form resembling that of the Goddesses; that Venus and the Graces imparted something to her; and that a different divinity bestowed on her a different gift.

And lastly, that from the gift, and all the givers, she was called Pandora. For all the Gods gave something to this figment, which was produced by a certain *providence*.[1] But what else is signified by Prometheus warning his brother

[1] The recondite meaning of this fable, is thus beautifully unfolded by Olympiodorus in his MS. Scholia, "On the Gorgias of Plato:" "*Prometheus* is the inspective guardian of the descent of rational souls: for to exert a *providential energy* is the employment of the rational soul, and prior to any thing else to know itself. Irrational natures, indeed, perceive through percussion, and prior to impulsion know nothing; but the rational nature is able, prior to information from another, to know what is useful. Hence, *Epimetheus* is the inspective guardian of the irrational soul, because it knows through percussion, and not prior to it. Prometheus, therefore, is that power which presides over the descent of rational souls. But the *fire* which he stole from heaven, signifies the rational soul itself; because as fire tends upward, so the rational soul pursues things on high. But you will say, why is this fire said to have been stolen? I answer, that which is stolen is transferred from its proper place to one that is foreign. Since, therefore, the rational soul is sent from its proper place of abode on high, to earth as to a foreign region, on this account the fire is said to be stolen. But why was it concealed in a reed? Because a reed is cavernous, and therefore signifies the fluid body in which the soul is carried. Why, however, was the fire stolen, contrary to the will of Jupiter? Again, the fable speaks as a fable. For both Prometheus and Jupiter are willing that the soul should abide on high; but as it is requisite that she should descend, the fable fabricates particulars accommodated to the persons. And it represents, indeed, the superior character, which is Jupiter, as unwilling; for he wishes the soul always to abide on high: but the inferior character, Prometheus, obliges her to descend. Jupiter, therefore, ordered Pandora to be made. And what else is this than *the irrational soul*, which is of a feminine characteristic? For as it was necessary that the soul should descend to these lower regions, but being incorporeal and divine, it was impossible for her to be conjoined with body without a medium; hence she becomes united with it through the irrational soul. But this irrational soul was called Pandora, because each of

Epimetheus, not to accept the gift[1] [Pandora], than that the choice of that which is in the intelligible, is more excellent [than of that which is in the sensible world]? The maker, however, Prometheus, was afterwards bound, because in a certain respect he comes into contact with the thing generated by him. A bond, also, of this kind is external, and the solution of it is by Hercules; because he possesses a liberating power. Of these things, however, any one may form whatever opinion he pleases. But it is evident that the gifts imparted to the world are indicated by this fable, and that it accords with what has been before said.

XV. Souls, therefore, fall from the intelligible world, in the first place indeed, into the heavens, and there receiving a body, they now proceed through it into more terrene bodies, so far as their progressions are more extended in length. And some of them indeed, proceed from the heavens into inferior bodies, but others pass from certain bodies into others; these being such as have not a power sufficient to raise themselves from hence, on account of the great weight and oblivion which they have attracted, and which draw them downward by their oppressive influence.

---

the Gods bestowed on it some particular gift. And this signifies that the illuminations which terrestrial natures receive, take place through the celestial bodies." *

[1] Ficinus, in what is here said of Prometheus, appears to have entirely mistaken the meaning of Plotinus, and also not to have attended to what is asserted in the fable itself. For the translation of Ficinus is: "Quod autem Epimetheus ei donum dederit nullum." But the Greek is: ὁ δὲ προμηθεὺς ἀποποιούμενος τὸ δῶρον αὐτοῦ. See the Works and Days of Hesiod.

---

* For the irrational soul is an *immaterial body*, or in other words, *vitalized extension*, such as the mathematical bodies which we frame in the phantasy or imagination; and the celestial bodies are of this kind.

But souls become different from each other, either through the diversity into which they are introduced, or through the difference of their fortunes and educations; or again, they have a difference from themselves; or they differ in all these respects, or in some of them. And some of them, indeed, entirely fall under the dominion of the fate which is here; but others, at one time are subject to fate, and at another are dependent only on themselves. Others again grant that such things as are necessary must indeed be endured, but that such things as are their own works belong to themselves, and that living according to another legislation which comprehends in itself all beings, they give themselves to another more sacred law. This legislation, however, is a contexture consisting of all the reasons and causes that are here, of psychical motions and the laws derived from thence. It also accords with these, thence receives its principles, and weaves together with them whatever is of a consequent nature. And such things indeed, as are able to save themselves according to their proper habit, it preserves unshaken; but it conducts other things to that condition of being to which they are naturally adapted, so as to be the cause in their descent of the different situations of different things.

XVI. The punishments, therefore, which are inflicted with justice on the wicked, it is proper to refer to the order which leads every thing in a becoming manner. Such things, however, as happen to the good without justice, as punishments, or poverty, or disease, may be said to take place through offences committed in a former life. For these things are woven together, and are pre-signified, so that they are also produced according to reason. Or shall we say that these are not effected according to physical reasons, nor to be ranked among things which have a precedaneous subsistence, but among such as are consequent to them? As if some edifice should fall, the animal upon which it falls would be killed, whatever it might be. Or as if two certain things moving with an orderly motion, or even one thing thus moving, that which happens to fall at the time, should be broken or trampled on. Or it may be said, that this unjust circumstance is not an evil to him who suffers it, and is useful to the connexion of the whole of things. Or that neither is it unjust, things having a just retribution from antecedent transactions. For it is not proper to think that some things are co-ordinated, but that others are to be referred to the impulse of arbitrary will. For if it is necessary that things should be generated according to causes and physical consequences, and according to one reason and one order, it is also necessary to think that the smallest things are co-ordinated, and woven together. Hence the unjust conduct of one man towards another, is indeed unjust to the doer, and the agent is not without blame, yet being co-ordinated in the universe, it is not unjust with reference to it, nor to him who suffers the injury, but it was thus fit that it should take place. But if he who is injured is a worthy man, the end of these things is good to him.[1] For it is necessary to think, that this co-ordination of things is not without divinity, and is not unjust, but is accurate in the retribution of that which is appropriate; but that it has immanifest causes, and on this account is the occasion of blame to the ignorant.

[1] Conformably to this, it is divinely said by Plato in the Republic: "Whatever comes from the Gods to the man who is beloved by the Gods, will all be the best possible, unless he has some necessary ill from former miscarriage. Hence, if the just man happens to be in poverty, or disease, or in any other of those seeming evils, these things issue to him in something good either whilst alive or dead. For never at any time is he neglected by the Gods, who inclines earnestly to endeavour to become just, and practises virtue, as far as it is possible for man to resemble God."

XVII. That souls, however, first descend from the intelligible into the heavens, may be rationally inferred from the following considerations. If the heaven is in the sensible place that which is most excellent, it will be proximate to the extremities of intelligibles. Hence, the celestial bodies are first animated from thence, and participate of them, as being more adapted to participation. But a terrestrial body is the last of bodies, is naturally adapted to participate of soul in a less degree, and is more remote from an incorporeal nature. All the celestial souls indeed illuminate heaven, and impart as it were much of themselves, and the first procession from themselves to it, but other things become fulgid through posterior natures. The souls, however, which descend below the heavens, illuminate another inferior nature, but their condition is not ameliorated by proceeding to a greater extent. For there is something which is as it were a centre; but after this is a circle shining from the centre; and after this, another circle, which is a light emanating from a light. External to these, however, there is no longer another circle of light, but that which is posterior to them is indigent of its proper light, through the want of a foreign splendour. But let this be a rhombus, or rather a sphere, of such a kind as to participate of the second of these circles, to which it is the next in order, and through proximity to which it becomes resplendent. The great light, therefore, [*i.e.* intellect] illuminates abiding, and the light which emanates from it proceeds according to [or is characterized by] reason. But the other things co-illuminate, some indeed abiding, but others being abundantly attracted by the splendour of that which is illuminated. In the next place, since the illuminated natures require much guardian attention, like ships in a storm at sea, the pilots of which incessantly watch over them, and neglecting their own concerns, forget that they are frequently in danger of perishing together with the ships; thus also these souls are abundantly hurried away from their own concerns, and afterwards are detained in the bonds of enchantment, being held in durance through their attention to nature. But if each animal was such as the universe, having a body sufficient and perfect, and free from the danger of passivity, in this case, the soul which is said to be present with body, would not be present with it, but entirely abiding on high would impart life to the body [which is suspended from it].

XVIII. Again, shall we say that the soul employed the discursive energy of reason, before she came into body, and will also after her departure from it? Or shall we say that a reasoning process is employed by her here, in consequence of her being involved in doubt and filled with care, through which she becomes debilitated in a greater degree? For through a diminution of intellect, she requires the discursive energy of reason in order to be sufficient to herself; just as reasoning is requisite in the arts, through the artists being involved in doubts. But when there is no difficulty, then art subdues [its subject matter] and operates. If, however, souls live in the intelligible world without reasoning, how can they be any longer rational? In answer to this, it may be said, that they are still rational, because they are able to employ a reasoning process whenever circumstances render it necessary. It is necessary, however, to assume a ratiocination of this kind; since if some one should consider the discursive energy of reason as a disposition always subsisting from intellect in souls, and a stable energy which is as it were an evolution of intellectual light, and if in the intelligible souls also use the reasoning power, yet as it appears to me, we must not think that voice is employed by them there, so long as they entirely subsist in the intelligible world. But when they have bodies in the heavens, they do not use the dialect which they employ here through indigence or ambiguity; but performing every thing in an orderly manner, and according to nature, they neither command any thing to be done, nor consult about it. They also mutually know the objects of their knowledge through a consciousness of perception; since even here likewise we know many things through the eyes, pertaining to those that are silent. *There, however, every body is pure, and each inhabitant as it were an eye.* Nothing likewise is there concealed, or fictitious, but before one can speak to another, the latter knows what the former intended to say. But there is no absurdity in admitting that dæmons and souls that dwell in the air use voice; for such as these are animals.

XIX. Shall we however say that the impartible and partible, are to be considered according to the same thing [in the soul], as if they were mingled together; or that the impartible is to be assumed according to one thing, but the partible as something successive, and another part of the soul? Just as we say the rational part is one thing, but the irrational another. This, however, will be known, when we have explained what we say each of these is. The impartible, therefore, is simply assumed by Plato, but the partible not simply; [for he says that the soul is a medium between an essence impartible] and an essence which is divisible about bodies, and that the soul is not on this account generated. It is requisite, therefore, to consider after what manner the nature of body is indigent of soul for the purposes of living; and to see that it is necessary the soul should every where be present with the body, and also with the whole of it. Every sensitive power indeed, if it perceives through the whole body, arrives at the whole by being divided. For being every where in the body, it may be said to be divided; but appearing every where a whole, it may be said that it is not entirely distributed into parts; but that it becomes partible about bodies.

If, however, some one should say that the soul is not divided in the other senses, but in the touch alone, to this we reply, that the soul is also divided in the other senses, since it is the body which receives it, but that it is less divided than in the touch. The physical and augmentative powers also of the soul, are divided in a similar manner. And if desire dwells about the liver, but anger about the heart, the same thing must also be asserted of these. Perhaps however, these were not assumed in that mixture; or perhaps they were assumed, but after another manner, and these were produced from some one of the assumed particulars. But the reasoning power and intellect, do not give themselves to body; for their work is not effected through corporeal instruments; since these are an impediment when they are employed in contemplations. Hence the impartible is different from the partible, and they are not mingled as one thing, but as a whole consisting of parts, each of which is pure, and separate in power. If, however, that which becomes partible about bodies, has the impartible from a more sublime power, this very same thing may be both impartible and partible, as being mingled from the partible, and the power which proceeds into it from on high.

XX. It is requisite, however, to consider whether these, and what are called the other parts of the soul are in place, or these in short are not, but the other parts are, and if they are where they are, or whether none of them is in place. For if we do not assign a certain place to the several parts of the soul, but admit that each of them is no where, and thus make them to be no more within, than without the body, we shall render the body inanimate, and shall not be able to show how those works are effected which are performed through the corporeal organs. Or if we admit that some of the parts of the soul are in place, but others not, we shall not appear to grant those parts to be in us which we exclude from place, so that neither shall we admit that the whole of our soul is in us. In short, therefore, we must neither assert that any one of the parts of the soul, nor that the whole of it is in body. For place is that which comprehends, and is comprehensive of body; and where each thing is that is divided, there it is situated in such a way that the whole is not in any thing indiscriminately. Soul, however, is not body, and is not rather that which is comprehended than that which comprehends. Nor yet is it in body as in a vessel; for if it were, the body would become inanimate, whether it comprehended the soul as a vessel, or as place; unless it should be said that the soul is collected in itself, and by a certain distribution transmits something of itself into its vessel the body, and thus as much as the vessel participates, so much will be taken away from the soul. Place, however, properly so called, is incorporeal, and not body. So that in what will it be indigent of soul? Body also, not by itself, but by the boundary of itself, will approximate to soul. Many other objections, likewise, may be urged against him who asserts that soul is in place. For place will always be co-introduced with soul; and [it may still be asked] what will that be which introduces together with itself place? If place also is interval, much less will soul be in the body as in place. For it is necessary, that interval should be a vacuum. Body, however, is not a vacuum, but perhaps that will be a vacuum in which body is; so that body will be in a vacuum. Moreover, neither will soul be in the body as in a subject. For that which is in a subject, is a passion of that in which it is, as colour and figure. But soul is separable from the body. Nor yet, is soul in the body, as a part in the whole: for soul is not a part of the body. But if some one should say that soul is a part as in the whole animal, in the first place indeed, the same doubt will remain how it is in the whole. For it is not proper to conceive that it subsists either as wine in a vessel of wine, or as a vessel in a vessel; nor in the same manner as a thing is in itself. Nor again, will it be in body as a whole in the parts. For it is ridiculous to say that the soul is a whole, but the body parts. Neither is it as form in matter: for the form which is in matter, is inseparable from matter. And matter now existing, form afterwards accedes to it. But soul produces the form in matter, being itself something different from material form. If, however, it should be said that soul is not a generated, but a separate form, it will not yet be manifest how this form is in body; and soul will be separate from body. How then is it said by all men, that the soul is in the body? Shall we say it is because not the soul but the body is visible? Perceiving therefore the body, and conceiving it to be animated because it is moved and has sensible perception, we say that the body has the soul. Hence, therefore, we say that the soul is in the body. If, however, the soul were visible and sensible, so as to be perceived to be full of life, to comprehend entirely the body in life, and to extend itself equally to the extremities of it, we should no longer say that the soul is in the body, but that in the more principal nature that which is not such subsists, in that which contains, the thing contained, and that which flows in that which does not flow.

XXI. What then shall we say, if some one should ask us how the soul is present with the body, without giving us any information himself on the subject? And also if he should ask us whether the whole soul is similarly present, or a different part is differently present with the body? Since, therefore, none of the above-mentioned modes of the subsistence of one thing in another[1] is adapted to the subsistence of the soul in the body; but

---

[1] And these modes are enumerated by Aristotle in his "Physics."

the soul is said to be in the body in such a way as the pilot in a ship, this is well said so far as pertains to the power by which the soul is able to separate itself from the body; yet it does not entirely exhibit to us the mode which we are now investigating. For the pilot, so far as he is a sailor, will be from accident a pilot in the ship. But if the soul is present with the body in the same manner as the pilot alone with the ship, how is this effected? For the pilot is not in all the ship, in the same manner as the soul is in all the body. Shall we, therefore, say, that the soul is in the body, in the same way as art is in the instruments of art? For instance, as art in the rudder, if the rudder was animated, so that the piloting art is within it, moving it artificially. Now, however, there is this difference between the two, that art operates externally. If, therefore, we admit that the soul is in the body, conformably to the paradigm of the pilot within the rudder, as in a natural instrument; for he thus will move it, in whatever he wishes to effect; shall we make any accession to the object of our investigation? Or shall we again be dubious how the soul is in the instrument? And though this mode is different from the former modes, yet we still desire to discover [something farther], and to accede still nearer to the thing proposed.

XXII. Shall we therefore say, that when the soul is present with the body, it is present in the same manner as light is with the air? For again, this when present is [in reality] not present. And being present through the whole, is mingled with no part of it. It is also itself permanent, but the air flows by it. And when the air becomes situated out of that in which there is light, it departs possessing nothing luminous; but as long as it is under the light, it is illuminated. Hence, here also, it may be rightly said, that air is in light, rather than light in air. On this account, likewise, Plato [in the "Timæus"] does not place soul in the body of the universe, but the body of the universe in soul. And he says, that there is something of soul in which body is contained, and also something in which there is nothing of body; meaning by the latter those powers of the soul, of which the body is not indigent. The same thing, likewise, must be said of other souls. Hence, we must assert, that the other powers of the soul are not present with the body; but that those powers are present with it of which it is indigent; and that they are present, without being established either in the parts, or in the whole of the body. We must also say, that for the purpose of sensation indeed, the sensitive power is present with the whole of the sentient [organs]; but that with respect to energies, a different energy is present with a different part of the body. But my meaning is as follows:

XXIII. Since the animated body is illuminated by the soul, a different part of the body differently participates of it; and the power fitted to effect a certain work, is denominated according to the aptitude of the organ to the work. Thus the power in the eyes is denominated visive, in the ears acoustic, in the tongue gustic, and in the nostrils olfactive; but we say that the power of the touch is present with the whole body. For in order to effect this perception, the whole body is present as an instrument with the soul. Since, however, the instruments of the touch are in the nerves first, which also have the power of moving the animal, this power imparts itself from the nerves. But the nerves beginning from the brain, which is the principle of sense and impulse, and in short of the whole animal, as they are derived from hence to the other parts of the body, that which uses these instruments is considered as subsisting there where the principles of the instruments subsist. It is better, however, to say, that the principle of the energy of the power is there; for from whence the instrument is to be moved, there it is requisite that the power of the artificer, which is adapted to the instrument, should be as it were firmly fixed; or rather not the power, since power is every where. But the principle of energy is there, where the principle of the instrument exists. Since, therefore, the power of sensible perception, and the power of impulse, pertain to the sensitive soul, and the nature of the phantasy, which as being nearer to that which is beneath, have reason situated above them;—this being the case, where this principle is in the supreme part, there reason was placed by the ancients in the summit of the whole animal, viz. in the head; not as being [immediately] situated in the brain, but in this sensitive power, through which [as a medium] reason is established in the brain. For it is requisite to assign the sensitive power to the body, and to that which is especially the recipient of the energy of the body. But it is necessary that the form of the soul which is able to receive apprehensions from reason, should communicate with reason which has no communication with the body. For the sensitive power is in a certain respect judicial; and the fantastic power is at it were intellectual. Impulse and appetite also follow the phantasy and reason. Hence the reasoning power is there, not as in place, but because that which is [locally] there, enjoys this power [by participation]. But how that which is there subsists, has been shown in the sensitive power. Since, however, the vegetative, and also the augmentative and nutritive powers never fail, but each of them nourishes through the blood, and the blood which nourishes is in the veins, but the principle of the veins and the blood is in the liver, in which these powers are firmly fixed;—this being the case, the ancients assigned this place to a portion of the epithymetic soul. For that which generates, nourishes, and increases, must necessarily desire these [viz. the veins and blood]. But as attenuated, light, acute, and pure blood, is an instrument adapted to anger, the fountain of the blood, the heart, was considered by the ancients as a fit habitation for anger. For here a blood of this kind is secreted, which is adapted to the effervescence of anger.

XXIV. Souls, however, still having a body undergo corporeal punishments. But where does the soul dwell on its departure from body? It will not indeed be here, where there is not any thing to receive it. For it is not able to abide in that which is not naturally adapted to receive it, unless the recipient has something of an unwise and insane nature which attracts the soul to it. But the soul is in such a recipient as this, if it has something besides itself; and it there follows where this recipient is naturally adapted to be and to be generated. Since, however, each place is ample, it is necessary that a difference should be produced both from the disposition of the soul, and the justice which has dominion in things. For no one can ever fly from the punishment which it becomes him to suffer for unjust deeds. For the divine law is inevitable, containing at once in itself the power of accomplishing what it has now judged to be fit. In the mean time, he who suffers is ignorantly led to that which it is proper he should suffer, being every where in his wanderings conducted in a circuitous course [1] by an unstable motion, but at length, like one wearied by the resistance which he has made, falling into a place adapted to him, he undergoes an involuntary suffering through a voluntary motion. In the law, however, it is promulgated how much and how long it is necessary to suffer. And again, at the same time a remission of punishment concurs with the power of flying from those places [in which the punishment is inflicted] through a power of harmony by which all things are de-

---

[1] Instead of αἰωρούμενος in this place, it appears from the version of Ficinus, that we should read περιαγόμενος. And indeed, the sense of the passage requires this emendation.

tained. But to souls that have bodies, it also pertains to undergo corporeal punishments. Souls, however, that are pure, and attract nothing whatever to themselves of body, are also necessarily unconfined by the body. *If, therefore, they are not at all in body, for neither have they a body, they are there where essence and being, and that which is divine, subsist, viz. in God.* Hence, a soul of this kind will be here, and together with these, and in deity. If, however, you still inquire where it will be, you must also inquire where they are. But in exploring this, do not explore it with the eyes, nor as if you were investigating bodies.

XXV. With respect to memory, it must be considered whether souls on departing from these places recollect [what happened to them on the earth]; or whether this is the case with some souls, but not with others; and likewise, whether they have a recollection of all things, or of certain things only. And in a similar manner, it deserves to be investigated whether they always remember, or for a certain time near to their departure from hence. If, however, we intend to investigate these things rightly, what that is which remembers must be first assumed. I do not mean that we must inquire what memory is, but what that is in which it is naturally adapted to subsist. For we have elsewhere shown what memory[1] is, and it has been frequently mentioned; but it must now be more accurately assumed what that is which is naturally adapted to remember. If, therefore, the power of memory is something adventitious, or something belonging to discipline or passion, remembrance will not happen to beings which are impassive and superior to time. Hence, memory must not be placed in deity, or in being, or intellect. For to these nothing accedes; nor does time, but eternity subsist about being.

---

[1] Memory is summarily, *stability of knowledge;* just as immortality is stability of life, and eternity is stability of being.

Nor is either temporal priority or that which is successive there; but each of these always subsists as it is, in sameness, receiving no mutation. How, therefore, can that which is in the same and the similar be in want of memory? For it is not at all disposed in futurity in a way different from what it was before; nor has it one intelligence after another, in order that it may abide in another, or that it may remember another intellection which it formerly possessed. But what prevents it from knowing the mutations of other things, without being changed itself, such as the periods of the world? Shall we say it is because it intellectually perceives one thing as prior, but another as posterior which is consequent to the mutations of that which is convolved? Besides, remembrance is different from intellectual perception: and it must not be said that the intellection of itself is recollection. For it does not proceed in its energy for the purpose of detaining it, lest it should depart; for thus it might fear lest the essence of itself should depart from itself. Neither, therefore, must it be said that soul remembers after the same manner, as we say it recollects those things which it innately possesses. But having descended hither, it possesses these innate conceptions, yet does not [always] energize according to them, and especially when it has profoundly descended into body. The ancients, however, appear to have considered memory and reminiscence to be the same thing as for the soul to energize according to those things which it now possesses; so that this is another species of memory. Hence, time is not present with memory thus denominated. Perhaps, however, these things are considered by us lightly, and not accurately. For perhaps it may be doubted, whether memory and reminiscence belong to such a soul as this [which we are now considering] or whether they do not rather pertain to another more obscure soul, or to this animal which is a composite of soul and body. And if they belong to another soul, it may also be doubted when and how it received what it recollects; and a similar doubt will arise if they are said to pertain to the composite of soul and body. Hence, that must be investigated which was the subject of our inquiry from the first, what that is which possesses in us the power of remembering. And if, indeed, it is the soul which remembers, it must be considered what part or power of the soul it is; but if it is the sentient power, as to some it has appeared to be, what the mode is of its subsistence must be investigated, and what ought to be called the animal. And again, whether it is proper to admit that the same thing apprehends both sensibles and intelligibles, or that one thing perceives the former, but another the latter of these.

XXVI. If, therefore, the animal is both at one and the same time in the senses according to energy, it is also necessary that sensible perception should be a thing of this kind. Hence, likewise, it is said to be common, in the same manner as to bore with an auger and to weave; in order that soul may subsist comformably to the artificer, in sensible perception, but the body according to the instrument; the body indeed suffering and being ministrant, but the soul receiving the impression of the body, or that which is effected through the body. Or the soul must receive the judgment arising from the passion of the body; where, indeed, sense may thus be said to be the common work, but memory will not be compelled to pertain to that which is common, the soul now receiving the impression, and either preserving or ejecting it; unless some one should infer that remembrance also is something common, because we acquire a good memory, and likewise become forgetful from the temperaments of the body. It may also be said, that the body either impedes or does not impede reminiscence, but that remembrance will nevertheless be the province of the soul. And with respect to disciplines, how will the remembrance of these pertain to that which is common [or to the animal which is the composite of soul and body], and not rather belong to the soul? But if the animal is both at once in such a way that another thing is produced from both, in the first place indeed, it will be absurd to say that the animal is neither body nor soul. For both being changed, [the animal will not be something different from both; nor again, both being mingled, will the soul be in the animal in capacity only; though even in this case, remembrance will nevertheless belong to the soul. Just as in the mixture of honey with wine, if there is still something of sweetness in it, this will be derived from the honey. What then, if it should be said that the soul indeed herself remembers, yet in consequence of being in the body, and therefore not being pure, but as it were affected with quality, she is able to impress in the body the types of sensibles, and to establish as it were a seat in it, for the purpose of receiving forms, and preventing them from gliding away? To this we reply, in the first place indeed, these types are not magnitudes; nor in the second place, are they like impressions from a seal, or resistances, or figurations, because neither is there any impulsion there, nor does the same thing take place as in wax; but the mode even in sensibles resembles that of intellection. In intellection, however, what resistance can there be? Or what need is there of body, or corporeal quality in intellectual energy? Moreover, it is necessary that soul should remember its own motions, such as its tendencies to the objects of its desire, and to things which it has not obtained, and which have not arrived at the body. For how could the body speak of things which have not arrived to it? Or how can the soul recollect in conjunction with body, that which the body is not at all naturally adapted to know? But it must be said, indeed, that some things end in the soul; and these are such as enter through the body; but that others pertain to the soul alone, if it is necessary that the soul should be something, and that there is a certain nature and work of it. If, however, this be the case, and it desires, and remembers its desire, it will also remember the attainment, or non-attainment of the object of its desire, since its nature does not rank among things of a flowing condition. For if this is not admitted, we must neither grant that it has a co-sensation, nor a power of following the conceptions of intellect, nor a certain conspiration, and as it were consciousness of itself. For unless the soul naturally possessed these things, it would not obtain them through its union with the body; but it would indeed have certain energies, the works of which would require the assistance of corporeal organs; and of some things it would bring with itself the powers; but of others it would also bring the energies. With respect to memory, however, the body is an impediment to it; since even now also oblivion is produced from the addition of certain things; but through ablation and purification, memory frequently emerges. When the soul, therefore, is alone, it is necessary that the moveable and flowing nature of the body, should be the cause of oblivion and not of memory. Hence, also, body may be understood to be the river of Lethe. Let, therefore, this passion [*i.e.* memory] belong to the soul.

XXVII. To what soul, however, does memory pertain? Does it belong to that more divine soul according to which we subsist, or to the other which we derive from the universe? May we not say, that memory pertains to each of these; but that one kind of memory is peculiar, and another common? and that when they are conjoined, all the species of memory subsist at once; but that when they are separated, if both should exist and remain, each soul will preserve for a long time the remembrance of things pertaining to itself, but for a short time the recollection of things foreign to its nature? The image, therefore, of Hercules, is in Hades.[1] For it appears to me requisite to think, that this image has a recollection of every thing that has been transacted in life. For to this image life especially pertained. Other souls, however, being both these together, have nothing more to say than what pertains to this life, and in consequence of being the composite of soul and body, know the concerns of the present state of existence, or besides this, something belonging to justice. But we have not yet shown what Hercules himself, who is without the image, will say. What, therefore, will the other soul say that is liberated and alone? For the soul, indeed, which is attracted by body, will recollect every thing which the man did or suffered [in the present life]. In the course of time, however, after death, the recollection of other things also from former lives will arise, so that some of these will be dismissed and despised. For the soul becoming in a greater degree purified from the body, will recollect those things, the remembrance of which she had lost in the present life. But when she becomes situated in another body, she will then indeed departing [from an intellectual] speak of the concerns of an external life. She will, likewise, speak of the things which she has just left, and also of many things pertaining to a superior life. But as many adventitious circumstances will arise in the course of time, she will always be oppressed with oblivion. What, however, will the soul which becomes alone remember? Or should we not first consider to what power of the soul remembrance belongs?

XXVIII. Do we, therefore, remember through the powers by which we perceive sensibly and learn? Or do we remember the objects of desire through the power by

[1] *i.e.* The irrational, which is the image of the rational soul, is in the obscurity of the sensible life.

which we desire, and the objects of anger through the irascible power? For it may be said, that it is not one thing which enjoys, and another which remembers what that thing enjoyed. The epithymetic power, therefore, is again moved through memory to the objects which it once enjoyed, when they present themselves to its view. For why is it not moved by another object, or not after the same manner? What hinders us, therefore, from granting to it a sensation of things of this kind? And why may we not, therefore, attribute desire to the sensitive power, and this in every respect, so that every thing may be named according to that which predominates? Or shall we say, that we ascribe sense to each thing in a different manner? Thus, for instance, it is sight indeed that perceives, and not the power which desires. But the power which desires is moved by sense, as it were in succession; yet not in such a way as that sense can tell what the quality is of the desire, but so as to suffer without perceiving what it is. Thus also with respect to anger, sight sees the author of the injury, but anger rises in opposition to the injurer; just as when a shepherd sees a wolf among his flock, the dog, though he does not himself see the wolf, yet is excited by impulse, or by the noise [which this circumstance produces]. For the power, indeed, which desires, possesses in itself a vestige of what it formerly enjoyed, not as memory, but as a disposition and passion. But it is another thing which perceives the enjoyment, and possesses in itself the remembrance of what has been done. That it is so, however, this is an argument, that memory frequently does not know what the things are of which desire participates, though they still reside in it.

XXIX. Shall we, therefore, ascribe memory to the sensitive power, and will the sensitive power be the same thing with us as that which remembers? If, however, the image of the soul remembers, as we have said, the sensitive power will be twofold. And if the sensitive power does not remember, but something else, this something else will have the power of remembering in a twofold respect. Farther still, if the sensitive power is capable of apprehending disciplines, it will also apprehend the objects of the dianoetic power [*i.e.* the discursive power of reason], or something else will apprehend the objects of each of these. Shall we, therefore, by admitting that the power which apprehends is common, attribute to it the remembrance of both these? If, however, one and the same thing apprehended sensibles and intelligibles, something to the purpose would perhaps be asserted. But if it is divided in a twofold respect, there will nevertheless be two things. And if we ascribe both to each soul, four things will be produced. In short, what necessity is there that we should remember through the same power by which we perceive, and that both sensible perception and recollection should be effected by the same power, and also that we should remember dianoetic objects through the power by which we energize dianoetically? For the same persons do not excel in dianoetically energizing and remembering, and those whose sensible perceptions are equally acute, do not remember equally. Some also excel in sensible perception, but others in memory whose sensations are not acute. Again, however, if each is different, it will be requisite that the power also should be different which remembers what sense had before perceived, and it will be necessary to perceive that which it is requisite to remember. Or may we not say that nothing hinders a sensible perception from being a phantasm to him who remembers, and that memory and retention may belong to the power of the phantasy, which is something different from memory. For it is this power in which sense ends; and when sense no longer energizes, the sensible spectacle is present with the phantastic power. If, therefore, the imagination of an absent object is present with this, it will now remember it. And if it remains, indeed, but for a little time, the remembrance will be little; but if for a long time the remembrance will be greater, in consequence of this power being stronger, so that not being easily perverted, it will not be compelled to lose its remembrance. Memory, therefore, belongs to the power of the phantasy, and to remember will consist of things of this kind. We say, however, that souls are differently disposed with respect to memory, either through differently possessing the powers of it, or by frequently or not frequently exercising it; or by corporeal temperaments being or not being inherent, and producing or not producing a change in quality, and causing as it were perturbation. These things, however, must be elsewhere discussed.

XXX. What, however, shall we say of the conceptions of the dianoetic power? Does the phantastic power pertain also to these? If, indeed, imagination followed every intellection, perhaps this imagination remaining, and being as it were an image of the dianoetic conception, there will thus be a remembrance of the thing known; but if not, something else must be investigated. Perhaps, however, memory will be a reception into the phantastic power of reason following the conception. For a conception is impartible, and not yet having proceeded as it were outwardly, it latently remains within. But reason evolving and educing into the phantastic power from each conception, exhibits the conception as it were in a mirror: and thus the apprehension, permanency, and remembrance of it are effected. Hence, since the soul is always moved to intelligence, when it perceives intellectually, then the apprehension of what it perceives is produced in us. For intelligence is one thing, and the apprehension of intelligence another. And we always indeed perceive intellectually, but we do not always apprehend that we do so.

This, however, is because the recipient not only receives intellections, but also the senses, and this alternately.

XXXI. If, however, memory pertains to the phantastic power, but each soul is said to remember, there will be two powers of the phantasy. The two souls, therefore, being separate, each will possess a phantastic power. But since they are with us in the same thing, how will they be two, and in which of them will memory be ingenerated? For if in both, there will always be twofold imaginations. For it must not be said, that the remembrance of intelligibles pertains to the one, but of sensibles to the other; since thus there will in every respect be two animals, having nothing in common with each other. If, therefore, there is memory in both what will be the difference? In the next place, what should hinder us from knowing this? Shall we say that we are then ignorant of the difference, when the one power is in symphony with the other; the phantastic powers not being separate, but that which is the more excellent of the two prevailing, one phantasm is produced, since the one follows the other like a shadow, and is subservient to it like a less to a greater light. When, however, there is a contest and dissonance between the two, then the one shines forth through itself; but it is concealed in the other, because in short that there are two souls is concealed from us. For both coalesce in one, and the one is diffused but not the other. The one, therefore, sees all things, and possesses some things indeed, proceeding from it, but dismisses others, as pertaining to the other power. Just as when we have sometimes conversed with persons of a viler character, and afterwards betake ourselves to those who are more worthy, we remember but little of our conversation with the former, but much of it with the latter.

XXXII. What, however, ought we to say concerning the remembrance of friends, and children, and wives; and also of our country, and other things which it is not absurd to recollect? Shall we say that the image of the soul will remember each of these accompanied with passion, but that the superior soul will recollect these impassively? For passion, perhaps, was from the first in this image. And such of the passions as are of an elegant nature, are in the worthy [*i.e.*, the superior] soul, so far as it communicates with the other. It is fit, however, that the inferior soul should also desire the recollection of the energies of the other soul, and especially when it has likewise become itself elegant and worthy. But this inferior soul may from the first become better, in consequence of being disciplined by the more excellent soul. The latter, however, will gladly resign to oblivion the concerns of the former. For it may happen, that the latter soul being worthy, the former which is of an inferior nature, may be forcibly restrained by the superior soul. And in proportion as this more excellent soul hastens to the intelligible, it will forget the concerns of this world, unless the whole of its life here, has been such as to preserve the remembrance alone of things of the most exalted nature. For here also it is beautiful to abandon human pursuits: [and this is the work of perfect virtue [1]]. A forgetfulness, therefore, of such pursuits, is necessary in another life. Hence, he who says that the worthy soul is oblivious, will in such a way as we have mentioned speak rightly. For it will fly from the many, and will collect multitude into one, dismissing that which is infinite. For thus it will not associate with multitude, but expelling it will live by itself: since here also, when it wishes to be in the intelligible world, while an inhabitant of earth, it dismisses all other concerns. Hence, when it is there, it

[1] It appears from the version of Ficinus, that the words καὶ τοῦτο τῆς τελείας ἀρετῆς ἔργον, are wanting in the original in this place.

remembers but few things of a terrestrial nature; but it remembers more of them when it is in the heavens. And Hercules, indeed, [when in Hades] may speak of his own fortitude; but in the intelligible world, he will consider these things as trifling, being transferred into a more sacred place, and strenuously engaging even above himself, in those contests in which the wise wish to engage.

XII.

ON THE GENERATION AND ORDER OF THINGS AFTER THE FIRST.

V. ii.

I. *THE one* is all things, and yet no one of all. For the principle of all is not all things; but *the one* is all, because all things run as it were into it, or rather do not as yet exist, but will be. How, therefore, [does multitude proceed] from *the one* which is simple, and in which no variety, nor any duplicity present themselves to the view? Is it because there was nothing in it, on this account all things are from it? Hence, in order that being might exist, *the one* is not being, but being is the progeny of it, and as it were its first-born. For *the one* being perfect, in consequence of not seeking after, or possessing, or being in want of any thing, it becomes as it were overflowing, and the superplenitude of it produces something else. That, however, which is generated from it is converted to it, and is filled, and was generated looking to it. But this is intellect. And the permanency indeed of it about *the one*, produced being; but its vision of *the one*, intellect. When, therefore, it is established about *the one*, in order that it may see it, then it becomes at once intellect and being. Hence, being in the same manner as *the one* produces things similar to itself, through an effusion of abundant power. Its offspring also has the form of it, in the same manner as prior to this it likewise flowed forth from *the one.* And this energy from essence is soul, which was generated from intellect permanently abiding. For intellect also was generated, that which is prior to it abiding. Soul, however, does not produce abiding, but being moved generates an image of itself. Soul, therefore, looking thither whence it was generated, is filled. But proceeding into another and contrary motion, it generates an image of itself, viz., sense, and the nature which is in plants. Nothing, however, is separated or cut off from that which is prior to itself. Hence, also, the soul of man is seen to proceed as far as to plants. For after *a certain* manner it proceeds into them, because that which is in plants is derived from it. Nevertheless, the whole of the human soul is not in plants, but it is thus ingenerated in plants, because it so far proceeds into an inferior nature, having made another hypostasis by its progression into and propensity to that which is subordinate; since the soul which is prior to this, being suspended from intellect, permits intellect to abide in itself.

II. The procession, therefore, of these is from the principle to the extremity, each thing at the same time being always left in its proper seat. But that which is generated receives another order, which is subordinate. Nevertheless, each thing becomes the same with that which it follows, as long as it follows it. When, therefore, soul [*i.e.* the human soul] is ingenerated in a plant, there is one part, viz., the part which is in the plant, which is most rash and insane; and as far as to this soul proceeds. But when the soul is in a brute,[1] it is led by the sentient power, which then has

[1] "When human souls," says Sallust, in his golden treatise "On the Gods and the World," "transmigrate into irrational animals, they follow externally, in the same manner as our presiding dæmons attend us in their beneficent operations. For the rational part never becomes the soul of the irrational nature."

dominion. When, however, it is ingenerated in man, then in short, either the motion is in the rational nature, or from intellect, in consequence of the soul having its proper intellect, and deriving from itself the power of intellection, or of being moved. Again, therefore, returning [whence we digressed], when some one cuts off either the germinations, or certain branches of a plant, whither does the soul that is in the plant depart? Shall we say, to that from whence it came? For it is not distant by place from its source. It is, therefore, in its principle. But if you cut off or burn the root, where is the life which was in the root? In soul, not proceeding to another place, but it may also be in the same place. It will, however, be in another place, if it should run back. But if not, it will be in another vegetable nature. For it is not contracted into a narrow space. But if it should run back, it will be in the power which is prior to it. Where, however, is this power situated? In the power prior to itself. And this again in another, as far as to intellect. But not in place. For no one of these was in place. And much less is intellect in place; so that neither is soul. Hence, soul being no where, in that which is no where it is thus also every where. But if soul proceeding to the supernal realms, should stop in its progression in that which is between, before it has entirely arrived at the summit, it will have a middle life, and will be established in that part of itself. Intellect, however, is all these, and yet it is not. It is, indeed, because they are from it; and again, it is not, because abiding in itself, it gave them to exist. Hence, there is an abundant life in the universe, which is as it were extended into length, and has each of its parts in a successive order. The whole, however, is in continuity with itself, but the parts are distinguished by a proper difference, that which

This doctrine, which originated from Syrianus and Proclus, was universally adopted by all the succeeding Platonists.

is prior not being destroyed in that which is posterior. What then is the soul which is ingenerated in plants? And does it generate nothing else than that in which it is? How this is effected, however, must be considered by us, assuming for this purpose another principle.

XIII.
ON GNOSTIC HYPOSTASES, AND THAT WHICH IS BEYOND THEM.

V. iii.

I. Is it therefore necessary, that intellect should be in itself various, in order that by one of the things contained in itself, having surveyed the rest, it may be thus said to understand itself, as if it would not be able to be converted to, and have an intellectual perception of itself, if it was entirely simple? Or is it also possible for that which is not a composite, to have the intellection of itself? For that which is said to perceive itself intellectually because it is a composite, and because by one of the things in itself it understands the rest, just as if by sense we should apprehend the form[1] of ourselves, and the other nature of the body, will not have a truly intellectual perception of itself. For in a thing of this kind, the whole will not be known, unless that which understands other things that are with itself, understands also itself; since otherwise we shall not have the object of investigation, viz., that which perceives itself, but we shall have one thing perceiving another. It is necessary, therefore, to admit that the intellectual perception of itself is the province of a simple nature, and how

[1] The word used here by Plotinus is μορφή, which, as we have elsewhere observed, pertains to the colour, figure, and magnitude of superficies.

this is effected must, if possible, be considered; or we must abandon the opinion that there is something which truly intellectually perceives itself. To abandon, however, this opinion is not easy, since the rejection of it is attended with many absurdities. For if we do not admit that to assign this power to the soul is not very absurd, yet not to ascribe it to the nature of intellect is perfectly absurd; viz., if we grant that it has indeed a knowledge of other things, but has no knowledge and science of itself. For sense, and not intellect, will have an apprehension of things external; and if you are willing to grant it, this will also be the case with the dianoetic power and opinion. But whether intellect has a knowledge of these or not, it is fit to consider. It is evident, indeed, that intellect knows such things as are intelligible. Does it, therefore, know these alone, or also itself that know these? And does it thus far know itself, that it knows these alone, but does not know what itself is? Hence, it will perceive that it knows some things belonging to itself, but it will not know what itself is; or it will both know the things which are its own, and itself. And what the mode of this knowledge is, and how far it extends, must be considered.

II. In the first place, however, we must inquire concerning the soul, whether the knowledge of itself is to be attributed to it, what the gnostic power of it is, and how it subsists. With respect to the sensitive power, therefore, of the soul, we must immediately say that its energy is directed to externals alone. For though there is a co-sensation of things which inwardly take place in the body, yet here the apprehension is of things which are external to sense: for then there is a sensation of the passions which are in the body. But the power in the soul which reasons, and which forms a judgment of the phantasms adjacent from sense, collects and divides them, surveys the impressions as it were which are derived from intellect, and possesses about these the same power [as intellect]. It likewise assumes intelligence, as knowing and adapting new and recently acceding impressions to those in itself which are ancient. And this knowledge and adaptation, we say, are the reminiscences of the soul. The intellect of the soul, also, stops as far as this in its power. [It must be investigated, therefore, whether the reasoning power also,[1]] is converted to, and knows itself, or whether this must be referred to intellect. For if we attribute a knowledge of itself to this part, we must admit that it is intellect; and in this case, we must investigate in what it differs from a superior intellect. But if we do not grant that it has a knowledge of itself, by a reasoning process we must proceed to the intellect which is superior, and we must consider what it is for this to know itself. And if we grant that this is also the province of the reasoning power, we must investigate what the difference is between the two in self-knowledge. For if there is no difference, then this our intellect is the highest. This dianoetic part, therefore, of the soul, is it converted to itself, or not? Or has it [only] a knowledge of the impressions which it receives both from intellect and sense? And in the first place, it must be investigated how it possesses this knowledge.

III. For sense, indeed, sees a man, and transmits the figure of him to the dianoetic part. But what does this part say? Perhaps it does not yet say any thing, but only knows that it is a man, and there stops. Unless, indeed, it should consider with itself, who this is, if it happens that it has before met with him, and should say, employing memory for this purpose, that it is Socrates. If, however, it should also evolve the form of the man, it will then distribute into parts those things which it received from

[1] It appears from the version of Ficinus, that it is necessary here after the word δυνάμει in the original, to supply and read as follows: ζητητέον ἄρα, εἰ τὸ λογιζόμενον καὶ εἰς ἑαυτὸν, κ. λ.

the imagination. And if it should also say, Is he a good man? it will make this inquiry from the information which it derived through sense. But that which it says on this occasion, it will now possess from itself, containing in itself a rule by which it forms a judgment of good. How then does it contain the good in itself? May we not say, so far as it is boniform, and is corroborated to the perception of a thing of this kind, in consequence of intellect shining upon it? For the pure part of the soul is this, and receives the supervening vestiges of intellect. Why, however, is not this intellect, but the rest beginning from the sensitive power is soul? May we not say, because it is necessary that soul should consist in the discursive energies of reason? But all these are the works of the reasoning power. Why, however, do we not grant to this part the power of intellectually perceiving itself, and thus become liberated from doubt? Is it because we assign to it the office of considering, and being busily employed about externals; but we conceive it to be the province of intellect, to survey both itself, and the forms which it contains? If, however, some one should say, what therefore prevents this part from considering things pertaining to itself, by another power? He who says this, does not investigate either the dianoetic or reasoning power, but assumes a pure intellect. What then prevents a pure intellect from existing in the soul? We reply, nothing prevents this. But farther still, it is necessary to inquire, whether this pure intellect is something belonging to soul?[1] We reply, it does not belong to the soul, and yet it is our intellect, being different from the dianoetic power, and proceeding on its summit. At the same time, however, it is ours, though we must not connumerate it with the parts of the soul. Or we may say,

[1] Both the sense of this passage, and the version of Ficinus require that instead of ἀλλ' ἔτι δεῖ λέγειν, ψυχῆς τοῦτο, we should read ἀλλ' ἔτι δεῖ λέγειν, εἰ τι ψυχῆς τοῦτο;

that it is ours, and yet not ours. Hence we use, and do not use it; but we always employ the dianoetic power. And it is ours indeed, when we use it, but not ours when we do not use it.[1] But what is it to use a pure intellect? Is it

[1] The intellect which is ours when we use it, and not ours when we do not, is a partial intellect of the Minerval series, which is proximately participated by dæmoniacal souls, and illuminates ours when we convert ourselves to it, and render our rational part intellectual. This in the "Phædrus" is said to be the governor of the soul, and to be the only thing which perceives real being. But the soul also perceives it in conjunction with this intellect, when she is nourished by the summit of her reasoning power and by science. This intellect, likewise, is spoken of in the "Timæus," and is denominated intelligence. For it is there said, that *true being is apprehended by intelligence in conjunction with reason.* Hence, as Proclus beautifully observes, "when reason intellectually perceives eternal being, as *reason* indeed, it energizes transitively, but as *perceiving intellectually*, it energizes with simplicity, understanding each thing as simple, yet not understanding all things at once, but passing from some things to others. At the same time, however, it perceives each of the things which it sees transitively as one simple thing."

In another part of his Commentary on the "Timæus" (p. 321), he also admirably observes respecting this partial intellect as follows: "What the impartible is in each partial soul (*i.e.* in a soul such as ours) is truly dubious. For it must not be admitted, that there is an intellect in each, and this partial. May we not say, therefore, that each partial soul is essentially suspended from a certain dæmon; and as every dæmon has a dæmoniacal intellect above itself, a partial soul also has this same intellect arranged as an impartible essence prior to itself? Hence, the dæmoniacal soul participates primarily of this intellect; but the partial souls that are under it, secondarily; and which also causes them to be partial. For each partial soul has the partible as its peculiarity, but has the impartible in common with the dæmons that are above these souls and whose peculiarity is the impartible. Hence, too, dæmons remain on high, but partial souls at a certain time descend, and divide themselves about bodies, as being more adapted to these. For if in partial souls, the genus of difference is exuberant, which is the reason why they are not always able to

to pronounce ourselves as becoming either such an intellect, or conformable to it? For we are not intellect. We subsist, therefore, conformable or according to it, the first reasoning power being the recipient of it. For we are sentient through sense, and we ourselves perceive sensibly. Are we therefore thus dianoetically perceived, and do we thus dianoetically energize? Or shall we say that we indeed are reasoning beings, and that we intellectually perceive the conceptions which are in dianoia? For we are this. But the conceptions arising from the energies of intellect, are in such a way above us, as those arising from the energies of sense are beneath us. And we are this peculiarity of soul, viz., the middle of a twofold power, the worse and the better; sense

energize according to all their powers, it is necessary that they should be in a greater degree adapted to a life divisible about body, and in a greater degree be separated from an impartible essence; by this means preserving an analogy to each of the extremes. Just as it is necessary that the most divine of souls, through their similitude to intellect, should in a greater degree be exempt from partible natures, but be more united to the impartible essences above them, and from which they are counascently suspended. They also have an intellectual arrangement among souls. And it is reasonable to suppose, that the intellect of each dæmon, so far as it is a whole and one, is the intellect of the dæmon which proximately [*i.e.* immediately] participates it, but that it comprehends in itself the number of souls that are under it, and the intellectual paradigms of them. Each partial soul, therefore, will have its appropriate paradigm in this intellect, and not simply the whole of this intellect, in the same manner as the dæmon who is essentially the leader of these souls. Defining, therefore, more accurately, we may say, that the impartible of each partial soul, is the form that is above it, which is comprehended in the one intellect that is allotted the government of the dæmoniacal series, under which each partial soul is arranged. And thus both the assertions are true, viz. that the intellect alone of each of these souls ranks among things which are always established on high, and that every partial soul is the medium of the impartible above it, and the partible nature posterior to it."

being the worse, but intellect the better power. And with respect to sense, indeed, it seems that we always grant it to be ours; for we are always sentient; but this is dubious with respect to intellect, because we do not always use it[1] and because it is separate. But it is separate because it does not verge to us, but we rather looking on high, tend to it. Sense, however, is our messenger, but intellect is our king.

IV. We also reign when we energize according to it. But we energize according to it in a twofold respect; either because letters as it were, which are as laws, are inscribed in us by intellect; or because we are filled with it; or when it is present, are able to see and be sentient of it. We also know by such a spectacle, that we are able to learn other things through a thing of this kind; so that we either learn the nature of the power which knows such an object as this, learning by the power itself; or we become a thing of this kind.[2] Hence, that which knows itself is twofold; one indeed being the dianoetic part of the soul, but the other being superior to this. And, therefore, that which knows itself has a subsistence conformable to pure intellect itself. It also intellectually perceives itself through this, not as any longer man, but as having entirely become something else; and hastily withdrawing itself to that which is on high, it alone draws upward together with itself, the more excellent part of the soul, which is alone able to be winged with intelligence, in order that he who possesses it may there deposit what he knew. Does not the dianoetic part, therefore, know that it is dianoetic, and that it receives the knowledge of things external; that it forms a judgment also of the things which it investigates, and this by the rules in itself which it derives from intellect? Does it not also know that there is something

---

[1] Instead of καὶ ὅτε μὴ αὐτὸ ἀεί in this place, it is necessary to read καὶ ὅτι μὴ αὐτῷ χρώμεθα ἀεί.

[2] I.e. We become intellect.

better than itself which does not[1] investigate, but possesses every thing in itself? If, therefore, it says that it is from intellect, and is the second after, and the image of intellect, having all things as it were written in itself, as there he who writes and has written, will he, who thus knows himself, stop as far as to these things? Shall we, however, employing another power, survey intellect knowing itself, or shall we assuming it, since it also is ours, and we are of it, thus both know intellect, and ourselves? Or is not the latter of these necessary, if we are to know what that is in intellect, for itself to know itself? Then, however, some one becomes himself intellect, when dismissing other things pertaining to himself, he beholds intellect through intellect, and by it also surveys himself, just as intellect likewise beholds itself.

V. Does intellect, therefore, by one part of itself behold another part? In this case, however, one part will be that which sees, but another, that which is seen. And this is not for the same thing to see itself. What then? If the whole is a thing of such a kind as to consist of similar parts, so that the perceiver differs in no respect from the thing perceived, in this case, the perceiver seeing that part which is the same with itself, will also see itself. For the perceiver does not at all differ from the thing perceived. Or may we not indeed in the first place say that this division of intellect is absurd? For how is the division to be made? since it cannot be casually. Who likewise is it that divides it? Is it he who arranges himself in the order of the perceiver, or he who arranges himself as the thing perceived? In the next place, how will the perceiver know himself, when in perceiving he arranges himself in the order of that which is seen? For that which sees was not supposed to be in that which is seen. Or will not he

---

[1] For ὃ ζητεῖ here, it is necessary to read ὃ μὴ ζητεῖ.

who thus knows himself, understand himself to be that which is perceived, but not that which perceives? So that he will not know all, nor the whole of himself. For that which he knows he knows as a thing seen, but not as a thing that sees, and thus he will be the perceiver of another thing, and not of himself. May he not, however, of himself add, that he is also that which sees, in order that he may perfectly know himself? But if he comprehends in himself that which sees, he also at the same time comprehends the things that are seen. If, therefore, in the perceiver the things perceived are contained, if indeed, they are impressions of the things seen, he will not contain the things themselves. But if he possesses the things themselves, he does not see them through dividing himself [into the perceiver and the thing perceived]; but prior to the division of himself, he both beheld and possessed them. If, however, this be the case, it is necessary that contemplation should be the same with the object of contemplation, and intellect the same with the intelligible. For if it is not the same, there will not be truth. For unless this is admitted, he who is said to possess beings, will only possess an impression different from beings, which is not truth. For truth ought not to be of another thing, but that which it says, that also it should be. Thus, therefore, intellect, the intelligible, and being are one; and this is the first being, and the first intellect, possessing beings; or rather, it is the same with beings. If, however, intelligence and the intelligible are one, how on this account does that which is intellective intellectually perceive itself? For intelligence, indeed, as it were, comprehends the intelligible, or is the same with it. Intellect, however, which intellectually perceives itself, is not yet manifest. But intelligence and the intelligible are the same; for the intelligible is a certain energy, since it is neither power, nor void of life, nor again is its life adventitious, nor its intellection in something different from itself, as in a stone, or a certain inanimate thing, and it is also the first essence. If, therefore, it is energy, and the first energy, intelligence likewise will be most beautiful, and will be essential intelligence. For intelligence of this kind is most true, is the first, and subsists primarily, and will therefore be the first intellect. For this intellect is not in capacity, nor is this one thing, but intelligence another; since thus again, the essential of it would be in capacity. If, therefore, it is energy, and the essence of it is energy, it will be one and the same with energy. Since, however, being and the intelligible are one and the same with energy, all will be at the same time one, viz., intellect, intelligence, and the intelligible. If, therefore, the intelligence of it is the intelligible, but it is the intelligible, hence it will itself intellectually perceive itself. For it will perceive itself by intelligence, which it is, and will understand the intelligible which also it is. According to each of these, therefore, it will intellectually perceive itself, both so far as it is intelligence, and so far as it is the intelligible, and will understand by intelligence, which it is.

VI. Reason, therefore, demonstrates that there is something which properly and principally itself intellectually perceives itself. This, however, when it is in soul, intellectually sees in one way, but in intellect more principally. For soul, indeed, knows itself, that it is the progeny of another thing; but intellect knows that it is from itself, and what its nature is, and who it is; and this by a natural conversion to itself. For beholding beings it beholds itself and beholding is in energy; and the energy is itself. For intellect and intelligence are one. With the whole of itself also it perceives the whole, and not a part by a part. Does, therefore, reason demonstrate it to be a thing of such a kind as to have an energy which is merely an object of belief; or is it indeed necessary that it should be such as it is, but that it should not have persuasion? For *necessity indeed is in intellect, but persuasion in soul.* Hence we investigate as it seems, rather for the purpose of persuading ourselves, than to behold truth in a pure intellect. For as long as we continued on high, and adhered to the nature of intellect we were satisfied, energized intellectually, and contemplated, collecting all things into one. For it was intellect that then energized, and spoke of itself. But soul was quiet, yielding to the energy of intellect. When, however, we descended hither, we were desirous of producing persuasion in the soul, wishing to behold the archetype in an image. Perhaps, therefore, it is requisite to teach our soul, how its intellect once beheld itself; and to teach that part of the soul this, which is in a certain respect intellectual, and which we assume to be dianoetic; by this appellation latently signifying, that it is a certain intellect, or that it is a power *through intellect,* and that it derives its subsistence from intellect. It is fit, therefore, that this part should know, that it also knows such things as it sees, and such things as it says. And if it were the things which it says, it would after this manner know itself. Since, however, the things which it sees are present with, or are supernally imparted to it from that region whence it also originates, it happens to this part likewise since it is reason, and receives things allied to itself, that by an adaptation of the vestiges which it contains, it is enabled to know itself. It may, therefore, transfer the image to true intellect which is the same with the things that are truly the objects of intellectual perception, and which have a real and primary subsistence. For it is not possible that such an intellect as this should be external to itself. Hence, if it is in and with itself, and is [truly] that which it is, it is intellect. But intellect can never be deprived of intellect; so that the knowledge of itself is necessarily present with it; and this because it is in itself, and its employment and essence consist in being intellect alone. For this is not a practical intellect, as looking to that which pertains to external action, and which in consequence of not abiding in itself, is a certain knowledge of externals. There is, however, no necessity if intellect is practic, that it should know itself; but this is the province of that intellect which is not engaged in practical affairs. For appetite is not in pure intellect; but this being absent, the consequent conversion to itself, not only demonstrates that the knowledge of itself is reasonable, but also necessary. For otherwise what would be the life of it, when liberated from action, and established in intellect?

VII. It may however, be said, that pure intellect beholds deity. But if it is acknowledged that it knows God, he who grants this, must also necessarily admit that it knows itself. For such things as it possesses from deity it knows, and also what he imparts, and what he is able to impart. But learning and knowing these things, it will likewise through this know itself. For divinity is one of the things imparted, or rather he is all that is imparted. If, therefore, intellect also knows him, and learns the powers that he possesses, it will likewise know itself to be generated from thence; and that it derives from him all that it is able to receive. If, however, it is unable to see him clearly, since to see is perhaps the very thing that is seen, on this account especially that which remains to it, will be to see and know itself, if to see is to be the very thing itself which is seen. For what else can we confer upon it? By Jupiter, quiet. The quiet of intellect however, is not mental alienation, but is the tranquil energy of intellect, withdrawing itself from other things; since to other natures also that are at rest from other employments, their own proper energy remains; and especially to those things whose existence is not in capacity, but in energy.

Where, therefore, existence is energy, and there is nothing else to which energy is directed, there energy is directed to itself. Hence intellect perceiving itself, is thus with itself, and has its energy directed to itself. For if something else is suspended from it, that something else is in itself, because its energy is directed to itself. For it is necessary that it should first be in itself, and afterwards that its energy should be directed to something else, or that something else should proceed from it, assimilated to it: just as fire, which is first in itself, and has the energy of fire, and thus is enabled to produce the vestigie of itself in something else. For again, intellect indeed, is energy in itself; but soul is so in proportion as it tends as it were internally to its own intellect. But so far as it departs from intellect, so far it tends to that which is external. And partly indeed, it is assimilated to that from whence it came; but partly, though it becomes dissimilar, yet here also it retains a similitude to it, whether it acts, or produces. For when it acts, at the same time it contemplates; and when it produces, it produces forms, which are as it were intellections derived from first intelligibles. Hence, all things are vestigies of intelligence and intellect, proceeding conformably to their archetype; those that are near to it, imitating it in a greater degree; but such things as are last preserving only an obscure image of it.

VIII. What kind of intelligible, however, does intellect see, and what does it perceive itself to be? With respect to the intelligible indeed, it is not proper to investigate such a thing as colour or figure in bodies: for intelligibles are prior to these. And the reason [or productive principle] in seeds which produces these, is not these. For these seminal principles also, are naturally invisible, and still more so are intelligibles. There is likewise the same nature of them and of the things that possess them, after the same manner as the reason which is in seed, and soul which participates of these. The vegetable soul however does not see the things which it possesses: for neither did it generate these,[1] but both itself, and the reasons it contains are an image. But that from whence it came is manifest and true, and primary. Hence, also, it is of itself, and with itself. The vegetable soul however, unless it pertained to, and was in another thing, would not remain what it is. For it belongs to an image, since it is of another thing, to be generated in something different from itself, unless it is suspended from it. Hence, neither does it see as not having sufficient light for this purpose. And if it should see, since it is perfected in another thing, it would behold another thing, and not itself. Nothing, however, of this kind takes place with pure intellect; but vision is there, and that which is visible is consubsistent with it. Such also is the visible, as is the vision; and the vision as the visible. Who is it therefore, that will speak of the visible such as it is? He who sees it. But intellect sees it; since in the sensible region also, sight being light, or rather being united to light, sees light; for it sees colour. There, however, sight does not perceive through another thing, but through itself, because there is nothing external to it. With another light, therefore, and not through another, it sees another light. Hence, light sees another light; and therefore itself beholds itself. This light however, when it shines forth in the soul illuminates it, *i.e.*, it causes it to be intellectual. And in consequence of this, the soul is in itself, similarly with supernal light. If such, therefore, is the vestige of light ingenerated in the soul, by conceiving supernal light[2] to be of this kind, and to be still more beautiful and clear, you will approach nearer to the nature of intellect and the intelligible. For this when

---

[1] Ταῦτα is omitted in the original.
[2] *I.e.* Intelligible light.

it shines forth, imparts to the soul a clearer, but not a generative life. For on the contrary it converts the soul to itself, and does not suffer it to be dissipated, but causes it to love and joyfully receive the splendour which is in it. Neither does it impart a sensitive life. For this looks to externals, but does not on this account perceive more acutely. He, however, who receives that light which is the fountain[1] of truth, beholds as it were more acutely visible objects; but the contrary is not true.[2] It remains, therefore, for the soul to assume an intellectual life which is a vestige of the life of intellect. For there realities subsist. But the life and energy which are in intellect, are the first light primarily shining in itself, and a splendour directed to itself, which at one and the same time illuminates, and is illuminated. This also is that which is truly intelligible, is intellect, and the object of intellect, and is seen by itself. Nor is it in want of another thing in order that it may see, but for the purpose of perceiving is sufficient to itself. For that which sees is itself the thing which is seen. This very thing also takes place with us, so that the knowledge of it by us, is effected through it. Or whence should we be able to speak concerning it? For it is a thing of such a kind as to have a clearer apprehension of itself, and we likewise more clearly perceive ourselves through it. Through arguments, however, of this kind, we should elevate our soul to it, considering also that our soul and its life are an image; a resemblance, and an imitation of it; and likewise that when it sees intellectually, it becomes deiform, and has the form of intellect. And if some one should inquire what the nature is of this perfect intellect, which is every intel-

[1] Πηγὴν is omitted in the original, but is added from the version of Ficinus.

[2] Instead of ἀλλὰ τοὐναντίον, it is necessary to read ἀλλ' οὐ τοὐναντίον. The meaning of Plotinus is, that intelligible light is not seen more acutely by the perception of visible objects.

lect, and primarily knows itself, such a one should first become established in intellect, or should yield that energy of his soul to intellect, which is employed about things of which he retains the memory in himself. But it will be possible for the soul thus disposed, to show that it is able through itself as an image to behold after a certain manner that pure intellect, through [a life] more accurately assimilated to it, as far as a part of the soul is capable of arriving at a similitude to intellect.

IX. It is necessary, therefore, as it seems, that the soul in order that it may see the most divine part of soul, ought to consider what that is which intellect may know. Perhaps, however, this may be effected, if you first separate body from the man, viz. from yourself. And if after this, you separate the soul which fashions the body, and as much as possible take away sense, desire and anger, and other trifles of this kind, as very much verging to the mortal nature. For then, that which remains of the soul, is what we have denominated the image of intellect, and which preserves something of its light; so as to resemble the light proximate to the sphere of the sun which emanating from, diffuses its light about the sun. No one therefore, will admit that light to be the sun, which proceeds from, and shines about it. For this light originates from the sun, and permanently surrounds it; but another light always proceeds from another prior to it, until it arrives as far as to us and the earth. All the light, however, which is about the sun, must be admitted to be situated in something else, in order that there may be no interval void of body after the sun. But soul is a light derived from, and subsisting about intellect. It also is suspended from intellect, which it surrounds, and is not in any other thing. Nor is there any place in which it is received; for neither is intellect in place. Hence, the light of the sun indeed, is in the air; but soul of this kind is so pure, that it is visible of itself, so that it is seen by itself, and by another soul similarly pure. Soul indeed, must reason about [in order to perceive] intellect, and must investigate from itself what the nature of it is. But intellect beholds itself without reasoning about itself. For it is always present with itself. But we are present with ourselves and with intellect when we tend to it. For our life is divided, and consists of many lives. But intellect is not at all in want of another life, or of other things; but what it imparts, it imparts to others, and not to itself. For it is not indigent of things inferior to itself; nor, since it possesses the universe, does it confer on itself that which is less. Nor does it contain first natures in itself as vestiges; or rather, it does not contain, but is itself these very things. If, however, some one is incapable of having such a primary soul, which perceives intellectually with purity, let him assume a doxastic soul, and afterwards, from this ascend [to intellect]. But if he cannot even assume this, let him employ sense, bringing with itself more dilated forms: I mean sense in itself, together with the things which it is able to contain, and which now exists in forms. If some one however, wishes to descend, let him proceed to the generative power, and as far as to its effects. Afterwards, let him from hence ascend from the last to the last forms, or rather to those that are the first.

X. And thus much concerning these particulars. If, however, not[1] only forms that are produced, are in intellect, for they are not the last of things [when they are considered as having an intellectual subsistence]; but their productive forms are the first of things, whence also they are first;—if this be the case, it is necessary, that the producing cause of forms should also be there, and that both the productive cause and the forms produced should be

---

[1] οὐ is omitted in the original.

one. For if this is not admitted, intellect will again be in want of something else. What then, will that which is beyond this be again in want? Or is not this, indeed, which is indigent intellect? Will not, therefore, that which is beyond intellect see itself? Or must we not rather say, that this is not at all in want of vision? But of this hereafter. Now, however, we shall resume what we were before discussing. For the speculation is not about a casual thing. Again, therefore, we must say that this intellect is in want of the vision of itself; or rather that it possesses the perception of itself. And in the first place, it sees that it is manifold. In the next place it sees that it is the perception of something else [*i.e.* of the intelligible], and hence, that it is necessarily perceptive of the intelligible. It likewise sees that the essence of itself is vision. For in consequence of there being a certain other thing, it is necessary there should be vision; since if there were nothing else, vision would be in vain. Hence, it is necessary that in intellect there should be more things than one, in order that there may be vision. It is also necessary that vision should concur with the visible; and that what is seen by intellect should be multitude, and not entirely one. For that which is entirely one has not any thing about which it may energize? but being alone and solitary, it is perfectly quiescent. For so far as it energizes, it is another and another. For if it were not another and another, what would it do, or where would it proceed? Hence it is necessary that the nature which energizes, should either energize about another thing, or be itself something manifold, if it intends to energize in itself. If, however, it does not proceed into any thing else, it will be quiescent. But when t is entirely quiescent, it will not perceive intellectually. Hence it is necessary that the nature which is intellective, should, when it perceives intellectually, be in two things; and that either one of the two should be external, or that both should be in the same thing, and that intelligence should always subsist in difference, and also from necessity in sameness. Those things also which are properly the objects of intellectual perception are the same and different. And again, each of the intelligibles co-introduces with itself this sameness and difference. Or what will that perceive intellectually, which does not contain in itself another and another? For if each of the objects of intellectual vision is reason,[1] it is a multitude. Intellect, therefore, will learn that it is itself a various eye, or that it consists as it were of various colours. For if it should apply itself to *the one*, and to be impartible, it would be silent. For what would it have to say, or discuss about it? Indeed, if it were requisite that the impartible should entirely speak of itself, it would be necessary that it should first say what it is not. So that thus it would be many in order that it may be one[2] [which is absurd]. In the next place, when it says "I am[3] this thing," if it says *this thing* as something different from itself, it asserts what is false; but if as an accident to itself, it says that it is a multitude. Or it will say this, *I am, I am,* and *I, I.* What then, if it should be alone two things, and should say I, and this?[4] Will it not in this case necessarily be more than two things? For these two are to be considered as different from each other, and different in a certain respect. Hence, there will now be number and many other things. It is necessary, therefore, that the nature which is intellective, should receive another and another, and that the objects of its perception

[1] *I.e.* If it is a distributed cause. For this is what reason and reasoning signify when ascribed to intelligible, and intellectual, or divine essences.
[2] For in this case, it would be at least two things; since in addition to the impartible it would have speech. And the duad is the first multitude.
[3] Instead of εἰ μή here, it is necessary to read εἰμι.
[4] The words καὶ τοῦτο are omitted in the original.

being intelligible, should be various; for otherwise there will not be an intellectual perception of, but a contact with it. There will likewise be as it were, an adhesion only ineffable, and without intellection, possessing an energy prior to intelligence, intellect not yet existing, in consequence of that which adheres not perceiving intellectually. It is necessary, however, that the nature which sees intellectually, should not itself remain simple, and especially when it perceives itself. For it will itself divide itself, even though it should be silently intellective. In the next place, that which is entirely simple will not be in want of a busy energy, as it were, about itself. For what will it learn by intellectual perception? For prior to this perception, it exists that which it is to itself. For again, knowledge is a certain desire and as it were, an investigating discovery. Hence, that which is without any difference [1] in itself with respect to itself, is quiescent, and investigates nothing respecting itself. But that which evolves itself, will also be multitudinous.

XI. Hence this intellect becomes manifold, when it wishes to understand that which is beyond intellect. Endeavouring, therefore, to come into contact with it as with that which is simple, it falls from it always receiving another multiplied nature in itself. Hence, it originates from [2] it not as intellect, but as sight not yet seeing. But it proceeds from it containing in itself that which it has multiplied. Hence, it indefinitely desires another thing, possessing at the same time a certain phantasm in itself. It proceeds, however, receiving another thing in itself, which causes it to be multitudinous. For again, it has an impression [3] of the vision [of that which is beyond itself],

[1] For διάφορον here, it is necessary to read ἀδιάφορον.
[2] Instead of ἐπ' αὐτῷ in this place, both the sense and the version of Ficinus require that we should read ἀπ' αὐτοῦ.
[3] This impression is *the one* of intellect, the summit and as it

or it would never become the recipient of it. Thus, therefore, it becomes manifold from *the one;* and thus as intellect it sees itself, and then becomes sight perceiving. This, however, is then intellect when it possesses; and as intellect it possesses.[1] But prior to this, it is desire alone, and a formless sight. This intellect, therefore, projects itself towards that which is beyond intellect: and when it receives it, it becomes [perceptive] intellect. But it is always the recipient [of the ineffable], and always becomes intellect, essence, and intelligence, when it perceives intellectually. For prior to this it was not intelligence, in consequence of not possessing the intelligible; nor intellect, because it was not yet intellective. That, however, which is prior to these, is the principle of these, but not as inherent in them. For the first principle, or the *from which*, is not inherent in that of which it is the principle, but the things *of which* a thing consists, are inherent in that thing. That, however, *from which* each thing is derived, is not each thing, but is different from all things. Hence, it is not some one of all things, but is prior to all things; so that on this account, it is also prior to intellect. For again, all things are within intellect; so that for this reason likewise, it is prior to intellect. If, also, the natures which are posterior to it have the order of all things, and on this account likewise it is prior to all things, it is not proper that it should be a certain one of those things to which it is prior. You must not, therefore, denominate it intellect. Hence, neither must you call it *the good*, if *the good* signifies some one of all things. But if it signifies that which is prior to all things, let it be thus denomi-

---

were flower of its nature, and a vestige of the ineffable. For by seeing the ineffable, it becomes stamped as it were with its superessential nature.

[1] Conformably to this, Aristotle says of intellect in his Metaphysics, ἐνέργει δὲ ἔχων, i.e., "It energizes possessing."

nated. If, therefore, intellect is intellect because it is multitudinous, and the intellection of itself as it were intervening, though it is from itself, multiplies itself, it is necessary that the nature which is perfectly simple, and the first of all things, should be beyond intellect. For if it possessed intelligence, it would not be beyond, but would be intellect. But if it were intellect, it would also be multitude.

XII. What however hinders [it may be said, the first principle of things] from being thus multitude, so long as it is one essence? For multitude here is not composition; but the energies of it are multitude. If, however, the energies of it are not essences, but it proceeds from capacity into energy, it will not be multitude indeed, yet it will be imperfect in essence before it energizes. But if the essence of it is energy, and the energy of it is multitude, its essence will be as multitudinous as its energy. We admit, however, that this is the case with intellect, to which we attribute the intellection of itself; but we do not assert this of the principle of all things. For it is necessary that prior to multitude there should be *the one*, from which multitude proceeds; since in every number *the one* is first. Our opponents, however, may say, that this is indeed the case in number. For the things which are in a consequent order to unity are compositions; but what necessity is there in beings, that there should be a certain one from which the many proceed? To this we reply, that the many without *the one* would be devised from each other, one thing casually proceeding to another, in order to the composition of multitude. Hence, they also say, that energies proceed from one intellect which is simple; so that they now admit there is something simple prior to energies. And in the next place, they should know that energies which are always permanent are hypostases. Energies, however, being hypostases, are different from that from which they proceed; since this indeed remains simple, but that which proceeds from it, is in itself multitude, and is suspended from its simple cause. For if they subsist, that from which they proceed at the same time in a certain respect energizing, there also there will be multitude. But if they are first energies producing that which is secondary, nothing prevents that which is prior to the energies from abiding in itself, and from conceding energies to that which is second, and which consists of energies. For that which is prior to energies is one thing, but the energies which proceed from it another; because from that not energizing [these derive their subsistence]. For if this were not the case, intellect would not be the first energy. For [that which is entirely simple] did not as it were desire that intellect should be generated, and afterwards intellect was generated, this desire subsisting between the simple principle, and its offspring intellect. Nor in short, did this principle desire. For thus it would be imperfect, and the desire would not yet have that which it wished to obtain. Nor again, does it partly obtain the object of its wish, and partly not. For there is nothing to which the extension [of its desire is directed]. But indeed, if any thing subsists after it, it subsists in consequence of this principle abiding in its accustomed habit. It is necessary, therefore, in order that something else may subsist, that this principle should be every where quiescent in itself. For if not, either it will be moved prior to being moved, and will perceive intellectually prior to intellectual perception, or its first energy will be imperfect, being an impulse alone. To what, therefore, can it thus be impelled? For either we must admit that the energy flowing as it were from it, is analogous to the light proceeding from the sun, which energy is every intelligible and intellectual nature, and that this principle being established at the summit of the intelligible world reigns over it, without separating from itself, that which is unfolded into light from it; or we must admit that there is another light prior to this light, which emits its splendour, perpetually abiding in the intelligible. For that which proceeds from this principle is not separated from it, nor again, is the same with it. Nor is it a thing of such a kind as not to be essence. Nor is it, as it were, blind; but it sees and knows itself, and is primarily gnostic. The principle itself, however, as it is beyond intellect, so likewise it is beyond knowledge. And as it is not in want of any thing, it is not in want of knowledge; but knowledge subsists in the nature which is next to this. For to know is *one certain* thing; but this principle is *one* without the addition of *certain*. For if it was a *certain one*, it would not be *the one itself*. For *itself* is prior to a *certain* or *some particular thing*.

XIII. Hence, it is in reality ineffable. For of whatever you speak, you speak of as a certain thing. But of that which is beyond all things, and which is beyond even most venerable intellect, it is alone true to assert that it has not any other name [than the ineffable], and that it is not some one of all things. Properly speaking, however, there is no name of it, because nothing can be asserted of it. We, however, endeavour as much as possible to signify to ourselves something respecting it. But when we say doubting, it has therefore no perception nor intellection of itself, and consequently does not know itself, we ought to consider this, that when we assert these things, we should convert ourselves to their contraries. For we make it to be multitudinous, when we admit that it is knowable and has knowledge: and by attributing intellection to it, we make it to be in want of intelligence. But if it subsists together with intellection, intellectual perception will be superfluously added to it. For in short, intellection appears to be the co-sensation of the whole [of that which is intellective] many things concurring in one and the same, when any thing itself intellectually perceives itself, in which also intellection properly so called consists. Each of these many, however, is itself one certain thing unattended with investigation. But if intelligence is of that which is external, it will be something indigent, and not properly intellectual perception. That, however, which is perfectly simple, and truly self-sufficient, is not in want of any thing. But that which is secondarily self-sufficient, being in want of itself, is in want of the intellectual perception of itself. And that which is indigent with respect to itself, produces from the whole of itself the self-sufficient, becoming sufficient from all [the particulars of which it consists], dwelling with itself, and being conversant with itself by intellection; since co-sensation also, is the sensation of a certain multitude, as its name testifies. Intelligence, likewise, which is prior to sense, converts that which is intellective, and which is evidently multitudinous, to itself. For if it should alone say this, *I am being*, it would say this, as having discovered that it is so. And it would make this assertion reasonably. For being is multitudinous; since when it extends itself to that which is simple, and says, I am being, it does not meet either with itself, or with being. For it does not speak of being as of a stone, when it speaks of it truly: but by one word it pronounces many things.[1] For this existence, which is truly existence, is not spoken of as having nothing more than a vestige of being; since this is not being, and therefore may be said to have the relation of an image to its archetype. Hence, true being contains in itself multitude. What then? will it not intellectually perceive each of the many it contains? May we not say, that if you wish to assume the solitary and alone, you will not have intellectual perception?

[1] Instead of ἀλλ' οὐκ εἴρηκε μιᾷ ῥήσει πολλά in this place, it is necessary to read ἀλλ' οὖν εἴρηκε κ λ.

Existence itself, however, is in itself multitudinous. And though you should speak of something else, that something else has existence. If, however, this be the case, if there is something which is the most simple of all things, it will not have an intellectual perception of itself. For if it had [it would also have a subsistence somewhere].[1] Neither, therefore, does it intellectually perceive itself, nor is there any intellectual perception of it.

XIV. How, therefore, can we speak of it? We are able indeed to say something *of* it, but we do not speak *it*. Nor have we either any knowledge, or intellectual perception of it. How, therefore, do we speak of it, if we do not possess it? May we not say, that though we do not possess it by knowledge, yet we are not entirely deprived of the possession of it; but we possess it in such a way that we can speak *of* it, but cannot speak *it?* For we can say what it is not, but we cannot say what it is; so that we speak *of* it from things posterior to it. We are not, however, prevented from possessing it, though we cannot say what it is. But in the same manner as those who energize enthusiastically, and become divinely inspired, perceive indeed, that they have something greater in themselves, though they do not know what it is; but of the things by which they are excited they speak, and from these receive a certain sensation of the moving power, which is different from them;—in this manner also we appear to be affected about that which is perfectly simple,

---

[1] The words within the brackets are wanting in the original, and are supplied from the version of Ficinus. After εἰ γὰρ ἕξει, therefore, it is requisite to add ἔχει καὶ ποῦ εἶναι. But the meaning of Plotinus in this place is, that if the most simple of all things had an intellectual perception of itself, it would be in itself; and consequently would be *somewhere*. For an intellectual essence because self-subsistent, is said to be in itself. For so far as it is the cause of, it comprehends itself; but so far as it is caused, it is comprehended by itself.

when possessing a pure intellect we employ it, and conclude that this is the inward intellect which is the source of essence, and of other things which belong to this arrangement. We are sensible, therefore, that the nature which is perfectly simple is not these things, but that it is something more excellent, more ample, and great, than that which we denominate being, because it is also superior to reason, intellect, and sense, imparting, but not being these.

XV. But how does it impart them? Shall we say by possessing, or by not possessing them? If, however, it indeed possesses them, it is not simple. But if it does not possess them, how does multitude proceed from it? For perhaps some one may admit that one simple thing may proceed from it, though even in this case it may be inquired how any thing can proceed from that which is entirely one. At the same time, however, it may be said, that one simple thing may flow from it, in the same manner as a surrounding splendour from light. But how do many things proceed from it? May we not say, that what proceeds from is not the same with it? If, therefore, it is not the same with, it is not better than it. [For what is better, or in short, more excellent than *the one?* It is therefore inferior to it. But this is more indigent.]¹ For what is in a greater degree indigent than *the one*, except that which is not one? This, therefore, that is more indigent is many. At the same time, however, it aspires after *the one*. Hence it is *one many*. For *the one* saves every thing which is not one; and every thing is what it is through *the one*. For unless it becomes one, though it should consist of many things, it cannot yet be

¹ The words within the brackets are supplied from the version of Ficinus; so that in the original, after οὐδέ γε βέλτιον, it is necessary to supply τί γὰρ βέλτιον τοῦ ἑνός, ἢ ὅλως κρεῖττον; χεῖρον ἄρα, τοῦτο δὲ ἐνδεέστερον.

denominated being. And though it may be possible to say what each thing is, yet this is only in consequence of each thing being one, and participating of sameness. That, however, which has not multitude in itself, is not one by the participation of one, but is *the one itself*, not from another, but because it is this; from which other things also derive their subsistence, some indeed, proximately, but others remotely. But since that which is next to *the one* is characterized by sameness, and is posterior to *the one*, it is evident that the multitude of it is every where one. For being multitude at the same time it subsists in sameness, and without separation, because all things in it exist collectively at once [in impartible union]. Each also of the natures which proceed from it, as long as it participates of life, is *one many*. For it cannot exhibit itself to the view as *one all*. That, however, from which this originates is *one all*, because it is a great principle. For the principle is in reality and truly one. But that which is next to the principle, being thus after a manner [exuberantly full of] and heavy with *the one*, becomes all things through its participation of *the one*; and whatever it contains is again all and one. What therefore is this all? Is it not those things of which *the one* is the principle? But how is *the one* the principle of all things? Is it not because it is the saviour of them, causing each of them to be one? Or is it also because it gave subsistence to them? After what manner therefore? Is it not because it antecedently contained them? We have however before observed, that thus it will be multitude. They are contained in it, therefore, in such a way as to subsist without distinction and separation.[1] But the things contained in the second principle [after *the one*] are separated by reason: for they are now in energy. *The one*, however, is the power of all

[1] As all things proceed from *the one*, hence *the one* is all things prior to all.

things. But what is the mode of this power? For it is not said to be in power or capacity in the same manner as matter, because it receives: for matter suffers [in consequence of being passive]; and thus the power of matter has an arrangement opposite to that of efficiency. How, therefore, does it produce the things which it has not? For it does not produce them casually; nor having considered what it is to do, does it then produce them. It has been said, therefore, by us, that if any thing proceeds from *the one*, it is different from it; but being different, it is not one. For this is what *the one* was. If, however, that which proceeds from *the one* is not one, it is now necessary that it should be two things, and should be multitude. For it is now same and different, quality, and other things. That the offspring of *the one*, therefore, is not one [alone] has been now demonstrated. But that it is multitude, and a multitude of such a kind as that which is surveyed in what is posterior to it, is deservedly a subject of doubt. And the necessity of the subsistence of that which is posterior to it, still remains to be investigated.

XVI. That it is necessary, therefore, there should be something after the first, has been elsewhere asserted by us. And, in short, we have said that this which is next to the first [principle of things] is power, and an inestimable power. This, likewise, is rendered credible from all other things, because there is nothing even among the last of things which has not a generative power. Now, however, we must say, that in things which are generated, the progression is not to the upward, but to the downward, and to a greater multitude, and that the principle of particulars is itself more simple [than its effects]. Hence, that which produced the sensible world will not be itself the sensible world, but intellect and the intelligible world. Hence, too, that which is prior to the intelligible world, and which generated it, is something more simple than intellect and the intelligible world. For that which is multitudinous does not originate from multitude, but from that which is not multitude. For if the source of it was multitudinous, it would not be the principle, but the principle would be some other thing prior to it. It is necessary, therefore, to refer all things to that which is truly one, and which is superior to all multitude, and to every kind of [participable] simplicity, if it is truly simple. But how is that which is generated from it, multitudinous and universal reason, since it is evident it is not itself reason ? If however it is not reason, how can reason proceed from that which is not[1] reason ? And how can that which is boniform proceed from *the good ?* For what does it possess in itself that can cause it to be denominated boniform ? Is it because it subsists with invariable sameness? But what does this contribute to *the good?* For we seek after a sameness of subsistence when good is present. Or do we not first investigate that from which it is not proper to depart, because it is good? But if it is not good, it is better to abandon the pursuit of it. Is it therefore considered by us as boniform, to live abiding in good voluntarily, and with invariable sameness? Hence, if intellect is satisfied with living after this manner, it evidently seeks after nothing else. It appears, therefore, that a sameness of subsistence is desirable, because what is present is sufficient. All things, however, being now present to intellect, to live is desirable; and this when all things are in such a manner present with it, as not to be different from it. But if all life is present with this, and a life perspicuous and perfect; in this, soul and every intellect subsist, and nothing is wanting to it either of life or intellect. Hence it is sufficient to itself, and seeks after

---

[1] μὴ is omitted in the original.

nothing farther. But if this be the case, it possesses in itself, that which it would investigate if it were not present. It possesses, therefore, in itself *the good*, or a thing of such a kind as we call life and intellect, or something else which is accidental to these. If, however, this is *the good*, there will be nothing beyond these. But if *the good* is beyond these, a life tending to this, suspended from it, having its subsistence from, and living according to it, will evidently be good. For *the good* is the principle of intellect. It is necessary, therefore, that *the good* should be more excellent than life and intellect. For thus intellect, and the life which it contains, will be converted to it, since the life of intellect possesses in itself an imitation of *the good*, according to which intellect lives, and this is also the case with intellect itself, whatever this imitation may be.

XVII. What then is better than a most wise, irreprehensible, and unerring life ? What more excellent than an intellect possessing all things ? Or than all life, and every intellect ? If, therefore, we should say that the maker of these is more excellent, and should relate how he made them, and show that nothing better than him can present itself to our view, our reasoning will not proceed to any thing else, but will stop there. It is necessary, however, to ascend, both on account of many other considerations, and because self-sufficiency to this intellect is the result of all the things of which[1] it consists. But each of these is evidently indigent, because each participates of the same one, and participates of one in consequence of not being

[1] Instead of ἐκ πάντων ἔξω ἐστίν, it is necessary to read ἐκ πάντων ἐξ οὗ ἐστιν. The necessity of this emendation was not seen by Ficinus, whose translation of this part is consequently very erroneous. For how can the sufficiency of intellect consist of an accumulation of all things *externally?* But the translation of Ficinus is, "tum etiam quia sufficientia huic ex cunctis accumulata pendet extrinsecus."

the one itself. What then is that of which this intellect participates, and which causes it to exist, and to be all things at once? If, however, it causes it to be every thing, and the multitude of it is sufficient to itself through the presence of *the one,* and if also it is evidently effective of essence and self-sufficiency, it will not be essence, but beyond this, and beyond self-sufficiency. Is what we have said therefore sufficient, or is the soul yet parturient with something else, and in a still greater degree? Perhaps, therefore, it is requisite that the soul should now become impelled towards *the one,* being filled with parturient conceptions about it. Again, however, let us try if we cannot find a certain charm for this parturiency. Perhaps, indeed, he will accomplish this, who frequently enchants himself from what has now been said. What other new enchantment, therefore, as it were, is there? For the charm which runs above all realities, and above the truths which we participate, immediately flies away from him who wishes to speak of and energize discursively about *the one;* since it is necessary that the dianoetic power, in order that it may speak of any thing, should assume another and another thing. For thus there will be a discursive energy. In that, however, which is perfectly simple, there is nothing[1] discursive; but it is sufficient to come into contact with it intellectually. That, however, which comes into contact with it, when it is in contact, is neither able to say any thing, nor has leisure to speak; but afterwards [when it falls off from this contact] reasons about it. Then also it is requisite to believe that we have seen it, when the soul receives a sudden light. For this light is from him, and is him. And then it is proper to think that he is present, when like another God entering into the house of some one who invokes him, he fills it with splendour.[2] For unless

[1] It is necessary here to supply *ou*.
[2] Plotinus, in what he here says, doubtless alludes to the following

he entered, he would not illuminate it. And thus the soul would be without light, and without the possession of this God. But when illuminated, it has that which it sought for. This likewise is the true end to the soul, to come into contact with his light, and to behold him through it; not by the light of another thing; but to perceive that very thing itself through which it sees. For that through which it is illuminated, is the very thing which it is necessary to behold. For neither do we see the sun through any other than the solar light. How, therefore, can this be accomplished? By an ablation of all things.

lines in the 19th book of the "Odyssey," when Ulysses and Telemachus remove the weapons out of the armory:
"Minerva preceded them, having a golden lamp, with which she produced a very beautiful light; on perceiving which, Telemachus thus immediately addressed his father: O father, this is certainly a most admirable thing which presents itself to my eyes. For the walls of the house, the beautiful spaces between the rafters, the fir beams, and the columns, appear to me to rise in radiance, as if on fire. Certainly some one of the Gods is present who inhabit the extended heaven. But the wise Ulysses thus answered him: Be silent, repress your intellect, and do not speak. For this is the custom of the Gods who dwell in Olympus." Homer, therefore, indicates by this, that to the reception of divine illumination, silence, and a cessation of all mental energy, are requisite.

XIV.
THAT THE NATURE WHICH IS BEYOND BEING IS NOT INTELLECTIVE;
AND WHAT THAT IS WHICH IS PRIMARILY, AND ALSO THAT WHICH IS SECONDARILY, INTELLECTIVE.

V. vi.

ONE kind of intelligence is the intellectual perception of another thing, but another is the perception of a thing by itself, or when a thing perceives itself; the latter of which flies in a greater degree from duplicity, or doubleness in intellection. But the former wishes also to avoid this diversity, but is less able to accomplish its wish. For it has indeed with itself that which it sees, but it is different from itself. That, however, which intellectually perceives itself, is not separated essentially from the object of its perception, but being co-existent with it sees itself. Both, therefore, become one being. Hence it perceives in a greater degree because it possesses that which it perceives. It is also primarily intellective, because that which perceives intellectually ought to be both one and two. For if it is not one, that which perceives will be one thing, and that which is intellectually perceived another. Hence it will not be primarily intellective, because in consequence of receiving the intellectual perception of another thing, it will not possess that which it perceives, as something belonging to itself; so that the thing perceived will not be the perceiver itself. Or if it should possess it as itself, in order that it may properly perceive intellectually, two things will be one. Hence it is necessary that both should be one. Or if there is indeed one thing, but again, this one does not consist of two things, it will not possess intelligence; so that neither will it perceive intellectually. Hence it is necessary that the nature which is intellective should be simple and at the same time not simple. He, however, who ascends from soul will in a greater degree apprehend that an intellective nature is a thing of this kind. For here [*i.e.* in soul] it is easy to divide, and duplicity may here be easily perceived. If some one, therefore, should make a twofold light, soul, indeed, according to the less pure, but the intelligible of it according to the purer light, and afterwards should cause that which sees to be a light equal to that which is seen, not having any further occasion to separate by difference,—he who does this, will admit that these two are one. And this perceives intellectually, indeed, because it is two things; but it sees because it is now one thing. Thus, therefore, such a one will apprehend intellect and the intelligible. Hence we, by a reasoning process, have made two things from one. On the contrary, however, it is two things from one, because it intellectually perceives, making itself to be two; or rather being two because it intellectually perceives; and because it is one thing [being intellective].

II. If, therefore, there is that which is primarily intellective, and also that which is after another manner [*i.e.* secondarily] intellective, that which is beyond the first intelligent nature, will not perceive intellectually. For it is necessary that it should become intellect in order that it may have intellectual perception. But being intellect it will also have the intelligible. And if it is primarily intellective, it will have the intelligible in itself. It is not, however, necessary that whatever is intelligible should have that which is intellective in itself, and perceive intellectually. For in this case, it will not only be intelligible, but also intellective. But being two things it will not be that which is first. Intellect, likewise, which possesses the intelligible, could not subsist without the existence of an essence which is purely intelligible; and which with respect to intellect, indeed, will be intelligible, but with reference to itself will be properly neither intellective, nor intelligible. For that which is intelligible, is intelligible to another thing. And intellect which darts itself forward by intelligence would have a vacuum, unless it received and comprehended in itself the intelligible which it intellectually perceives. For it is not intellective without the intelligible. Hence it is then perfect when it possesses the intelligible. It is necessary, however, prior to its perceiving intellectually, that it should have with itself a perfect essence. Hence, that with which the perfect is essentially [1] present, will be perfect prior to intellectual perception. To this, therefore, nothing of intellectual perception is necessary. For prior to this it is sufficient to itself. Hence it does not perceive intellectually. There is, therefore, that which is not intellective; there is also that which is primarily intellective; and there is that which is intellective in a secondary degree. Farther still, if that which is first perceives intellectually, something is present with it. Hence it is not the first, but that which is second. It is also not one, but is now [2] many; and is all such things as it intellectually perceives. For if it only intellectually perceived itself, it would be many.[3]

[1] There is an omission in the original here of κατ' οὐσίαν, but both the sense and the version of Ficinus require it should be inserted.

[2] For εἴδη here, it is necessary to read ἤδη.

[3] The intelligible is prior to intelligence; for the former is

III. If, however, it should be said, that nothing hinders this same thing which is the first from being many, we reply that in these many there will be a subject. For it is not possible for the many to subsist, unless *the one* exists, from which, or in which they subsist; or in short, unless there is a one which is prior to other things that are numbered among themselves, and which it is necessary to receive itself in itself alone. But if it subsists in conjunction with other things, it is necessary having received this with other things, but which at the same time is different from them, that we should suffer it to be with other things, but that we should also investigate this subject, no longer in conjunction with other things of which it is the subject, but itself by itself. For that which is the same in other things, will indeed be similar to *this*, but will not be *this*.[1] It is necessary, however, that it should be alone, if it is to be seen in other things, unless it should be said that the being of it has its hypostasis in conjunction with other things. Hence, there will not be that which is itself simple; nor will there be that which is composed of many things. For since that which is simple has no subsistence, neither will that which is a composite of many things subsist. For because each simple

characterized by *essence*, but the latter by *intellect*. And being is prior to intellect. The intelligible, however, contains in itself intellect casually. Hence it has a knowledge which is beyond intellect. Much more, therefore, is the ineffable principle of things, who is beyond the intelligible, above the possession of intellectual perception. For his knowledge like his nature is more impartible than every centre, and more ineffable than all silence. For it is, if it be lawful so to speak, a darkness which transcends all gnostic illumination. Hence by energizing about it, knowledge is refunded into ignorance.

[1] For the imparticipable or exempt *one*, is not consubsistent with any thing, but the participable one is consubsistent either with being, or life, or intellect, or soul, or body. See my translation of Proclus' "Elements of Theology."

thing is unable to exist, no one certain simple thing subsisting from itself, hence since that which is multitudinous is not able to have an hypostasis by itself, nor to impart itself to another thing, because it has no existence, how can there be that which is composed of all things, when it must consist of nonentities, which are not merely negations of a certain thing, but have no subsistence whatever? If, therefore, a certain thing is multitude, it is necessary there should be *one* prior to the *many*. Hence, if that which is intellective is a certain multitude, it is necessary that there should not be intellectual perception in that which is not[1] multitude. This, however, is the first [principle of things]. In the natures, therefore, posterior to it, there will be intellectual perception and intellect.

IV. Farther still, if it is necessary that *the good* should be simple and unindigent, it will not be in want of intellectual perception. But that which is not necessary to it, will not be present with it; since, in short, nothing is present with it. Intellectual perception, therefore, will not be inherent in it, because neither will any thing else. Besides, intellect is something different from *the good*. For it becomes boniform by the intellectual perception of *the good*. Again, as in two things where there is one and another thing, it is not possible for this one which subsists in conjunction with something else to be *the one itself*, but it is necessary that *the one* which is one by itself, should be prior to that which is with another; thus also it is necessary, that where a certain one which is in a certain respect simple subsists in conjunction with another thing, there should prior to it be *the one* which is perfectly simple, and which has nothing in itself of the things contained in that which subsists in conjunction with others. For whence could one thing be another, unless prior to these that had a separate sub-

---

[1] μὴ is omitted in the original.

sistence, from which the thing that is another is derived? For that which is simple, cannot be derived from another. But that which is multitudinous or two, must necessarily be suspended from another thing. Hence, that which is first may be assimilated to light; that which is next to it, to the sun; but that which is the third, to the moon, deriving light from the sun. For soul, indeed, has an adventitious intellect, which, as soul is of an intellectual nature, colours it [with a light derived from *the good*]. Intellect, however, contains in itself an appropriate light of its own; for it is not light alone, but that which is illuminated essentially. But that which imparts this light, since it is not any thing else, is a simple light, affording to intellect the power of existing that which it is. Why, therefore, should this simple light be in want of any thing? For it is not the same with that which is in another; since that which is in another is different from that which subsists itself by itself.

V. Farther still, that which is multitudinous will seek itself, and will wish to verge to and be co-sentient of itself. Where, however, will that which is entirely one proceed to itself? And where will it be in want of co-sensation? For this same thing is more excellent than all co-sensation and intellection. For intellectual perception is not the first of things, either with respect to existence, or dignity of nature; but it is the second thing, and generated posterior to the subsistence of *the good*. As soon as generated, also, it moved itself towards *the good*. But being moved towards, it also knew it. And *intellectual perception is this, viz. a motion towards the good, and an aspiration after it*. For desire generated intelligence, and is consubsistent with it. For sight is the desire of seeing. *The good*, therefore, is not at all in want of intellectual perception. For there is not any thing else beside itself which is the good of it; since when that also which is different from *the good* intellectually perceives it, it does this in consequence of being boniform, and possessing a similitude to *the good*. It likewise intellectually perceives that which it sees, as good and desirable to itself; and in consequence of receiving as it were the imagination of good. And if it is always thus affected, it is alway this [*i.e.* it is always boniform]. For again, in the intellection of itself, it accidentally perceives *the good*. For looking to *the good*, it intellectually sees it, and also sees itself energizing. But the energy of all things is directed to *the good*.

VI. If, therefore, these things are rightly asserted, intelligence will have no place whatever in *the good*. For the good which is present with an intellective [1] nature is different from *the good itself*. Hence *the good* is unenergetic. For why is it necessary that energy should energize? For in short, no energy whatever has again energy. But if to other energies which are directed to another thing, we attribute something else, it is however necessary, that the first energy from which other energies are suspended, should be that very thing which it is, and that nothing else should be added to it. An energy, therefore, of this kind is not intellectual perception. For it does not possess that which it intellectually perceives; since it is the first energy. In the next place, neither does intelligence intellectually perceive, but that which possesses intelligence. Again, therefore, two things take place in that which perceives intellectually. But that which is first is by no means two. Farther still, the truth of this may be seen in a still greater degree by him who considers how this twofold nature subsists in every thing which is more clearly intellective. For we say, indeed, that beings as beings, that each thing itself [by itself,] and truly existing beings, are in the intelligible

---

[1] Instead of τὸ νοῦν τὶ in this place, it is necessary to read τῷ νοοῦντι.

place; and this not merely because some things abide invariably the same in essence, but others, and these are such as are in the sensible region, continually flow and are not permanent.[1] For perhaps there are some things in sensibles of a permanent nature. But we assert this of intelligibles, because they possess the perfection of existence. For it is necessary that the essence which is primarily so called, should not be the shadow of existence, but should have the fulness of being. Existence, however, is then full, when it receives the form of intellectual perception, and of life. Hence, in [real] being, to perceive intellectually, to live, and to exist, are consubsistent. If, therefore, it is being, it is also intellect, and if it is intellect it is being. And intellectual perception is simultaneous with existence. Hence, to perceive intellectually is many things, and not one thing. It is necessary, therefore, that with the nature which is not a thing of this kind, there should not be intellectual perception. Hence, among the several forms contained in true beings, there are man, and the intellectual perception[2] of man; horse, and the intellectual perception of horse; the just, and the intellection of the just. Hence too, all things there are double, and *the one* is two. And again, two passes into one. But that which is the first of things is not either of these; nor does it consist of all the things which are two; nor is it, in short, two. It has been, however, elsewhere shown by us, how two derives its subsistence from *the one*. But since *the one* is beyond essence, it is also beyond intellectual perception. There will be no absurdity therefore, in asserting that *the one* does not know itself. For being one it does not possess with itself that which it may learn. But neither is it necessary that it should know other things. For it

---

[1] Instead of οὐ νεύει here, it is necessary to read οὐ μένει.
[2] It is requisite here, to supply the words ἀνθρώπου νόησις καί.

imparts to them something better and greater than the knowledge of them; and this is the good of other things. But it rather imparts to them the ability, as much as possible, of coming into contact with it in the same thing.

XV.
ON THE GOOD, OR THE ONE.
VI. ix.

I. ALL beings are beings through *the one*, both such as are primarily beings, and such as in any respect whatever are said to be classed in the order of beings. For what would they be, if they were not one? For if deprived of unity, they are no longer that which they were said to be. For neither would an army, or a choir, exist [as such], unless each of them was one. Nor would a herd exist, if it were not one. But neither would a house or a ship have an existence, unless they possess *the one;* since a house is one thing, and also a ship, which one if they lose, the house will no longer be a house, nor the ship a ship. Continued magnitudes, therefore, unless *the one* is present with them, will not have an existence. Hence, when they are divided, so far as they lose *the one*, they change their existence. The bodies, also, of plants and animals, each of which is one, if they fly from *the one*, in consequence of being broken into multitude, lose the essence which they before possessed, no longer being that which they were, but becoming instead of it other things, and continuing to be these so long as they are one. Health, likewise, then has a subsistence, when the body is congregated into one [*i.e.*, when it possesses symmetry], and beauty then flourishes when the nature of *the one* confines the parts of the body. Virtue also exists in the soul when the soul tends to unity, and is united in one concord. Since, therefore, the soul conducts all things to one, by fabricating, fashioning, forming and co-arranging them, is it necessary to assert when we have arrived as far as to soul, that she supplies *the one*, and that she is *the one itself?* Or must we not say, that as when she imparts other things to bodies, such as *morphe* and form, it is not herself which she imparts, but things different from herself, thus also it is requisite to think if she imparts *the one*, that she imparts it as something different from herself; and that looking to *the one*, she causes each of her productions to be one, in the same manner as looking to man, she fabricates man, assuming together with man *the one* contained in man.[1] For of the things which are denominated one, each is in such a manner one as is the being which it possesses.[2] So that things which are in a less degree beings, possess in a less degree *the one;* but those that have more of entity have also more of *the one*. Moreover, soul being different from *the one*, possesses more of it in proportion as it is more truly soul, yet is not *the one itself*. For soul is one, and in a certain respect *the one* which it possesses is an accident. And these are two things, soul and one, in the same manner as body and one. That indeed which is decrete multitude, as a choir, is more remote from *the one*, but that which is continuous is nearer to it. But soul which has more alliance with, participates more abundantly of *the one*. If, however, because soul cannot exist unless it is one, it should be said that soul and *the one* are the same, we reply in the first place, that other

[1] The original here is defective, which deficiency may be supplied from the version of Ficinus, by reading ὥσπερ καὶ πρὸς ἄνθρωπον βλέπουσαν ἄνθρωπον δημιουργεῖ, instead of ὥσπερ καὶ πρὸς ἄνθρωπον ἄνθρωπον.

[2] *I.e.* The nature of its being depends on the nature of the unity which it participates; so that its being is more or less excellent according as this unity partakes in a greater or less degree of *the one itself*.

things also are what they are in conjunction with being one, but at the same time *the one* is different from them. For body and one are not the same; but body participates of *the one*. In the next place, each soul is a multitude, though it does not consist of parts. For there are many powers in it, viz., those of reasoning, appetition, and apprehension, which are connected by unity as by a bond. Soul, therefore, being itself one imparts *the one*, to other things. But she also suffers [*i.e.* participates] this one from something else.

II. Shall we say, therefore, that in each of the things which subsist according to a part, the essence of it and *the one* are not the same? In true being indeed, and true essence, essence, being, and *the one*, are the same. So that he who discovers being in these, will also discover *the one*, and will find that essence itself is *the one itself*. Thus, for instance, if essence is intellect, *the one* also is here intellect, viz., an intellect which is primarily being, and primarily one. And when it imparts existence to other things, thus, and so far as it imparts this, it also imparts *the one*. For what else besides intellect and being, can *the one* of these be said to be? For either *the one* is the same with being, as a man is the same thing as one man; or it is as a certain number of each thing, as when you speak of a certain two. And thus *the one* is asserted of a certain thing alone. If, therefore, number pertains to beings, it is evident that *the one* also pertains to them: and what it is must be investigated. But if *the one* is nothing more than the energy of the soul attempting to number, *the one* will have no existence in things themselves. Reason however has said, that whatever loses *the one*, loses entirely at the same time its existence. It is necessary, therefore, to consider whether each thing that has a being, and each thing that is one are the same, and whether in short, *being* and *the one* are the same. If, however, the being of each thing is multitude, but it is impossible for *the one* to be multitude, each of these will be different from the other. Man, therefore, is an animal, is rational, and has many parts, and this multitude is bound together by unity. Hence, man is one thing, and unity another; since the former is partible, but the latter impartible. Moreover, being which ranks as a whole, and contains all beings in itself, will rather be many beings [than one], and will be different from *the one*. But by assumption and participation, it will possess *the one*. Being, likewise, has life and intellect: for it is not deprived of life. Hence, being is many things. If also it is intellect, it is thus again necessary that it should be multitudinous; and this in a still greater degree, if it comprehends in itself forms or ideas. For idea is not unity, but is rather number. And this is true both of each idea, and of that which is all ideas collectively. Idea, likewise, is in such a manner one, as the world is one. In short, *the one* is the first of things, but intellect, forms, and being are not the first. For each form consists of many things, and is a composite, and posterior. For those things from which each form consists have a priority of subsistence. But that it is not possible that intellect can be the first of things, is evident from the following considerations. It is necessary that intellect should consist in intellectual perception; and that the most excellent intellect, and which does not look to what is external to, should intellectually perceive that which is prior to itself. For being converted to itself, it is [at the same time] converted to the principle of itself. And if indeed it is both intellective and intelligible, it will be twofold and not simple, and therefore not *the one*. But if it looks to something different from itself, it will entirely look to that which is more excellent than, and prior to itself. If, however, it both looks to itself, and to that which is better than itself, it will thus also be secondary. And it is requisite to admit that such an intellect as this, is present indeed with *the good*, and with that which is first, and that it beholds it. It likewise associates with, and intellectually perceives itself, and knows that it is itself all things. By no means, therefore, since it is thus various, is it *the one*. Neither, therefore, will *the one* be all things;[1] since if it were, it would no longer be *the one*. Nor is it intellect. For thus it would be all things; intellect being all things. Nor is it being. For being likewise is all things.

III. What then will *the one* be; and what nature will it possess? Or may we not say that it is not at all wonderful, it should not be easy to tell what it is, since neither is it easy to tell what being is, or what form is. But our knowledge is fixed in forms. When, however, the soul directs its attention to that which is formless, then being unable to comprehend that which is not bounded, and as it were impressed with forms by a former of a various nature, it falls from the apprehension of it, and is afraid it will possess [nothing from the view]. Hence, it becomes weary in endeavours of this kind, and gladly descends from the survey frequently falling from all things, till it arrives at something sensible, and as it were rests in a solid substance; just as the sight also, when wearied with the perception of small objects, eagerly converts itself to such as are large. When, however, the soul wishes to perceive by itself, and sees itself alone, then in consequence of being one with the object of its perception, it does not think that it yet

[1] It is well observed by Damascius in his MS. treatise περί ἀρχῶν, that neither *the one* nor *all things* accords *in reality* with the nature of *the one*. For these are opposed to each other, and distribute our conceptions. For if we look to the simple and *the one*, we destroy its immensely great perfection: and if we conceive all things subsisting together, we abolish *the one* and the simple. But this is because we are divided, and look to divided peculiarities. In short, so far as it is *the one*, it is exempt from all things, and is without any multitude; but so far as it is the principle of all things, it is all things prior to all.

possesses that which it investigates, because it is not different from that which it intellectually perceives. At the same time, it is requisite that he should act in this manner, who intends to philosophize about *the one*. Since, therefore, that which we investigate is one, and we direct our attention to the principle of all things, to *the good*, and the first, we ought not to be far removed from the natures which are about the first of things, nor fall from them to the last of all things, but proceeding to such as are first, we should elevate ourselves from sensibles which have an ultimate subsistence. The soul, likewise, should for this purpose be liberated from all vice, in consequence of hastening to *the* [vision of the] *good;* and should ascend to the principle which is in herself, and become one instead of many things, in order that she may survey the principle [1] of all things, and *the one*. Hence it is requisite, that the soul of him who ascends to *the good* should then become intellect, and that he should commit his soul to, and establish it in intellect, in order, that what intellect sees, his soul may vigilantly receive, and may through intellect survey *the one;* not employing any one of the senses, nor receiving any thing from them, but with a pure intellect, and with the summit [and as it were, flower] of intellect, beholding that which is most pure. When, therefore, he who applies himself to the survey of a thing of this kind, imagines that there is either magnitude, or figure, or bulk about this nature, he has not intellect for the leader of the vision; because intellect is not naturally adapted to perceive things of this kind, but such an energy is the energy of sense, and of opinion following sense. But in order to perceive *the one*, it is necessary to ¦receive from intellect a declaration of what intellect is able to accomplish. Intel-

[1] For ἀρχήν here, it is necessary to read ἀρχῆς; and it is also requisite to alter the punctuation conformably to the above translation.

lect, however, is able to see either things prior to itself, or things pertaining to itself, or things effected by itself. And the things indeed contained in itself, are pure; but those prior to itself are still purer and more simple; or rather this must be asserted of that which is prior to it. Hence, that which is prior to it, is not intellect, but something more excellent. For intellect is a *certain* one among the number of beings; but that is not a *certain* one, but is prior to every thing. Nor is it being; for being has, as it were, the form of *the one*.[1] But that is formless, and is even without intelligible form. For the nature of *the one* being generative of all things, is not any one of them. Neither, therefore, is it a certain thing, nor a quality, nor a quantity, nor intellect, nor soul, nor that which is moved, nor again that which stands still. Nor is it in place, or in time; but is by itself uniform, or rather without form, being prior to all form, to motion and to permanency. For these subsist about being which also cause it to be multitudinous. Why, however, if it is not moved, does it not stand still? Because it is necessary that one or both of these should subsist about being. And that which stands still, stands still through permanency, and is not the same with it. Hence permanency is accidental to it, and it no longer remains simple. For when we say that *the one* is the cause of all things, we do not predicate anything as an accident to it, but rather as something which happens to us, because we possess something from it, *the one* in the mean time subsisting in itself. It is necessary, however, when speaking accurately of *the one*, neither to call it *that*, nor *this*. But we running as it were externally round it, are desirous of explaining the manner in which we are

[1] Instead of τοῦ ὄντος here, it is necessary to read τοῦ ἑνός. For it is absurd to suppose Plotinus would say, *that being has as it were the form of being*, and yet Ficinus so translates it: " Nam ens velut formam ipsam entis habet."

x

affected about it. And at one time, indeed, we draw near to it, but at another time fall from it, by our doubts about it.

IV. In this affair, however, a doubt especially arises, because the perception of the highest God is not effected by science, nor by intelligence, like other intelligibles, but by the presence of him, which is a mode of knowledge superior to that of science. But the soul suffers an apostasy from *the one*, and is not entirely one when it receives scientific knowledge. For science is reason, and reason is multitudinous. The soul, therefore, in this case, deviates from *the one*, and falls into number and multitude. Hence it is necessary to run above science, and in no respect to depart from a subsistence which is profoundly one; but it is requisite to abandon science, the objects of science, every other thing, and every beautiful spectacle. For every thing beautiful is posterior to the supreme, and is derived from him, in the same manner as all diurnal light is derived from the sun. Hence Plato says, he is neither effable, nor to be described by writing. We speak however, and write about him, extending ourselves to him, and exciting others by a reasoning process to the vision of him; pointing out, as it were, the way to him who wishes to behold something [of his ineffable nature]. For doctrine extends as far as to the way and the progression to him. But the vision of him is now the work of one who is solicitous to perceive him. He, however, will not arrive at the vision of him, and will not be affected by the survey, nor will have in himself as it were an amatory passion from the view, (which passion causes the lover to rest in the object of his love) nor receive from it a true light, which surrounds the whole soul with its splendour, in consequence of becoming nearer to it; he, I say, will not behold this light, who attempts to ascend to the vision of the supreme while he is drawn downwards by those things which are an impediment to the vision. He will likewise not ascend by himself alone, but will be accompanied by that which will divulse him from *the one*, or rather he will not be himself collected into one. For *the one* is not absent from any thing, and yet is separated from all things; so that it is present, and yet not present with them. But it is present with those things that are able, and are prepared to receive it, so that they become congruous, and as it were pass into contact with it, through similitude and a certain inherent power allied to that which is imparted by *the one*. When, therefore, the soul is disposed in such a way as she was when she came from *the one*, then she is able to perceive it, as far as it is naturally capable of being seen. He, therefore, who has not yet arrived thither, but either on account of the above-mentioned obstacle is deprived of this vision, or through the want of reason which may conduct him to it, and impart faith respecting it; such a one may consider himself as the cause of his disappointment through these impediments, *and should endeavour by separating himself from all things to be alone.* But with respect to arguments in the belief of which he is deficient, he should conceive as follows:

V. Whoever fancies that beings are governed by fortune and chance, and are held together by corporeal causes, is very remote from God, and the conception of *the one*. Our arguments, likewise, are not addressed to these, but to those who admit that there is another nature besides bodies, and who ascend [at least] as far as to soul. It is necessary, therefore, that these should be well acquainted with the nature of soul, both as to other things, and to its being derived from intellect; from which also participating of reason, it possesses virtue. After these things, however, he should admit the subsistence of another intellect, different from that which reasons, and which is denominated rational. He should likewise consider reasonings to subsist now as it were in interval and motion, and sciences to be such-like reasons in the soul, with an [evolved] and manifest subsistence; in consequence of intellect which is the cause of sciences being now infused into the soul. Hence in this case, the soul has as it were a sensible perception of intellect, through apprehending it incumbent on soul, and containing in itself the intelligible world, a tranquil intellect, and a quiet motion, and having and being all things,—a multitude without separation, and again a separate multitude. For it is neither separated like the reasons [*i.e.* forms or ideas in the human soul] which are perceived by our intellect one at a time,[1] [and not simultaneously,] nor is it a confused multitude. For each of the forms contained in it proceeds separate from the rest; in the same manner as in the sciences, where all things subsisting in an impartible nature, at the same time each is separate from the rest. This multitude, therefore, subsisting at once is the intelligible world, which is immediately united to the first principle of things, and which the same reason that demonstrates the existence of soul says has a necessary subsistence. This, however, has a more principal subsistence than soul, yet is not the first of things, because it is not [profoundly] one, and simple. But *the one*, and the principle of all things, is simple. Hence that which is prior to the most honourable thing among beings,[2] if it is necessary there should be something prior to intellect, which wishes indeed to be one, yet is not one, but has the form of one, because intellect is not in

[1] In the original, οὔτε γὰρ διακέκριται ὡς οἱ λόγοι οἱ ἤδη καθ' ἓν νοούμενοι, which Ficinus not understanding has erroneously translated as follows: "Neque enim discernitur sicut rationes in probatione solent, sed tanquam rationes jam secundum unum quiddam excogitante." For the human intellect perceives only one form or idea at a time; but a divine intellect sees all forms at once.

[2] Instead of τὸ δὴ πρὸ τοῦ ἐν τοῖς οὐ δ' τιμιώτατον here, it is necessary to read τὸ δὴ πρὸ τοῦ ἐν τοῖς οὖσιν τιμιώτατου.

itself dispersed, but is truly present with itself, and does not, in consequence of its proximity to *the one*, divulse itself, though in a certain respect it dares to depart from *the one;*—that, I say, which is prior to intellect and is *the one*, is a prodigy, and is not being, lest here also *the one* should be predicated of another thing, to which no name is in reality adapted. But if it is necessary to give it a name, it may appropriately be called in common *one*, yet not as being first something else, and afterwards one. It is indeed on this account difficult to be known; but is principally to be known from its offspring essence. And intellect leads to essence. The nature also of *the one* is such, that it is the fountain of the most excellent things, and a power generating beings, abiding in itself without diminution, and not subsisting in its progeny. But we denominate it *the one* from necessity, in order that we may signify it to each other by a name, and may be led to an impartible conception, being anxious that our soul may be one.[1] We do not, however, here speak of *the one* and the impartible in such a way as when we speak of a point or the monad. For that which is after this manner one, is the principle of quantity, which could not subsist unless essence had a prior existence, and also that which is antecedent to essence. It is necessary therefore to project the dianoetic power to these; but we should consider the monad and a point as having an analogical similitude to *the one*, on account of their simplicity, and their flying from multitude and division.

VI. How, therefore, can we speak of *the one*, and how can we adapt it to intellectual conception? Shall we say that this may be accomplished, by admitting that it is more transcendently one than the monad and a point? For in these, indeed, the soul taking away magnitude and

---

[1] Instead of καὶ τὴν ψυχὴν ἓν οὐ θέλοντες in this place, it is requisite to read καὶ τὴν ψυχὴν ἓν εἶναι ἐίλοντες.

the multitude of number, ends in that which is smallest, and fixes itself in a certain thing which is indeed impartible, but which was in a partible nature, and is in something different from itself. But *the one* is neither in another thing, nor in that which is partible. Nor is it impartible in the same way as that which is smallest. For it is the greatest of all things, not in magnitude, but in power. So that it is without magnitude in power. For the natures also which are [immediately] posterior to it, are impartible in powers, and not in bulk. The principle of all things likewise must be admitted to be infinite, not because he is magnitude or number which cannot be passed over, but because the power of him is incomprehensible.[1] For when you conceive him to be intellect or God, he is more [excellent] than these. And again, when by the dianoetic power you equalize him with *the one*, or conceive him to be God, by recurring to that which is most united in your intellectual perception, he even transcends these appellations. For he is in himself, nor is any thing accidental to him. By that which is sufficient to itself also the unity of his nature may be demonstrated. For it is necessary that the principle of all things should be most sufficient both to other things, and to itself, and that it should also be most un-indigent. But every thing which is multitudinous and not one, is indigent; since consisting of many things it is not one. Hence the essence of it requires to be one. But *the one* is not in want of itself. For it is *the one*. Moreover, that which is many, is in want of as many things as it is. And each of the things that are in it, as it subsists in conjunction with others, and is not in itself, is indigent of other things; and thus a thing of this kind exhibits indigence, both according to parts and according to the whole. If, therefore, it is necessary there should be something

---

[1] For περιληπτῷ here, it is necessary to read ἀπεριληπτῷ.

which is most sufficient to itself, it is necessary there should be *the one*, which alone is a thing of such a kind, as neither to be indigent with reference to itself, nor with reference to another thing.[1] For it does not seek after any thing in order that it may be, nor in order that it may be in an excellent condition, nor that it may be there established. For being the cause of existence to other things, and not deriving that which it is from others, nor its happiness, what addition can be made to it external to itself? Hence its happiness, or the excellency of its condition, is not accidental to it. For it is itself [all that is sufficient to itself]. There is not likewise any place for it. For it is not in want of a foundation, as if it were not able to sustain itself. For that which is established in another thing is inanimate, and a falling mass, if it is without a foundation. But other things are established on account of *the one*, through which also they at the same time subsist, and have the place in which they are arranged. That, however, which seeks after place is indigent. But the principle is not indigent of things posterior to itself. The principle, therefore, of all things is unindigent of all things. For that which is indigent, is indigent in consequence of aspiring after its principle. But if *the one* was indigent of any thing it would certainly seek not to be *the one*; so

---

[1] As, however, a thing cannot be said to be a principle or cause without the subsistence of the things of which it is the principle or cause; hence *the one*, so far as it is a principle or cause, will be indigent of the subsistence of these. "Indeed," as Damascius says, "how is it possible it should not be indigent so far as it is *the one*? Just as it is all other things which proceed from it. For the indigent also is something belonging to all things." Hence there is something even beyond *the one*, which has no kind of indigence whatever, which is in every respect incapable of being apprehended, and about which we must be perfectly silent. See the Introduction to my "Plato," and the additional notes to the 3rd Volume of it.

that it would be indigent of its destroyer. Every thing, however, which is said to be indigent, is indigent of a good condition, and of that which preserves it. Hence to *the one* nothing is good, and, therefore, neither is the wish for any thing good to it. But it is *super-good*. And it is not good to itself, but to other things, which are able to participate of it. Nor does *the one* possess intelligence, lest it should also possess difference; nor motion. For it is prior to motion, and prior to intelligence. For what is there which it will intellectually perceive? Shall we say itself? Prior to intellection, therefore, it will be ignorant, and will be in want of intelligence in order that it may know itself, though it is sufficient to itself. It does not follow, however, that because *the one* does not know itself, and does not intellectually perceive itself, there will be ignorance in it. For ignorance takes place where there is diversity, and when one thing is ignorant of another. That, however, which is *alone* neither knows any thing, nor has any thing of which it is ignorant. But being one, and associating with itself, it does not require the intellectual perception of itself; since neither is it necessary, in order that you may preserve *the one*, to adapt to it an association with itself. But it is requisite to take away intellectual perception, an association with itself, and the knowledge of itself, and of other things. For it is not proper to arrange it according to the act of perceiving intellectually, but rather according to intelligence. For intelligence does not perceive intellectually, but is the cause of intellectual perception to another thing. Cause, however, is not the same with the thing caused. But the cause of all things is not any one of them. Hence neither must it be denominated that good which it imparts to others; but it is after another manner *the good*, in a way transcending other goods.

VII. If, however, because it is none of these things, you become indefinite in your decision, in this case establish yourself in the above mentioned particulars, and from these [ascend to] and fix yourself in God. But for this purpose you must not extend the dianoetic power outwardly. For God is not in a certain place, so as to desert other things; but wherever any thing is able to come into contact with him, there he is present. Hence, as in other things, it is not possible to perceive something intellectually, while understanding and attending to another thing, but it is necessary not to introduce any thing else to the object of intellectual vision, in order that the perceiver may be the thing itself which is perceived;—thus also here, it is not possible for the soul to perceive God, while it retains the impression of something else, and energizes according to that impression. Nor again, is it possible for the soul while occupied and detained by other things to be impressed with the form of something contrary to them. But as it is said of matter, that it ought to be void of all qualities, in order that it may receive the impressions of all things; thus also, and in a much greater degree, it is necessary that the soul should become formless, in order that there may be no impediment to its being filled and illuminated by the first principle of things. If, however, this be the case, it is requisite that the soul, dismissing all externals, should be entirely converted to its inmost recesses, and should not be called to any thing external, but should be unintellective of all things; and prior to this indeed, in inclination, but then also it should be without the perception of forms. It is likewise necessary that the soul, being ignorant of herself, should dwell on the contemplation of God, and associating, and as it were sufficiently conversing with him, should announce, if possible, the conference which it there held to another; which Minos perhaps having accomplished, was on this account said to be the familiar of Jupiter. Calling to mind also this conference, he established laws which were the images of it, being filled through the contact with divinity with materials for the institution of laws. Or may we not say that the soul, if she wishes to abide on high, will consider political concerns as unworthy to be the subject of conference with deity? For this indeed will be the language of him who has seen much of divinity. *For, as it is said, God is not external to any one, but is present with all things, though they are ignorant that he is so.* For they fly from him, or rather from themselves. They are unable, therefore, to apprehend that from which they fly. And having destroyed themselves, they are incapable of seeking after another. For neither will a child, when through insanity he becomes out of himself, recognize his father. But he who knows himself, will also know from whence he was derived.

VIII. If, therefore, a certain soul has known itself at another time, it will also know that its motion is not rectilinear, but that its natural motion is as it were in a circle about a certain thing, not externally, but about a centre. The centre, however, is that from which the circle proceeds; and therefore such a soul will be moved about the source of its existence. It will also be suspended from this, eagerly urging itself towards that to which all souls ought to hasten. But the souls of the Gods always tend thither; and by tending to this they are Gods. For whatever is conjoined to this is a God. But that which is very distant from it, is a multitudinous man and a brute. Is, therefore, that in the soul which is as it were a centre, the object of investigation? Or is it necessary to think that it is something else, in which as it were all centres concur? This centre, however, and this circle are assumed by us according to analogy. For the soul is not a circle in the same way as a figure; but because an ancient nature is in it and about it. And because the soul is suspended from a thing of this kind, and in a still greater degree when it is wholly separated from the body. Now, however, since a part of us is detained by the body; just as if some one should have his feet in the water, but with the rest of his body should be above it;—thus also being elevated by that part which is not merged in body, we are conjoined to that which is as it were the centre of all things; after the same manner as we fix the centres of the greatest circles in the centre of the sphere by which they are comprehended. If, therefore, the circles were corporeal and not psychical, they would be conjoined to the centre locally, and the centre being situated in a certain place, the circles would revolve about it. Since, however, these souls are themselves intelligible, and this centre is above intellect, it must be admitted that this contact is effected by other powers than those by which an intellective nature is adapted to be conjoined to the object of intellectual perception. The contact, also, is greater than that by which intellect is present [with the intelligible] through similitude and sameness, and is conjoined with a kindred nature, nothing intervening to separate the conjunction. For bodies, indeed, are prevented from being united to each other; but incorporeal natures are not separated from each other by bodies. Hence, one is not distant from the other by place, but by *otherness* and difference. When, therefore, difference is not present, then the natures which are not different are present with each other. The principle of all things, therefore, not having any difference, is always present; but we are present with it when we have no difference. And it indeed does not aspire after us, in order that it may be conversant with us; but we aspire after it, in order that we may revolve about it. We indeed perpetually revolve about it, but we do not always behold it. As a band of singers, however, though it moves about the coryphæus, may be diverted to the survey of something foreign to the choir [and thus become discordant], but when it converts itself to him, sings well, and truly subsists about him;—thus also we perpetually revolve about the principle of all things, even when we are perfectly loosened from it, and have no longer a knowledge of it. Nor do we always look to it; but when we behold it, then we obtain the end of our wishes, and rest [from our search after felicity]. Then also we are no longer discordant, but form a truly divine dance about it.

IX. In this dance, however, the soul beholds the fountain of life, the fountain of intellect, the principle of being, the cause of good, and the root of soul. And these are not poured forth from this fountain, so as to produce in it any diminution. For it is not a corporeal mass; since if it were, its progeny would be corruptible. But now they are perpetual, because the principle of them abides with invariable sameness; not being distributed into them, but remaining whole and entire. Hence, they likewise remain, just as if the sun being permanent, light also should be permanent. For we are not cut off from this fountain, nor are we separated from it, though the nature of body intervening, draws us to itself. But we are animated and preserved by an infusion from thence, this principle not imparting, and afterwards withdrawing itself from us; since it always supplies us with being, and always will as long as it continues to be that which it is. Or rather, we are what we are by verging to it. Our well-being also consists in this tendency. And to be distant from it is nothing else than a diminution of existence. Here, likewise, the soul rests, and becomes out of the reach of evils, running back to that place which is free from ill. And here also, she energizes intellectually, is liberated from perturbations, and lives in reality. For the present life, and which is without God, is a vestige of life, and an imitation of that life which is real. But the life in the intelligible world consists in the energy of intellect. Energy also generates Gods, through a tranquil and quiet contact with the principle of all things. It likewise generates beauty, justice, and virtue. For the soul being filled with deity, brings forth these. And this is both the beginning and end to the soul. It is the beginning indeed, because she originates from thence; but it is the end, because *the good* is there, and because when the soul is situated there, she becomes what she was before. For the good which is here, and in sensible concerns, is a lapse, a flight, and a defluxion of the wings of the soul. But that *the good* is there, is indicated by the love which is connascent with the soul; conformably to which Love is conjoined in marriage with souls, both in writings and in fables.[1] For since the soul is different from God, but is derived from him, she necessarily loves him, and when she is there she has a celestial love; but the love which she here possesses is common and vulgar. For in the intelligible world the celestial Venus reigns; but here the popular Venus,[2] who

[1] See my translation of the fable of Cupid and Psyche; for to this fable Plotinus now evidently alludes.
[2] The celestial Venus, says Proclus (in Schol. MSS. in Cratylum), is supermundane, leads upwards to intelligible beauty, is the supplier of an unpolluted life, and separates from generation. But the Venus that proceeds from Dione governs all the co-ordinations in the celestial world and the earth, binds them to each other, and perfects their generative progressions, through a kindred conjunction. He likewise informs us, that this goddess proceeds from foam, according to Orpheus, as well as the more ancient [or celestial] Venus; and that both proceed from generative powers; one from that of Heaven, but the other from that of Jupiter the Demiurgus. He adds, that by the sea (from which they rose) we must understand an expanded and circumscribed life; by its profundity, the universally-extended progression of such a life; and by the foam, the greatest purity of nature, that which is full of prolific light and power, that which swims upon all life, and is as it were its highest flower.

is as it were meretricious.[1] Every soul also is a Venus. And this the nativity of Venus, and Love who was born at the same time with her, obscurely signify.[2] The soul, therefore, when in a condition conformable to nature, loves God, wishing to be united to him, being as it were the desire of a beautiful virgin to be conjoined with a beautiful Love. When, however, the soul descends into generation, then being as it were deceived by [spurious] nuptials, and associating herself with another and a mortal Love, she becomes petulant and insolent through being absent from her father. But when she again hates terrene wantonness and injustice, and becomes purified from the defilements which are here, and again returns to her father, then she is affected in the most felicitous manner. And those indeed who are ignorant of this affection, may from terrene love form some conjecture of divine love, by considering how great a felicity the possession of a most beloved object is conceived to be; and also by considering that these earthly objects of love are mortal and noxious, that the love of them is nothing more than the love of images, and that they lose their attractive power because they are not truly desirable, nor our real good, nor that which we investigate. In the intelligible world, however, the true object of love is to be found, with which we may be conjoined, which we may participate, and truly possess, and which is not externally enveloped with flesh. *He however who knows this, will know what I say,* and will be convinced that the soul has then another life. The soul also proceeding to, and having now arrived at the desired end, and participating of deity, will know that the supplier of true life is then present. She will likewise then require nothing farther; for on the contrary, it will be requisite to lay

[1] Plotinus says this, looking to the illegitimate participations of this Venus by mankind.
[2] See the speech of Diotima in the "Banquet of Plato."

aside other things, to stop in this alone, and to become this alone, amputating every thing else with which she is surrounded. Hence, it is necessary to hasten our departure from hence, and to be indignant that we are bound in one part of our nature, in order that with the whole of our [true] selves, we may fold ourselves about divinity, and have no part void of contact with him. When this takes place therefore, the soul will both see divinity and herself, as far as it is lawful for her to see him. And she will see herself indeed illuminated, and full of intelligible light; or rather, she will perceive herself to be a pure light, unburthened, agile, and becoming to be a God, or rather being a God, and then shining forth as such to the view.[1] But if she again becomes heavy, she then as it were wastes away.

X. How does it happen, therefore, that the soul does not abide there? Is it not because she has not yet wholly migrated from hence? But she will then, when her vision of deity possesses an uninterrupted continuity, and she is no longer impeded or disturbed in her intuition by the body. That however which sees divinity, is not the thing

[1] Hence Aristotle in his "Politics" also says, that he who surpasses beyond all comparison the rest of his fellow-citizens in virtue, ought to be considered as a God among men. He also observes, that such a one is no longer a part of the city, that law is not for him, since he is a law to himself, and that it would be ridiculous in any one to subject him to the laws. Let no one, however, who is not thus transcendently virtuous, fancy that law also is not for him; for this fancy in such a one is not only idle, but if not suppressed may lead to sedition, and the destruction of himself and others. In short, the man who has not completely subdued his passions, is so far from being above law, that, as Proclus well observes, "the universe uses him as a brute." Observe, too, that when Plotinus calls the man who is able in this life to see divinity a God, he means that he is a God only according to *similitude;* for in this way, men transcendently wise and good are called by Plato, Gods and divine.

which is disturbed, but something else; when that which perceives him is at rest from the vision. But it is not then at rest according to a scientific energy, which consists in demonstrations, in credibilities, and a discursive process of the soul. For here vision, and that which sees, are no longer reason, but greater than and prior to reason. And in reason, indeed, they are as that is which is perceived. He therefore who sees himself, will then, when he sees, behold himself to be such a thing as this, or rather he will be present with himself thus disposed, and becoming simple, will perceive himself to be a thing of this kind. Perhaps, however, neither must it be said that he sees, but that he is the thing seen; if it is necessary to call these two things, *i.e.* the perceiver and the thing perceived. But both are one;[1] though it is bold to assert this. Then, indeed, the soul neither sees, nor distinguishes by seeing, nor imagines that there are two things; but becomes as it were another thing, and not itself. Nor does that which pertains to itself contribute any thing there. But becoming wholly absorbed in deity, she is one, conjoining as it were centre with centre. For here concurring, they are one; but they are then two when they are separate. For thus also we now denominate that which is another. Hence this spectacle is a thing difficult to explain by words. For how can any one narrate that as something different from himself, which when he sees he does not behold as different, but as one with himself?

XI. This, therefore, is manifested by the mandate of the mysteries, which orders that they shall not be divulged to those who are uninitiated. For as that which is divine cannot be unfolded to the multitude, this mandate forbids the attempt to elucidate it to any one but him who is fortunately able to perceive it. Since, therefore, [in this con-

[1] From the conclusion of this section, it is evident that instead of ἀλλὰ μή, in this place, we should read ἀλλὰ μήν.

junction with deity] there were not two things, but the perceiver was one with the thing perceived, as not being [properly speaking] vision but union; whoever becomes one by mingling with deity, and afterwards recollects this union, will have with himself an image of it. But he was also himself one, having with respect to himself no difference, nor with respect to other things. For then there was not any thing excited with him who had ascended thither; neither anger, nor the desire of any thing else, nor reason, nor a certain intellectual perception, nor, in short, was even he himself moved, if it be requisite also to assert this; but being as it were in an ecstasy, or energizing enthusiastically, he became established in quiet and solitary union, not at all deviating from his own essence, nor revolving about himself, but being entirely stable, and becoming as it were stability itself. Neither was he then excited by any thing beautiful; but running above the beautiful, he passed beyond even the choir of the virtues. Just as if some one having entered into the interior of the adytum should leave behind all the statues in the temple, which on his departure from the adytum will first present themselves to his view, after the inward spectacle, and the association that was there, which was not with a statue or an image, but with the thing itself [which the images represent], and which necessarily become the second objects of his perception. Perhaps, however, this was not a spectacle, but there was another mode of vision, viz. ecstasy, and an expansion and accession of himself, a desire of contact, rest, and a striving after conjunction, in order to behold what the adytum contains. But nothing will be present with him who beholds in any other way. The wise prophets, therefore, obscurely signified by these imitations how this [highest] God is seen. But the wise priest understanding the enigma, and having entered into the adytum, obtains a true vision of what is there. If, however, he has not entered, he will conceive this adytum to be a certain invisible thing, and will have a *knowledge* of the fountain and principle, as the principle of things. But when situated there, he will *see* the principle, and will be conjoined with it, by a union of like with like, neglecting nothing divine which the soul is able to possess. Prior to the vision also it requires that which remains from the vision. But that which remains to him who passes beyond all things, is that which is prior to all things. For the nature of the soul will never accede to that which is entirely non-being. But proceeding indeed downwards it will fall into evil; and thus into non-being, yet not into that which is perfect nonentity. Running, however, in a contrary direction, it will arrive not at another thing, but at itself. And thus not being in another thing, it is not on that account in nothing, but is in itself. *To be in itself alone, however, and not in being, is to be in God.* For God also is something which is not essence, but beyond essence. Hence the soul when in this condition associates with him. He, therefore, who perceives himself to associate with God, will have himself the similitude of him. And if he passes from himself as an image to the archetype, he will then have the end of his progression. But when he falls from the vision of God, if he again excites the virtue which is in himself, and perceives himself to be perfectly adorned; he will again be elevated through virtue, proceeding to intellect and wisdom, and afterwards to the principle of all things. *This, therefore, is the life of the Gods, and of divine and happy men, a liberation from all terrene concerns, a life unaccompanied with human pleasures, and a flight of the alone to the alone.*[1]

[1] From this *solitary* subsistence of *the one*, the solitariness of all other divine natures is derived, and their ineffable association with themselves. Hence Plato in the "Timæus" says, "that the Demiurgus established heaven (*i.e.* the world) one, only, solitary

nature, able through virtue to converse with itself, indigent of nothing external, and sufficiently known and friendly to itself." Proclus, in his Commentaries on this dialogue, admirably illustrates these words as follows : " To comprehend the whole blessedness of the world in three appellations, is most appropriate to that which subsists according to a triple cause, viz. the final, the paradigmatic, and the demiurgic. For of the appellations themselves, the first of them, viz. *one*, is assumed from the final cause ; for *the one* is the same with *the good*. But the second, viz. *only*, is assumed from the paradigmatic cause. For the *only-begotten* and *onlyness* (μόνωσις) were, prior to the universe, in all-perfect animal. And the third, viz. the *solitary*, is assumed from the demiurgic cause. For the ability of using itself, and through itself governing the world, proceeds from the demiurgic goodness. The world, therefore, is *one*, so far as it is united and is converted to the *one*. But it is *only*, so far as it participates of the intelligible, and comprehends all things in itself. And it is *solitary*, so far as it is similar to its father, and is able to save itself. From the three, however, it appears that it is a God. For *the one*, the *perfect*, and the *self-sufficient*, are the elements of deity. Hence, the world receiving these, is also itself a God ; being *one* indeed, according to hyparxis ; but *alone*, according to a perfection which derives its completion from all sensible natures ; and *solitary* through being sufficient to itself. For those that lead a solitary life, being converted to themselves, have the hopes of salvation in themselves. And that this is the meaning of the term *solitary*, is evident from the words, " able through virtue to converse with itself, indigent of nothing external, and sufficiently known and friendly to itself." For in these words Plato clearly manifests what the solitariness is which he ascribes to the world, and that he denominates that being solitary, who looks to himself, to that with which he is furnished, and to his own proper measure. For those that live in solitary places, are the saviours of themselves, so far as respects human causes. The universe, therefore, is likewise after this manner solitary, as being sufficient to itself, and preserving itself, not through a diminution but from an exuberance of power ; for self-sufficiency is here indicated ; and as he says, through virtue. For he alone among partial animals [such as we are] who possesses virtue, is able to associate with, and love himself with a parental affection. *But the vicious man looking to his inward baseness, is indignant with himself and with his own essence, is astonished with externals, and pursues an association with others, in consequence of his inability to behold himself. On the contrary, the worthy man perceiving himself beautiful, rejoices and is delighted, and producing in himself beautiful conceptions, gladly embraces an association with himself.* For we are naturally domesticated to the beautiful, but hastily withdraw ourselves from deformity. Hence, if the world possesses virtue adapted to itself, in its intellectual and psychical essence, and in the perfection of its animal nature, looking to itself, it loves itself, and is present with, and sufficient to itself.

ADDITIONAL NOTES.

PAGE 3. *Intellectual Prudence.* The following account of the virtues is extracted from the Notes to my Translation of the "Phædo" of Plato: The first of the virtues are the physical, which are common to brutes, being mingled with the temperaments, and for the most part contrary to each other; or rather pertaining to the animal. Or it may be said that they are illuminations from reason, when not impeded by a certain bad temperament: or that they are the result of energies in a former life. Of these Plato speaks in the "Politicus" and the "Laws." The ethical virtues, which are above these, are ingenerated by custom and a certain right opinion, and are the virtues of children when well educated. These virtues also are to be found in some brute animals. They likewise transcend the temperaments, and on this account are not contrary to each other. These virtues Plato delivers in the "Laws." They pertain however at the same time both to reason and the irrational nature. In the third rank above these are the political virtues, which pertain to reason alone; for they are scientific. But they are the virtues of reason adorning the irrational part as its instrument; through prudence adorning the gnostic, through fortitude the irascible, and through temperance the epithymetic power (or the power which is the source of desire); but adorning all the parts of the irrational nature through justice. And of these virtues Plato speaks much in the "Republic." These virtues too follow each other. Above these are the cathartic virtues, which pertain to reason alone, withdrawing from other things to itself, throwing aside the instruments of sense as vain, repressing also the energies through these instruments, and liberating the soul from the bonds of generation. Plato particularly unfolds these virtues in the "Phædo." Prior to these however are the theoretic virtues, which pertain to the soul, introducing itself to natures superior to itself, not only gnostically, as some one may be induced to think from the name, but also orectically: for it hastens to become, as it were, intellect instead of soul; and intellect possesses both desire and knowledge. These virtues are the converse of the political: for as the latter energize about things subordinate according to reason, so the former about things more excellent according to intellect. These virtues Plato delivers in the "Theætetus."

According to Plotinus, there is also another gradation of the virtues besides these, viz. the paradigmatic. For, as our eye, when it is first illuminated by the solar light, is different from that which illuminates, as being illuminated, but afterwards is in a certain respect united and conjoined with it, and becomes as it were solar-form; so also our soul at first indeed is illuminated by intellect, and energizes according to the theoretic virtues, but afterwards becomes, as it were, that which is illuminated, and energizes uniformly according to the paradigmatic virtues. And it is the business indeed of philosophy to make us intellect; but of theurgy to unite us to intelligibles, so that we may energize paradigmatically. And as when possessing the physical virtues, we know mundane bodies (for the subjects to virtues of this kind are bodies); so from possessing the ethical virtues, we know the fate of the universe, because fate is conversant with irrational lives. For the rational soul is not under fate; and the ethical virtues are irrational, because they pertain to the irrational part. According to the political virtues we know mundane affairs, and according to the cathartic super-mundane; but as possessing the theoretic we know intellectual, and from the paradigmatic intelligible natures. Temperance also pertains to the ethical virtues; justice to the political, on account of compacts; fortitude to the cathartic, through not verging to matter; and prudence to the theoretic. Observe too, that Plato in the "Phædo" calls the physical virtues servile, because they may subsist in servile souls; but he calls the ethical σκιογραφίαι *adumbrations*, because their possessors only know *that* the energies of such virtues are right, but do not know *why* they are so. It is well observed too here, by Olympiodorus, that Plato calls the cathartic and theoretic virtues, those which are in reality true virtues. He also separates them in another way, viz. that the political are not telestic, *i.e.* do not pertain to mystic ceremonies, but that the cathartic and theoretic are telestic. Hence, Olympiodorus adds, the cathartic virtues are denominated from the purification which is used in the mysteries; but the theoretic from perceiving things divine. On this account he accords with the Orphic verses, that

> The soul that uninitiated dies,
> Plung'd in the blackest mire in Hades lies.

For initiation is the divinely-inspired energy of the virtues. Olympiodorus also further observes, that by the thyrsus-bearers, Plato means those that energize according to the political virtues, but by the Bacchuses those that exercise the cathartic virtues. For we are bound in matter as Titans, through the great partibility of our nature; but we rise from the dark mire as Bacchuses. Hence we become more prophetic at the time of death: and Bacchus is the inspective guardian of death, because he is likewise of every thing pertaining to the Bacchic sacred rites.

All the virtues likewise exhibit their proper characters, these being every where common, but subsisting appropriately in each. For the characteristic property of fortitude is the not declining to things subordinate; of temperance, a conversion from an inferior nature; of justice, a proper energy, and which is adapted to being; and of prudence, the election and selection of things good and evil. Olympiodorus farther observes, that all the virtues are in the Gods. For many Gods, says he, are adorned with their appellations; and all goodness originates from the Gods. Likewise, prior to things which sometimes participate the virtues, as is our case, it is necessary there should be natures which always participate them. In what order, therefore, do the virtues first appear? Shall we say in the psychical? For virtue is the perfection of the soul; and election and pre-election are the energies and projections of the soul. Hence the Chaldæan oracles conjoin fontal virtue with fontal soul, or in other words, with soul subsisting according to cause. But may it not also be said, that the virtues naturally wish to give an orderly arrangement to that which is disordered? If this be admitted, they will originate from the demiurgic order. How then will they be cathartic there? May we not say, Olympiodorus adds, that through the cathartic virtues considered according to their casual subsistence in Jupiter the demiurgus, he is enabled to abide in his accustomed mode, as Plato says in the "Timæus"? And farther still, according to ancient theologists, he ascends to the tower of Saturn, who is a *pure* intellect.

As this distribution of the virtues, however, is at present no less novel than important, the following discussion of them from the 'Αφορμαὶ πρὸς τὰ νοητὰ, or AUXILIARIES TO INTELLIGIBLES, of Porphyry, is added both for the sake of the philosophic reader, and because it elucidates what is said by Plotinus on this subject. The substance of it is indeed evidently derived from Plotinus.

"There is one kind of virtues pertaining to the political character, and another to the man who tends to contemplation, and on this account is called theoretic, and is now a beholder. And there are also other virtues pertaining to intellect, so far as it is intellect, and separate from soul. The virtues indeed of the political character, and which consist in the moderation of the passions, are characterised by following and being obedient to the reasoning about that which is becoming in actions. Hence, looking to an innoxious converse with neighbours, they are denominated, from the aggregation of fellowship, political. And prudence indeed subsists about the reasoning part; fortitude about the irascible part; temperance, in the consent and symphony of the opithymotic with the reasoning part; and justice in each of these performing its proper employment with respect to governing and being governed. But the virtues of him who proceeds to the contemplative life, consist in a departure from terrestrial concerns. Hence also, they are called purifications, being surveyed in the refraining from corporeal actions, and avoiding sympathies with the body. For these are the virtues of the soul elevating itself to true being. The political virtues, therefore, adorn the mortal man, and are the forerunners of purifications. For it is necessary that he who is adorned by these, should abstain from doing any thing precedaneously in conjunction with body. Hence in purifications, not to opine with body, but to energize alone, gives subsistence to prudence; which derives its perfection through energizing intellectually with purity. But not to be similarly passive with the body, constitutes temperance. Not to fear a departure from body as into something void, and nonentity, gives subsistence to fortitude. But when reason and intellect are the leaders, and there is no resistance [from the irrational part], justice is produced. The disposition therefore, according to the political virtues, is surveyed in the moderation of the passions; having for its end to live as man conformable to nature. But the disposition according to the theoretic virtues, is beheld in apathy;[1] the end of which is a similitude to God.

"Since, however, of purification one kind consists in purifying, but another pertains to those that are purified, the cathartic virtues are surveyed according to both these significations of purification; for they purify the soul, and are present with purification. For the end of purification is to become pure. But since purification, and the being purified, are an ablation of every thing foreign, the good resulting from them will be different from that which purifies; so that if that which is purified was good prior to the impurity with which it is defiled, purification is sufficient. That, however, which remains after purification, is good, and not purification. The nature of the soul also was not good, but is that which is able to partake of good, and is boniform. For if this were not the case, it would not have become situated in evil. The good, therefore, of the soul consists in being united to its generator; but its evil, in an association with things subordinate to itself. Its evil also is twofold; the one arising from an association with terrestrial natures; but the other from doing this with an excess of the passions. Hence all the political virtues, which liberate the soul from one evil, may be denominated virtues, and are honourable. But the cathartic are more honourable, and liberate it from evil, so far as it is soul. It is necessary, therefore, that the soul when purified should associate with its generator. Hence the virtue of it after its conversion consists in a scientific knowledge of [true] being; but this will not be the case unless conversion precedes.

"There is therefore another genus of virtues after the cathartic and political, and which are the virtues of the soul energizing intellectually. And here, indeed, wisdom and prudence consist in the contemplation of those things which intellect possesses. But justice consists in performing what is appropriate in a conformity to, and energizing according to intellect. Temperance is an inward conversion of the soul to intellect. And fortitude

[1] This philosophic apathy is not, as is stupidly supposed by most of the present day, insensibility, but a perfect subjugation of the passions to reason.

is apathy; according to a similitude of that to which the soul looks, and which is naturally impassive. These virtues also, in the same manner as the others, alternately follow each other.

"The fourth species of the virtues, is that of the paradigms subsisting in intellect; which are more excellent than the psychical virtues, and exist as the paradigms of these; the virtues of the soul being the similitudes of them. And intellect indeed is that in which all things subsist at once as paradigms. Here, therefore, prudence is science; but intellect that knows [all things] is wisdom. Temperance is that which is converted to itself. The proper work of intellect, is the performance of its appropriate duty [and this is justice [1]]. But fortitude is sameness, and the abiding with purity in itself, through an abundance of power. There are therefore four genera of virtues; of which, indeed, some pertain to intellect, concur with the essence of it, and are paradigmatic. Others pertain to soul now looking to intellect, and being filled from it. Others belong to the soul of man, purifying itself, and becoming purified from the body, and the irrational passions. And others are the virtues of the soul of man, adorning the man, through giving measure and bound to the irrational nature, and producing moderation in the passions. And he, indeed, who has the greater virtues has also necessarily the less; but the contrary is not true, that he who has the less has also the greater virtues. Nor will he who possesses the greater, energize precedaneously according to the less, but only so far as the necessities of the mortal nature require. The scope also of the virtues, is, as we have said, generically different in the different virtues. For the scope of the political virtues, is to give measure to the passions in their practical energies according to nature. But the scope of the cathartic virtues, is entirely to obliterate the remembrance of the passions. And the scope of the rest subsists analogously to what has been before said. Hence, he who energizes according to the practical virtues, is a *worthy* man; but he who energizes according to the cathartic virtues, is *a dæmoniacal man*, or is also *a good dæmon*. He who energizes according to the intellectual virtues alone, is *a God.* But he who energizes according to the paradigmatic virtues, is *the father of the Gods.* We, therefore, ought especially

[1] The words καὶ δικαιοσύνη are omitted in the original. But it is evident from Plotinus, that they ought to be inserted.

to pay attention to the cathartic virtues, since we may obtain these in the present life. But through these, the ascent is to the more honourable virtues. Hence it is requisite to survey to what degree purification may be extended. For it is a separation from body, and from the passive motion of the irrational part. But how this may be effected, and to what extent, must now be said.

"In the first place, indeed, it is necessary that he who intends to acquire this purification, should, as the foundation and basis of it, know himself to be a soul bound in a foreign thing, and in a different essence. In the second place, as that which is raised from this foundation, he should collect himself from the body, and as it were from different places, so as to be disposed in a manner perfectly impassive with respect to the body. For he who energizes uninterruptedly according to sense, though he may not do this with an adhering affection, and the enjoyment resulting from pleasure, yet at the same time his attention is dissipated about the body, in consequence of becoming through sense[1] in contact with it. But we are addicted to the pleasures or pains of sensibles, in conjunction with a promptitude, and converging sympathy; from which disposition it is requisite to be purified. *This, however, will be effected by admitting necessary pleasures, and the sensations of them, merely as remedies, or as a liberation from pain, in order that [the rational part] may not be impeded [in its energies].* Pain also must be taken away. But if this is not possible, it must be mildly diminished. And it will be diminished, if the soul is not copassive with it. Anger, likewise, must as much as possible be taken away; and must by no means be premeditated. But if it cannot be entirely removed, deliberate choice must not be mingled with it, but the unpremeditated motion must be the impulse of the irrational part. *That however which is unpremeditated is imbecile and small.* All fear, likewise, must be expelled. For he who requires this purification, will fear nothing. Here, however, if it should take place, it will be unpremeditated. Anger therefore and fear must be used for the purpose of admonition. But the desire of every thing base must be exterminated. Such a one also, so far as he is a cathartic philosopher, will not desire meats and drinks.

---

[1] Instead of κατ' αὐτήν here, it is necessary to read κατ' αἴσθησιν.

Neither must there be the unpremeditated in natural venereal connexions; *but if this should take place, it must be only as far as to that precipitate imagination which energizes in sleep.* In short, the intellectual soul itself of the purified man, must be liberated from all these [corporeal propensities]. He must likewise endeavour that what is moved to the irrational nature of corporeal passions, may be moved without sympathy, and without animadversion; so that the motions themselves may be immediately dissolved, through their vicinity to the reasoning power. This, however, will not take place while the purification is proceeding to its perfection; but will happen to those in whom reason rules without opposition. Hence in these, the inferior part will so venerate reason, that it will be indignant if it is at all moved, in consequence of not being quiet when its master is present, and will reprove itself for its imbecility. These, however, are yet only moderations of the passions, but at length terminate in apathy. For when co-passivity is entirely exterminated, then apathy is present with him who is purified from it. For passion becomes moved, when reason imparts excitation, through verging [to the irrational nature]."

PAGE 11. *The endeavour is not to be without sin, but to be a God.* That is, to be a God according to a similitude to divinity itself. For through this similitude, good men are also called by Plato Gods. Hence, too, Empedocles says of himself,

χαίρετ' ἐγώ δ' ὕμμιν, θεὸς ἄμβροτος οὐχ' ἔτι θνητὸς.
" Farewell, no mortal, but a God am I."

From this magnificent conception of human nature by the Pythagoreans and Plato, considered according to its true condition, the lofty language of the Stoics about their wise man was doubtless derived. For they assert of him that he possesses continual hilarity, and sublime joy; that he is blessed even in torments; that he is without perturbation, because he is stable and remote from error; that he does not opine, because he does not assent to anything false; that nothing happens to him contrary to his expectation; and that he is sufficient to himself, or is contented with himself alone, so far as pertains to living blessedly, and not to merely living; for to the latter many things are necessary, but to the former nothing is requisite but a sane and erect mind which looks down upon fortune with contempt. They farther add, that all things are the property of the wise man, and that he alone is to be considered rich, because he uses all things in the way which they ought to be used, and because he alone possesses the virtues, which are more precious than all treasures. That he alone is free, but that all bad men are slaves: for he neither fears any thing, nor does any thing cause him to grieve, nor is he subservient to any subordinate nature. That he alone is a king; for he governs both himself, and others. Hence Seneca, "Are you willing to have great honour, I will give you *a great empire:* obtain dominion over yourself." And lastly they add, that the wise man is obnoxious to no injury. For, as Seneca says in his treatise " De Constantia Sapientis," " Fortune takes away nothing except that which she gave ; but she does not give virtue, and therefore does not take it away. Virtue is free, inviolable, unmoved, unshaken, and so hardened against casualties, that she cannot even be made to incline, much less can she be vanquished. Hence the wise man loses nothing of which he will perceive the loss ; for he is in the possession of virtue, from which he can never be driven, and he uses every thing else as something different from his proper good. If, therefore, an injury cannot hurt any of those things which are the property of a wise man, because they are safe through virtue, an injury cannot be done to a wise man." And afterwards, speaking of Stilpo the philosopher, who on being asked by Demetrius whether he had lost any thing by the capture of Megara, answered that he had lost nothing; for, said he, *all that is mine is with me ;* and yet his patrimony was a part of the plunder, and the enemy had ravished his daughters, and conquered his country; speaking of this very extraordinary man, he observes as follows, " Stilpo shook off victory from the conqueror, and testified that though the city was taken, he himself was not only unconquered, but without loss ; for he had with him true goods, upon which no hand can be laid. Whatever may be dissipated and plundered, he did not consider as his own, but as a thing adventitious, and which follows the nod of fortune, and hence he did not love it as his proper good. It must therefore be admitted that this perfect man, who was full of human and divine virtues, lost nothing. His goods were begirt with solid and insurmountable fortifications. You must not compare with these the walls of Babylon, which Alexander entered; nor the walls of Carthage or Numantia, which were captured by one hand; nor the Capitol, or the citadel; for these possess an hostile vestige. But the walls which defend the wise man are safe from flames and incursion; they afford no entrance, are unconquerable, and so lofty that they reach even to the Gods." Agreeably to this, also, the great Socrates said with a magnanimity which has seldom been equalled, and never surpassed, ἐμὲ δὲ "Ανυτος καὶ Μέλιτος ἀποκτεῖναι μὲν δύνανται, βλάψαι δὲ οὐ δύνανται. "Anytus and Melitus may indeed put me to death, but they cannot injure me."

These magnificent conceptions, and this elevated language arising from the cultivation of true virtue and wisdom, were no longer to be found when the hand of barbaric despotism abolished the schools of the philosophers. For then, as a necessary consequence, a night of ignorance succeeded, which is without a parallel in the history of any period; and Philosophy, accompanied by all the great virtues, retired from the Cimmerian darkness into the splendid and dignified solitude in which the Genius of antiquity resides.

PAGE 14. *Dialectic.* For the sake of the truly philosophic reader who may not have my translation of Plato in his possession, the following additional observations on that master science, dialectic, are extracted from the 3rd volume of that translation, and principally from the notes on the Parmenides.

The method of reasoning employed by the dialectic of Plato, was invented by the Eleatic Zeno the disciple of Parmenides, and is as follows: Two hypotheses being laid down, viz. *if a thing is,* and *if it is not,* each of these may be tripled, by considering in each *what happens, what does not happen, what happens and at the same time does not happen;* so that six cases will be the result. But since, *if a thing is,* we may consider itself either with respect to itself, or itself with respect to others; or we may consider others themselves with respect to themselves, or others with respect to that thing itself, and so likewise if a thing is not: hence the whole of this process will consist of eight triads, which are the following. 1. *If a thing is,* what happens to itself with respect to itself, what does not happen, what happens and at the same time does not happen. 2. *If a thing is,* what happens to itself with respect to others, what does not happen, what happens and at the same time does not happen.

ADDITIONAL NOTES. 335

3. *If a thing is*, what happens to others with respect to themselves, what does not happen, what happens and at the same time does not happen. 4. *If a thing is*, what happens to others with respect to that thing, what does not happen, what happens and at the same time does not happen. And the other four, which are founded on the hypothesis *that a thing is not*, are to be distributed in exactly the same manner as those we have just enumerated. Such (says Proclus in MS. "Commen. in Parmenid.") is the whole form of the dialectic method, which is both intellectual and scientific; and under which those four powers the *definitive* and *divisive*, the *demonstrative* and *analytic*, receive their consummate perfection.

The "Parmenides" of Plato gives a specimen of this method logically and synoptically; comprehending in eight the above-mentioned four and twenty modes. Plato also adds, that the end of this exercise is the perception of truth. "We must not, therefore," says Proclus, "consider him as simply speaking of scientific truth, but of that which is intelligible, or which, in other words, subsists according to a superessential characteristic. For the whole of our life is an exercise to the vision of this; and the wandering through dialectic hastens to that as its port. Hence Plato in a wonderful manner uses the word $\delta\iota o\psi\epsilon\sigma\theta\alpha\iota$, to *look through*: for souls obtain the vision of intelligibles through many media."

That the dialectic method, however, may become conspicuous to the reader, the two following specimens of it are subjoined from the above-mentioned admirable Commentary of Proclus. The first of these is an investigation of the four and twenty modes in providence. If then providence is, there will follow to itself with respect to itself, the beneficent, the infinitely powerful, the efficacious; but there will not follow, the subversion of itself, the privation of counsel, the unwilling. That which follows and does not follow is, that it is one and not one. There will follow to itself with respect to other things, to govern them, to preserve every thing, to possess the beginning and the end of all things, and to bound the whole of sensibles. That which does not follow is, to injure the objects of its providential care, to supply that which is contrary to expectation, to be the cause of disorder. There will follow and not follow, the being present to all things, and an exemption from them; the knowing, and not knowing them. For it knows them in a different manner, and not with powers co-ordinate to the things known. There will follow to other things with respect to themselves, to suffer nothing casually from each other, and that nothing will be [really] injured by any thing. There will not follow, that any thing pertaining to them will be from fortune, and the being unco-ordinated with each other. There will follow and not follow, that all things are good; for this will partly pertain to them, and partly not. To other things with respect to it there will follow, to be suspended from it, on all sides to be guarded and benefited by it. There will not follow, an opposition to it, and the possibility of escaping it. For there is nothing so small that it can be concealed from it, nor so elevated that it cannot be vanquished by it. There will follow and not follow, that every thing will participate of providence. For in one respect they partake of it, and in another not of it, but of the goods which are imparted to every thing from it.

But let providence not have a subsistence, again there will follow to itself with respect to itself the imperfect, the unprolific, the inefficacious, a subsistence for itself alone. There will not follow, the unenvying, the transcendently full, the sufficient, the assiduous. There will follow, and not follow, the unsolicitous, and the undisturbed. For in one respect these will be present with that which does not providentially energize, and in another respect will not, in consequence of secondary natures not being governed by it. But it is evident that there will follow to itself with respect to other things, the unmingled, the privation of communion with all things, the not knowing any thing. There will not follow, the assimilating other things to itself, and the imparting to all things the good that is fit. There will follow and not follow, the being desirable to other things; for this in a certain respect is possible and not possible. For if it should be said, that through a transcendency exempt from all things, it does not providentially energize, nothing hinders but that it may be an object of desire to all secondary natures; but yet, considered as deprived of this power, it will not be desirable. To other things with respect to themselves there will follow, the unadorned, the casual, the indefinite in passivity, the reception of many things adventitious in their nature, the being carried in a confused and disordered manner. There will not follow, an allotment with respect to one thing, a distribution according to desert, and a subsistence according to intellect. There will follow and not follow, the being good. For so far as they are beings, they must necessarily be good; and yet, providence not having a subsistence, it cannot be said whence they possess good. But to other things with respect to providence there will follow, the not being passive to it, and the being unco-ordinated with respect to it. There will not follow, the being measured and bounded by it. There will follow and not follow, the being ignorant of it. For it is necessary they should know that it is not, if it is not; and it is also necessary they should not know it; for there is nothing common to them with respect to providence.

In the next place, let it be proposed to consider the consequences of admitting or denying the perpetual existence of soul.

If then soul always is, the consequences to itself with respect to itself, are, the self-motive, the self-vital, and the self-subsistent. But the things which do not follow to itself with respect to itself, are, the destruction of itself, the being perfectly ignorant, and knowing nothing of itself. The consequences which follow and do not follow are, the impartible and the partible (for in a certain respect it is partible, and in a certain respect impartible), perpetuity and non-perpetuity of being. For so far as it communicates with intellect, it is eternal; but so far as it verges to a corporeal nature, it is mutable.

Again, if soul is, the consequences to itself with respect to other things, *i.e.* bodies, are communication of motion, the connecting of bodies, as long as it is present with them, together with dominion over bodies, according to nature. That which does not follow, is to move externally. For it is the property of animated bodies to be moved inwardly; and to be the cause of rest and immutability to bodies. The consequences which follow and do not follow are to be present with bodies, and yet to be present separate from them. For soul is present with them by its providential energies, but is exempt from them by its essence, because this is incorporeal. And this is the first hexad.

The second hexad is as follows: If soul is, the consequence to other things, *i.e.* bodies, with respect to themselves, is sympathy; for according to a vivific cause, bodies sympathize with each other. But that which does not follow, is the non-sensitive. For in consequence of there being such a thing as soul, all things must necessarily be sensitive; some things peculiarly so, and others as parts of the whole. The consequences which follow and do not follow to bodies with respect to themselves are, that in a certain respect they move themselves, through being animated, and in a certain respect do not move themselves; for there are many modes of self-motion.

Again, if soul is, the consequences to bodies with respect to soul, are, to be moved internally and vivified by soul, to be preserved and connected through it, and to be entirely suspended from it. The consequences which do not follow are, to be dissipated by soul, and to be filled from it with a privation of life; for bodies receive from soul, life and connection. The consequences which follow and do not follow are, that bodies participate, and do not participate of soul. For so far as soul is present with bodies, so far they may be said to participate of soul; but so far as it is separate from them, so far they do not participate of soul. And this forms the second hexad.

The third hexad is as follows: If soul is not, the consequences to itself with respect to itself are, the non-vital, the unessential, and the non-intellectual; for not having any subsistence, it has neither essence,[1] nor life, nor intellect. The consequences which do not follow are, the ability to preserve itself, to give subsistence to, and be motive of itself, with every thing else of this kind. The consequences which follow and do not follow are, the unknown and the irrational. For not having a subsistence, it is in a certain respect unknown and irrational with respect to itself, as neither reasoning nor having any knowledge of itself; but in another respect, it is neither irrational nor unknown, if it is considered as a certain nature, which is not rational, nor endued with knowledge.

Again, if soul is not, the consequences which follow to itself with respect to bodies are, to be unprolific of them, to be unmingled with, and to employ no providential energies about them. The consequences which do not follow are, to move, vivify, and connect bodies. The consequences which follow and do not follow are, that it is different from bodies, and that it does not

---

[1] *I.e.* Not being soul, it has not the essence of soul; but this does not prevent it from being something else. For the hypothesis is, *if soul is not*, which is equivalent to the assertion that if a thing is not soul, it is something else.

communicate with them. For this in a certain respect is true, and not true, if that which is not soul is considered as having indeed a being, but unconnected with soul. For thus it is different from bodies, since these are perpetually connected with soul: and again, it is not different from bodies, so far as it has no subsistence, and is not. And this forms the third hexad.

In the fourth place then, if soul is not, the consequences to bodies with respect to themselves are, the immovable, privation of difference according to life, and the privation of sympathy with each other. The consequences which do not follow are, a sensible knowledge of each other, and to be moved from themselves. That which follows and does not follow is, to be passive to each other. For in one respect they would be passive, and in another not; since they would be alone corporeally and not vitally passive.

Again, if soul is not, the consequences to other things with respect to it are, not to be taken care of, not to be moved by soul. The consequences which do not follow are, to be vivified and connected by soul. The consequences which follow and do not follow are, to be assimilated and not assimilated to soul. For so far as soul having no subsistence, neither will bodies subsist, so far they will be assimilated to soul; for they will suffer the same with it; but so far as it is impossible for that which is not to be similar to any thing, so far bodies will have no similitude to soul. And this forms the fourth and last hexad.

Hence we conclude, that soul is the cause of life, sympathy and motion to bodies; and in short, of their being and preservation. For soul subsisting, these are at the same time introduced: but not subsisting, they are at the same time taken away.

P. 122. Note. Hence there is something even beyond *the one*. —The most sublime of the arcane dogmas of the Platonic Theology is this, that the ineffable principle of things is something even beyond *the one*, as is demonstrated by Proclus in his second book "On the Theology of Plato," and particularly by Damascius in his MS. treatise περὶ ἀρχῶν, " On Principles." See my translation of the former of these works, and of an extract from the latter in the Additional Notes at the end of the third Volume of my Plato, and in my "Dissertation on the

Philosophy of Aristotle." From this extract, the following observations are selected. "*The one* is not *the one* as that which is smallest, but it is *the one* as all things. For by its own simplicity it accedes to all things, and makes all things to be one. Hence all things proceed from it, because it is itself all things prior to all. And as that which has an united subsistence is prior to things which are separated from each other, so *the one* is *many* prior to *the many*. All things, therefore, are from *the one*, and with reference to *the one*, as we are accustomed to say. If then according to a more usual manner of speaking, we call things which consist in multitude and separation *all things*, we must admit that *the united*, and in a still greater degree *the one*, are the principles of these. But if we consider these two as all things, and assume them in conjunction with all other things, according to habitude and co-ordination with them, we must then investigate another principle prior to all things, which it is no longer proper to consider in any way as all things, nor to co-arrange with its progeny. For if some one should say that *the one*, though it is all things which have in any respect a subsistence, yet is *one* prior to *all things*, and is more one than *all things*; since it is *one* by itself, but *all things* as the cause of all, and according to a co-ordination with all things;—if this should be said, *the one* will thus be doubled, and we ourselves shall become doubled, and multiplied about its simplicity. For, by being *the one* it is all things after the most simple manner. At the same time also, though this should be said, it is necessary that the principle of all things should be exempt from all things, and consequently that it should be exempt from the most simple *allness*, and from a simplicity absorbing all things, such as is that of *the one*. Our soul, therefore, prophesies that the principle which is beyond all things that can in any respect be conceived, is uncoordinated with all things. Neither, therefore, must it be called principle nor cause, nor that which is first nor prior to all things, nor beyond all things. By no means, therefore, must we celebrate it as all things, nor, in short, is it to be celebrated, or recalled into memory. We may also add, that *the one* is the summit of *the many*, as the cause of the things proceeding from it: and that we form a conception of *the one* according to a purified suspicion extended to that which is most simple and most comprehensive. But that which is most venerable must necessarily be incomprehensible by all conceptions and suspicions; since also in other things, that which always soars beyond our conceptions is more honourable than that which is more obvious; so that what flies from all our suspicions will be *most* honourable. But if this be the case, it is nothing. Let however *nothing* be twofold, one better than *the one*, the other posterior to sensibles. If also we strive in vain in asserting these things, striving in vain is likewise twofold; the one falling into the ineffable, the other into that which in no respect whatever has any subsistence. For the latter also is ineffable, as Plato says, yet according to the worse, but the former according to the better. If, too, we search for a certain advantage arising from it, this is the most necessary advantage of all others, that all things proceed as from an adytum, from the ineffable, and in an ineffable manner. For neither do they proceed as *the one* produces *the many*, nor as *the united* things *separated*, but as the ineffable similarly produces all things *ineffably*. But if in asserting these things concerning it, that it is ineffable, that it is no one of all things, that it is incomprehensible, we subvert what we say, it is proper to know that these are the names and words of our parturitions, daring anxiously to explore it, and which, standing in the vestibules of the adytum, announce indeed nothing pertaining to the ineffable, but signify the manner in which we are affected about it, our doubts and disappointments; nor yet this clearly, but through indications to such as are able to understand these investigations. We also see that our parturitions suffer these things about *the one*, and that in a similar manner they are solicitous and subverted. For *the one*, says Plato, if it *is*, is not *the one*. But if it is not, no assertion can be adapted to it: so that neither can there be a negation of it, nor can any name be given to it; for neither is a name simple. Nor is there any opinion nor science of it. For neither are these simple; nor is intellect itself simple. So that *the one* is in every respect unknown and ineffable.

"What then? Shall we investigate something else beyond the ineffable? Or perhaps, indeed, Plato leads us ineffably through *the one* as a medium, to the ineffable beyond *the one* which is now the subject of discussion; and this by an ablation of *the one*, in the same manner as he leads us to *the one* by an ablation of other things. But if having ascended as far as to *the one* he is silent, this also is becoming in Plato to be perfectly silent, after the manner of the ancients, concerning things in every respect unspeakable; for the discourse was indeed most dangerous in consequence of falling on idiotical ears. Hence that which is beyond *the one* is to be honoured in the most perfect silence, and prior to this, by the most perfect ignorance, which despises all knowledge."[1]

And in another part of the same admirable work, he further observes: " Ascending therefore to *the one*, shall we meet with it as that which is known? Or wishing to meet with it as such shall we arrive at the unknown? May we not say that each of these is true? For we meet with it afar off as that which is far known; and when we are united to it from afar, passing beyond that in our nature which is gnostic of *the one*, then are we brought to be one, that is to be unknown instead of being gnostic. This contact, therefore, as of one with one, is above knowledge, but the other is as of that which is gnostic with that which is known. As, however, the crooked is known by the straight, so we form a conjecture of the unknown by the known. And this indeed is a mode of knowledge. *The one*, therefore, is so far known, that it does not admit of an approximating knowledge, but appears afar off as known, and imparts a gnostic indication of itself. Unlike other things, however, the nearer we approach to it, it is not the more, but on the contrary less known; knowledge being dissolved by *the one* into ignorance, since as we have before observed where there is knowledge there is also separation. But separation approaching to *the one* is inclosed in union; so that knowledge also is refunded into ignorance. This, too, the analogy of Plato requires. For first, we endeavour to see the sun, and we do indeed see it afar off; but by how much the nearer we approach to it, by so much the less do we see it: and at length, we neither see other things nor it, the eye becoming spontaneously dazzled by its light. Is therefore *the one* in in its proper nature unknown, though there is something else un-

[1] As that which is below all knowledge is an ignorance worse than knowledge, so the silence in which our ascent to the ineffable terminates, is succeeded by an ignorance superior to all knowledge. Let it, however, be carefully remembered, that such an ignorance is only to be obtained after the most scientific and intellectual energies.

known beside *the one?* *The one* indeed wills to be by itself, but with no other; but the unknown, beyond *the one*, is perfectly ineffable, which we acknowledge we neither know, nor are ignorant of, but which has about itself *super-ignorance*. Hence by proximity to this *the one itself* is darkened: for being very near to the immense principle, if it be lawful so to speak, it remains as it were in the adytum of that truly mystic silence. On this account, Plato in speaking of it finds all his assertions subverted: for it is near to the subversion of every thing, which takes place about the first. It differs from it however in this, that it is *one* simply, and that according to *the one* it is also at the same time all things. But the first is above *the one* and *all things*, being more simple than either of these."

ALPHABETICAL LIST

OF

BOHN'S LIBRARIES.

November, 1895.

'I may say in regard to all manner of books, Bohn's Publication Series is the usefullest thing I know.'—THOMAS CARLYLE.

'The respectable and sometimes excellent translations of Bohn's Library have done for literature what railroads have done for internal intercourse.'—EMERSON.

'An important body of cheap literature, for which every living worker in this country who draws strength from the past has reason to be grateful.'
Professor HENRY MORLEY.

BOHN'S LIBRARIES.

STANDARD LIBRARY	343 VOLUMES.
HISTORICAL LIBRARY	23 VOLUMES.
PHILOSOPHICAL LIBRARY . . .	17 VOLUMES.
ECCLESIASTICAL LIBRARY . . .	15 VOLUMES.
ANTIQUARIAN LIBRARY . , . .	36 VOLUMES.
ILLUSTRATED LIBRARY	75 VOLUMES.
SPORTS AND GAMES	16 VOLUMES.
CLASSICAL LIBRARY	108 VOLUMES.
COLLEGIATE SERIES	10 VOLUMES.
SCIENTIFIC LIBRARY	46 VOLUMES.
ECONOMICS AND FINANCE . . .	5 VOLUMES.
REFERENCE LIBRARY	30 VOLUMES.
NOVELISTS' LIBRARY	13 VOLUMES.
ARTISTS' LIBRARY	10 VOLUMES.
CHEAP SERIES	55 VOLUMES.
SELECT LIBRARY OF STANDARD WORKS	31 VOLUMES.

'Messrs. Bell are determined to do more than maintain the reputation of "Bohn's Libraries."'—*Guardian.*

'The imprint of Bohn's Standard Library is a guaranty of good editing.'
Critic (N.Y.)

'This new and attractive form in which the volumes of Bohn's Standard Library are being issued is not meant to hide either indifference in the selection of books included in this well-known series, or carelessness in the editing.'
St. James's Gazette.

'Messrs. Bell & Sons are making constant additions of an eminently acceptable character to "Bohn's Libraries."'—*Athenæum.*

ALPHABETICAL LIST OF BOOKS

CONTAINED IN

BOHN'S LIBRARIES.

748 Vols., Small Post 8vo. cloth. Price £160.

Complete Detailed Catalogue will be sent on application.

Addison's Works. 6 vols. 3s. 6d. each.
Aeschylus. Verse Trans. by Anna Swanwick. 5s.
—— Prose Trans. by T. A. Buckley. 3s. 6d.
Agassiz & Gould's Comparative Physiology. 5s.
Alfieri's Tragedies. Trans. by Bowring. 2 vols. 3s. 6d. each.
Alford's Queen's English. 1s. & 1s. 6d.
Allen's Battles of the British Navy. 2 vols. 5s. each.
Ammianus Marcellinus. Trans. by C. D. Yonge. 7s. 6d.
Andersen's Danish Tales. Trans. by Caroline Peachey. 5s.
Antoninus (Marcus Aurelius). Trans. by George Long. 3s. 6d.
Apollonius Rhodius. The Argonautica. Trans. by E. P. Coleridge. 5s.
Apuleius, The Works of. 5s.
Ariosto's Orlando Furioso. Trans. by W. S. Rose. 2 vols. 5s. each.
Aristophanes. Trans. by W. J. Hickie. 2 vols. 5s. each.
Aristotle's Works. 5 vols, 5s. each; 2 vols, 3s. 6d. each.
Arrian. Trans. by E. J. Chinnock. 5s.
Ascham's Scholemaster. (J. E. B. Mayor.) 1s.
Bacon's Essays and Historical Works, 3s. 6d.; Essays, 1s. and 1s. 6d.; Novum Organum, and Advancement of Learning, 5s.
Ballads and Songs of the Peasantry. By Robert Bell. 3s. 6d.
Bass's Lexicon to the Greek Test. 2s.

Bax's Manual of the History of Philosophy. 5s.
Beaumont & Fletcher. Leigh Hunt's Selections. 3s. 6d.
Bechstein's Cage and Chamber Birds. 5s.
Beckmann's History of Inventions. 2 vols. 3s. 6d. each.
Bede's Ecclesiastical History and the A. S. Chronicle. 5s.
Bell (Sir C.) On the Hand. 5s.
—— Anatomy of Expression. 5s.
Bentley's Phalaris. 5s.
Björnson's Arne and the Fisher Lassie. Trans. by W. H. Low. 3s. 6d.
Blair's Chronological Tables. 10s.
—— Index of Dates. 2 vols. 5s. each.
Bleek's Introduction to the Old Testament. 2 vols. 5s. each.
Boethius' Consolation of Philosophy, &c. 5s.
Bohn's Dictionary of Poetical Quotations. 6s.
Bond's Handy - book for Verifying Dates, &c. 5s.
Bonomi's Nineveh. 5s.
Boswell's Life of Johnson. (Napier). 6 vols. 3s. 6d. each.
—— (Croker.) 5 vols. 20s.
Brand's Popular Antiquities. 3 vols. 5s. each.
Bremer's Works. Trans. by Mary Howitt. 4 vols. 3s. 6d. each.
Bridgewater Treatises. 9 vols. Various prices.
Brink (B. Ten). Early English Literature. 2 vols. 3s. 6d. each.
—— Five Lectures on Shakespeare 3s.6d.

ALPHABETICAL LIST OF

Browne's (Sir Thomas) Works. 3 vols. 3s. 6d. each.

Buchanan's Dictionary of Scientific Terms. 6s.

Buckland's Geology and Mineralogy. 2 vols. 15s.

Burke's Works and Speeches. 8 vols. 3s. 6d. each. The Sublime and Beautiful. 1s. & 1s. 6d. Reflections on the French Revolution. 1s.

—— Life, by Sir James Prior. 3s. 6d.

Burney's Evelina. 3s. 6d. Cecilia 2 vols. 3s. 6d. each.

Burns' Life by Lockhart. Revised by W. Scott Douglas. 3s. 6d.

Burn's Ancient Rome. 7s. 6d.

Butler's Analogy of Religion, and Sermons. 3s. 6d.

Butler's Hudibras. 5s.; or 2 vols., 5s. each.

Caesar. Trans. by W. A. M'Devitte. 5s.

Camoens' Lusiad. Mickle's Translation, revised. 3s. 6d.

Carafas (The) of Maddaloni. By Alfred de Reumont. 3s. 6d.

Carpenter's Mechanical Philosophy 5s. Vegetable Physiology. 6s. Animal Physiology. 6s.

Carrel's Counter Revolution under Charles II. and James II. 3s. 6d.

Cattermole's Evenings at Haddon Hall. 5s.

Catullus and Tibullus. Trans. by W. K. Kelly. 5s.

Cellini's Memoirs. (Roscoe.) 3s. 6d.

Cervantes' Exemplary Novels. Trans. by W. K. Kelly. 3s. 6d.

—— Don Quixote. Motteux's Trans. revised. 2 vols. 3s. 6d. each.

—— Galatea. Trans. by G. W. J. Gyll. 3s. 6d.

Chalmers On Man. 5s.

Channing's The Perfect Life. 1s. and 1s. 6d.

Chaucer's Works. Bell's Edition, revised by Skeat. 4 vols. 3s. 6d. ea.

Chess Congress of 1862 By J. Löwenthal. 5s.

Chevreul on Colour. 5s. and 7s. 6d.

Chillingworth's The Religion of Protestants. 3s. 6d.

China: Pictorial, Descriptive, and Historical. 5s.

Chronicles of the Crusades. 5s.

Cicero's Works. 7 vols. 5s. each. 1 vol., 3s. 6d.

—— Friendship and Old Age. 1s. and 1s. 6d.

Clark's Heraldry. (Planché.) 5s. and 15s.

Classic Tales. 3s. 6d.

Coleridge's Prose Works. (Ashe.) 6 vols. 3s. 6d. each.

Comte's Philosophy of the Sciences. (G. H. Lewes.) 5s.

—— Positive Philosophy. 3 vols. 5s. each.

Condé's History of the Arabs in Spain. 3 vols. 3s. 6d. each.

Cooper's Biographical Dictionary. 2 vols. 5s. each.

Cowper's Works. (Southey.) 8 vols. 3s. 6d. each.

Coxe's House of Austria. 4 vols. 3s. 6d. each. Memoirs of Marlborough. 3 vols. 3s. 6d. each. Atlas to Marlborough's Campaigns. 10s. 6d.

Craik's Pursuit of Knowledge. 5s.

Craven's Young Sportsman's Manual. 5s.

Cruikshank's Punch and Judy. 5s. Three Courses and a Dessert. 5s.

Cunningham's Lives of British Painters. 3 vols. 3s. 6d. each.

Dante. Trans. by Rev. H. F. Cary. 3s. 6d. Inferno. Separate, 1s. and 1s. 6d. Purgatorio. 1s. and 1s. 6d. Paradiso. 1s. and 1s. 6d.

—— Trans. by I. C. Wright. (Flaxman's Illustrations.) 5s.

—— Inferno. Italian Text and Trans. by Dr. Carlyle. 5s.

—— Purgatorio. Italian Text and Trans. by W. S. Dugdale. 5s.

De Commines' Memoirs. Trans. by A. R. Scoble. 2 vols. 3s. 6d. each.

Defoe's Novels and Miscel. Works. 6 vols. 3s. 6d. each. Robinson Crusoe (Vol. VII). 3s. 6d. or 5s. The Plague in London. 1s. and 1s. 6d.

Delolme on the Constitution of England. 3s. 6d.

Demmins' Arms and Armour. Trans. by C. C. Black. 7s. 6d.

Demosthenes' Orations. Trans by C. Rann Kennedy. 4 vols. 5s., and 1 vol. 3s. 6d.
—— Orations On the Crown. 1s. and 1s. 6d.
De Stael's Corinne. Trans. by Emily Baldwin and Paulina Driver. 3s. 6d.
Devey's Logic. 5s.
Dictionary of Greek and Latin Quotations. 5s.
—— of Poetical Quotations (Bohn). 6s.
—— of Scientific Terms. (Buchanan.) 6s.
—— of Biography. (Cooper.) 2 vols. 5s. each.
—— of Noted Names of Fiction. (Wheeler.) 5s.
—— of Obsolete and Provincial English (Wright.) 2 vols. 5s. each.
Didron's Christian Iconography. 2 vols. 5s. each.
Diogenes Laertius. Trans. by C. D. Yonge. 5s.
Dobree's Adversaria. (Wagner). 2 vols. 5s. each.
Dodd's Epigrammatists. 6s.
Donaldson's Theatre of the Greeks. 5s.
Draper's History of the Intellectual Development of Europe. 2 vols. 5s. each.
Dunlop's History of Fiction. 2 vols. 5s. each.
Dyer's History of Pompeii. 7s. 6d.
—— The City of Rome. 5s.
Dyer's British Popular Customs. 5s.
Early Travels in Palestine. (Wright.) 5s.
Eaton's Waterloo Days. 1s. and 1s. 6d.
Eber's Egyptian Princess. Trans. by E. S. Buchheim. 3s. 6d.
Edgeworth's Stories for Children. 3s. 6d.
Ellis' Specimens of Early English Metrical Romances. (Halliwell.) 5s.
Elze's Life of Shakespeare. Trans. by L. Dora Schmitz. 5s.
Emerson's Works. 3 vols. 3s. 6d. each, or 5 vols. 1s. each.
Ennemoser's History of Magic. 2 vols. 5s. each.
Epictetus. Trans. by George Long. 5s.
Euripides. Trans. by E. P. Coleridge. 2 vols. 5s. each.
Eusebius' Eccl. History. Trans. by C. F. Cruse. 5s.

Evelyn's Diary and Correspondence. (Bray.) 4 vols. 5s. each.
Fairholt's Costume in England. (Dillon.) 2 vols. 5s. each.
Fielding's Joseph Andrews. 3s. 6d. Tom Jones. 2 vols. 3s. 6d. each. Amelia. 5s.
Flaxman's Lectures on Sculpture. 6s.
Florence of Worcester's Chronicle. Trans. by T. Forester. 5s.
Foster's Works. 10 vols. 3s. 6d. each.
Franklin's Autobiography. 1s.
Gesta Romanorum. Trans. by Swan & Hooper. 5s.
Gibbon's Decline and Fall. 7 vols. 3s. 6d. each.
Gilbart's Banking. 2 vols. 5s. each.
Gil Blas. Trans. by Smollett. 6s.
Giraldus Cambrensis. 5s.
Goethe's Works and Correspondence, including Autobiography and Annals, Faust, Elective affinities, Werther, Wilhelm Meister, Poems and Ballads, Dramas, Reinecke Fox, Tour in Italy and Miscellaneous Travels, Early and Miscellaneous Letters, Correspondence with Eckermann and Soret, Zelter and Schiller, &c. &c. By various translators. 16 vols. 3s. 6d. each.
—— Faust. Text with Hayward's Translation. (Buchheim.) 5s.
—— Faust. Part I. Trans. by Anna Swanwick. 1s. and 1s. 6d.
—— Boyhood. (Part I. of the Autobiography.) Trans. by J. Oxenford. 1s. and 1s. 6d.
—— Reinecke Fox. Trans. by A. Rogers. 1s. and 1s. 6d.
Goldsmith's Works. (Gibbs.) 5 vols. 3s. 6d. each.
—— Plays. 1s. and 1s. 6d. Vicar of Wakefield. 1s. and 1s. 6d.
Grammont's Memoirs and Boscobel Tracts. 5s.
Gray's Letters. (D. C. Tovey.) [*In the press.*
Greek Anthology. Trans. by E. Burges. 5s.
Greek Romances. (Theagenes and Chariclea, Daphnis and Chloe, Clitopho and Leucippe.) Trans. by Rev. R. Smith. 5s.

Greek Testament. 5s.
Greene, Marlowe, and Ben Jonson's Poems. (Robert Bell.) 3s. 6d.
Gregory's Evidences of the Christian Religion. 3s. 6d.
Grimm's Gammer Grethel. Trans. by E. Taylor. 3s. 6d.
—— German Tales. Trans. by Mrs. Hunt. 2 vols. 3s. 6d. each.
Grossi's Marco Visconti. 3s. 6d.
Guizot's Origin of Representative Government in Europe. Trans. by A. R. Scoble. 3s. 6d.
—— The English Revolution of 1640. Trans. by W. Hazlitt. 3s. 6d.
—— History of Civilisation. Trans. by W. Hazlitt. 3 vols. 3s. 6d. each.
Hall (Robert). Miscellaneous Works. 3s. 6d.
Handbooks of Athletic Sports. 8 vols. 3s. 6d. each.
Handbook of Card and Table Games. 2 vols. 3s. 6d. each.
—— of Proverbs. By H. G. Bohn. 5s.
—— of Foreign Proverbs. 5s.
Hardwick's History of the Thirty-nine Articles. 5s.
Harvey's Circulation of the Blood. (Bowie.) 1s. and 1s. 6d.
Hauff's Tales. Trans. by S. Mendel. 3s. 6d.
—— The Caravan and Sheik of Alexandria. 1s. and 1s. 6d.
Hawthorne's Novels and Tales. 4 vols. 3s. 6d. each.
Hazlitt's Lectures and Essays. 7 vols. 3s. 6d. each.
Heaton's History of Painting. (Cosmo Monkhouse.) 5s.
Hegel's Philosophy of History. Trans. by J. Sibree. 5s.
Heine's Poems. Trans. by E. A. Bowring. 3s. 6d.
—— Travel Pictures. Trans. by Francis Storr. 3s. 6d.
Helps (Sir Arthur). Life of Thomas Brassey. 1s. and 1s. 6d.
Henderson's Historical Documents of the Middle Ages. 5s.
Henfrey's English Coins. (Keary.) 6s.
Henry (Matthew) On the Psalms. 5s.
Henry of Huntingdon's History. Trans. by T. Forester. 5s.

Herodotus. Trans. by H. F. Cary. 3s. 6d.
—— Wheeler's Analysis and Summary of. 5s. Turner's Notes on. 5s.
Hesiod, Callimachus and Theognis. Trans. by Rev. J. Banks. 5s.
Hoffmann's Tales. The Serapion Brethren. Trans. by Lieut.-Colonel Ewing. 2 vols. 3s. 6d.
Hogg's Experimental and Natural Philosophy. 5s.
Holbein's Dance of Death and Bible Cuts. 5s.
Homer. Trans. by T. A. Buckley. 2 vols. 5s. each.
—— Pope's Translation. With Flaxman's Illustrations. 2 vols. 5s. each.
—— Cowper's Translation. 2 vols. 3s. 6d. each.
Hooper's Waterloo. 3s. 6d.
Horace. Smart's Translation, revised, by Buckley. 3s. 6d.
Hugo's Dramatic Works. Trans. by Mrs. Crosland and F. L. Slous. 3s. 6d.
—— Hernani. Trans. by Mrs. Crosland. 1s.
—— Poems. Trans. by various writers. Collected by J. H. L. Williams. 3s. 6d.
Humboldt's Cosmos. Trans. by Otté, Paul, and Dallas. 4 vols. 3s. 6d. each, and 1 vol. 5s.
—— Personal Narrative of his Travels. Trans. by T. Ross. 3 vols. 5s. each.
—— Views of Nature. Trans. by Otté and Bohn. 5s.
Humphreys' Coin Collector's Manual. 2 vols. 5s. each.
Hungary, History of. 3s. 6d.
Hunt's Poetry of Science. 5s.
Hutchinson's Memoirs. 3s. 6d.
India before the Sepoy Mutiny. 5s.
Ingulph's Chronicles. 5s.
Irving (Washington). Complete Works. 15 vols. 3s. 6d. each; or in 18 vols. 1s. each, and 2 vols. 1s. 6d. each.
—— Life and Letters. By Pierre E. Irving. 2 vols. 3s. 6d. each.
Isocrates. Trans. by J. H. Freese. Vol. 1. 5s.
James' Life of Richard Cœur de Lion. 2 vols. 3s. 6d. each.
—— Life and Times of Louis XIV. 2 vols. 3s. 6d. each.

BOHN'S LIBRARIES.

Jameson (Mrs.) Shakespeare's Heroines. 3s. 6d.
Je sse (E.) Anecdotes of Dogs. 5s.
Jesse (J. H.) Memoirs of the Court of England under the Stuarts. 3 vols. 5s. each.
—— Memoirs of the Pretenders. 5s.
Johnson's Lives of the Poets. (Napier). 3 vols. 3s. 6d. each.
Josephus. Whiston's Translation, revised by Rev. A. R. Shilleto. 5 vols. 3s. 6d. each.
Joyce's Scientific Dialogues. 5s.
Jukes-Browne's Handbook of Physical Geology. 7s. 6d. Handbook of Historical Geology. 6s. The Building of the British Isles. 7s. 6d.
Julian the Emperor. Trans by Rev. C. W. King. 5s.
Junius's Letters. Woodfall's Edition, revised. 2 vols. 3s. 6d. each.
Justin, Cornelius Nepos, and Eutropius. Trans. by Rev. J. S. Watson. 5s.
Juvenal, Persius, Sulpicia, and Lucilius. Trans. by L. Evans. 5s.
Kant's Critique of Pure Reason. Trans. by J. M. D. Meiklejohn. 5s.
—— Prolegomena, &c. Trans. by E. Belfort Bax. 5s.
Keightley's Fairy Mythology. 5s. Classical Mythology. Revised by Dr. L. Schmitz. 5s.
Kidd On Man. 3s. 6d.
Kirby On Animals. 2 vols. 5s. each.
Knight's Knowledge is Power. 5s.
La Fontaine's Fables. Trans. by E. Wright. 3s. 6d.
Lamartine's History of the Girondists. Trans. by H. T. Ryde. 3 vols. 3s. 6d. each.
—— Restoration of the Monarchy in France. Trans. by Capt. Rafter. 4 vols. 3s. 6d. each.
—— French Revolution of 1848. 3s. 6d.
Lamb's Essays of Elia and Eliana. 3s. 6d., or in 3 vols. 1s. each.
—— Memorials and Letters. Talfourd's Edition, revised by W. C. Hazlitt. 2 vols. 3s. 6d. each.
—— Specimens of the English Dramatic Poets of the Time of Elizabeth. 3s. 6d.

Lanzi's History of Painting in Italy, Trans. by T. Roscoe. 3 vols. 3s. 6d. each.
Lappenberg's England under the Anglo-Saxon Kings. Trans. by B. Thorpe. 2 vols. 3s. 6d. each.
Lectures on Painting. By Barry, Opie and Fuseli. 5s.
Leonardo da Vinci's Treatise on Painting. Trans. by J. F. Rigaud. 5s.
Lepsius' Letters from Egypt, &c. Trans. by L. and J. B. Horner. 5s.
Lessing's Dramatic Works. Trans. by Ernest Bell. 2 vols. 3s. 6d. each. Nathan the Wise and Minna von Barnhelm. 1s. and 1s. 6d. Laokoon, Dramatic Notes, &c. Trans. by E. C. Beasley and Helen Zimmern. 3s. 6d. Laokoon separate. 1s. or 1s. 6d.
Lilly's Introduction to Astrology. (Zadkiel.) 5s.
Livy. Trans. by Dr. Spillan and others. 4 vols. 5s. each.
Locke's Philosophical Works. (J. A. St. John). 2 vols. 3s. 6d. each.
—— Life. By Lord King. 3s. 6d.
Lodge's Portraits. 8 vols. 5s. each.
Longfellow's Poetical and Prose Works. 2 vols. 5s. each.
Loudon's Natural History. 5s.
Lowndes' Bibliographer's Manual. 6 vols. 5s. each.
Lucan's Pharsalia. Trans. by H. T. Riley. 5s.
Lucian's Dialogues. Trans. by H. Williams. 5s.
Lucretius. Trans. by Rev. J. S. Watson. 5s.
Luther's Table Talk. Trans. by W. Hazlitt. 3s. 6d.
—— Autobiography. (Michelet). Trans. by W. Hazlitt. 3s. 6d.
Machiavelli's History of Florence, &c. Trans. 3s. 6d.
Mallet's Northern Antiquities. 5s.
Mantell's Geological Excursions through the Isle of Wight, &c. 5s. Petrifactions and their Teachings. 6s. Wonders of Geology. 2 vols. 7s. 6d. each.
Manzoni's The Betrothed. 5s.
Marco Polo's Travels. Marsden's Edition, revised by T. Wright. 5s.

ALPHABETICAL LIST OF

Martial's Epigrams. Trans. 7s. 6d.
Martineau's History of England, 1800–15. 3s. 6d.
—— History of the Peace, 1816–46. 4 vols. 3s. 6d. each.
Matthew Paris. Trans. by Dr. Giles. 3 vols. 5s. each.
Matthew of Westminster. Trans. by C. D. Yonge. 2 vols. 5s. each.
Maxwell's Victories of Wellington. 5s.
Menzel's History of Germany. Trans. by Mrs. Horrocks. 3 vols. 3s. 6d. ea.
Michael Angelo and Raffaelle. By Duppa and Q. de Quincy. 5s.
Michelet's French Revolution. Trans. by C. Cocks. 3s. 6d.
Mignet's French Revolution. 3s. 6d.
Mill (John Stuart). Selected Essays. [*In the press.*]
Miller's Philosophy of History. 4 vols. 3s. 6d. each.
Milton's Poetical Works. (J. Montgomery.) 2 vols. 3s. 6d. each.
—— Prose Works. (J. A. St. John.) 5 vols. 3s. 6d. each.
Mitford's Our Village. 2 vols. 3s. 6d. each.
Molière's Dramatic Works. Trans. by C. H. Wall. 3 vols. 3s. 6d. each.
—— The Miser, Tartuffe, The Shopkeeper turned Gentleman. 1s. & 1s. 6d.
Montagu's (Lady M. W.) Letters and Works. (Wharncliffe and Moy Thomas.) 2 vols. 5s. each.
Montaigne's Essays. Cotton's Trans. revised by W. C. Hazlitt. 3 vols. 3s. 6d. each.
Montesquieu's Spirit of Laws. Nugent's Trans. revised by J. V. Prichard. 2 vols. 3s. 6d. each.
Morphy's Games of Chess. (Löwenthal.) 5s.
Motley's Dutch Republic. 3 vols. 3s. 6d. each.
Mudie's British Birds. (Martin.) 2 vols. 5s. each.
Naval and Military Heroes of Great Britain. 6s.
Neander's History of the Christian Religion and Church. 10 vols. Life of Christ. 1 vol. Planting and Training of the Church by the Apostles. 2 vols. History of Christian Dogma.

2 vols. Memorials of Christian Life in the Early and Middle Ages. 16 vols. 3s. 6d. each.
Nicolini's History of the Jesuits. 5s.
North's Lives of the Norths. (Jessopp.) 3 vols. 3s. 6d. each.
Nugent's Memorials of Hampden. 5s.
Ockley's History of the Saracens. 3s. 6d.
Ordericus Vitalis. Trans. by T. Forester. 4 vols. 5s. each.
Ovid. Trans. by H. T. Riley. 3 vols. 5s. each.
Pascal's Thoughts. Trans. by C. Kegan Paul. 3s. 6d.
Pauli's Life of Alfred the Great, &c. 5s.
—— Life of Cromwell. 1s. and 1s. 6d.
Pausanias' Description of Greece. Trans. by Rev. A. R. Shilleto. 2 vols. 5s. each.
Pearson on the Creed. (Walford.) 5s.
Pepys' Diary. (Braybrooke.) 4 vols. 5s. each.
Percy's Reliques of Ancient English Poetry. (Prichard.) 2 vols. 3s. 6d. ea.
Petrarch's Sonnets. 5s.
Pettigrew's Chronicles of the Tombs. 5s.
Philo-Judæus. Trans. by C. D. Yonge. 4 vols. 5s. each.
Pickering's Races of Man. 5s.
Pindar. Trans. by D. W. Turner. 5s.
Planché's History of British Costume. 5s.
Plato. Trans. by H. Cary, G. Burges, and H. Davis. 6 vols. 5s. each.
—— Apology, Crito, Phædo, Protagoras. 1s. and 1s. 6d.
—— Day's Analysis and Index to the Dialogues. 5s.
Plautus. Trans. by H. T. Riley. 2 vols. 5s. each.
—— Trinummus, Menæchmi, Aulularia, Captivi. 1s. and 1s. 6d.
Pliny's Natural History. Trans. by Dr. Bostock and H. T. Riley. 6 vols. 5s. each.
Pliny the Younger, Letters of. Melmoth's trans. revised by Rev. F. C. T. Bosanquet. 5s.
Plotinus : Select Works of. 5s.

Plutarch's Lives. Trans. by Stewart and Long. 4 vols. 3s. 6d. each.
—— Moralia. Trans. by Rev. C. W. King and Rev. A. R. Shilleto. 2 vols. 5s. each.
Poetry of America. (W. J. Linton.) 3s. 6d.
Political Cyclopædia. 4 vols. 3s. 6d. ea.
Polyglot of Foreign Proverbs. 5s.
Pope's Poetical Works. (Carruthers.) 2 vols. 5s. each.
—— Homer. (J. S. Watson.) 2 vols. 5s. each.
—— Life and Letters. (Carruthers.) 5s.
Pottery and Porcelain. (H. G. Bohn.) 5s. and 10s. 6d.
Propertius. Trans. by Rev. P. J. F. Gantillon. 3s. 6d.
Prout (Father.) Reliques. 5s.
Quintilian's Institutes of Oratory. Trans. by Rev. J. S. Watson. 2 vols. 5s. each.
Racine's Tragedies. Trans. by R. B. Boswell. 2 vols. 3s. 6d. each.
Ranke's History of the Popes. Trans. by E. Foster. 3 vols. 3s. 6d. each.
—— Latin and Teutonic Nations. Trans. by P. A. Ashworth. 3s. 6d.
—— History of Servia. Trans. by Mrs. Kerr. 3s. 6d.
Rennie's Insect Architecture. (J. G. Wood.) 5s.
Reynold's Discourses and Essays. (Beechy.) 2 vols. 3s. 6d. each.
Ricardo's Political Economy. (Gonner.) 5s.
Richter's Levana. 3s. 6d.
—— Flower Fruit and Thorn Pieces. Trans. by Lieut.-Col. Ewing. 3s. 6d.
Roger de Hovenden's Annals. Trans. by Dr. Giles. 2 vols. 5s. each.
Roger of Wendover. Trans. by Dr. Giles. 2 vols. 5s. each.
Roget's Animal and Vegetable Physiology. 2 vols. 6s. each.
Rome in the Nineteenth Century. (C. A. Eaton.) 2 vols. 5s. each.
Roscoe's Leo X. 2 vols. 3s. 6d. each.
—— Lorenzo de Medici. 3s. 6d.
Russia, History of. By W. K. Kelly. 2 vols. 3s. 6d. each.
Sallust, Florus, and Velleius Paterculus. Trans. by Rev. J. S. Watson. 5s.

Schiller's Works. Including History of the Thirty Years' War, Revolt of the Netherlands, Wallenstein, William Tell, Don Carlos, Mary Stuart, Maid of Orleans, Bride of Messina, Robbers, Fiesco, Love and Intrigue, Demetrius, Ghost-Seer, Sport of Divinity, Poems, Aesthetical and Philosophical Essays, &c. By various translators. 7 vols. 3s. 6d. each.
—— Mary Stuart and The Maid of Orleans. Trans. by J. Mellish and Anna Swanwick. 1s. and 1s. 6d.
Schlegel (F.). Lectures and Miscellaneous Works. 5 vols. 3s. 6d. each.
—— (A. W.). Lectures on Dramatic Art and Literature. 3s. 6d.
Schopenhauer's Essays. Selected and Trans. by E. Belfort Bax. 5s.
—— On the Fourfold Root of the Principle of Sufficient Reason and on the Will in Nature. Trans. by Mdme. Hillebrand. 5s.
Schouw's Earth, Plants, and Man. Trans. by A. Henfrey. 5s.
Schumann's Early Letters. Trans. by May Herbert. 3s. 6d.
—— Reissmann's Life of. Trans. by A. L. Alger. 3s. 6d.
Seneca on Benefits. Trans. by Aubrey Stewart. 3s. 6d.
—— Minor Essays and On Clemency. Trans. by Aubrey Stewart. 5s.
Sharpe's History of Egypt. 2 vols. 5s. each.
Sheridan's Dramatic Works. 3s. 6d.
—— Plays. 1s. and 1s. 6d.
Sismondi's Literature of the South of Europe. Trans. by T. Roscoe. 2 vols. 3s. 6d. each.
Six Old English Chronicles. 5s.
Smith (Archdeacon). Synonyms and Antonyms. 5s.
Smith (Adam). Wealth of Nations. (Belfort Bax.) 2 vols. 3s. 6d. each.
—— Theory of Moral Sentiments. 3s. 6d.
Smith (Pye). Geology and Scripture. 5s.
Smollett's Novels. 4 vols. 3s. 6d. each.
Smyth's Lectures on Modern History. 2 vols. 3s. 6d. each.

Socrates' Ecclesiastical History. 5s.
Sophocles. Trans. by E. P. Coleridge, B.A. 5s.
Southey's Life of Nelson. 5s.
—— Life of Wesley. 5s.
—— Life, as told in his Letters. By J. Dennis. 3s. 6d.
Sozomen's Ecclesiastical History. 5s.
Spinoza's Chief Works. Trans. by R. H. M. Elwes. 2 vols. 5s. each.
Stanley's Dutch and Flemish Painters, 5s.
Starling's Noble Deeds of Women. 5s.
Staunton's Chess Players' Handbook. 5s. Chess Praxis. 5s. Chess Players' Companion. 5s. Chess Tournament of 1851. 5s.
Stöckhardt's Experimental Chemistry. (Heaton.) 5s.
Strabo's Geography. Trans. by Falconer and Hamilton. 3 vols. 5s. each.
Strickland's Queens of England. 6 vols. 5s. each. Mary Queen of Scots. 2 vols. 5s. each. Tudor and Stuart Princesses. 5s.
Stuart & Revett's Antiquities of Athens. 5s.
Suetonius' Lives of the Caesars and of the Grammarians. Thomson's trans. revised by T. Forester. 5s.
Sully's Memoirs. Mrs. Lennox's trans. revised. 4 vols. 3s. 6d. each.
Tacitus. The Oxford trans. revised. 2 vols. 5s. each.
Tales of the Genii. Trans. by Sir. Charles Morell. 5s.
Tasso's Jerusalem Delivered. Trans. by J. H. Wiffen. 5s.
Taylor's Holy Living and Holy Dying. 3s. 6d.
Terence and Phædrus. Trans. by H. T. Riley. 5s.
Theocritus, Bion, Moschus, and Tyrtæus. Trans. by Rev. J. Banks. 5s.
Theodoret and Evagrius. 5s.
Thierry's Norman Conquest. Trans. by W. Hazlitt. 2 vols. 3s. 6d. each.

Thucydides. Trans by Rev. H. Dale. 2 vols. 3s. 6d. each.
—— Wheeler's Analysis and Summary of. 5s.
Trevelyan's Ladies in Parliament. 1s. and 1s. 6d.
Ulrici's Shakespeare's Dramatic Art. Trans. by L. Dora Schmitz. 2 vols. 3s. 6d. each.
Uncle Tom's Cabin. 3s. 6d.
Ure's Cotton Manufacture of Great Britain. 2 vols. 5s. each.
—— Philosophy of Manufacture. 7s. 6d.
Vasari's Lives of the Painters. Trans. by Mrs. Foster. 6 vols. 3s. 6d. each.
Virgil. Trans. by A. Hamilton Bryce, LL.D. 3s. 6d.
Voltaire's Tales. Trans. by R. B. Boswell. 3s. 6d.
Walton's Angler. 5s.
—— Lives. (A. H. Bullen.) 5s.
Waterloo Days. By C. A. Eaton. 1s. and 1s. 6d.
Wellington, Life of. By 'An Old Soldier.' 5s.
Werner's Templars in Cyprus. Trans. by E. A. M. Lewis. 3s. 6d.
Westropp's Handbook of Archæology. 5s.
Wheatley. On the Book of Common Prayer. 3s. 6d.
Wheeler's Dictionary of Noted Names of Fiction. 5s.
White's Natural History of Selborne. 5s.
Wieseler's Synopsis of the Gospels. 5s.
William of Malmesbury's Chronicle. 5s.
Wright's Dictionary of Obsolete and Provincial English. 2 vols. 5s. each.
Xenophon. Trans. by Rev. J. S. Watson and Rev. H. Dale. 3 vols. 5s. ea.
Young's Travels in France, 1787-89. (M. Betham-Edwards.) 3s. 6d.
—— Tour in Ireland, 1776-9. (A. W. Hutton.) 2 vols. 3s. 6d. each.
Yule-Tide Stories (B. Thorpe.) 5s.

www.ingramcontent.com/pod-product-compliance
Lightning Source LLC
Chambersburg PA
CBHW022104290426
44112CB00008B/550